AN INTRODUCTORY BIBLIOGRAPHY FOR JAPANESE STUDIES

Vol. XII, Part 1
Social Sciences
1996–97

Compiled by the Tōhō Gakkai

THE JAPAN FOUNDATION

2000

FOREWORD

The present work constitutes the twenty-third publication in our bibliographical series entitled *An Introductory Bibliography for Japanese Studies* and is the twelfth title devoted to the area of the social sciences. The intent of this series is to introduce to foreign scholars the kind of research that their Japanese counterparts have been conducting in various disciplines making up the vast field of Japanese studies. Each volume in the series is made up of two parts, and in principle, covers on a biennial basis the most recent research being carried out in the field. It has been the custom in the editing process to devote Part 1 to research in the social sciences and Part 2 to the humanities. Previously published volumes include:

Volume I, Part 1, Social Sciences: 1969-72 (Published 1974)
Volume I, Part 2, Humanities: 1970-73 (1975)
Volume II, Part 1, Social Sciences: 1973-74 (1976)
Volume II, Part 2, Humanities: 1974-75 (1977)
Volume III, Part 1, Social Sciences: 1975-76 (1978)
Volume III, Part 2, Humanities: 1976-77 (1980)
Volume IV, Part 1, Social Sciences: 1977-78 (1982)
Volume IV, Part 2, Humanities: 1978-79 (1982)
Volume V, Part 1, Social Sciences: 1979-80 (1986)
Volume V, Part 2, Humanities: 1980-82 (1986)
Volume VI, Part 1, Social Sciences: 1981-85 (1988)
Volume VI, Part 2, Humanities: 1983-86 (1990)

Volume VII, Part 1, Social Sciences: 1986-87 (1991)
Volume VII, Part 2, Humanities: 1987-88 (1991)
Volume VIII, Part 1, Social Sciences: 1988-89 (1992)
Volume VIII, Part 2, Humanities: 1989-90 (1994)
Volume IX, Part 1, Social Sciences: 1990-91 (1994)
Volume IX Part 2, Humanities: 1991-92 (1995)
Volume X, Part 1, Social Sciences: 1992-93 (1996)
Volume X, Part 2, Humanities: 1993-94 (1998)
Volume XI, Part 1, Social Sciences: 1994-95 (1998)
Volume XI Part 2, Humanities: 1995-96 (1999)

The present title covers the social sciences over the two-year period 1996-97; the categories covered are Law, Political Sciences, International Relations, Economics, Business Administration, Sociology, Geography, Cultural Anthropology, and Education. Each of these nine social science categories is accompanied by an essay describing the major research trends in the particular field during the review period and a select bibliographical list with annotations on the more important works published during the same period. Since the aim of this particular series is to mainly introduce research written by Japanese scholars in their own language, we recommend that the reader interested in English-language Japanese studies refer to the bibliographies published by the Association for Asian Studies in the United States.

Beginning with Volume VI, Part 1 (Social Sciences), we have entrusted the Tōhō Gakkai (The Institute of Eastern Culture) with the entirety of the editing tasks for the series. We would like to express our heartfelt appreciation to Dr. Hattori Masaaki, Chairman of the Board of Directors of the Tōhō Gakkai. We would also like to thank the actual contributors to the volume for graciously taking time out of their busy research activities in order to make the introduction of these nine categories a truly important scholarly achievement. Last but not least we would like to express our deep gratitude to the staff of the Tōhō Gakkai for their strenuous efforts to prepare English texts for publication.

All opinions expressed in the text are to be attributed to the respective authors, and do not necessarily correspond to the views of the Japan Foundation. Moreover, we sincerely urge our readers to express their opinions regarding the volume's contents and to make suggestions for improving the presentation and format of the bibliography, in order that it may better serve them. Please address all correspondence to: Publishing Division, Media Department, The Japan Foundation, Ark Mori Bldg. 20F, 1-12-32 Akasaka, Minato-ku, Tokyo 107-6021, Japan.

The Japan Foundation
November 2000

CONTENTS

EDITORIAL NOTES

1. Romanization: The Hepburn system with minor modification has been employed for Japanese words.
2. Personal names: In accordance with Japanese practice, the family name precedes the given name.
3. Brackets in the bibliographical listings indicate series title.

LAW

Hamano Ryō
Rikkyō University
Koyanagi Shun'ichirō
Dokkyō University
Nomura Toyohiro and Kansaku Hiroyuki
Gakushūin University
Kanda Hideki, Araki Takashi, Hasebe Yasuo
and Yamaguchi Atsushi
The University of Tokyo

I. SOCIOLOGY OF LAW

In 1997 the Japanese Association of Sociology of Law celebrated its fiftieth anniversary. As is evidenced by the Bibliography, increasing numbers of younger researchers are beginning to publish more work, and it would seem that the study of the sociology of law in Japan is entering a new era.

During the review period (1996–97), as in previous years, the field of sociology of law saw sound progress in both empirical and theoretical research. With respect to empirical research, studies were published on subjects including the judicial process [I-01, 02], dispute processes [I-03], the invocation of law [I-04, 05], legal consciousness [I-06~08], the legal profession [I-09~11], corporate legal departments [I-12], and the administrative process [I-13, 14]. As for theoretical research, there appeared studies on subjects such as methodology [I-15], sociological theories of law [I-16, 17], the judicial process [I-18, 19], dispute processes [I-20 ~24], and the legal profession [I-25~28].

In addition, a commemorative collection of articles [I-29] was published, and the symposiums and individual presentations at the annual meetings of the Japanese Association of Sociology of Law resulted in two volumes of articles [I-30, 31].

II. LEGAL HISTORY

The study of Japan's legal history during the review period was characterized by a profusion of research on the Edo period and modern history, but there also appeared important research on ancient history and medieval history.

On the subject of the history of laws related to land, there appeared a compilation covering the period from ancient times down to the present day [II-01]. In the area of ancient history, Ōtsu Tōru [II-02] produced a study of the relationship between the Japanese *ritsuryō* and Chinese *lü-ling*. Ōtsu is a leading scholar of Japanese ancient history and legal history, and in this article he argues that although the emperor's position as initially laid down in Japan's *ritsuryō* differed from that in China, by the ninth century the acceptance of T'ang customs and rites had advanced to a considerable degree. There also appeared a study of the influence of Chinese law around the time of the compilation of the Taihō Code [II-03].

With regard to medieval history, there appeared a study of family law [II-04], while in the field of modern history Takahashi Satoshi [II-05] vividly describes the nature of civil suits during the Edo period with reference to an actual case and points out the importance of the judicial system in dispute resolution. A distinctive feature of lawsuits in the Edo period was the distinction between ordinary civil suits and money suits, and this distinction is dealt with in relation to *bakufu* law [II-06] and *han* law [II-07]. There were also published collections of materials on *bakufu* law [II-08] and *han* law [II-09].

In the area of modern history, mention should first be made of a study of the process of state formation in the early part of the Meiji era [II-10]. The judicial system is discussed in [II-11], and it is shown that the judicial conciliation system played an important role in the first half of the Meiji era. Debt law is dealt with in [II-12], which points out that the French civil code served an important function as a judicial norm in the first half of the Meiji era. Property law is discussed with reference to the Special Law on Large-Scale Disasters and Leased Land and Houses, which attracted renewed interest as a result of the Great Hanshin Earthquake of 1995 [II-13, 14], and it is argued that the Law Providing Special Measures as to Leased Land and Leased Buildings in Cities Damaged by Disaster, recognizing the right of tenants visited by a disaster to lease land and build a house, was premised on the difficult economic and social conditions obtaining after World War II.

III. CIVIL LAW

When compared with earlier periods, there do not seem to have been any noticeable changes in the years 1996-97 regarding general research trends in the field of civil law. That is to say, in all areas of civil law there was published research on the enactment process, attempting to clarify the content of the provisions of Japan's Civil Code by tracing them back to their respective mother laws; comparative research comparing civil law in other countries with Japanese civil law; research dealing purely with the various institutions of civil law in other countries; and legal research on new social problems (in particular, research on how to apply existing legal theory and on whether or not new legislation is necessary). Among this research, the following comments are restricted to some of the more noteworthy topics in the study of Japanese civil law.

Firstly, there appeared some studies on the methodology of civil jurisprudence and basic theories of civil law [III-01~03]. Although they are written by scholars of civil law, in content they are not necessarily confined to civil law and include ideas applicable to the study of law in general. In addition, as already noted, there appeared a considerable amount of research on the enactment process, but the works listed in the Bibliography are restricted to historical research on the period up to the establishment of the Civil Code [III-04~09].

Secondly, in research dealing with almost every area of civil law, studies on basic contract theory [III-10~12] and studies on the transfer of real rights [III-13~16] were especially conspicuous.

Thirdly, there was produced much research on questions that the recent enactment of new laws is intended to resolve, questions that are already being examined by the Legislative Council of the Ministry of Justice, and questions that it is hoped will be resolved by future legislation. This includes research on the Products Liability Law passed in 1994, research on marriage and divorce (retention of maiden names by married women, causes of divorce, etc.), and research on legal questions concerning the elderly, especially the system of majority guardianship [III-17~24]. Under current law, the right of tenants to continue their tenancy if desired after the termination of the contract period is protected by the system of just cause, but there has been some discussion of whether or not to revise the Leased Land and House Law and introduce fixed-term residential tenancy, whereby the lease is considered to end with the termination of the agreed period. In contrast to economists, who support its active introduction, legal scholars are critical of this proposal [III-25~27].

Fourthly, there has also been considerable interpretative and legislative research on whether or not problems created by relatively recent social changes can be resolved through existing legal theory and, if not, what form of legislation might be desirable. This includes, for example, research on electronic money [III-28, 29].

Fifthly, as always, the proceedings of symposiums held by the Japan Association of Private Law were published. The themes of the Civil Law Section of its annual conference were "Issues Facing Security Jurisprudence" (1995) and "Malfeasance in Business Relations and Its Legal Treatment" (1996), and the Association's journal carried papers and records of discussions on these topics [III-30, 31].

Lastly, in addition to the above, there also appeared much other important research [III-32~36]. In particular, volumes published in honour of the sixtieth and seventieth birthdays of well-known scholars [III-37~42], as well as monographs and collected works of individual scholars [III-43~45], all contain outstanding pieces of research.

IV. COMMERCIAL LAW

In 1997 the Commercial Code was revised three times with regard to stock companies, and as a result (1) the rules regarding company mergers were simplified and rationalized [IV-01], (2) the stock option system was introduced [IV-02], and (3) penalties for according benefits (*rieki-kyōyo*) were established and tightened. Among these revisions, the introduction of the stock option system was made by a Diet member's bill, which was the first time this had occurred with respect to amendments to the Commercial Code. This led to a spate of research on the stock option system [IV-03, 04] and restrictions on stock repurchases [IV-05, 06], including discussions of the merits and demerits of legislating through Diet member's bills.

In addition, the Liberal Democratic Party's Commercial Law Subcommittee made public in September 1997 its "Main Points of a Draft Plan for the Revision of Commercial Code Regarding Corporate Governance" [IV-07], and it proposed the tightening of the auditor system and a review of stockholder representative suits. Not only did academics respond directly to this draft plan of the LDP [IV-08, 09], but there also appeared a great deal of research on corporate governance [IV-10~12] and representative suits [IV-13~15]. The significance and functions of auditing by auditors and the supervising of corporate directors and boards of directors in the execution of their duties also attracted considerable attention [IV-16~20]. A distinctive feature of this research was that discussion of corporate governance attained greater depth with respect to management controls for efficient company operations. Lastly, following the lifting of the ban on pure holding companies as a result of the revision of the Act Concerning Prohibition of Private Monopoly and Maintenance of Fair Trade, it is expected that corporate groups in the form of holding companies will be formed in the near future, and there has been a focus on important points that had hitherto remained dormant, especially the legal problems that will arise in such combined corporations (or corporate groups) [IV-21, 22].

There was an upsurge of interest in interdisciplinary fields and hybrid fields such as corporate accounting law and the impact of capital markets on company law. The symposiums of the Commercial Law Section at the annual conference of the Japan Association of Private Law dealt with "Developments in Capital Markets and the Transformation of Company Law" (1996) [IV-23] and "Corporate Accounting and Company Law" (1997) [IV-24], and these topics too were a reflection of this trend [IV-25, 26].

There also appeared several outstanding historical studies concerning the course of events leading to the revision of the Commercial Code and the history of theories of commercial law [IV-27 ~30]. In addition to important research on the basic principles of company law such as the legal personality [IV-31] and the system of general stockholder meetings [IV-32], comparative research on company law, chiefly British and American company law [IV-33], was also actively pursued. It is further worth noting that a comparative study of ostensible legal principles in commercial law was published [IV-34].

Many important studies were published in the fields of securities law [IV-35~38] and insurance law and maritime commercial law [IV-39~42], and systematic commentaries on the Insurance Business Law were also published [IV-43, 44]. With the imminent reform of the financial system, legal issues pertaining to the expansion of bank services [IV-45], changes in the basic structure of mutual companies [IV-46], and the liberalization of commissions for stock brokerage [IV-47] were examined, and there were also published a noteworthy commentary [IV-48] and several studies [IV-49~51] on the Securities and Exchange Law.

V. LABOR LAW

During the review period there occurred major law revisions in the fields of equal employment law [V-01] and labor market law, and many studies relating to these revisions were published. Firstly, the Equal Employment Opportunity Law, passed in 1985, underwent a radical revision in 1997 [V-02~06]. In concrete terms, all sexual discrimination in recruitment, engagement, placement and promotion was prohibited; it became possible for mediation (which had previously required the agreement of both parties) to be initiated upon application by workers alone; a system for publishing the names of corporations that violated the equal employment opportunity law was introduced; and provisions regarding positive action and sexual harassment were also established [V-07, 08]. At the same time, provisions for the protection of women in the Labor Standards Law (restrictions on overtime and holiday working hours, and prohibition on working late at night) were abolished. These all came into effect from 1 April 1999.

In conjunction with the government's deregulation policies, sections of the Worker Dispatching Law and Employment Security Law (restrictions on fee-charging employment exchange services) were liberalized [V-09]. In the context of this trend towards deregulation, there was much lively discussion of labor laws and deregulation [V-10～13].

With regard to labor law in general, it is worth noting that there appeared a detailed review of the development of postwar labor jurisprudence [V-14] and a systematic study of a new type that repositions the functions of the law in the light of the actual state of the labor market and labor-management relations [V-15].

In the field of individual labor relations, valuable research into the legislative history of the Labor Standards Law on the basis of hitherto unpublished materials was published [V-16, 17]. A new study that takes into account proof of allegations in lawsuits [V-18] and an outstanding legislative and interpretative study of part-time work [V-19] were also published. As a reflection of the fluidization of the Japanese labor market, there appeared articles on dismissal restrictions [V-20, 21], the duty not to compete [V-22, 23], and the resolution of individual employment disputes [V-24, 25]. In addition, as a consequence of the stagnation of Japan's post-bubble economy, the question of modifying working conditions [V-26～28], dismissal to modify terms and conditions of employment [V-29, 30], wage systems commensurate with individual achievement (reflecting the individualization of personnel management) [V-31], death from overwork (*karōshi*) among white-collar workers [V-32, 33], and the protection of personal rights in the workplace [V-34] all became important subjects of legal inquiry.

In the area of collective labor relations, new issues were examined with regard to unfair labor practices [V-35~37] and collective bargaining and collective agreements [V-32, 38]. Special mention should be made of the fact that middle-aged workers, who have been made a target of down-sizing on account of the high salaries that they were paid under the seniority-based wage system, have formed a union for those in managerial positions in order to protect their own interests, and this move has also been addressed from a legal perspective [V-29]. In commemoration of the fiftieth anniversary of the inauguration of the labor relations commissions, a comprehensive examination of the system of labor relations commissions was also undertaken [V-39].

As for questions relating to internationalization, there appeared with regard to the question of foreign workers a comprehensive study that also covers issues outside labor law [V-40] and a book that discusses in comparison with German law the question of the choice of governing laws for foreign workers [V-41].

VI. PUBLIC LAW

3 May 1997 marked the fiftieth anniversary of the coming into effect of the Constitution of Japan, and there were published several works that review its history and consider its future [VI-01, 06~08]. In particular, *Kōhō Kenkyū* (Public Law Review), No. 59 [VI-01], contains papers and discussions from the annual conference of the Japan Public Law Association held at the University of Tokyo in October 1996 on the theme of "Five Decades of the Constitution of Japan: Retrospection and Future Prospects," as well as the texts of commemorative lectures by Professors Ashibe Nobuyoshi and Itō Masami.

On 2 April 1997 the Supreme Court ruled on the Ehime Shinto Offerings (*Tamagushi-ryō*) Case that the action of Ehime prefectural government in making offerings at religious ceremonies performed by Yasukuni Shrine and Gokoku Shrine gave the impression that the prefectural government was especially supporting a particular religious group and aroused interest in a particular religion, and this corresponded to religious activity by public bodies prohibited in Article 20 of the Constitution (*Minshū* [Supreme Court Civil Procedure Law Report], Vol. 51, No. 4, p. 1673). This was the first judgement of unconstitutionality by the Supreme Court in the sphere of freedom of conscience. This ruling applied the so-called purpose-effect standard, and it gave rise to considerable debate on the significance of this standard. [VI-15] includes a round-table discussion and several articles by scholars on the subject of this ruling.

The Administrative Reform Committee made public draft guidelines for a Freedom of Information Bill, and this prompted the publication of some literature on this subject [VI-18,19]. In the field of constitutional scholarship there is a strong view that "the right to know" should be written into the objectives of the bill, but the Administrative Reform Committee took the stance that, because the concept of "the right to know" has many meanings and is of indeterminate content, it should not be written into the bill. Further articles relating to this topic are to be found in Vol. 10 of [VI-17]. The Freedom of Information Bill was passed into law in May 1999.

Following the publication of several recommendations by the Decentralization Promotion Committee, there appeared two special issues on this subject [VI-31, 32]. The Committee's 1st Recommendation proposed the abolition of agency-delegated work performed by local government under strong central supervision.

The final report of the Administrative Reform Council, proposing the reorganization of central government, was published in December 1997, and the Basic Act for Reorganizing the Central Government, drafted on the basis of this report, was passed in June 1998. As concrete reforms are put into effect, including the strengthening of the cabinet's functions and the introduction of autonomous administrative agencies, it is to be expected that there will be considerable discussion of the rights and wrongs of these reforms. Vol. 1 of [VI-17] includes articles on decentralization and central government reform.

VII. CRIMINAL LAW

The review period saw a steady accumulation of research in the various spheres of criminal law [VII-01~04, 14, 15]. Particularly noticeable as an overall trend was the growth and development of discussion relating to moves towards legislation against organized crime that would allow for the introduction of wiretapping [VII-05~07]. The debate surrounding the state of juvenile justice also showed a marked increase in depth [VII-08~13].

In the area of the general theory of criminal law, a number of important studies were published in the fields of methodology, the constituent elements of offences, illegality, and responsibility [VII-16~28]. Here one can see evidence of steady theoretical development. Also important is the debate about the Organ Transplant Law, which finally passed into law in 1997 [VII-29].

As for specialized areas of criminal law, a variety of research results were produced [VII-30~32], and it is worth noting that a start has been made on research into illegal acts that have arisen in recent years with the growth of Internet-based communications, such as crimes of obscenity [VII-33~35]. Research on economic crimes has also been progressing [VII-36~39].

In the area of criminal procedure law, there appeared a great variety of both theoretical and factual research in all fields, and a number of important works were published [VII-40~48]. Mention should also be made of research on victims in criminal justice [VII-49~51].

BIBLIOGRAPHY

I. Sociology of Law
    01 太田勝造・岡本浩一・松村良之 Ōta Shōzō, Okamoto Kōichi and Matsumura Yoshiyuki, 裁判官の判断におけるスジとスワリ (1)~(11・未完) "*Suji* and *Suwari* in the Decisions of Judges," 「判例タイムズ」 911 号, pp. 89-96; 912 号, pp. 60-65; 916 号, pp. 49-58; 919 号, pp. 65-74; 921 号, pp. 67-74; 923 号, pp. 88-97; 925 号, pp. 100-106; 927 号, pp. 79-84; 937 号, pp. 89-91; 941 号, pp. 87-92; 946 号, pp. 64-69, 判例タ

イムズ社, 1996-97.

A quantitative analysis, based on empirical data, of the process whereby judges form their decisions.

02 菅原郁夫 Sugawara Ikuo,『民事裁判心理学序説』*An Introduction to the Psychology of Civil Adjudication*, 366 pp., 信山社, 1997.

03 村山眞維 Murayama Masayuki, "British and Japanese Mediation," *Family Law*, Vol. 27, pp. 419-421, Jordan Publishing, 1997.

04 尾崎一郎 Ozaki Ichirō, 都市の公共性と法 (1) ~ (4) "Public Spheres in Urban Life and the Law,"「法学協会雑誌」113 巻 9 号, pp. 60-120; 10 号, pp. 73-126; 11 号, pp. 1-58; 12 号, pp. 35-72, 法学協会, 1996.

An analysis based on empirical research conducted on the inhabitants of apartment blocks in the suburbs of Tokyo.

05 佐藤岩夫 Satō Iwao, 公共圏の形成をめぐる社会運動と法 (1・未完) "Social Movements Concerning the Formation of the Public Sphere and the Law,"「法学雑誌」43 巻 4 号, pp. 1-26, 大阪市立大学法学会, 1997.

06 吉田 勇 Yoshida Isamu, 近隣紛争の社会的波紋 (1) (2) "The Social Repercussions of Neighbourhood Disputes, "「熊本法学」86 号, pp. 31-91; 87 号, pp. 37-87, 熊本大学法学会, 1996.

07 木下麻奈子 Kinoshita Manako, 援助行動と法に関する規範意識の構造 "The Structure of Normative Consciousness Relating to Helpful Behavior and the Law,"「香川法学」16 巻 3-4 号, pp. 280-372, 香川大学法学会, 1997.

08 木下麻奈子 Kinoshita Manako, 援助行動と法に関する日本人の規範認識 "Japanese Normative Perceptions Relating to Helping Behavior and the Law,"「香川法学」17 巻 3 号, pp. 115-220, 香川大学法学会, 1997.

09 濱野 亮 Hamano Ryō, "Lawyers in Tokyo and Their Work for Businesses,"「立教法学」43 号, pp. 218-235, 立教法学会, 1996.

10 神長百合子 Kaminaga Yuriko,『法の象徴的機能と社会変革』*The Symbolic Functions of Law and Social Change*, 325 pp., 勁草書房, 1996.

An empirical study of cause lawyering in the United States.

11 村山眞維 Murayama Masayuki, 法律業務の社会組織と刑事弁護 "The Social Organization of Legal Practice and Criminal Defence,"「千葉大法学論集」10 巻 3 号, pp. 161-312, 千葉大学法学会, 1996.

12 米田憲市 Yoneda Ken'ichi, 企業法務体制における法的役割 "The Legal Role in the System of Corporate Law Departments,"「神戸法学雑誌」47 巻 1 号, pp. 57-124, 神戸法学会, 1997.

13 長谷川貴陽史 Hasegawa Kiyoshi, 事前調整指導の法社会学的考察 "A Consideration of Prior Reconciliatory Guidance from the Perspective of the Sociology of Law,"「本郷法政紀要」5 号, pp. 207-237, 東京大学大

学院法学政治学研究科, 1996.

14 北村喜宣 Kitamura Yoshinobu,『行政執行過程と自治体』*The Process of Administrative Implementation and Local Government*, 313 pp., 日本評論社, 1997.

15 和田仁孝 Wada Yoshitaka,『法社会学の解体と再生』*The Dismantlement and Rebirth of the Sociology of Law*, 245 pp., 弘文堂, 1996.
    An analysis of developments in the interpretive sociology of law in the United States.

16 千葉正士 Chiba Masaji, 法文化の操作的定義 "Operational Definitions of Legal Culture,"「東海法学」16 巻, pp. 1-27, 東海大学法学部, 1996.

17 広渡清吾 Hirowatari Seigo, 日本社会の法化 "Legalization in Japanese Society,"『岩波講座　現代の法 15』pp. 141-176, 岩波書店, 1997.

18 阿部昌樹 Abe Masaki, 中央―地方関係における司法府の位置づけをめぐって (1) ~ (3) "On the Position of the Judiciary in Central-Local Relations,"「法学雑誌」43 巻 3 号, pp. 1-38; 4 号, pp. 27-62; 44 巻 1 号, pp. 1-37, 大阪市立大学法学会, 1997.

19 渡辺千原 Watanabe Chihara, 事実認定における「科学」(1) (2) "'Science' in Fact-Finding,"「民商法雑誌」116 巻 3 号, pp. 19-60; 4-5 号, pp. 189-223, 有斐閣, 1997.

20 西田英一 Nishida Eiichi, 新たな法主体の可能性 (1) (2) "The Possibilities of a New Legal Subject,"「法学論叢」137 巻 1 号, pp. 74-98; 139 巻 1 号, pp. 65-88, 京都大学法学会, 1995-96.

21 棚瀬孝雄 (編) Tanase Takao (ed.),『紛争処理と合意』*Dispute Resolution and Agreement*, 261 pp., ミネルヴァ書房, 1996.

22 守屋 明 Moriya Akira, 紛争処理論からみた民事司法の現状と課題 "The Present State of Civil Justice and Related Issues as Seen from Theories of Dispute Resolution,"「法学会雑誌」46 巻 3-4 号, pp. 235-261, 岡山大学法学会, 1997.

23 守屋 明 Moriya Akira, 裁判外紛争解決手続 "Procedures for Out-of-Court Dispute Resolution,"『岩波講座　現代の法 5』, pp. 301-332, 岩波書店, 1997.

24 吉田 勇 Yoshida Isamu, 社会的な交渉規範の一断面 (1) (2) "One Aspect of Social Bargaining Norms,"「熊本法学」89 号, pp. 213-254; 91 号, pp. 23-69, 熊本大学法学会, 1997.

25 濱野 亮 Hamano Ryō, 経済社会における弁護士の基本的機能 "The Basic Functions of Lawyers in the Economy,"「立教法学」44 号, pp. 190-155, 立教法学会, 1996.

26 棚瀬孝雄 Tanase Takao, 弁護士倫理の言説分析 (1) ~ (4) "An Analysis of Discourse on Lawyers' Ethics,"「法律時報」68 巻 1 号, pp. 52-61; 2

号，pp. 47–56; 3 号，pp. 72–76; 4 号，pp. 55–63，日本評論社，1996.

27   村山眞維 Murayama Masayuki, 弁護士活動とその社会的基盤 "Lawyers'
Activities and Their Social Basis,"『岩波講座　現代の法 5』, pp. 129–160,
岩波書店，1997.

28   日本弁護士連合会編集委員会（編）Japan Federation of Bar Associations
Editorial Committee (ed.),『あたらしい世紀への弁護士像』 *Images of
Lawyers for the New Century*, 293 pp., 有斐閣，1997.

29   宮澤節生・神長百合子（編）Miyazawa Setsuo and Kaminaga Yuriko
(eds.),『法社会学コロキウム』 *A Colloquium on the Sociology of Law*,
478 pp., 日本評論社，1996.

　　　A collection of articles in commemoration of the 70th birthday of
Professor Ishimura Zensuke 石村善助 with contributions by 23 researchers
in the sociology of law and related fields.

30   日本法社会学会（編）Japanese Association of Sociology of Law (ed.),
『土地・環境問題と法社会学』 *Land and Environmental Problems and
the Sociology of Law* [『法社会学』48 号], 257 pp., 有斐閣，1996.

31   日本法社会学会（編）Japanese Association of Sociology of Law (ed.),
『紛争処理と法社会学』 *Dispute Resolution and the Sociology of Law*
[『法社会学』49 号], 257 pp., 有斐閣，1997.

32   日本法社会学会創立 50 周年記念事業実行委員会（編）Executive Com-
mittee for Events Commemorating the 50th Anniversary of the Japanese
Association of Sociology of Law (ed.),『法社会学への出発』 *Embarking
on the Sociology of Law*, 87 pp., 日本法社会学会事務局，1997.

II. Legal History

01   国土庁土地局土地情報課（監修）・土地総合研究所（編）Land Informa-
tion Section, Land Bureau, National Land Agency (supvr.), Land Institute of Japan (ed.),『日本の土地——その歴史と現状』 *Japan's Land: Its
History and Present State*, 255 pp., ぎょうせい，1996.

　　　Divided into an introduction (服藤弘司 Harafuji Hiroshi) and chapters
on the ancient period (梅田康夫 Umeda Yasuo), medieval period (伊藤一
義 Itō Kazuyoshi), early modern period (藤原明久 Fujiwara Akihisa),
modern period (小柳春一郎 Koyanagi Shun'ichirō), postwar period (島
本富夫 Shimamoto Tomio), and present conditions (益本圭太郎
Masumoto Keitarō), this book reflects the results of recent research, and as
well as containing a bibliography, it is also easy to read.

02   大津　透 Ōtsu Tōru, 天皇制と律令・礼の継受——衣服令・喪葬令をめ
ぐる覚書 "The Emperor System and the Acceptance of *Lü-ling* and *Li*;
Notes on Rules for Official Costume and Rules for Funerals and Mourn-
ing,"『日中文化交流叢書（2）——法律制度』, pp. 100–142, 大修館書店，

1997.

03 坂上康俊 Sakaue Yasutoshi, 大宝律令制定前後における日中間の情報伝
播 "The Transmission of Information between Japan and China Around
the Time of the Formulation of the Taihō Code," 『日中文化交流叢書 (2)
——法律制度』, pp. 49–99, 大修館書店, 1997.

04 高橋秀樹 Takahashi Hideki, 『日本中世の家と親族』*The Household (Ie)
and Kindred in Medieval Japan*, 313 pp., 吉川弘文館, 1996.

05 高橋　敏 Takahashi Satoshi, 『江戸の訴訟——御宿村一件顛末』 *Litigation in Edo: The Story of a Case in Onjuku Village*, 220 pp., 岩波書店,
1996.

   An official in the village of Onjuku in present-day Shizuoka prefecture
was once punished for having lodged vagrants in violation of a *bakufu*
ban on providing village lodgings for such people, and this book deals
with records concerning the village headman (*nanushi* 名主) who went to
Edo in an attempt to resolve the matter. Making use of pictorial and other
materials, the author provides a lucid description of contemporary society
and the judicial system.

06 神保文夫 Jimbo Fumio, 江戸幕府出入筋の裁判における本公事・金公事
の分化について "On the Separation of Main Suits (*Hon-kuji*) and
Money Suits (*Kane-kuji*) in the Civil Litigation of the Edo *Bakufu*," 「法
制史研究」45 号, pp. 1–38, 日本法制史学会, 1996.

07 吉田正志 Yoshida Masashi, 享保・元文期における仙台藩金銀出入取捌
仕法の確立 "The Establishment of Laws for Treating Money Suits in
Sendai *Han* during the Kyōhō and Gembun Eras," 「法学」60 巻 5 号,
pp. 1–51, 東北大学法学会, 1996.

08 石井良助・服藤弘司（編）Ishii Ryōsuke and Harafuji Hiroshi (eds.), 『幕
末御触書集成』 *Collected Proclamations (Ofuregaki) Issued by the
Bakufu after 1837*, 岩波書店, 1997.
　『別巻　解題』*Separate Volume: Explanatory Comments*, 419 pp.
　『別巻　事項目録・編年目録』*Separate Volume: Itemized Table of
　Contents and Chronological Table of Contents*, 427 pp.
　The first of these two volumes provides explanatory comments by
Harafuji on the materials contained in the volumes of this collection, and
it constitutes a full-scale study of *bakufu* laws.

09 小林　宏・高塩　博（編）Kobayashi Hiroshi and Takashio Hiroshi
(eds.), 『熊本藩法制資料集』*Collected Materials on the Laws of
Kumamoto Han*, 1303 pp., 創文社, 1996.

10 吉井蒼生夫 Yoshii Tamio, 『近代日本の国家形成と法』*State Formation
and the Law in Modern Japan*, 390 pp., 日本評論社, 1996.

11   林　真貴子 Hayashi Makiko, 紛争解決制度形成過程における勧解前置の
役割 "The Role of the Conciliation Preamble in the Formation of the
Dispute Resolution System,"「阪大法学」45 巻 6 号，pp. 951-980, 大阪大
学法学会，1997.

12   藤原明久 Fujiwara Akihisa, 明治前半期における連帯債務法——フラン
ス民法継受の諸相 "Joint and Several Obligation Law in the First Half of
the Meiji Era: Various Aspects of the Acceptance of the French Civil
Code,"「神戸法学雑誌」46 巻 3 号，pp. 455-528, 神戸大学法学会，1996.
　　　On the basis of an analysis of judicial precedents and government
ordinances relating to deliberations on proposed legislation, Fujiwara
shows that in the first half of the Meiji era the French civil code served as
the standard of judicial proceedings and was in effect the source of
Japanese law.

13   小柳春一郎 Koyanagi Shun'ichirō, 関東大震災と借地借家臨時措置法
（大正 13 年法律第 16 号） "The Great Kantō Earthquake of 1923 and the
Leased Land and Houses Emergency Measures Law (Law No. 16, 1924),"
「獨協法学」41 号，pp. 235-283; 42 号，pp. 217-296; 43 号，pp. 231-300,
獨協大学法学会，1995-96.

14   小柳春一郎 Koyanagi Shun'ichirō, 大規模災害と借地借家の立法史
"Large-Scale Disasters and the History of Legislation for Leased Land
and Leased Houses,"「不動産研究」38 巻 2 号，pp. 1-9, 日本不動産研究
所，1996.

III. Civil Law

01   広中俊雄 Hironaka Toshio, 日本民法編纂史とその資料 "The History of
the Compilation of Japan's Civil Code and Related Materials,"「民法研
究」1 巻，pp. 137-170, 信山社，1997.

02   七戸克彦 Shichinohe Katsuhiko, 旧民法・現行民法の条文対照 (1) "A
Comparison of the Articles of the Old Civil Code and the Current Civil
Code,"「法学研究」69 巻 9 号，pp. 135-187, 慶應義塾大学，1996.

03   七戸克彦 Shichinohe Katsuhiko, 旧民法・現行民法の条文対照表 (2) (3)
"A Comparative Table of the Articles of the Old Civil Code and the
Current Civil Code,"「法学研究」69 巻 10 号，pp. 131-171; 11 号，pp.
97-129, 慶應義塾大学，1996-97.

04   森田　修 Morita Osamu, 私法学における歴史認識と規範認識 (1) (2)
"Historical Perceptions and Normative Perceptions in the Study of Private
Law,"「社会科学研究」47 巻 4 号，pp. 171-248 (1995); 6 号，pp. 221-
271(1996), 東京大学社会科学研究所.

05   シンポジウム　民法学の方法・思想・思考様式 "Symposium: The
Methods, Ideas and Thought Patterns of Civil Jurisprudence,"「北大法学

論集」47 巻 6 号, pp. 1813-1904, 北海道大学, 1997.

The proceedings of a symposium at the 1997 conference of the Japan Association of Private Law; it includes: 瀬川信久 Segawa Nobuhisa, はじめに "Introduction"; 平井宜雄 Hirai Yoshio, 「法的思考様式」を求めて —35 年の回顧と展望 "In Search of 'Legal Thought Patterns": 35 Years in Retrospect and Future Prospects"; 吉田邦彦 Yoshida Kunihiko, 現代思想から見た民法解釈方法論——平井教授の研究を中心として "The Methodology of Interpreting Civil Law as Seen from Contemporary Thought: With a Focus on Professor Hirai's Research"; and a record of the subsequent discussion.

06　山本敬三　Yamamoto Keizō, 民法における動的システムの検討 "An Examination of the Dynamic System in Civil Law," 「法学論叢」138 巻 1-3 号, pp. 208-298, 京都大学, 1996.

07　来栖三郎 Kurusu Saburō, フィクションとしての自由意志 "Free Will as a Fiction," 「法学協会雑誌」112 巻 11 号, pp. 1459-1502, 法学協会, 1996.

08　大江　忠 Ōe Tadashi, 『要件事実民法』 Civil Law Concerning Facts to Be Proved, 3 vols., ii＋385 pp., 第一法規出版, 1995.

09　伊藤滋夫 Itō Shigeo, 裁判規範としての民法に関する一考察 "A Consideration of Civil Law as a Judicial Norm," 『21 世紀の民法』[III-41], pp. 3-34, 法学書院, 1996.

10　野村豊弘　Nomura Toyohiro, ボアソナードの契約に関する基礎理論 "Boissonade's Basic Theory on Contracts," 『日本民法学の形成と課題』 [III-37], Vol. 1, pp. 257-292, 有斐閣, 1996.

11　沖野眞已　Okino Masami, いわゆる例文解釈について "On So-called Interpretation of Examples," 『日本民法学の形成と課題』[III-37], Vol. 1, pp. 603-649, 有斐閣, 1996.

12　藤田寿夫 Fujita Hisao, 契約締結上の過失 "Negligence in the Conclusion of Contracts," 『契約責任の現代的諸相』[III-38], Vol. 1, pp. 131-166, 東京布井出版, 1996.

13　滝沢聿代 Takizawa Itsuyo, 物権変動論のその後の展開 (1) (2) "Subsequent Developments in Theories on the Transfer of Real Rights," 「成城法学」50 号, pp. 1-32 (1995); 52 号, pp. 175-228 (1996), 成城大学法学会.

14　滝沢聿代 Takizawa Itsuyo, 民法 94 条 2 項と民法 177 条の適用関係 "The Relationship between the Application of Article 94, Clause 2, and Article 177 of the Civil Code," 『日本民法学の形成と課題』[III-37], Vol. 1, pp. 195-225, 有斐閣, 1996.

15　石田　剛 Ishida Takeshi, 不動産二重売買における公序良俗 "Public

Policy in the Double Sale of Real Estate," 『民事法理論の諸問題』 [III-39], Vol. 2, pp. 129-183, 成文堂, 1996.

16 松岡久和 Matsuoka Hisakazu, 民法177条の第三者・再論 "The Third Party in Article 177 of the Civil Code Reconsidered," 『民事法理論の諸問題』 [III-39], Vol. 2, pp. 185-220, 成文堂, 1996.

17 小林秀之・鎌田　薫・升田　純・林田　学・伊藤滋夫 Kobayashi Hideyuki, Kamata Kaoru, Masuda Jun, Hayashida Manabu and Itō Shigeo, 座談会製造物責任法 (PL法) の検討 "Round-Table Discussion: An Examination of the Products Liability Law," 「判例タイムズ」907号, pp. 4-31, 判例タイムズ社, 1996.

A discussion of the Products Liability Law one year after it had come into effect.

18 星野英一 Hoshino Eiichi, 家族法改正問題 "Problems in the Revision of Family Law," 「法学教室」184号, pp. 44-48, 有斐閣, 1996.

19 中川　淳 Nakagawa Jun, 婚姻制度審議の中間報告案の注目点 "Points of Note in the Draft Interim Report on Deliberations on Marriage Procedures," 「民事研修」464号, pp. 11-20, 法務総合研究所, 1996.

20 須永　醇 (編) Sunaga Jun (ed.), 『被保護成年者制度の研究』 *Studies in the System of Adult Dependants*, xvi+626+xxii pp., 勁草書房, 1996.

21 丸山　健 Maruyama Takeshi, 新しい成年後見制度の創設に向けて "Towards the Creation of a New System of Majority Guardianship," 「NBL」590号, pp. 15-20, 商事法務研究会, 1996.

22 成年後見をめぐる諸問題 "Problems Concerning Majority Guardianship," 「家族〈社会と法〉」12号, pp. 48-143, 日本家族〈社会と法〉学会, 1996.

23 特集　成年後見法の展望 "Special Feature: A Review of Majority Guardianship Law," 「自由と正義」47巻7号, pp. 23-54, 日本弁護士会連合会, 1996.

Includes: 新井　誠 Arai Makoto, 高齢社会の成年後見法——先輩諸外国に学ぶ "Majority Guardianship Law in an Aging Society: Learning from Other Countries"; 西岡清一郎 Nishioka Seiichirō, 東京家庭裁判所における禁治産・準禁治産宣告の事情 "Reasons for Interdictions of Incompetence and Quasi-Incompetence at the Tokyo Family Court"; and 吉田勧 Yoshida Susumu, 成年後見制度はどのような場面で必要とされているか——「権利擁護センターすてっぷ」の経験から "In What Situations Is the System of Majority Guardianship Needed ?: From My Experiences with the Step Centre for the Protection of Rights."

24 道垣内弘人 Dōgauchi Hiroto, 成年後見制度私案 (1) 〜(7) "My Own Proposals for a Majority Guardianship System," 「ジュリスト」1074号,

pp. 117-121; 1075 号， pp. 93-98; 1076 号，pp. 122-129; 1077 号，pp. 120-127; 1078 号，pp. 76-81; 1079 号，pp. 112-117; 1080 号，pp. 82-85, 有斐閣，1995.

25　澤野順彦 Sawano Yorihiko,「定期借家権」構想の問題点 "Problems in the Plan for 'Fixed-Term Residential Tenancy',"「NBL」585 号，pp. 11-17, 商事法務研究会，1996.

26　鈴木禄弥 Suzuki Rokuya, いわゆる「定期借家権構想」(上・下) "The So-called 'Plan for Fixed-Term Residential Tenancy',"「NBL」586 号，pp. 6-16; 587 号，pp. 25-30, 商事法務研究会，1996.

27　特集　定期借家権の検討 "Special Feature: An Examination of Fixed-Term Residential Tenancy,"「ジュリスト」1088 号，pp. 30-41, 有斐閣，1996.
　　　　Includes: 本田純一 Honda Jun'ichi, 定期借家権導入論とその問題点 "Arguments for the Introduction of Fixed-Term Residential Tenancy and Associated Problems."

28　森田宏樹 Morita Hiroki, 電子マネーの法的構造 (1) ～(5) "The Legal Structure of Electronic Money,"「NBL」616 号，pp. 6-12; 617 号，pp. 23-30; 619 号，pp. 30-37; 622 号，pp. 33-39; 626 号，pp. 48-56, 商事法務研究会，1997.

29　内田　貴 Uchida Takashi, 情報化社会の継続的取引 "Continuous Transactions in an Informationalized Society,"『日本民法学の形成と課題』[III-37], Vol. 2, pp. 725-766, 有斐閣，1996.

30　担保法学の当面する課題 "Issues Facing Security Jurisprudence,"「私法」58 号，pp. 3-87, 日本私法学会，1996.
　　　　Contains contributions by 椿寿夫 Tsubaki Toshio, 伊藤進 Itō Susumu, 鎌田薫 Kamata Kaoru, 吉田眞澄 Yoshida Masumi, 加藤雅信 Katō Masanobu, 角紀代恵 Kado Kiyoe, 鳥谷部茂 Toriyabe Shigeru, 國井和郎 Kunii Kazurō, and 寺田正春 Terada Masaharu.

31　取引関係における違法行為とその法的処理——制度間競合論の視点から "Malfeasance in Business Relations and Its Legal Treatment: From the Perspective of the Theory of Intersystem Competition,"「私法」59 号，pp. 3-85, 日本私法学会，1997.
　　　　Contains contributions by 奥田昌道 Okuda Masamichi, 道垣内弘人 Dōgauchi Hiroto, 山田誠一 Yamada Seiichi, 磯村保 Isomura Tamotsu, and 山本敬三 Yamamoto Keizō.

32　山田誠一 Yamada Seiichi, 法人の理事と代理権の制限 "The Directors of a Body Corporate and Limits to Their Agency,"『日本民法学の形成と課題』[III-37], Vol. 1, pp. 123-152, 有斐閣，1996.

33　加藤雅信 Katō Masanobu, 総有論，合有論のミニ法人論的構造 "The Mini-Corporative Structure of Theories of Combined Ownership and

Joint Ownership," 『日本民法学の形成と課題』 [III-37], Vol. 1, pp. 153-193, 有斐閣, 1996.

34 古積健三郎 Furuzumi Kenzaburō, 従物上に存在する複数の担保権の優劣関係 "The Relative Relationship between Several Security Rights Existing on an Appurtenance," 『民事法理論の諸問題』 [III-39], Vol. 2, pp. 221-273, 成文堂, 1996.

35 窪田充見 Kubota Atsumi, 金銭債務の不履行と損害賠償 "Debt Default and Damage Compensation," 『民事法理論の諸問題』 [III-39], Vol. 2, pp. 327-375, 成文堂, 1996.

36 平井宜雄 Hirai Yoshio, いわゆる継続的契約に関する一考察 "A Consideration of So-called Continuous Contracts," 『日本民法学の形成と課題』 [III-37], Vol. 2, pp. 697-724, 有斐閣, 1996.

37 『星野英一先生古稀祝賀——日本民法学の形成と課題』 *Collected Papers Celebrating the 70th Birthday of Professor Hoshino Eiichi: The Formation of Japanese Civil Jurisprudence and Related Issues,* 2 vols., vol. 1: xi+649 pp.; vol. 2: vi+773 pp., 有斐閣, 1996.

38 『北川善太郎先生還暦記念——契約責任の現代的諸相』 *Collected Papers Commemorating the 60th Birthday of Professor Kitagawa Zentarō: Contemporary Aspects of Contractual Liability,* Vol. 1, viii+440 pp., 東京布井出版, 1996.

39 『奥田昌道先生還暦記念——民事法理論の諸問題』 *Collected Papers Commemorating the 60th Birthday of Professor Okuda Masamichi: Issues in Civil Law Theory,* 2 vols., vol. 1: 2+2+474 pp.; vol. 2: 3+590 pp., 成文堂, 1996.

40 『広中俊雄先生古稀祝賀論集——民事法秩序の生成と展開』 *Collected Papers Celebrating the 70th Birthday of Professor Hironaka Toshio: The Genesis and Development of Civil Law Order,* v+762 pp., 創文社, 1996.

41 『小野幸二教授還暦記念論集——21世紀の民法』 *Collected Papers Commemorating the 60th Birthday of Professor Ono Kōji: Civil Law in the 21st Century,* 970 pp., 法学書院, 1996.

42 『森島昭夫先生還暦記念——不法行為法の現代的課題と展開』 *Collected Papers Commemorating the 60th Birthday of Professor Morishima Akio: Contemporary Issues and Developments in Tort Law,* vi+542 pp., 日本評論社, 1977.

43 瀬川信久 Sagawa Nobuhisa, 『日本の借地』 *Leasehold in Japan,* 250 pp., 有斐閣, 1996.

44 大村敦志 Ōmura Atsushi, 『法源・解釈・民法学』 *Sources of Law, Interpretation, and Civil Jurisprudence,* 476 pp., 有斐閣, 1996.

45　田高寛貴 Tadaka Hirotaka,『担保体系の新たな展開——譲渡担保を中心に』 *New Developments in the Security System: With a Focus on Transferred Security*, ix＋332 pp., 勁草書房, 1997.

IV. Commercial Law

01　菊池洋一 Kikuchi Yōichi, 平成 9 年改正商法の解説（1）～（4）"An Exposition of Commercial Code Revisions in 1997,"「商事法務」1462 号, pp. 2-8; 1463 号, pp. 7-15; 1464 号, pp. 20-29; 1465 号, pp. 42-46, 商事法務研究会, 1997.

02　保岡興治 Yasuoka Okiharu, ストック・オプション制度等に係る商法改正の経緯と意義 "The Circumstances and Significance of the Revision of Commercial Code Relating to the Stock Option System, etc.,"「商事法務」1458 号, pp. 2-10, 商事法務研究会, 1997.

03　森本　滋 Morimoto Shigeru, 議員立法によるストック・オプション制度 "The Stock Option System Based on a Diet Member's Bill,"「商事法務」1459 号, pp. 2-10, 商事法務研究会, 1997.

04　伊藤靖史 Itō Yasushi, 業績連動型報酬と取締役の報酬規制（1）（2）"Performance-Related Remuneration and Regulations for the Remuneration of Directors,"「民商法雑法」116 巻 2 号, pp. 222-254; 3 号, pp. 401-425, 有斐閣, 1997.

05　龍田　節 Tatsuta Misao, 会社の計算による自己株式の取得 "The Acquisition of Treasury Stocks on the Account of the Company,"「法学論叢」138 巻 4-6 号, pp. 1-32, 京都大学法学会, 1996.

06　小林　量 Kobayashi Ryō, 自己株式の取得と取締役の責任 "The Acquisition of Treasury Stocks and the Liability of Directors,"『企業の健全性確保と取締役の責任』, pp. 243-268, 有斐閣, 1997.

07　太田誠一 Ōta Seiichi, コーポレイト・ガバナンスに関する商法等改正試案骨子 "Main Points of a Draft Plan for the Revision of Commercial Code Regarding Corporate Governance,"「商事法務」1470 号, pp. 4-11, 商事法務研究会, 1997.

08　株式代表訴訟研究会 Stockholder Representative Suits Study Group, 株主代表訴訟に関する自民党の商法等改正試案骨子に対する意見 "A View of the LDP's Main Points of a Draft Plan for the Revision of Commercial Code Regarding Stockholder Representative Suits,"「商事法務」1471 号, pp. 2-22, 商事法務研究会, 1997.

09　黒沼悦郎・近藤光男・志谷匡史・正井章筰・行澤一人 Kuronuma Etsurō, Kondō Mitsuo, Shitani Masashi, Masai Shōsaku and Yukizawa Kazuhito, コーポレート・ガバナンスに関する商法等改正試案骨子の検討 "An Examination of the Main Points of a Draft Plan for the Revision of Commercial Code Regarding Corporate Governance,"「商事法務」

1477 号, pp. 11-21, 商事法務研究会, 1997.

10　奥島孝康 (編) Okushima Takayasu (ed.),『コーポレートガバナンス――新しい危機管理の研究』*Corporate Governance: Studies on a New Form of Crisis Management*, 267 pp., 金融財政事情研究会, 1996.

11　森本　滋　Morimoto Shigeru, 大会社の経営機構と取締役の法的地位 "The Management Structure of Large Companies and the Legal Position of Directors,"「法学論叢」140 巻 5-6 号, pp. 109-154, 京都大学法学会, 1997.

12　梅本剛正 Umemoto Yoshimasa, コーポレート・ガバナンスにおける機関投資家の位置付け "The Position of Institutional Investors in Corporate Governance,"「甲南法学」37 巻 3 号, pp. 169-214, 甲南大学法学会, 1997.

13　周　劍龍　Chou Chien-lung,『株主代表訴訟制度論』*The System of Stockholder Representative Suits*, 312 pp., 信山社, 1996.

14　畠田公明 Hatada Kōmei, 株主代表訴訟の終了 "The Termination of Stockholder Representative Suits,"「福岡大学法学論集」41 巻 3-4 号, pp. 505-551, 福岡大学法学会, 1997.

15　吉原和志 Yoshihara Kazushi, 法令違反行為と取締役の責任 "Actions in Violation of Law and Directors' Liability,"「法学」60 巻 1 号, pp. 1-55, 東北大学法学会, 1996.

16　山村忠平 Yamamura Chūhei,『監査役制度の生成と発展』*The Origins and Development of the Auditor System*, 183 pp., 国際書院, 1997.

17　森　淳二朗　Mori Junjirō, 監査役の構成原理とシステム "The Organizational Principles and System behind the Auditor,"『企業の健全性確保と取締役の責任』, pp. 53-79, 有斐閣, 1997.

18　加藤　修 Katō Osamu, 会計監査人の機関性 "The Organic Nature of the Auditor,"「法学研究」70 巻 1 号, pp. 31-44, 慶應義塾大学, 1997.

19　川浜　昇　Kawahama Noboru, 取締役会の監督機能 "The Supervisory Functions of the Board of Directors,"『企業の健全性確保と取締役の責任』, pp. 3-52, 有斐閣, 1997.

20　山田純子 Yamada Junko, 取締役の監視義務――アメリカ法を参考にして "The Supervisory Duties of Directors: With Reference to American Law,"『企業の健全性確保と取締役の責任』, pp. 221-242, 有斐閣, 1997.

21　江頭憲治郎 Egashira Kenjirō, 純粋持株会社をめぐる法的諸問題 "Legal Problems Surrounding Pure Holding Companies,"「商事法務」1426 号, pp. 2-7, 商事法務研究会, 1996.

22　藤田友敬 Fujita Tomotaka, 持株会社の設立 "The Establishment of a Holding Company,"「商事法務」1431 号, pp. 4-12, 商事法務研究会, 1996.

23 シンポジウム　資本市場の展開と会社法の変貌 "Symposium: Developments in Capital Markets and the Transformation of Company Law,"「私法」58 号, pp. 88-151, 日本私法学会, 1996.

　　Contains: 神田秀樹 Kanda Hideki, 資本市場からみた会社法 "Company Law as Seen from Capital Markets"; 西山芳喜 Nishiyama Yoshiki, 資本市場の発達と企業会計・開示・監査 "The Growth of Capital Markets and Corporate Accounts, Disclosure, and Auditing"; 小林量 Kobayashi Ryō, 資本制度と額面株式制度の変容 "Changes in the Capital System and Par-Value Stock System"; 吉原和志 Yoshihara Kazushi, 敵対的企業買収と資本市場 "Hostile Corporate Takeovers and Capital Markets"; and 浜田道代 Hamada Michiyo, 企業金融と多数決の限界 "Corporate Finance and the Limitations of Majority Decisions."

24 シンポジウム　企業会計と会社法 "Symposium: Corporate Accounting and Company Law,"「私法」59 号, pp. 86-117, 日本私法学会, 1997.

　　Contains: 川村正幸 Kawamura Masayuki, 会社会計法の課題——問題提起 "Issues in Company Accounting Law: Some Problems"; 白鳥栄一 Shiratori Eiichi, 国際会計基準とわが国の会社法 "International Accounting Standards and Japan's Company Law"; 安藤英義 Andō Hideyoshi, 外貨建取引・金融派生商品等の会計基準 "Accounting Standards for Transactions in Foreign Currency, Derivatives, etc."; 伊藤邦雄 Itō Kunio, 連結財務諸表と商法 "Consolidated Financial Statements and Commercial Law"; 中里実 Nakazato Minoru, 租税法と企業会計（商法・会計学）"Tax Law and Corporate Accounting (Commercial Law and Accounting)"; and 中村忠 Nakamura Tadashi, 合併法制の会計的側面 "Accounting Aspects of Legislation on Mergers."

25 弥永真生 Yanaga Masao,『企業会計法と時価主義』*Corporate Accounting Law and the Market Value Principle* 350 pp., 日本評論社, 1996.

26 松井秀征 Matsui Hideyuki, 取締役の新株発行権限 (1) (2) "The Power of Directors to Issue New Shares,"「法学協会雑誌」114 巻 4 号, pp. 58-105; 6 号, pp. 89-142, 法学協会, 1997.

27 淺木愼一 Asagi Shin'ichi, 明治 32 年会社法制定の歴史的展開 "Historical Developments in the Enactment of the Company Law in 1899,"「神戸学院法学」26 巻 2 号, pp. 1-88, 神戸学院法学会, 1996.

28 淺木愼一 Asagi Shin'ichi, 明治 32 年会社法制定の歴史的展開・補論 "Historical Developments in the Enactment of the Company Law in 1899: Supplementary Remarks,"「神戸学院法学」26 巻 3 号. pp. 1-32, 神戸学院法学会, 1996.

29 中東正文 Nakahigashi Masafumi, 昭和 25 年商法改正 (1) ～ (4) "The Revision of the Commercial Code in 1950,"「中京法学」30 巻 3 号, pp.

1-69; 31 巻 1 号, pp. 129-173; 2 号, pp. 21-65; 3 号, pp. 107-137, 中京大学法学会, 1995-97.

30 倉沢康一郎・奥島孝康 (編) Kurasawa Yasuichirō and Okushima Takayasu (eds.),『岩崎稜先生追悼論文集——昭和商法学史』 Collected Papers in Memory of the Late Professor Iwasaki Ryō: The History of Commercial Jurisprudence in the Shōwa Era, 782 pp., 日本評論社, 1996.

31 村上淳一 Murakami Jun'ichi, 会社の法人格——比較法史の断章 "The Legal Personality of Companies: An Episode in Comparative Legal History,"「桐蔭法学」4 号, pp. 1-23, 桐蔭学園横浜大学, 1996.

32 前田重行 Maeda Shigeyuki,『株主総会制度の研究』 A Study of the System of General Stockholder Meetings, 351 pp., 有斐閣, 1997.

33 『長濱洋一教授還暦記念——現代英米会社法の諸相』 Collected Papers Commemorating the 60th Birthday of Professor Nagahama Yōichi: Various Aspects of Contemporary Anglo-American Company Law, 460 pp., 成文堂, 1996.

34 『岩本慧先生傘寿記念論文集——商法における表見法理』 Collected Papers Commemorating the 80th Birthday of Professor Iwamoto Satoshi: Ostensible Legal Principles in Commercial Law, 340 pp., 中央経済社, 1996.

35 高窪利一 Takakubo Toshikazu,『有価証券法研究』 A Study of Negotiable Securities Law (2 vols.), 853 pp., 信山社, 1996.

36 倉沢康一郎 Kurasawa Yasuichirō, 「修正発行説」の意義と機能 "The Significance and Functions of the 'Revised Issue Doctrine',"『田中誠二先生追悼論文集——企業の社会的役割と商事法』, pp. 621-631, 経済法例研究会, 1996.

37 福瀧博之 Fukutaki Hiroyuki, 手形授受 (交付) の合意に関する覚書 "Notes on Agreement about the Transfer (Delivery) of Bills of Exchange,"「関西大学法学論集」46 巻 4-6 号, pp. 319-387, 関西大学法学会, 1997.

38 高田晴仁 Takada Haruhito, 指図債権の裏書譲渡と権利移転的効力について——民法 469 条論・序説 "On the Endorsement Transfer of Obligations to Order and the Effect of the Transfer of Rights: An Introductory Study of Article 469 of the Civil Code,"『現代企業法の諸問題』, pp. 193-250, 日本評論社, 1996.

39 坂口光男 Sakaguchi Mitsuo,『保険契約法の基本問題』 Basic Problems in Insurance Contract Law, 221 pp., 文眞堂, 1996.

40 甘利公人 Amari Kimihito,『会社役員賠償責任保険の研究』 A Study of Liability Insurance for Company Directors, 272 pp., 多賀出版, 1997.

41 山下友信 Yamashita Tomonobu, 保険契約と詐害行為取消権・否認権

(上・下) "Insurance Contracts and the Right to Rescind Fraudulent Transactions or Preference," 「金融法務事情」1452 号, pp. 30-36; 1453 号, pp. 24-32, きんざい, 1996.

42 原茂太一 Haramo Taichi, ヘイグ・ヴィスビー規則第 3 条第 2 項の位置付けについて "On the Position of Article 3, Clause 2 of the Hague-Visby Rules," 「青山法学論集」38 巻 3-4 号, pp. 63-92, 青山学院法学会, 1997.

43 石田　満 Ishida Mitsuru, 『保険業法』 *Insurance Business Law*, 326 pp., 損害保険事業総合研究所, 1996.

44 江頭憲治郎・小林　登・山下友信 Egashira Kenjirō, Kobayashi Noboru and Yamashita Tomonobu, 『損害保険実務講座補巻・保険業法』 *Lectures on Nonlife Insurance Practice, Supplementary Volume: Insurance Business Law*, 275 pp., 有斐閣, 1997.

45 川村正幸 Kawarura Masayuki, 銀行の業務拡大と金融商品説明義務 "The Expansion of Bank Services and the Obligation to Explain Financial Products," 「一橋論叢」118 巻 1 号, pp. 1-17, 一橋大学, 1997.

46 大塚英明 Ōtsuka Hideaki, 相互会社の新たな社員配当法理 "New Legal Principles for Dividends of Mutual Companies to Members," 「保険学雑誌」552 号, pp. 11-27, 日本保険学会, 1996.

47 行澤一人 Yukizawa Kazuhito, 証券手数料の自由化と証券市場改革 (上・下) "The Liberalization of Securities Commissions and the Reform of the Securities Market," 「商事法務」1449 号, pp. 12-15; 1450 号, pp. 30-34, 商事法務研究会, 1997.

48 神田秀樹 (監修) Kanda Hideki (supvr.), 『注解証券取引法』 *Annotated Securities and Exchange Law*, 1510 pp., 有斐閣, 1997.

49 岸田雅雄 Kishida Masao, 不実の情報開示——商法 266 条ノ 3 を含む "The False Disclosure of Information: Including Article 266-3 of the Commercial Code," 『企業の健全性確保と取締役の責任』, pp. 411-437, 有斐閣, 1997.

50 並木和夫 Namiki Kazuo, 『内部者取引の研究』 *A Study of Insider Trading*, 214 pp., 慶應義塾大学法学研究会, 1996.

51 黒沼悦郎 Kuronuma Etsurō, 取引による相場操縦の悪性について "On the Malignancy of Market Manipulation by Trading," 『企業の健全性確保と取締役の責任』, pp. 480-515, 有斐閣, 1997.

V. Labor Law

01 浅倉むつ子・今野久子 Asakura Mutsuko and Konno Hisako, 『女性労働判例ガイド』 *A Guide to Judicial Precedents Concerning Women's Labor*, 373 pp., 有斐閣, 1997.

02 特集　男女雇用機会均等法 10 年 "Special Feature: Ten Years under the Equal Employment Opportunity Law," 「ジュリスト」1079 号, pp. 4-43,

有斐閣, 1996.

03   特集　均等法 10 年を問う "Special Feature: Questioning Ten Years under the Equal Employment Opportunity Law,"「日本労働研究雑誌」433 号, pp. 1-48, 日本労働研究機構, 1996.

04   特集　性差別禁止立法への提言 "Proposals for Legislation Prohibiting Sexual Discrimination,"「季刊労働法」178 号, pp. 12-81, 総合労働研究所, 1996.
　　　V-02～04 discuss the situation prior to the revision of the Equal Employment Opportunity Law.

05   特集　男女雇用機会均等法の改正 "Special Feature: The Revision of the Equal Employment Opportunity Law,"「ジュリスト」1116 号, pp. 39-71, 有斐閣, 1997.

06   浜田冨士郎 Hamada Fujio, 改正男女雇用機会均等法の課題 "Issues in the Revised Equal Employment Opportunity Law,"「日本労働研究雑誌」451 号, pp. 27-37, 日本労働研究機構, 1997.

07   特集　セクシャルハラスメント "Special Issue: Sexual Harassment,"「ジュリスト」1097 号, pp. 56-75, 有斐閣, 1996.
　　This discusses the situation prior to the revision of the Equal Employment Opportunity Law.

08   山川隆一 Yamakawa Ryūichi, "'Personal Rights' in the Workplace: The Emerging Law Concerning Sexual Harassment in Japan," *Japan Labor Bulletin*, Vol. 36, No. 9, pp. 5-9, 日本労働研究機構, 1997.

09   日本労働法学会（編）Japan Labor Law Association (ed.),『雇用の流動化と労働法の課題』 *The Fluidization of Employment and Issues in Labor Law* [「日本労働法学会誌」87 号], 223 pp., 総合労働研究所, 1996.

10   特集　規制緩和と労働法 "Special Issue: Deregulation and Labor Law,"「季刊労働法」183 号, pp. 6-82, 総合労働研究所, 1997.

11   特集　雇用・労働の規制緩和をめぐる動向 "Special Issue: Moves Surrounding the Deregulation of Employment and Labor,"「法律のひろば」50 巻 8 号, pp. 4-48, ぎょうせい, 1997.

12   馬渡淳一郎 Mawatari Jun'ichirō, 職業紹介事業・労働者派遣事業の規制緩和 "Deregulation of Employment Exchange Services and Worker Dispatching Services,"「日本労働研究雑誌」446 号, pp. 33-41, 日本労働研究機構, 1997.

13   荒木尚志 Araki Takashi, "Changing Japanese Labor Law in Light of Deregulation Drives: A Comparative Analysis," *Japan Labor Bulletin*, Vol. 36, No. 5, pp. 5-10, 日本労働研究機構, 1997.

14   籾井常喜（編）Momii Tsuneki (ed.),『戦後労働法学説史』 *The History*

of Postwar Labor Law Theory, 865 pp., 労働旬報社, 1996.

15 菅野和夫 Sugeno Kazuo,『雇用社会の法』 *Laws for an Employment Society*, 366 pp., 有斐閣, 1996.

16 渡辺　章（編）Watanabe Akira (ed.),『労働基準法（昭和 22 年）(1)』 *The Labor Standards Law (1947)* (1), 645 pp., 信山社, 1996.

17 渡辺　章（編）Watanabe Akira (ed.),『労働基準法（昭和 22 年）(3)』*The Labor Standards Law (1947) (3)* (2 vols.), 955 pp., 信山社, 1997.

18 山川隆一 Yamakawa Ryūichi,『雇用関係法』 *Laws Related to Employment*, 311 pp., 新世社, 1996.

19 水町勇一郎 Mizumachi Yūichirō,『パートタイム労働の法律政策』*Legal Policy for Part-Time Work*, 257 pp., 有斐閣, 1997.

20 道幸哲也 Dōkō Tetsunari, 職場における自立と協調性——協調性欠如を理由とする解雇の法理 "Independence and Cooperativeness in the Workplace: The Legal Principles of Dismissal Due to a Lack of Cooperativeness,"「季刊労働法」177 号, pp. 86-97, 総合労働研究所, 1996.

21 小宮文人 Komiya Fumito, 解雇制限法 "Dismissal Restrictions Law,"「日本労働研究雑誌」446 号, pp. 24-32, 日本労働研究機構, 1997.

22 小畑文子 Obata Fumiko, 労働者の退職後の競業避止義務 "The Duty of Workers Not to Compete (*Konkurrenzverbot*) After Retirement,"「日本労働研究雑誌」441 号, pp. 25-33, 日本労働研究機構, 1997.

23 田村善之 Tamura Yoshiyuki, 労働者の転職・引抜きと企業の利益（上・下）"Workers' Job-Changing and Head-Hunting and Corporate Interests,"「ジュリスト」1102 号, pp. 75-80; 1103 号, pp. 106-115, 有斐閣, 1997.

24 特集　個別紛争処理システム "Special Feature: Systems for Resolving Individual Disputes,"「日本労働研究雑誌」436 号, pp. 2-37, 日本労働研究機構, 1996.

25 中窪裕也 Nakakubo Hiroya, "Procedures for Resolving Individual Employment Disputes," *Japan Labor Bulletin*, Vol. 35, No. 6, pp. 5-8, 日本労働研究機構, 1996.

26 野田　進 Noda Susumu,『労働契約の変更と解雇——フランスと日本』 *Modifying Labor Contracts and Dismissal: France and Japan*, 536 pp., 信山社, 1997.

27 菅野和夫 Sugeno Kazuo, 就業規則変更と労使交渉——判例法理の発展のために "The Modification of Work Rules and Labor-Management Bargaining: In the Interests of the Growth of Case Law,"「労働判例」718 号, pp. 6-14, 産労総合研究所, 1997.

28 盛　誠吾 Mori Seigo, 労働条件変更の法理——判例の動向と理論的課題 "The Legal Principles of Modifying Labor Conditions: Precedent Trends

and Theoretical Issues," 「自由と正義」48 巻 11 号, pp. 96-107, 日本弁護士連合会, 1997.

29 日本労働法学会 Japan Labor Law Association, 管理職組合・変更解約告知・チェック・オフ "The Managers Union, Notice to Modify Terms and Conditions of Employment, and Checkoff," 「日本労働法学会誌」88 号, pp. 139-215, 総合労働研究所, 1996.

30 土田道夫 Tsuchida Michio, 変更解約告知と労働者の自己決定（上・下）"Notice to Modify Terms and Conditions of Employment and Workers' Self-Determination," 「法律時報」68 巻 2 号, pp. 39-46; 3 号, pp. 55-63, 日本評論社, 1996.

31 日本労働法学会 Japan Labor Law Association, 賃金処遇制度の変化と法 "Changes in the Wage and Benefits System and the Law," 「日本労働法学会誌」89 号, pp. 5-121, 総合労働研究所, 1997.

32 日本労働法学会 Japan Labor Law Association, パートと均等待遇・協約の拡張適用・過労死 "Part-Time Work and Equal Treatment, Extended Application of Agreements, and Death from Overwork," 「日本労働法学会誌」90 号, pp. 170-211, 総合労働研究所, 1997.

33 岩出　誠 Iwade Makoto, 従業員の健康管理をめぐる法的諸問題 "Legal Problems Surrounding Employees' Health Care," 「日本労働研究雑誌」441 号, pp. 12-24, 日本労働研究機構, 1997.

34 道幸哲也　Dōkō Tetsunari, 職場における人権保障法理の新たな展開 "New Developments in Legal Principles for the Protection of Personal Rights in the Workplace," 「日本労働研究雑誌」441 号, pp. 2-11, 日本労働研究機構, 1997.

35 道幸哲也 Dōkō Tetsunari, 組合併存下における労働条件の決定過程と団結権保障（上・下）"The Process for Deciding Labor Conditions and Guarantees of the Right to Organize under the Coexistence of Unions," 「法律時報」68 巻 7 号, pp. 32-41; 8 号, pp. 65-69, 日本評論社, 1996.

36 倉田　聡 Kurata Satoshi, チェック・オフと不当労働行為 "Checkoff and Unfair Labor Practices," 「日本労働法学会誌」88 号, pp. 235-250, 総合労働研究所, 1996.

37 道幸哲也　Dōkō Tetsunari, 不当労働行為救済法理の独自性（上・下）"The Originality of the Legal Principles of Remedies for Unfair Labor Practices," 「判例時報」1589 号, pp. 21-31; 1590 号, pp. 15-26, 判例時報社, 1997.

38 鈴木　隆 Suzuki Takashi, チェック・オフと協約法理 "Checkoff and the Legal Principles of Collective Agreements," 「日本労働法学会誌」88 号, pp. 219-234, 総合労働研究所, 1996.

39 特集　労働委員会の課題と展望 "Special Issue: Issues in Labor Relations

Commissions and Future Prospects," 「別冊中央労働時報」897 号, pp. 2-64, 労委協会, 1996.

40 手塚和彰 Tezuka Kazuaki, 『外国人と法』 *Foreigners and the Law*, 318 pp., 有斐閣, 1996.

41 米津孝司 Yonezu Takashi, 『国際労働契約法の研究』 *A Study of International Labor Contract Law*, 230 pp., 尚学社, 1997.

VI. Public Law

01 日本公法学会 Japan Public Law Association, 「公法研究」 *Public Law Review*, 58 号, 342 pp. (1996); 59 号, 438 pp. (1997), 有斐閣.

The annual bulletin of the Japan Public Law Association. No. 58 deals with "The Right to Pursue Happiness: Its Structure and Development" and "Effective Enforcement of Public Administration," while No. 59 features "Five Decades of the Constitution of Japan: Retrospection and Future Prospects."

02 1996 年学界回顧 "Legal Studies in Japan, 1996," 「法律時報」68 巻 13 号, 日本評論社, 1996.

小林武・清田雄治 Kobayashi Takeshi and Kiyota Yūji, 憲法 "Constitutional Law" (pp. 6-23); 渡名喜庸安・本田滝夫 Tonaki Yōan and Honda Takio, 行政法 "Administrative Law" (pp. 24-31).

03 学界展望 (1996) "Legal Studies in Japan (1996)," 「公法研究」, 58 号, 有斐閣, 1996.

初宿正典 Shiyake Masanori, 憲法 "Constitutional Law" (pp. 274-301); 高木光 Takagi Hikaru, 行政法 "Administrative Law" (pp. 302-329).

04 1997 年学界回顧 "Legal Studies in Japan, 1997," 「法律時報」69 巻 13 号, 日本評論社, 1997.

小林武・清田雄治 Kobayashi Takeshi and Kiyota Yūji, 憲法 "Constitutional Law" (pp. 6-24); 渡名喜庸安・白藤博行 Tonaki Yōan and Shirafuji Hiroyuki, 行政法 "Administrative Law" (pp. 25-32).

05 学界展望 (1997) "Legal Studies in Japan (1997)," 「公法研究」, 59 号, 有斐閣, 1997.

岡田信弘 Okada Nobuhiro, 憲法 "Constitutional Law" (pp. 373-390); 高木光 Takagi Hikaru, 行政法 "Administrative Law" (pp. 391-420).

06 特集 日本国憲法 50 年と 21 世紀への展望 "Special Issue: Fifty Years under the Constitution of Japan and Prospects for the 21st Century," 「法律時報」68 巻 6 号, pp. 6-179, 日本評論社, 1996.

07 特集 日本国憲法 50 年の軌跡と展望 "Special Issue: The Course of Fifty Years under the Constitution of Japan and Future Prospects," 「ジュリスト」1089 号, pp. 10-302, 有斐閣, 1996.

08 樋口陽一・森 英樹・高見勝利・辻村みよ子 (編) Higuchi Yōichi, Mori

Hideki, Takami Katsutoshi and Tsujimura Miyoko (eds.),『憲法理論の
50年』Fifty Years of Constitutional Theory, 375 pp., 日本評論社, 1996.

09 樋口陽一 Higuchi Yōichi,『転換期の憲法？』The Constitution at a
Turning Point?, 260 pp., 敬文堂, 1996.

A collection of 12 articles published by the author in the early 1990s. He
examines what has changed and what has not changed (or should not
change) with respect to basic concepts of constitutionalism such as
"nation-state" and "human rights."

10 深瀬忠一 Fukase Tadakazu, 戦後50年の世界の「諸憲法と国際平和」の
新たな展望 (1)～(7) "Fresh Prospects for 'Constitutions and World
Peace' in the World 50 Years after World War II,"「法律時報」68巻1号
～9号, 日本評論社, 1996.

11 大石　眞 Ōishi Makoto,『憲法と宗教制度』The Constitution and Religious Institutions, 308 pp., 有斐閣, 1996.

12 君塚正臣 Kimizuka Masaomi,『性差別司法審査基準論』A Study of
Standards for Judicial Reviews of Sexual Discrimination, 353 pp., 信山
社, 1996.

An examination of constitutional review standards regarding questions
of sexual discrimination, with reference chiefly to American case law
theory.

13 藤井俊夫 Fujii Toshio,『経済規制と違憲審査』Economic Regulations
and Constitutional Review, 360 pp., 成文堂, 1996.

14 本　秀紀 Moto Hideki,『現代政党国家の危機と再生』The Crisis and
Rebirth of the Contemporary Party State, 374 pp., 日本評論社, 1996.

A study of the system of state assistance for political parties with
reference to the German system.

15 特集　愛媛玉串料訴訟最高裁大法廷判決 "Special Issue: The Decision by
the Grand Bench of the Supreme Court on the Ehime Shinto Offerings
(Tamagushi-ryō) Case,"「ジュリスト」1114号, pp. 4-68, 有斐閣, 1997.

16 特集　憲法学の可能性を探る "Special Issue: Exploring the Possibilities
of the Study of Constitutional Law,"「法律時報」69巻6号, pp. 8-63, 日
本評論社, 1997.

Four constitutional scholars of the younger generation (水島朝穂
Mizushima Asaho, 長谷部恭男 Hasebe Yasuo, 石川健治 Ishikawa Kenji
and 蟻川恒正 Arikawa Tsunemasa) present their views on and debate
about the topics of state sovereignty and peace; popular sovereignty,
parliament, and local autonomy; human rights, state power, and societal
power; and the legitimacy of judges and democracy.

17 『岩波講座　現代の法1』Iwanami Lecture Series: Contemporary Law,

岩波書店，1997．

Vol. 1,『現代国家と法』*The Contemporary State and the Law*, 328 pp.
　　　Contains 10 articles that examine basic legal theory concerning the
　　state and the nature of the administrative reforms currently underway.

Vol. 3,『政治過程と法』*The Political Process and the Law*, 312 pp.
　　　Contains 10 articles on the universality and peculiarities of Japan's
　　political process.

Vol. 10,『情報と法』*Information and the Law*, 327 pp.
　　　Contains articles dealing with subjects such as information disclo-
　　sure, protection of the confidentiality of personal information, and new
　　developments in broadcasting and communications legislation.

Vol. 11,『ジェンダーと法』*Gender and the Law*, 347 pp.
　　　Contains articles that explore the possibilities of feminist jurispru-
　　dence in Japan.

18　特集　情報公開法制定の論点 "Special Issue: Moot Points Regarding the
　　Enactment of the Freedom of Information Bill,"「法律時報」69 巻 1 号,
　　pp. 6-88, 日本評論社，1997．
　　　Includes a discussion about the "Draft Guidelines of the Freedom of
　　Information Bill" by Okudaira Yasuhiro 奥平康弘 and Shiono Hiroshi 塩
　　野宏.

19　特集　情報公開法要綱案をめぐって "Special Issue: On the Draft Guide-
　　lines of the Freedom of Information Bill,"「ジュリスト」1107 号, pp. 4-
　　72, 有斐閣，1997．

20　特集　住民記録システムネットワークへの課題 "Special Issue: Issues for
　　the Residents' Records System Network,"「ジュリスト」1092 号, pp. 5-
　　36, 有斐閣，1996．
　　　Examines a proposal to improve administrative efficiency by systemati-
　　cally assigning a number to every person in Japan on the basis of informa-
　　tion recorded in the Residents' Basic Register.

21　田村　理 Tamura Osamu,『フランス革命と財産権――財産権の「神聖不
　　可侵」と自然権思想』*The French Revolution and Property Rights: The
　　"Sacred Inviolability" of Property Rights and Natural Rights Thought*,
　　520 pp., 創文社，1997．

22　時國康夫 Tokikuni Yasuo,『憲法訴訟とその判断の手法』*Constitutional
　　Litigation and Methods of Adjudication*, 307 pp., 第一法規出版，1997．
　　　A collection of articles that brings together pioneering research on
　　theoretical aspects of constitutional litigation, such as methods for demon-
　　strating legislative facts and the standing necessary for raising issues of
　　unconstitutionality.

23 笹田栄司 Sasada Eiji,『裁判制度』 *The Judicial System*, 260 pp., 信山社, 1997.

24 芦部信喜 Ashibe Nobuyoshi,『憲法〔新版〕』 *Constitutional Law (New Edition)*, 370 pp., 岩波書店, 1997.

    A new edition of a widely used standard textbook on constitutional law.

25 長谷部恭男 Hasebe Yasuo,『憲法』 *Constitutional Law*, 454 pp., 新世社, 1997.

26 樋口陽一・佐藤幸治・中村睦男・浦部法穂 Higuchi Yōichi, Satō Kōji, Nakamura Mutsuo and Urabe Noriho,『憲法 II』 *The Constitution II*, 403 pp., 青林書院, 1997.

    An article-by-article commentary on Articles 21-40 (freedom of expression, economic freedom, personal freedom, etc.).

27 奥平康弘 Okudaira Yasuhiro,『ジャーナリズムと法』 *Journalism and the Law*, 363 pp., 新世社, 1997.

    A textbook that explains judicial precedents and legal theory relating to the mass media.

28 大橋洋一 Ōhashi Yōichi,『行政法学の構造的変革』 *Structural Changes in Administrative Law*, 346 pp., 有斐閣, 1996.

29 高橋　滋 Takahashi Shigeru,『行政手続法』 *Administrative Procedure Law*, 470 pp., 弘文堂, 1996.

30 阿部泰隆 Abe Yasutaka,『政策法学の基本指針』 *Basic Guidelines for Policy-Related Jurisprudence*, 394 pp., 有斐閣, 1996.

31 特集　地方分権と国・地方関係 "Special Issue: Decentralization and National-Regional Relations,"「ジュリスト」1090 号, pp. 4-72, 有斐閣, 1996.

32 特集　地方分権推進委員会第 1 次勧告 "Special Issue: The 1st Recommendation of the Decentralization Promotion Committee,"「ジュリスト」1110 号, pp. 3-89, 有斐閣, 1997.

33 兼子　仁 Kaneko Masashi,『行政法学』 *Administrative Law*, 336 pp., 岩波書店, 1997.

    A textbook that covers administrative law in general.

34 見上崇洋 Mikami Takahiro,『行政計画の法的統制』 *Legal Control of Administrative Plans*, 440 pp., 信山社, 1997.

35 宇賀克也 Uga Katsuya,『国家補償法』 *State Compensation Law*, 531 pp., 有斐閣, 1997.

    A comprehensive study of compensation for illegal acts performed by the state or public bodies and indemnity for lawful expropriation.

36 西埜　章 Nishino Akira,『国家賠償法』 *State Redress Law*, 584 pp., 青

林書院, 1997.

An article-by-article commentary on the State Redress Law.

37　原野　魁 Harano Akira,『行政の公共性と行政法』 *The Public Nature of Administration and Administrative Law*, 325 pp., 法律文化社, 1997.

VII. Criminal Law

01　内藤　謙・芝原邦爾・西田典之（編）Naitō Ken, Shibahara Kuniji and Nishida Noriyuki (eds.),『刑事法学の課題と展望──香川達夫博士古稀祝賀』 *Issues in and Prospects for Criminal Jurisprudence: Collected Papers Celebrating the 70th Birthday of Dr. Kagawa Tatsuo*, 450 pp., 成文堂, 1996.

02　中山研一先生古稀祝賀論文集編集委員会（編）Collected Papers Celebrating the 70th Birthday of Professor Nakayama Ken'ichi Editorial Committee (ed.),『中山研一先生古稀祝賀論文集』 *Collected Papers Celebrating the 70th Birthday of Professor Nakayama Ken'ichi*, 成文堂, 1997.
Vol. 1,『生命と刑法』 *Life and Criminal Law*, 401 pp.
Vol. 2,『経済と刑法』 *The Economy and Criminal Law*, 373 pp.
Vol. 3,『刑法の理論』 *Theories of Criminal Law*, 341 pp.
Vol. 4,『刑法の諸相』 *Various Aspects of Criminal Law*, 328 pp.
Vol. 5,『刑法の展開』 *Developments in Criminal Law*, 343 pp.

03　西原春夫・松尾浩也・田宮　裕（編）Nishihara Haruo, Matsuo Kōya and Tamiya Hiroshi (eds.),『アメリカ刑事法の諸相──鈴木義男先生古稀祝賀』 *Various Aspects of American Criminal Law: Collected Papers Celebrating the 70th Birthday of Professor Suzuki Yoshio*, 598 pp., 成文堂, 1996.

04　井戸田　侃（編）Idota Akira (ed.),『新・生きている刑事訴訟法──佐伯千仞先生卆寿祝賀論文集』 *New Studies in Living Criminal Procedure Code: Collected Papers Celebrating the 90th Birthday of Professor Saeki Chihiro*, 340 pp., 成文堂, 1997.

05　特集　組織犯罪対策立法 "Special Issue: Proposed Legislation against Organized Crime,"「ジュリスト」1122 号, pp. 4-51, 有斐閣, 1997.

06　中山研一・小田中聰樹・川崎英明 Nakayama Ken'ichi, Odanaka Toshiki and Kawasaki Hideaki, 組織的犯罪対策立法の検討 "An Examination of Proposed Legislation against Organized Crime,"「法律時報」69 巻 3 号, pp. 39-50; 4 号, pp. 47-52, 日本評論社, 1997.

07　井上正仁 Inoue Masahito,『捜査手段としての通信・会話の傍受』 *Wiretapping in Criminal Investigation*, 297 pp., 有斐閣, 1997.

08　特集　少年法の現状と課題 "Special Issue: The Current State of Juvenile Law and Related Issues,"「ジュリスト」1087 号, pp. 9-95, 有斐閣, 1996.

09 特集 少年司法制度の再検討 "Special Issue: A Reexamination of the Juvenile Justice System," 「刑法雑誌」 36 巻 2 号, pp. 295-345, 日本刑法学会, 1997.

10 荒木伸怡 (編) Araki Nobuyoshi (ed.), 『非行事実の認定』 *Fact-Finding for Juvenile Delinquency*, 344 pp., 弘文堂, 1997.

11 斉藤豊治 Saitō Toyoji, 『少年法研究』 *A Study of Juvenile Law*, 228 pp., 成文堂, 1997.

12 後藤弘子 (編) Gotō Hiroko (ed.), 『少年犯罪と少年法』 *Juvenile Crime and Juvenile Law*, 233 pp., 明石書店, 1997.

13 木村裕三 Kimura Yūzō, 『イギリスの少年司法制度』 *The System of Juvenile Justice in Great Britain*, 403 pp., 成文堂, 1997.

14 鈴木義男 Suzuki Yoshio, 『日本の刑事司法再論』 *Japan's Criminal Justice Reconsidered*, 249 pp., 成文堂, 1997.

15 吉岡一男 Yoshioka Kazuo, 『刑事制度論の展開』 *Developments in Criminal Institution Theory*, 291 pp., 成文堂, 1997.

16 内田博文 Uchida Hirofumi, 『刑法学における歴史研究の意義と方法』 *The Significance and Methods of Historical Research in Criminal Jurisprudence*, 563 pp., 九州大学出版会, 1997.

17 山口 厚 Yamaguchi Atsushi, 犯罪論の基礎 "Foundations of Criminal Law Theory," 「法学教室」 184 号, pp. 61-67; 185 号, pp. 74-80; 186 号, pp. 49-55; 187 号, pp. 60-66; 189 号, pp. 67-73; 190 号, pp. 40-47; 191 号, pp. 46-53; 192 号, pp. 63-70; 194 号, pp. 97-103; 195 号, pp. 60-67; 197 号, pp. 95-101; 198 号, pp. 71-78, 有斐閣, 1996-97.

18 山中敬一 Yamanaka Keiichi, 『刑法における客観的帰属の理論』 *The Theory of Objective Attribution in Criminal Law*, 852 pp., 成文堂, 1997.

19 特集 不作為犯論の再構成 "A Reconstruction of the Theory of Crimes of Omission," 「刑法雑誌」 36 巻 1 号, pp. 91-177, 日本刑法学会, 1996.

20 振津隆行 Furitsu Takayuki, 『刑事不法論の研究』 *A Study of the Theory of Criminal Unlawfulness*, 314 pp., 成文堂, 1996.

21 特集 正当防衛と過剰防衛 "Special Issue: Legitimate Self-Defence and Excessive Self-Defence," 「刑法雑誌」 35 巻 2 号, pp. 205-267, 日本刑法学会, 1996.

22 高山佳奈子 Takayama Kanako, 違法性の意識 "Consciousness of Illegality," 「法学協会雑誌」 114 巻 1 号, pp. 73-109; 2 号, pp. 147-206; 3 号, pp. 281-338; 4 号, pp. 357-413; 5 号, pp. 485-546, 法学協会事務所, 1997.

23 特集 刑事責任能力をめぐる最近の動向と問題点 "Special Issue: Recent Trends and Problems Concerning Criminal Responsibility," 「刑法雑誌」 36 巻 1 号, pp. 38-90, 日本刑法学会, 1996.

34

24 岩井宜子 Iwai Yoshiko,『精神障害者福祉と司法』 *The Welfare of the Mentally Disabled and Justice*, 354 pp., 尚学社, 1997.

25 松原芳博 Matsubara Yoshihiro,『犯罪概念と可罰性』 *The Concept of Crime and Punishability*, 462 pp., 成文堂, 1997.

26 特集 罪数論の現代的意義 "The Contemporary Significance of the Theory of Concurrence of Crimes,"「刑法雑誌」37巻1号, pp. 52-102, 日本刑法学会, 1997.

27 奥村正雄 Okumura Masao,『イギリス刑事法の動向』 *Trends in British Criminal Law*, 248 pp., 成文堂, 1996.

28 町野 朔・林 幹人（編）Machino Saku and Hayashi Mikito (eds.),『現代社会における没収・追徴』 *Forfeiture in Contemporary Society*, 375 pp., 信山社, 1996.

29 特集 臓器移植法 "Special Issue: The Organ Transplant Law,"「ジュリスト」1121号, pp. 4-62, 有斐閣, 1997.

30 芝原邦爾・堀内捷三・町野 朔・西田典之(編) Shibahara Kuniji, Horiuchi Shōzō, Machino Saku and Nishida Noriyuki (eds.),『刑法理論の現代的展開 各論』 *Contemporary Developments in Criminal Law Theory: Specific Topics*, 376 pp., 日本評論社, 1996.

31 町野 朔 Machino Saku,『犯罪各論の現在』 *The Present State of Specialized Topics in Crime Theory*, 446 pp., 有斐閣, 1996.

32 山口 厚 Yamaguchi Atsushi, 犯罪各論の基礎 "Foundations of Criminal Law Theory: Specific Topics,"「法学教室」199号, pp. 73-80; 200号, pp. 103-109; 202号, pp. 90-96; 203号, pp. 74-81; 204号, pp. 91-98; 206号, pp. 44-51; 207号, pp. 65-72, 有斐閣, 1997.

33 園田 寿 Sonoda Hisashi, サイバーポルノと刑法 "Cyberpornography and Criminal Law,"「法学セミナー」501号, pp. 4-8, 日本評論社, 1996.

34 前田雅英 Maeda Masahide, インターネットとわいせつ犯罪 "The Internet and Obscenity Offenses,"「ジュリスト」1112号, pp. 77-83, 有斐閣, 1997.

35 山口 厚 Yamaguchi Atsushi, コンピュータ・ネットワークと犯罪 "Computer Networks and Crime,"「ジュリスト」1117号, pp. 73-80, 有斐閣, 1997.

36 上嶌一高 Ueshima Kazutaka,『背任罪理解の再構成』 *A Reconstruction of the Crime of Breach of Trust*, 308 pp., 成文堂, 1997.

37 神山敏雄 Kamiyama Toshio,『日本の経済犯罪』 *Economic Crime in Japan*, 320 pp., 日本評論社, 1996.

38 西田典之（編）Nishida Noriyuki (ed.),『金融業務と刑事法』 *Financial Business and Criminal Law*, 247 pp., 有斐閣, 1997.

39 特集 企業犯罪をめぐる現代的諸問題 "Special Issue: Contemporary

Problems Surrounding Corporate Crime," 「刑法雑誌」36 巻 2 号, pp. 241-294, 日本刑法学会, 1997.

40 鈴木茂嗣 Suzuki Shigetsugu, 『続・刑事訴訟法の基本構造』 *The Basic Structure of Criminal Procedure Code (Contd.)* (2vols.), 366 pp., 408 pp., 成文堂, 1996-97.

41 渡辺 修（編）Watanabe Osamu (ed.),『刑事手続の最前線』 *The Forefront of Criminal Procedure*, 326 pp., 三省堂, 1996.

42 川崎英明 Kawasaki Hideaki,『現代検察官論』 *A Study of the Contemporary Public Prosecutor*, 297 pp., 日本評論社, 1997.

43 平良木登規男 Hiraragi Tokio,『捜査法』 *Criminal Investigation Law*, 340 pp., 成文堂, 1996.

44 特集 被疑者の逮捕・勾留 "Special Issue: The Arrest and Detention of Suspects," 「刑法雑誌」35 巻 2 号, pp. 269-333, 日本刑法学会, 1996.

45 特集 捜索・押収と令状主義 "Special Issue: Search, Seizure, and Warrant Requirements," 「刑法雑誌」36 巻 3 号, pp. 409-455, 日本刑法学会, 1997.

46 下村幸雄 Shimomura Yukio,『共犯者の自白』 *Admissions of Guilt by Criminal Accomplices*, 470 pp., 日本評論社, 1996.

47 田中輝和 Tanaka Terukazu, 『刑事再審理由の判断方法』 *Methods of Judging Reasons for the Reopening of Criminal Proceedings*, 464 pp., 信山社, 1996.

48 光藤景皎（編）Mitsudō Kageaki (ed.), 『事実誤認と救済』 *Erroneous Factual Determination and Remedies*, 306 pp., 成文堂, 1997.

49 宮沢浩一・田口守一・高橋則夫（編）Miyazawa Kōichi, Taguchi Morikazu and Takahashi Norio (eds.),『犯罪被害者の研究』 *Studies of Crime Victims*, 500 pp., 成文堂, 1996.

50 高橋則夫 Takahashi Norio,『刑法における損害回復の思想』 *The Idea of the Recovery of Damages in Criminal Law*, 232 pp., 成文堂, 1997.

51 特集 犯罪被害者と刑事司法 "Special Issue: Crime Victims and Criminal Justice," 「刑法雑誌」35 巻 3 号, pp. 383-433, 日本刑法学会, 1996.

POLITICAL SCIENCE

Iio Jun
National Graduate Institute for Policy Studies
Kanai Toshiyuki
Tokyo Metropolitan University

I. JAPANESE NATIONAL POLITICS AND RESEARCH TRENDS

Japanese politics in the review period (1996–97) began with the sudden announcement of his resignation by Prime Minister Murayama Tomiichi of the Social Democratic Party (SDP) on 5 January 1996, followed on 11 January by the appointment of Hashimoto Ryūtarō of the Liberal Democratic Party (LDP) as prime minister while still preserving the framework of the coalition government made up of the LDP, SDP and New Party Sakigake. By March Hashimoto had provisionally resolved the issue of bankrupt housing-loan corporations (*jūsen*), which had been pending since the previous year, and on the question of U.S. forces stationed in Okinawa he reached an agreement with the United States in April for the return of Futemma Air Station, which in turn led to the Japan-U.S. Joint Declaration on Security. In this fashion Hashimoto demonstrated his leadership and restored some vitality to politics, which had seemed to be in a state of stagnancy.

Then on 20 October he faced the electorate in a general election. The opposition Shinshintō (New Frontier Party) was unable to extend its support because of problems with internal unity, and although it attempted to launch some bold policies, these were announced rather abruptly just before the election and failed to gain the understanding of voters. In addition, on the government side a large number of Diet members from the SDP and Sakigake formed the Democratic Party (Minshutō) shortly before the elec-

38

tion, thereby obscuring the boundaries between the government and opposition parties, and voter turnout was low. In urban areas the Shinshintō and Democratic Party lost seats because of vote-splitting, and although the LDP did not win an outright majority, it increased the number of its seats and grew in stability.

It was on this basis that the 2nd Hashimoto Cabinet was inaugurated, and with what was in effect an LDP one-party cabinet (since no cabinet ministers came from the SDP and Sakigake, which had lost many seats) Hashimoto secured the political initiative for 1997, promising to implement six major reforms centered on the administrative reforms proposed by each party during the election campaign and focussing on administration, fiscal structure, social security, economic structure, financial system, and education. By way of contrast, leading members of the Shinshintō began leaving the party because of its defeat in the general elections, and in December 1997 Ozawa Ichirō, who had been elected party leader, finally decided to dissolve the party, and the Shinshintō, which had been formed to provide opposition to the LDP, fell apart.

In April 1997 the Hashimoto Cabinet raised the consumption tax in accordance with its prearranged programme. During the summer, definite plans for administrative reform and the reform of Japan's fiscal structure were drawn up. These achievements made it possible for Hashimoto to be reelected president of the LDP. His position would thus seem to have been rock-solid, but following internal discord on the occasion of a cabinet reshuffle in September, some party members rebelled against aspects of the proposed administrative reforms, and there was also increasing dissatisfaction with the sluggishness of the economy. This was compounded by a failure to deal effectively with a financial crisis that began surfacing towards the end of the year, and this resulted in a rapid decline in support for the government.

As a reflection of the advances being made in the study of Japanese politics, increasing numbers of textbooks on political science are drawing their examples from Japanese politics [I-01 ~03]. In research on the policy-making process too there have begun to appear textbooks compiled on the basis of Japanese examples [I-04, 05]. There were also published some examinations of the methodology of the study of Japanese politics [I-06, 07].

A distinctive feature of the study of Japanese politics during the review period was the emergence of research on the demise of the LDP's long-term one-party government and the start of a period of coalition government in 1993, the most important events in Japanese politics in recent years. Representative of this research was the 1996 issue of the annual bulletin of the Japanese Political Science Association [I-08]. In content it ranges from considerations of the political system as a whole to examinations of the actual policy process and discussions of changes in party support on the basis of public opinion polls, and the articles elucidate the shift in government and the transformation of Japan's political system from a variety of angles. The contributors take the view that political change does not come about merely by chance, but that social and economic changes prepare the way for political change, one manifestation of which was the political changes of 1993. There also appeared another study on the same subject [I-09], but in this case the focus is on the structural and ideological changes behind political change rather than on analyzing the actual process of change. In addition to further studies related to this topic [I-12 ~14], there also appeared some detailed research on the political process that merits attention [I-71~74] and a number of studies that approach the subject from the perspective of opinion polls [I-98~103]. There were also published testimonies by some of those directly involved in these events [I-52~54], as well as some reportages of related interest [I-50, 51].

There has also begun to appear research that reconsiders the significance of the political reform movement that brought about the political changes of 1993 and the resulting reform of the electoral system. A representative work, centered on case studies of the 1996 general elections, concludes that the effects of electoral reform have been questionable [I-10]. Those who take this standpoint tend to stress the adventitious nature of the political changes of 1993, but a different view has been put forward by one of the participants in these changes [I-55], and there also appeared a noteworthy study of the electoral system and party system in Japan from a more general perspective [I-92].

In addition, there appeared several works that explore the factors behind political change in general terms [I-17~20, 91], and I-19 and -20 merit attention in that they attempt to forge a link between the electoral process and the policy process, which have hitherto been treated separately. Also worth mentioning is I-22, which goes back to the time of the oil crisis in the 1970s and provides a comprehensive discussion of relations between the government and markets in Japan.

In research on individual political actors, the fruits of research on the Diet are continuing to be published at a constant rate [I-24~28]. With regard to political parties, systematic studies of party organization have appeared [I-30, 31], and an extension of this can be seen in research on supporters' associations (*kōenkai*) [I-33, 34]. Research on special-interest groups has been somewhat sluggish [I-39~41], and likewise there has appeared little research on individual politicians [I-46~48]; I-47 and -48 are collections of data on politicians' activities. A more unusual work is I-56, which adds relevant material to the testimony of a former Deputy Chief Cabinet Secretary. In contrast to previous years, there has been a sharp decline in the number of political commentaries being published, and among these about the only one to attract much attention was a study of the language used by politicians [I-62].

In research on the policy process, there appeared an analysis of the policy process surrounding the introduction of the consumption tax [I-65], and, focussing on the concept of limited rationality, it makes a major contribution to analysis of the current situation and theoretical formulations with respect to both politicians and bureaucrats in Japan. There also appeared a multifaceted study of Japan-U.S. trade negotiations [I-66], describing both the process and the consciousness of people in both countries, and a collection of articles dealing with the policy-making process [I-67], chiefly with respect to planning in the prewar and postwar periods. In addition, I-68 probes the political process behind the administrative reforms of the 1980s by adding discussions with participants to an account of the process itself, while I-69, exploring the factors behind the Ministry of Finance's loss of power with reference to the revision of the Bank of Japan Law and the reform of the Ministry of Finance, deals with a political process that was underway only several months to one year earlier, and it shows that researchers are beginning to acquire a sense of contemporaneity that is no less prompt in responding to current events than are journalists. In other publications on the political process listed in the Bibliography there is evidence of a growing tendency to conduct analyses on the basis of a specific theoretical framework, thus indicating that criticism of previous directionless descriptions of the political process has had an effect.

In the field of psephology and public opinion polls, the commencement of the publication of a series entitled "The Changing Voting Behavior of the Japanese" [1-86~88] merits special mention. A factor behind publications such as this is the increasing refinement of databases, resulting in a situation in which not only are there professionals who concentrate on collecting data, but large numbers of researchers vie with each other in interpreting the same data from different angles. In addition, there also appeared an outstanding study that emphasizes the existence of the ideological axis as an unchanging factor in politics [1-89].

II. PUBLIC ADMINISTRATION AND LOCAL GOVERNMENT

The establishment of a non-LDP government in 1993 led to the reinstatement of the power of bureaucrats *vis-à-vis* politicians. But the restoration of bureaucratic power was unable to bring about stability of governance through bureaucratic control as it had in the past, and instead the mistakes of bureaucrats were exposed in the absence of political leadership. This included revelations of time-honored patterns of bureaucratic corruption in a series of scandals involving the misuse of subsidies by leading officials of the Ministry of Health and Welfare, the wining and dining of officials of the Ministry of Finance, and the entertaining of central government officials by local bureaucrats with public funds. In addition, responses to crisis management on the occasion of the Great Hanshin Earthquake and the sarin-gas attack on Tokyo's subway system [II-01, III-30, 50, 51], cases of infection with the HIV virus through contaminated blood, the economic recession, and financial uneasiness [I-69] all served to highlight not only bureaucratic corruption but also failures in the operations of the administration *per se.* The Great Hanshin Earthquake also led to an upsurge of interest in volunteer activities, partly because of the contrast that they presented with the ineptitude of the bureaucracy [III-04, 42, 43].

It was in such circumstances that criticism of the bureaucracy increased both in the mass media and among the general public, and numerous reports on the subject were published [II-37~47, III-54~56]. The reconfirmation of the importance of the evaluation of administration [II-18, 20, 21, 34, III-34], the advocacy of accountability [II-19], and accounts of the "New Public Management" (NPM) administrative reforms being undertaken in Anglo-Saxon countries [II-12, 22, 30] were also reflected in research. Although public administration and local government are fields of study that are relatively independent of trends in the real world, with an inevitable time lag between such trends and research related to them, the increase in studies responding to contemporary issues in the midst of these major changes has nonetheless been a distinctive feature of research in recent years.

In the 1996 general elections administrative reform once again became an issue, being incorporated into the election pledges of all the major parties [II-12~14]. After the elections the Hashimoto Cabinet included administrative reform among its "six major reforms" and set up an Administrative Reform Council (28 Nov. 1996) with the prime minister as its chairman. Members included the chairmen of the Decentralization Promotion Committee and the Administrative Reform Committee, concerned with issues such as deregulation and freedom of information, and its aim was to develop comprehensive administrative reforms, although the real interests of the Hashimoto administration lay in the reorganization of central government and the strengthening of the cabinet's functions rather than in deregulation and decentralization. Consequently, after the Administrative Reform Council submitted its interim report on 3 September 1997 and its final report on 3

December 1997, it was agreed in general terms to reorganize central government (with a prime minister's office and twelve ministries and agencies) and strengthen cabinet functions. Deregulation and decentralization did not occupy a central position in the Hashimoto Cabinet's administrative reforms, and in this sense these issues lost their political drive at a government level, but they continued to be promoted quietly by third-party independent committees made up chiefly of people of learning and experience and members of the business world. The Administrative Reform Committee submitted its "Second Opinion on the Promotion of Deregulation: Towards a New Japan Built by Creativity" on 16 December 1996, and an administrative reform programme was decided on by the cabinet council on 25 December. Meanwhile, the Decentralization Promotion Committee submitted an interim report on 29 March 1996 and its first, second, third and fourth recommendations on 20 December 1996 and 8 July, 2 September and 9 October 1997. The Decentralization Promotion Committee has largely fulfilled its allotted task, and decentralization could be said to have now reached the stage of actual implementation [III-02, 11~20].

When one looks back on this period in later years, it may be found that these administrative reforms became a political issue only because of an apparent respite in Japan's economic woes. The same could be said about the inclusion of reform of the fiscal structure in the six major reforms promoted by the Hashimoto Cabinet, with plans for fiscal rebuilding by curbing annual expenditure. But from about autumn 1997 financial uncertainty and the economic recession progressively worsened, and in 1998 interest shifted to financial and economic issues.

BIBLIOGRAPHY

I. National Politics
I-1. General Works and Textbooks
    01 伊藤光利 (編) Itō Mitsutoshi (ed.),『ポリティカル・サイエンス事始め』 *The Beginnings of Political Science*, 239 pp., 有斐閣, 1996.

02 堀江　湛（編）Horie Fukashi (ed.),『日本の選挙と政党政治』 *Elections and Party Politics in Japan* [現代の政治学 I], 240 pp., 北樹出版, 1997.

03 真渕　勝・久米郁男・北山俊哉 Mabuchi Masaru, Kume Ikuo and Kitayama Toshiya,『はじめて出会う政治学』 *Encountering Political Science for the First Time*, 247 pp., 有斐閣, 1997.

04 草野　厚 Kusano Atsushi,『政策過程分析入門』 *An Introduction to the Analysis of the Policy Process*, 201 pp., 東京大学出版会, 1997.

05 磯野育男 Isozaki Ikuo,『政策過程の理論と実際』 *The Theory and Practice of the Policy Process*, 264 pp., 芦書房, 1997.

06 鈴木基史 Suzuki Motoshi, 合理的選択新制度論による日本政治の批判的考察 "A Critical Appraisal of the Rational-Choice Institutionalist Approach to Japanese Politics,"「レヴァイアサン」19 号, pp. 86-104, 木鐸社, 1996.

07 猪口　孝 Inoguchi Takashi, 現代日本政治研究の問題と展望 "Contemporary Japanese Political Studies: Problems and Future Prospects,"「レヴァイアサン」21 号, pp. 146-160, 木鐸社, 1997.

I-2. The Political System

08 日本政治学会（編）Japanese Political Science Association (ed.),『55 年体制の崩壊』 *The Collapse of the 1955 Regime* [「年報政治学」1996 年], 岩波書店, 1996.

Contains: 岡沢憲芙 Okazawa Norio, 政党政治システムの変容 "The Transformation of the Party Government System," pp. 3-30; 田中愛治 Tanaka Aiji, 国民意識における「55 年体制」の変容と崩壊 "The Transformation and Collapse of the '1955 Regime' in Public Attitudes," pp. 31-66; 岩井奉信 Iwai Tomoaki, 55 年体制の崩壊とマスメディア "The Collapse of the 1955 Regime and the Mass Media," pp. 67-88; 穴見明 Anami Akira, 55 年体制の崩壊と執政機能の強化 "The Collapse of the 1955 Regime and the Strengthening of the Executive Functions of Government," pp. 89-107; 伊藤光利 Itō Mitsutoshi, 自民党下野の政治過程 "The Political Process of the LDP's Fall from Power," pp. 109-128; 篠田徹 Shinoda Tōru, 再びニワトリからアヒルへ? "From Chicken to Duck Again?," pp. 129-149; 薮野祐三 Yabuno Yūzō, ナショナル・ポリティクスとローカル・ポリティクスの相克 "The Conflict between National Politics and Local Politics," pp. 151-172; 江上能義 Egami Takayoshi, 55 年体制の崩壊と沖縄革新県政の行方 "The Collapse of the 1955 Regime and the Future of Okinawa's Reformist Prefectural Government," pp. 173-188; and 後房雄 Ushiro Fusao, 制度改革と政治変動 "Institutional Reform and Political Change," pp. 189-212.

09 山口二郎・生活経済政策研究所（編）Yamaguchi Jirō and Economic

Policy Institute for Quality Life (eds.),『連立政治——同時代の検証』 *Coalition Government: A Contemporaneous Examination*, 254+6 pp., 朝日新聞社, 1997.

Includes: 山口二郎 Yamaguchi Jirō, 壮大な政治的実験？ "A Spectacular Political Experiment ?"; 後房雄 Ushiro Fusao, 戦後民主主義のバージョン・アップ "An Upgrade of Postwar Democracy"; 新川敏光 Shinkawa Toshimitsu, 歌を忘れたカナリア？ "A Canary That Has Forgotten How to Sing？"; 伊藤光利 Itō Mitsutoshi, 連立維持か党の独自性か "To Preserve the Coalition or Promote Party Originality?"; 坪郷實 Tsubogō Minoru, 市民活動の時代に "An Age of Citizens' Activities"; and 山口二郎 Yamaguchi Jirō, 経済構造の変化と遅れた政治の対応 "Changes in Economic Structure and the Tardy Political Response."

10 大嶽秀夫（編）Ōtake Hideo (ed.),『政界再編の研究——新選挙制度による総選挙』 *Studies in Party Realignment: General Elections under the New Electoral System*, 375 pp., 有斐閣, 1997.

Includes: 大嶽秀夫 Ōtake Hideo, 都市圏における個人後援会の変容と再編 "The Transformation and Reorganization of Personal Supporters' Associations (*Kōenkei*) in Urban Areas"; 山田真裕 Yamada Masahiro, 農村型選挙区における政界再編および選挙制度改革の影響 "The Influence of Party Realignment and Electoral System Reform in Rural Constituencies"; パク・チョルヒー Park Cheol Hee, 大都市の下町における選挙ネットワークの変化と連続 "Change and Continuity in Electoral Networks in the Downtown Areas of Large Cities"; 丹羽功 Niwa Isao, 大企業労使と選挙 "Labor and Management in Large Corporations and Elections"; 丹羽功 Niwa Isao, 自民党地方組織の活動 "The Activities of LDP Regional Organizations"; 谷聖美 Tani Satomi, ポスト55年体制期における地方レベルでの政治的再編 "Political Realignment at a Regional Level in the Post-1955-Regime Period"; 鈴木創 Suzuki Hajime, 地方レベルにおける社会党の再編 "The Reorganization of the Socialist Party at a Regional Level"; 鹿毛理恵子 Kage Rieko, 制度認識と政党システム再編 "Perceptions of the System and the Reorganization of the Party System"; and 片岡正昭 Kataoka Masaaki, 読売選挙版へのアンケート分析 "An Analysis of a Questionnaire on the *Yomiuri Newspaper*'s Election Issue."

11 五十嵐 仁 Igarashi Hitoshi,『徹底検証・政治改革神話』 *A Thorough Examination of the Myth of Political Reform*, 238 pp., 労働旬報社, 1997.

12 加藤淳子 Katō Junko, Michael Laver and Kenneth A. Shepsle, 日本における連立政権の形成 "The Formation of the Coalition Government in Japan,"「レヴァイアサン」19号, pp. 63-85, 木鐸社, 1996.

13 Jain, Purnendra C., 転換期の日本の政党政治 "Japan's Party Politics in Transition,"「レヴァイアサン」18号, pp. 29-41, 木鐸社, 1996.

14 中野　実 Nakano Minoru, 政界再編期の立法過程 "The Legislative Process at a Time of Party Realignment,"「レヴァイアサン」18号, pp. 71-95, 木鐸社, 1996.

15 金子　勝 Kaneko Masaru,「橋本行政改革」と日本国憲法──「日本型ファシズム」批判 "'Hashimoto's Administrative Reforms' and the Constitution of Japan: A Critique of 'Japanese-Style Fascism',"「立正法学論集」31巻1-2号, pp. 21-62, 立正大学法学会, 1997.

16 辻中　豊 Tsujinaka Yutaka, 日本政治体制のベクトル転換──コーポラティズム化から多元主義化へ "A Vector Change in Japan's Political Regime: From Corporatization to Pluralization,"「レヴァイアサン」20号, pp. 130-150, 木鐸社, 1997.

17 井下田　猛 Igeta Takeshi,『連立時代の政治学』Political Science in a Coalition Period, 226 pp., 北樹出版, 1996.

18 西川吉光 Nishikawa Yoshimitsu,『転換期日本の政治と社会』Politics and Society in Japan at a Time of Transition, 223 pp., 北樹出版, 1996.

19 堀　要 Hori Kaname,『日本政治の実証分析』A Factual Analysis of Japanese Politics, 289 pp., 東海大学出版会, 1996.

20 小林良彰 Kobayashi Yoshiaki,『現代日本の政治過程──日本型民主主義の計量分析』The Political Process in Contemporary Japan: A Quantitative Analysis of Japanese-Style Democracy, 288 pp., 東京大学出版会, 1997.

21 伊藤光利 Itō Mitsutoshi, 地方政府に媒介された多元主義 "Pluralism Mediated by Local Government,"「奈良法学会雑誌」8巻3-4号, pp. 23-85, 奈良産業大学法学会, 1996.

22 内山　融 Uchiyama Yū, 危機・国家・市場──70年代日本の経済危機・政治危機と市場の脱〈公的領域〉化 "Crisis, State and Markets: Japan's Economic Crisis and Political Crisis in the 1970s and the Markets' Shift away from Being a 'Public Sphere',"「国家学会雑誌」109巻9-10号, pp. 1-62; 110巻1-2号, pp. 1-57; 3-4号, pp. 49-259; 5-6号, pp. 95-157; 11-12号, pp. 1-59, 国家学会事務所, 1997.

23 森本哲郎 Morimoto Tetsuo, 民主主義への移行における正統性問題──戦後日本政治における正統性原理の転換について "The Problem of Legitimacy in the Transition to Democracy: On the Shift in the Principle of Legitimacy in Postwar Japanese Politics,"「奈良法学会雑誌」10巻2号, pp. 19-41, 奈良産業大学法学会, 1997.

I-3. Political Organizations and Political Actors

24 大山礼子 Ōyama Reiko,『国会学入門』An Introduction to the Study of

the Diet, 262 pp., 三省堂, 1997.

25 中村睦男・前田英昭 (編) Nakamura Mutsuo and Maeda Hideaki (eds.), 『立法過程の研究——立法における政府の役割』 *Studies in the Legislative Process: The Role of Government in Lawmaking*, 526 pp., 信山社, 1997.

26 大山礼子 Ōyama Reiko, 国会改革と議院内閣制——議員立法活用論を手がかりとして "Diet Reform and the Parliamentary Cabinet System: With Reference to the Advocacy of Greater Utilization of Members' Legislation," 「一橋論叢」 115 巻 1 号, pp. 129-150, 一橋大学一橋学会, 1996.

27 谷 勝宏 Tani Katsuhiro, 政策担当秘書の立法補佐活動の研究 "A Study of the Activities of Policy Secretaries as Legislative Advisors," 「名城法学」 46 巻 2 号, pp. 61-151, 名城大学法学会, 1996.

28 谷 勝宏 Tani Katsuhiro, 議員立法の機能化に関する実態分析 "A Fact-Finding Analysis of the Functionalization of Members' Legislation," 「名城法学」 47 巻 3 号, pp. 175-285, 名城大学法学会, 1997.

29 岸本一男・蒲島郁夫 Kishimoto Kazuo and Kabashima Ikuo, 合理的選択理論から見た日本の政党システム "Japan's Party System as Seen from the Perspective of the Theory of Rational Choice," 「レヴァイアサン」20 号, pp. 84-100, 木鐸社, 1997.

30 川人貞史 Kawato Sadafumi, シニオリティ・ルールと派閥 "The Seniority Rule and LDP Factions," 「レヴァイアサン」1996 年冬号, pp. 111-145, 木鐸社, 1996.

31 西川知一・河田潤一 (編) Nishikawa Tomokazu and Kawata Jun'ichi (eds.), 『政党派閥——比較政治学的研究』 *Party Factions: A Study from the Perspective of Comparative Political Science*, 581 pp., ミネルヴァ書房, 1996.

Includes: 居安正 Iyasu Tadashi, 自民党の派閥 "The Factions of the LDP," pp. 133-217; 武重雅文 Takeshige Masafumi, 新聞が描いた自民党派閥 "LDP Factions as Portrayed by Newspapers," pp. 219-240; and 福永文夫 Fukunaga Fumio, 日本社会党の派閥 "The Factions of the Social Democratic Party," pp. 241-290.

32 森本哲郎 Morimoto Tetsuo, 政治における「理念」の運命——55 年体制下の自民党「組織」問題を素材に "The Fate of 'Ideals' in Politics: On the Basis of the Question of LDP 'Organization' under the 1955 Regime," 「奈良法学会雑誌」8 巻 3-4 号, pp. 217-248, 奈良産業大学法学会, 1996.

33 山田真裕 Yamada Masahiro, 後援会政治の分析枠組み "The Analytical Framework of the Politics of Supporters' Associations (*Kōenkai*)," 「法と政治」48 巻 1 号, pp. 15-36, 関西学院大学法政学会, 1997.

34 喜志麻孝子 Kishima Takako, 町内会と後援会——西洋近代的政治シス

テムに対するアンチテーゼ "Chōnaikai (Neighbourhood Associations) and Kōenkai (Political Supporters' Associations): An Antithesis to the Modern Western Political System,"「レヴァイアサン」21 号, pp. 113-140, 木鐸社, 1997.

35 高橋　勉 Takahashi Tsutomu,『資料　社会党河上派の軌跡』 *Materials on the Course Taken by the Kawakami Faction of the Japan Socialist Party*, 531 pp., 三一書房, 1996.

36 信田智人 Shinoda Tomohito,『官邸の権力』 *The Power of the Prime Minister's Residence*, 238 pp., 筑摩書房, 1996.

37 中邨　章 (編) Nakamura Akira (ed.),『官僚制と日本の政治』 *The Bureaucracy and Japanese Politics*, 242 pp., 北樹出版, 1997.

38 猪口　孝 Inoguchi Takashi, 官僚制の歴史から見た日本政治 "Japanese Politics and the Bureaucracy: From the Tokugawa Period to the Present,"「レヴァイアサン」18 号, pp. 7-28, 木鐸社, 1996.

39 窪田　明 Kubota Akira, 日本におけるビッグビジネスと政治——1993-94 "Big Business and Politics in Japan, 1993-94,"「レヴァイアサン」18 号, pp. 42-60, 木鐸社, 1996.

40 辻中　豊 Tsujinaka Yutaka, 日本における利益団体システムの変化と今後の展望・課題 "Changes in the System of Interest Groups in Japan and Future Prospects and Issues,"「筑波法政」20 号, pp. 89-131, 筑波大学社会科学系, 1996.

41 新川敏光 Shinkawa Toshimitsu, もう一つの 55 年体制——交叉階級的連合と企業主義 "Another 1955 Regime: Cross-Class Alliances and Enterprise Labor Unions,"「北大法学論集」47 巻 1 号, pp.1-52, 北海道大学法学部, 1996.

42 小川恒夫 Ogawa Tsuneo, 報道の課題設定機能と記憶設定機能 "The Agenda-Setting Function and Memory-Setting Function of News Coverage,"「東海大学紀要・文学部」65 集, pp. 122-135, 東海大学文学部, 1996.

43 佐藤　毅 Satō Takeshi, 湾岸戦争とマス・メディア——報道規制と世論操作 (上・中) "The Gulf War and Mass Media: Press Restrictions and the Manipulation of Public Opinion,"「大東法学」26 号, pp. 1-37; 27 号, pp. 95-130, 大東文化大学法学会, 1996.

44 茨木正治 Ibaraki Masaharu,『「政治漫画」の政治分析』 *A Political Analysis of "Political Cartoons,"* 224 pp., 芦書房, 1997.

45 岩本美砂子 Iwamoto Misako, 女のいない政治過程 "A Political Process without Women,"「女性学」5 号, pp. 8-39, 日本女性学会, 1997.

46 吉田雅信 Yoshida Masanobu,『政治家の心理分析——竹下登, 小沢一郎, 羽田孜, 橋本龍太郎』 *A Psychological Analysis of Politicians: Takeshita*

Noboru, Ozawa Ichirō, Hata Tsutomu, and Hashimoto Ryūtarō, 197 pp., 近代文芸社, 1997.

47 日本有権者連盟（編）Japan Voter's League (ed.),『政治家の通信簿』*The Report Cards of Politicians*, 985+5 pp., 四谷ラウンド, 1996.

48 東京商工連盟（編）Tokyo Federation of Commerce and Industry (ed.), 『国会議員の公約と行動』*The Public Promises and Behavior of Diet Members*, 1172 pp., 四谷ラウンド, 1997.

I-4. The Political Situation, Biographies, and Political Commentary

49 読売新聞社政治部（編）Yomiuri Shimbun Political News Department (ed.),『政──まつりごと』*Politics as Ritual*, 358 pp., 読売新聞社, 1996.

50 井芹浩文・内田健三・蒲島郁夫・川戸恵子・近藤大博・曾根泰教・成田憲彦・早野 透 Iseri Hirofumi, Uchida Kenzō, Kabashima Ikuo, Kawado Keiko, Kondō Daihaku, Sone Yasunori, Narita Norihiko and Hayano Tōru,『日本政治は甦るか──同時進行分析』*Will Japanese Politics Recover?: A Contemporaneous Analysis*, 263 pp., 日本放送出版協会, 1997.

51 田原総一郎 Tahara Sōichirō,『頭のない鯨──政治劇の真実』*Whale Without a Head: The Truth Behind the Political Drama*, 197 pp., 朝日新聞社, 1997.

52 平野貞夫 Hirano Sadao,『小沢一郎との二十年──「政界再編」舞台裏』*Twenty Years Together with Ozawa Ichirō: Behind the Scenes of "Political Realignment,"* 316 pp., プレジデント社, 1996.

53 野中広務 Nonaka Hiromu,『私は戦う』*I Shall Fight*, 229 pp., 文藝春秋, 1996.

54 小沢一郎 Ozawa Ichirō,『語る』*Speaking My Mind*, 238 pp., 文藝春秋, 1996.

55 島 聡 Shima Satoshi,『選挙を変えなければ、日本はよくならない』*Unless Electoral Campaigns Are Changed, Japan Will Not Get Any Better*, 207 pp., 日本図書刊行会, 1997.

56 御厨 貴・渡邉昭夫（編）Mikuriya Takashi and Watanabe Akio (eds.), 『首相官邸の決断──内閣官房副長官石原信雄の 2600 日』*Decisions in the Prime Minister's Residence: Deputy Chief Cabinet Secretary Ishihara Nobuo's 2,600 Days*, 264 pp., 中央公論社, 1997.

57 麻生 幾 Asō Iku,『情報官邸に達せず』*The Information Did Not Reach the Prime Minister's Residence*, 276 pp., 文藝春秋, 1996.

58 俵 孝太郎 Tawara Kōtarō,『日本の政治家──親と子の肖像』*Japan's Politicians: Portraits of Parents and Children*, 381 pp., 中央公論社, 1997.

59 国正武重 Kunimasa Takeshige,『戦後政治の素顔──記者の証言』*The*

Real Face of Postwar Politics: A Reporter's Testimony, 277 pp., 近代文芸社, 1997.

60　石川真澄 Ishikawa Masumi, 『人物戦後政治』 *Figures in Postwar Politics*, 250 pp., 岩波書店, 1997.

61　三輪和雄 Miwa Kazuo, 『病める政治家たち──病気と政治家と権力』 *Ailing Politicians: Illness, Politicians, and Power*, 455 pp., 文藝春秋, 1996.

62　Arthy, Ian, 『政・官・財の国語塾』 *Classes for the Japanese Language Used by Politicians, Officials, and Financiers*, 286 pp., 中央公論社, 1996.

63　山口二郎 Yamaguchi Jirō, 『日本政治の課題──新・政治改革論』 *Issues in Japanese Politics: A New Proposal for Political Reform*, 205 pp., 岩波書店, 1997.

64　橋本晃和 Hashimoto Akikazu, 『「新・無党派」が政治を変える』 *"New Nonaligned Voters" Will Change Politics*, 199 pp., 勁草書房, 1996.

I-5. The Political Process

65　加藤淳子 Katō Junko, 『税制改革と官僚制』 *Tax Reform and the Bureaucracy*, 306＋17 pp., 東京大学出版会, 1997.

66　谷口将紀 Taniguchi Masaki, 『日本の対米貿易交渉』 *Japan's Trade Negotiations with the United States*, 296 pp., 東京大学出版会, 1997.

67　御厨　貴 Mikuriya Takashi, 『政策の総合と権力』 *Policy Integration and Power*, 250＋11 pp., 東京大学出版会, 1997.

68　大嶽秀夫 Ōtake Hideo, 『「行革」の発想』 *The Thinking Behind "Administrative Reform,"* 464 pp., TBS ブリタニカ, 1997.

69　真渕　勝 Mabuchi Masaru, 『大蔵省はなぜ追いつめられたのか──政官関係の変貌』 *Why Was the Ministry of Finance Cornered?: The Transformation of Relations Between Politicians and Bureaucrats*, 342 pp., 中央公論社, 1997.

70　中村昭雄 Nakamura Akio, 『日本政治の政策過程』 *The Policy Process in Japanese Politics*, 229 pp., 芦書房, 1996.

71　田中宗孝 Tanaka Munetaka, 『政治改革6年の過程』 *The Course of 6 Years of Political Reform*, 415 pp., ぎょうせい, 1997.

72　成田憲彦 Narita Norihiko, 「政治改革の過程」論の試み──デッサンと証言 "A Tentative Theory of the 'Process of Political Reform': Sketch and Testimony," 「レヴァイアサン」20 号, pp. 7-57, 木鐸社, 1997.

73　Reed, Steven R., ブームの政治 "A Story of Three Booms," 「レヴァイアサン」18 号, pp. 61-70, 木鐸社, 1996.

74　川口英俊 Kawaguchi Hidetoshi, 連座制と 1994 年政治改革──選挙における政治腐敗と腐敗防止法の運用 "The Guilt-by-Association System and the Political Reforms of 1994: Political Corruption in Elections and the Application of the Law to Prevent Corruption," 「法学政治学論究」28 号,

pp. 159-183, 慶應義塾大学大学院法学研究科, 1996.

75　谷　勝宏 Tani Katsuhiro, 被爆者援護法——議員立法のアジェンダ・セッテイング機能の検証 "The Atomic Bomb Victims' Relief Law: An Examination of the Agenda-Setting Functions of Member's Legislation," 「阿南工業高等専門学校研究紀要」32 号, pp. 79-99, 阿南工業高等専門学校, 1996.

76　加藤浩三 Katō Kōzō, 開発援助政策をめぐる日本とドイツの対照 "Japanese and German Development Cooperation Policies in Comparison," 「レヴァイアサン」18 号, pp. 96-118, 木鐸社, 1996.

77　斎藤　淳 Saitō Jun, 省益と援助——日本の ODA 国別配分政策の計量分析 "Ministry Interests and Foreign Aid: A Quantitative Analysis of Country Allocation Policies for Japan's ODA," 「レヴァイアサン」19 号, pp. 126-145, 木鐸社, 1996.

78　樋渡由美 Hiwatari Yumi, 国際化の国内政治基盤——日本の自動車産業と輸出自主規制 "The Domestic Political Basis of Internationalization: The Japanese Automobile Industry and Voluntary Export Restraints," 「レヴァイアサン」21 号, pp. 56-81, 木鐸社, 1997.

79　建林正彦 Tatebayashi Masahiko, 中小企業政策と選挙制度 "Policies for Small Business and the Electoral System," 『危機の日本外交』[「年報政治学」1997 年], pp. 177-196, 岩波書店, 1997.

80　大矢根　聡 Ōyane Satoshi, 日米半導体摩擦における「数値目標」形成過程 "The Formation of 'Numerical Targets' in Japan-U.S. Semiconductor Trade Friction," 『危機の日本外交』[「年報政治学」1997 年], pp. 155-175, 岩波書店, 1997.

81　久米郁男 Kume Ikuo, 鳩山・岸路線と戦後政治経済体制——市場の「政治性」への一考察 "The Hatoyama-Kishi Policy Line and the Postwar Political Economy: A Consideration of the 'Political Nature' of the Market," 「レヴァイアサン」20 号, pp. 151-172, 木鐸社, 1997.

82　山川雄巳 Yamakawa Katsumi, 阪神・淡路大震災における村山首相の危機管理リーダーシップ "Prime Minister Murayama's Crisis Management Leadership at the Time of the Great Hanshin Earthquake," 「関西大学・法学論集」47 巻 5 号, pp. 1-83, 関西大学法学会, 1997.

83　松井隆幸 Matsui Takayuki, 『戦後日本産業政策の政策過程』 The Policy Process in Postwar Japan's Industrial Policy, 155 pp., 九州大学出版会, 1997.

84　大山耕輔 Ōyama Kōsuke, 『行政指導の政治経済学——産業政策の形成と実施』 The Political Economics of Administrative Guidance: The Formation and Implementation of Industrial Policy, 284 pp., 有斐閣, 1996.

85　藤本一美 Fujimoto Kazumi, 『「解散」の政治学』 The Politics of "Dissolu-

tion of the Diet," 245 pp., 第三文明社, 1996.

I-6. Elections and Public Opinion

86 三宅一郎・綿貫譲治 Miyake Ichirō and Watanuki Jōji,『環境変動と態度変容』*Changes in the Environment and Changes in Attitude*, 224 pp., 木鐸社, 1997.

87 小林良彰 Kobayashi Yoshiaki,『日本人の投票行動と政治意識』*The Voting Behavior and Political Consciousness of the Japanese*, 242 pp., 木鐸社, 1997.

88 池田謙一 Ikeda Ken'ichi,『転変する政治のリアリティ』*The Reality of Ever-Changing Politics*, 222 pp., 木鐸社, 1997.

89 蒲島郁夫・竹中佳彦 Kabashima Ikuo and Takenaka Yoshihiko,『現代日本人のイデオロギー』*The Ideology of the Contemporary Japanese*, 402+15 pp., 東京大学出版会, 1997.

90 公平慎策 Kōhei Shinsaku,『現代日本人の政治意識』*The Political Consciousness of the Contemporary Japanese*, 182 pp., 慶應義塾大学出版会, 1997.

91 龍円恵喜二 Ryōen Ekiji,『日本政治を動かす基本動因』*The Basic Motives Driving Japanese Politics*, 151 pp., 北樹出版, 1996.

92 川人貞史 Kawato Sadafumi, 選挙制度と政党制――日本における5つの選挙制度の比較分析 "The Electoral System and the Party System: A Comparative Analysis of Five Electoral Systems Used in Japan,"「レヴァイアサン」20号, pp. 58-83, 木鐸社, 1997.

93 鈴木基史 Suzuki Motoshi, 日本とアメリカ合衆国における国政選挙のマクロ分析 "A Macro-Analysis of National Elections in Japan and the United States of America,"「選挙研究」11号, pp. 3-22, 北樹出版, 1996.

94 Reed, Steven R., 中選挙区における m+1 の法則 "The Rule of m+1 in Medium-Size Constituencies,"「総合政策研究」2号, pp. 235-244, 中央大学総合政策学部, 1997.

95 森 裕城 Mori Hiroki, 選挙過程における合理性の衝突――自民党政権の継続と社会党 "The Clash of Rationality in the Electoral Process: The Continuation of a LDP Government and the Social Democratic Party,"「筑波法政」23号, pp. 215-232, 筑波大学社会科学系, 1997.

96 三宅一郎 Miyake Ichirō, 対外国態度と有権者の政治意識 "Attitudes Towards Other Countries and the Political Consciousness of Voters,"「選挙研究」12号, pp. 41-58, 北樹出版, 1997.

97 中村 宏 Nakamura Hiroshi,『地方選挙――英国、日本、ヨーロッパ』*Local Elections: Great Britain, Japan, and Europe*, 206 pp., 日本評論社, 1996.

98 蒲島郁夫・山田真裕 Kabashima Ikuo and Yamada Masahiro, 政治変動

と有権者の政党認知の変容 "Political Change and the Transformation of Voters' Perceptions of Political Parties," 「レヴァイアサン」18 号, pp. 139-159, 木鐸社, 1996.

99　三宅一郎 Miyake Ichirō, 政治改革に対する不満と期待——1993 年総選挙の主要争点 "Dissatisfaction with and Expectations for Political Reform: The Main Points of Contention in the 1993 General Elections," 「大阪国際大学国際研究論叢」8 号特別号, pp. 17-32, 大阪国際大学, 1996.

100　市川太一 Ichikawa Taichi, 選挙制度改革と各界の意識 "Reform of the Electoral System and the Awareness of Different Social Groups," 「広島修道大学研究叢書」95 号, pp. 265-291, 広島修道大学総合研究所, 1996.

101　蒲島郁夫・石生義人・森　裕城 Kabashima Ikuo, Ishio Yoshito and Mori Hiroki, 新党の登場と投票行動 "The Emergence of New Parties and Voting Behavior," 「選挙研究」12 号, pp. 71-87, 北樹出版, 1997.

102　井田正道 Ida Masamichi, 政党再編期における農業者の政治意識 "The Political Consciousness of Farmers at a Time of Party Realignment," 「人間科学」14 巻 2 号, pp. 87-100, 常磐大学人間科学部, 1997.

103　田中愛治 Tanaka Aiji, 「政党支持なし」層の意識構造——政党支持概念再検討の試論 "The Attitudinal Structure of Nonaligned Voters: A Tentative Reexamination of the Concept of Partisanship," 「レヴァイアサン」20 号, pp. 101-129, 木鐸社, 1997.

104　岩淵美克 Iwabuchi Yoshikatsu, 東京都知事選における無党派層の投票行動 "The Voting Behavior of Nonaligned Voters in the Tokyo Gubernatorial Elections," 「選挙研究」11 号, pp. 61-70, 北樹出版, 1996.

105　牛山久二彦 Ushiyama Kunihiko, 過度期の地方政治——94-95 年地方選挙の概況 "Local Politics in Transition: The General Situation in the 1994-95 Local Elections," 「自治総研」22 巻 4 号, pp. 1-35, 地方自治総合研究所, 1996.

106　読売新聞社（編）Yomiuri Shimbun (ed.),『大変革への序章——検証・新制度下の 96 年衆院選』*The Prelude to Major Reforms: An Examination of the 1996 Lower House Elections under the New Electoral System*, 236＋33 pp., 読売新聞社, 1996.

II. Public Administration
II-1. General Studies

01　日本行政学会（編）Japanese Society for Public Administration (ed.),『比較の中の行政と行政観、災害と行政』*Public Administration and Views of Public Administration in Comparison; Disasters and Public Administration*[「年報行政研究」32 号], 172 pp., ぎょうせい, 1997.

02　行政管理研究センター（編）Institute of Administrative Management

(ed.),「季刊行政管理研究」*Administrative Management Research Quarterly*, 73 号～76 号 (1996), 77 号～80 号 (1997), 行政管理研究センター.

Each issue carries a variety of articles, representative of which are: 金井利之 Kanai Toshiyuki, オランダにおける財政調整プログラムの変更 "Modifications of the Fiscal Adjustment Programme in the Netherlands" (73 号, pp. 59-70); 衛藤幹子 Etō Mikiko, 自治体の政策形成力 "The Policy-Forming Powers of Local Government" (74 号, pp. 3-14); 斎藤友彦 Saitō Tomohiko, もうひとつの改革視点 "計画分権" "An Alternative Perspective on Reform: 'Decentralization of Planning'" (74 号, pp. 15-28); 竹下譲 Takeshita Yuzuru, 行政組織の改革——イギリスのシティズンズ・チャーターを事例に "The Reform of Administrative Organization: With Reference to the Citizens' Charter in Great Britain" (75 号, pp. 3-15); 山本清 Yamamoto Kiyoshi, 政官関係の比較制度分析 "A Comparative Institutional Analysis of Relations between Politicians and Bureaucrats" (75 号, pp. 16-25); 中邨章 Nakamura Akira, 分権論議の国際比較とわが国分権論の特色 "An International Comparison of the Decentralization Debate and Distinctive Features of the Debate about Decentralization in Japan" (77 号, pp. 3-15); 今川晃 Iamagawa Akira, イギリスの地方自治体における苦情処理システム政策形成・展開の背景 "The Background to Policy Formation and Development for a System for Dealing with Complaints in Local Bodies in Great Britain" (77 号, pp. 16-24); 中村虎彰 Nakamura Toraakira, アメリカ政府間規制と連邦強制事務 "Intergovernmental Regulations and Compulsory Federal Work in the United States" (77 号, pp. 33-43); 村上弘 Murakami Hiroshi, ドイツの政治システムと行政財政改革 "The Political System in Germany and Administrative and Fiscal Reform" (78 号, pp. 3-13); 笠京子 Ryū Kyōko, 行政執行活動の効率化——英国保守党政権の組織改革 "Increasing the Efficiency of the Executive Activities of Public Administration: Organizational Reform under the Conservative Government in Great Britain" (78 号, pp. 14-22); 武藤博己 Mutō Hiromi, 公務員制度と改革論議 "The Civil Service System and the Debate about Reform" (79 号, pp. 3-13); and 今里滋 Imazato Shigeru, 融解する政府職能——民間専門職と "プロクシィ・ガバメント" "The Dissolution of Government Functions: Private-Sector Professionals and 'Proxy Government'" (79 号, pp. 14-26). No. 80 contains the texts of public lectures, etc., presented at an international symposium on "International Trends in Administrative Reform and the Implementation of Administrative Reform in Japan," held to commemorate the 20th anniversary of the establishment of the Institute of Administrative Management.

03 森田　朗 Morita Akira,『現代の行政』 *Public Administration Today*, 166 pp., 放送大学教育振興会, 1996.

04 今村都南雄・武藤博己・真山達志・武智秀之 Imamura Tsunao, Mutō Hiromi, Mayama Tatsushi and Takechi Hideyuki,『ホーンブック行政学』 *Hornbook on Public Administration*, 273 pp., 北樹出版, 1996.

05 東京リーガルマインド Tokyo Legal Mind,『出る順・公務員ウォーク 問　体系別過去本試験問題集　地方上級国家 II 種編　行政学　第 2 版』 *Past Examination Questions from Civil Service Examinations on Upper Class Civil Service for Local Government and 2nd Class Civil Service for National Government: Public Administration (2nd ed.)*, 335 pp., 東京 リーガルマインド, 1997.

06 今村都南雄 Imamura Tsunao,『行政学の基礎理論』 *Basic Theories of Public Administration*, ix+420 pp., 三嶺書房, 1997.

07 今里　滋 Imazato Shigeru, アメリカ行政学の回顧的展望 "A Retrospective Review of American Public Administration,"「法政研究」63 巻 3-4 号, pp. 877-949, 九州大学法政学会, 1997.

08 武智秀之 Takechi Hideyuki,『行政過程の制度分析』 *An Institutional Analysis of the Administrative Process*, vii+287 pp., 中央大学出版部, 1996.

09 下條美智彦 Shimojō Michihiko,『フランスの行政』 *Public Administration in France*, xv+280 pp., 早稲田大学出版部, 1996.

10 城山英明 Shiroyama Hideaki,『国際行政の構造』 *The Structure of International Administration*, vii+284 pp., 東京大学出版会, 1997.

11 福田耕治 Fukuda Kōji, 欧州連邦主義と補完性原理 (1) – (3) "Euro-Federalism and the Principle of Subsidiarity," (1):「駒沢大学法学部研究紀要」55 号, pp. 1-24, 駒沢大学法学部；(2):「政治学論集」45 号, pp. 59-79, 駒沢大学法学部；(3):「法学論集」55 号, pp. 33-65, 駒沢大学法学部, 1997.

II-2. Administrative Reform

12 行政改革会議事務局（編）Administrative Reform Council Office (ed.),『諸外国の行政改革の動向』 *Trends in Administrative Reform in Other Countries*, 327 pp., 行政管理研究センター, 1997.

13 並河信乃 Namikawa Shino,『図解・行政改革のしくみ』 *The Mechanisms of Administrative Reform Illustrated*, 190 pp., 東洋経済新報社, 1997.

14 増島俊之 Masujima Toshiyuki,『行政改革の視点』 *Perspectives on Administrative Reform*, 211+6 pp., 良書普及会, 1996.

15 毛　桂榮 Mao Guirong,『日本の行政改革』 *Japan's Administrative Reform*, x+291 pp., 青木書店, 1997.

II-3. Administrative Control

16 毛　桂榮 Mao Guirong, 日本の議院内閣制 "Japan's Parliamentary Cabinet System,"「法学研究」62 号, pp. 85-129, 明治学院大学法学会, 1997.

17 原田　久 Harada Hisashi, 比較の中の政官関係論・序説 "An Introductory Discussion of Government-Bureaucracy Relations in Comparison,"「アドミニストレーション」4 巻 2 号, pp. 69-118, 熊本県立大学総合管理学部, 1997.

18 山本　清 Yamamoto Kiyoshi, 会計検査と政策科学 "Auditing and Policy Science,"『政策科学の新展開』, pp. 111-132, 東洋経済新報社, 1997.

19 宋　成植 Sŏng Sŏng-shik, 会計検査院におけるアカウンタビリティ確保の理論と現状——米・日・韓の比較研究の試み "Theories for Ensuring Accountability in Boards of Audit and the Current Situation: A Tentative Comparative Study of the United States, Japan and Korea,"「筑波法政」22 号, pp. 201-218, 筑波大学社会科学系, 1997.

20 潮見憲三郎 Shiomi Kenzaburō,『オンブズマンとは何か』What Is the Ombudsman?, 317 pp., 講談社, 1996.

21 宇都宮深志 Utsunomiya Fukashi, オンブズマン制度導入の可能性と課題 "The Possibility of Introducing the Ombudsman System and Related Issues,"「東海大学政治経済学部紀要」28 号, pp. 13-28, 東海大学, 1996.

II-4. Administrative Organization

22 笠　京子 Ryū Kyōko, 英国中央行政組織改革の現状 "The Present State of the Reform of Central Administrative Organization in Great Britain,"「香川法学」16 巻 3-4 号, pp. 195-203, 香川大学法学会, 1997.

23 牧原　出 Makihara Izuru, 内閣・官房・原局 (1) (2) "Cabinet, Ministerial Secretariat, and Directorate-General,"「法学」59 巻 3 号, pp. 1-29; 60 巻 3 号, pp. 1-76, 東北大学法学部, 1995-96.

24 金井利之 Kanai Toshiyuki, オランダ省庁機構の観察ノート (1) "Observational Notes on the Organization of Central Government in the Netherlands,"「法学会雑誌」38巻1号, pp. 127-155, 東京都立大学法学会, 1997.

25 金井利之 Kanai Toshiyuki, オランダ省庁再編の観察ノート "Observational Notes on the Reorganization of Central Government in the Netherlands,"「法学会雑誌」38 巻 2 号, pp. 75-122, 東京都立大学法学会, 1997.

II-5. Administrative Management

26 早川征一郎 Hayakawa Seiichirō,『国家公務員の昇進・キャリア形成』The Promotion and Career Formation of Civil Servants, ix+386 pp., 日本評論社, 1996.

27 稲継裕昭 Inatsugu Hiroaki,『日本の官僚人事システム』The Personnel System in Japan's Bureaucracy, viii+230 pp., 東洋経済新報社, 1996.

28 片岡寛光 Kataoka Hiromitsu,『官僚のエリート学』A Study of the

Bureaucratic Elite, viii+243 pp., 早稲田大学出版部, 1996.

29 坂本　勝 Sakamoto Masaru, アメリカ連邦公務員制度における人事行政の動向——メリット・システムと代表性を中心に "Trends in Personnel Administration in the U.S. Federal Public Service System: With a Focus on the Merit System and Representativeness,"「龍谷法学」29巻3号, pp. 1-112, 龍谷大学法学会, 1996.

30 西村美香 Nishimura Mika, New Public Management (NPM) と公務員制度改革 "New Public Management (NPM) and the Reform of the Civil Service System,"「成蹊法学」45号, pp. 352-405, 成蹊大学法学会, 1997.

Reflecting an increasing interest in bureaucrats in recent years, there has been a revival of research on the civil service system. II-27 is a meticulous study of the system of promotion in Japan's civil service system, while II-28 elucidates the Japanese personnel system. II-29 and -30 explore new directions in the civil service system with reference to overseas developments.

31 北村　亘 Kitamura Wataru, 現代英国における「省庁間調整」(1) (2) "'Interdepartmental Coordination' in Contemporary Great Britain,"「法学論叢」139巻5号, pp. 70-82; 142巻1号, pp. 53-81, 京都大学法学会, 1996-97.

32 趙　文富 Cho Moon-boo,『予算決定過程の構造と機能』 *The Structure and Functions of the Budget-Making Process*, 401+20 pp., 良書普及会, 1996.

33 西川伸一 Nishikawa Shin'ichi, 内閣法制局——その制度的権力への接近 "The Cabinet Legislation Bureau: An Approach to Its Institutional Power,"「政経論叢」65巻5-6号, pp. 185-251, 明治大学政治経済研究所, 1997.

II-6. Policy

34 山谷清志 Yamatani Kiyoshi,『政策評価の理論とその展開』 *Theories of Policy Evaluation and Their Development*, iv+214 pp., 晃洋書房, 1997.

35 風間規男 Kazama Norio, 公共政策論の新たな地平 "New Horizons in Public Policy Theory,"「近畿大学法学」45巻1号, pp. 55-122, 近畿大学法学会, 1997.

36 新藤宗幸 Shindō Muneyuki,『福祉行政と官僚制』 *Welfare Administration and the Bureaucracy*, viii+204 pp., 岩波書店, 1996.

II-7. Actual Conditions

37 週刊金曜日編集部（編）*Friday Weekly* Editorial Department (ed.),『環境を破壊する公共事業』 *Public Works That Destroy the Environment*, 280 pp., 緑風出版, 1997.

38 依田　薫 Yoda Kaoru,『これがお役所の正体だ！』 *This Is What Gov-*

ernment Offices Are Really Like!, 221 pp., 日本実業出版社, 1997.

39 週刊東洋経済編集部（編）*Weekly Tōyō Keizai* Editorial Department (ed.),『霞ヶ関を解体せよ』*Dismantle Kasumigaseki* (*Central Government Institutions*)*!*, 244 pp., 東洋経済新報社, 1997.

40 住田正二 Sumita Shōji,『役人につけるクスリ』*Some Medicine to Give Government Officials*, 206 pp., 朝日新聞社, 1997.

41 富岡　悠 Tomioka Hisashi,『公安調査庁の暴走』*The Excesses of the Public Security Investigation Agency*, 236 pp., 現代書館, 1996.

42 久保博司 Kubo Hiroshi,『日本警察』*The Japanese Police*, 263 pp., 講談社, 1997.

43 岸　宣仁 Kishi Nobuhito,『淋しい大蔵官僚』*The Lonely Officials of the Ministry of Finance*, 245 pp., 東洋経済新報社, 1997.

44 テリー伊藤 Itō, Terry,『お笑い大蔵省極秘情報』*The Laughable Top-Secret Information of the Ministry of Finance*, 190 pp., 飛鳥新社, 1996.

45 宮本政於 Miyamoto Masao,『お役所の精神分析』*A Psychoanalysis of Government Offices*, 325 pp., 講談社, 1997.

46 宝島社（編）Takarajimasha (ed.),『大蔵官僚の手口』*The Methods Used by Ministry of Finance Officials* ［別冊宝島 M］, 190 pp., 宝島社, 1996.

47 宝島社（編）Takarajimasha (ed.),『厚生省更正せず』*The Ministry of Health and Welfare Will Not Mend Its Ways* ［別冊宝島 M］, 190 pp., 宝島社, 1996.

III. Local Government

III-1. General Studies

01 日本地方自治学会（編）Japan Association for the Study of Local Government (ed.),『行政手続法と地方自治』*Administrative Procedure Law and Local Government*, iii＋206 pp., 敬文堂, 1996.

02 日本地方自治学会（編）Japan Association for the Study of Local Government (ed.),『機関委任事務と地方自治』*Agency-Delegated Tasks and Local Government*, ii＋268 pp., 敬文堂, 1997.

03 自治体学会（編）Japan Association of Local Government Policy Studies (ed.),『まちづくりを問い直す──防災と自治』*Reconsidering the Town-Building Movement: Disaster Prevention and Self-Government* ［「年報自治体学」9 号］, ii＋202 pp., 良書普及会, 1996.

04 自治体学会（編）Japan Association of Local Government Policy Studies (ed.),『自立する市民と自治体──新しい関係構築のために』*Increasingly Independent Citizens and Local Government: For the Building of a New Relationship* ［「年報自治体学」10 号］, ii＋248 pp., 良書普及会, 1997.

III-03 deals with the Great Hanshin Earthquake, while III-04 focusses on citizens' participation and NPOs (nonprofit organizations).

05 神奈川県自治総合研究センター（発行）Kanagawa Institute for Local Autonomy (pub.),「刊自治体学研究」*Local Government Studies Quarterly*, 68 号～71 号 (1996), 72 号～75 号 (1997), 公人社.

The special topics featured in each issue are as follows: Urban policy in a mature society (No. 68); Policy techniques for management of the environment (No. 69); Towards the building of a participatory society: Local revitalization through a partnership of citizens, corporations and administration (No. 70); Thinking about a society of fewer children (No. 71); Local government reform for a decentralized society (No. 72); Cities and the environment: Towards the preservation and restoration of the local environment (No. 73); The challenge of community networks (No. 74); The nurturing of human resources in 21st-century local government/ Towards the revival of making things (No. 75).

06 本間義人 Homma Yoshihito,『土木国家の思想』*The Thought behind the Civil Engineering State*, vii＋376 pp., 日本経済評論社, 1996.

07 中西啓之 Nakanishi Hiroyuki,『日本の地方自治』*Local Government in Japan*, 374 pp., 自治体研究社, 1997.

08 安島喜一 Ajima Kiichi,『変革期の地方自治』*Local Government at a Time of Change*, 234 pp., 三省堂, 1997.

09 秋月謙吾 Akizuki Kengo,「地域」をめぐる行政システム "The Administrative System Surrounding 'Localities'," 「法学論叢」140 巻 3-4 号, pp. 212-231, 京都大学法学会, 1997.

10 江藤俊昭 Etō Toshiaki, ローカル政治におけるグローバリゼーション "Globalization in Local Politics," 「法学論集」38 号, pp. 170-191, 山梨学院大学法学研究会, 1997.

III-2. Decentralization

11 日本行政学会（編）Japanese Society for Public Administration (ed.),『分権改革』*Decentralization Reforms* [「年報行政研究」31 号], 202 pp., ぎょうせい, 1996.

12 松下圭一 Matsushita Keiichi,『日本の自治・分権』*Self-Government and Decentralization in Japan*, iv＋225 pp., 岩波書店, 1996.

13 新藤宗幸 Shindō Muneyuki,『地方分権を考える』*Thinking about Decentralization*, 156 pp., NHK 出版, 1996.

14 重森 暁 Shigemori Akira,『地方分権』*Decentralization*, vi＋200 pp., 丸善ライブラリー, 1996.

15 並河信乃（編）Namikawa Shino (ed.),『分権社会の創造』*The Creation of a Decentralized Society*, 277 pp., 東洋経済新報社, 1996.

16 秋月謙吾 Akizuki Kengo, 地方制度改革分析に向けての一序説 "A Prologue to the Analysis of Reforms of the Local Government System," 「法

学論叢』140 巻 1-2 号, pp. 179-203, 京都大学法学会, 1996.

17 地方自治総合研究所（編）Japan Research Institute for Local Government (ed.),『地方分権の戦略』*Strategies for Decentralization*, 381 pp., 第一書林, 1996.

18 地方自治制度研究会（編）Local Government System Study Group (ed.),『地方分権推進ハンドブック』*Handbook for the Promotion of Decentralization*, 324 pp., ぎょうせい, 1996.

19 成田頼明 Narita Yoriaki,『地方分権への道程』*The Path to Decentralization*, 7+286 pp., 良書普及会, 1997.

20 朝日新聞社地域報道部 Asahi Shimbun Local News Department,『地方分権の足音』*The Footfall of Decentralization*, 301 pp., 公人の友社, 1997.

III-3. Local Government Management and Policies

21 打越綾子 Uchikoshi Ayako,『アメリカ州・地方政府における "Strategic Planning"』*"Strategic Planning" in American State and Local Government*, 129 pp., 東京大学都市行政研究会, 1996.

22 二宮厚美 Ninomiya Atsumi,『国家改造と自治体リストラ』*Remodelling of the State and Restructuring of Local Government*, 307 pp., 自治体研究社, 1997.

23 山崎 正 Yamazaki Tadashi,『地方分権と予算・決算』*Decentralization and Budgets and Settlement of Accounts*, vi+241 pp., 勁草書房, 1996.

24 清水江一 Shimizu Kōichi,『自治体の政策形成戦略』*Strategies for Policy Formation in Local Government*, 237 pp., ぎょうせい, 1997.

25 佐々木信夫 Sasaki Nobuo,『自治体政策学入門』*An Introduction to the Study of Local Government Policies*, 3+247 pp., ぎょうせい, 1996.

26 蓮池 穣 Hasuike Minoru, 北海道における地方自治体の人事行政 "Personnel Administration in Local Government in Hokkaido,"「札幌学院法学」12 巻 2 号, pp. 147-163, 札幌学院大学法学会, 1996.

27 北原鉄也 Kitahara Tetsuya, 線引き制度と市街化 "The Demarcation System and Urbanization,"「愛媛大学法文学部論集（総合政策学科編）」1-2 号, pp. 59-87, 愛媛大学法文学部, 1997.

28 竹村保治 Takemura Yasuharu, 神戸市の行政区再編成の研究 "A Study of the Reorganization of Kobe City's Administrative Districts,"「法学雑誌」42 巻 4 号, pp. 773-804, 大阪市立大学, 1996.

29 中井道夫 Nakai Michio, 都市計画における透明性 "Transparency in Urban Planning,"「法学論集」38 号, pp. 192-210, 山梨学院大学法学研究会, 1997.

30 魚谷増男 Uotani Masuo, 防災行政における危機管理システムの分析と評価について "On the Analysis and Assessment of Crisis Management Systems in Disaster-Prevention Administration,"「平成法政研究」1 巻 1

号, pp. 39-71, 平成国際大学法学会, 1996.

III-4. Intergovernmental Relations

31　伊藤正次 Itō Masatsugu,『中央周辺関係の比較政治学』 *The Comparative Political Science of Central-Peripheral Relations*, 137 pp., 東京大学都市行政研究会, 1996.

32　牧田義輝 Makita Yoshiteru,『アメリカ大都市圏の行政システム』 *The Administrative System in American Metropolitan Areas*, xiv+226 pp., 勁草書房, 1996.

33　広本政幸 Hiromoto Masayuki, 厚生行政と建設行政の中央地方関係(1)-(3)"Central-Local Relations in Welfare Administration and Construction Administration,"「法学雑誌」43 巻 1 号, pp. 99-127; 2 号, pp. 239-267; 3 号, pp. 494-526, 大阪市立大学, 1996-97.

34　日高昭夫 Hidaka Akio, 高齢者サービスの自治体間比較について "On a Comparison of Local Governments Regarding Services for the Elderly,"「法学論集」38 号, pp. 211-238, 山梨学院大学法学研究会, 1997.

35　小原隆治 Ohara Ryūji, 市町村合併論の論点 "Points at Issue in the Debate about the Amalgamation of Cities, Towns and Villages,"「成蹊法学」45 号, pp. 189-214, 成蹊大学法学会, 1997.

III-5. Relations Between the Public and Private Sectors

36　今村都南雄 (編) Imamura Tsunao (ed.),『公共サービスと民間委託』 *Public Services and Contracting-out to the Private Sector*, xii+333 pp., 敬文堂, 1997.

37　成瀬龍夫 (編) Naruse Tatsuo (ed.),『公社・第三セクターの改革課題』 *Issues for Reform in Public Corporations and the Third Sector*, 306 pp., 自治体研究社, 1997.

38　佐藤克廣 Satō Katsuhiro, オハイオ州デイトン (Daton) 市のプライオリティ委員会を通じた市民参加 "Citizens' Participation through the Priority Committee in Daton, Ohio,"「法学研究」33 巻 2 号, pp. 377-407, 北海学園大学法学会, 1997.

39　荒木昭次郎 Araki Shōjirō, 自治行政における公民協働論 "Theories of Public- and Private-Sector Cooperation in Local Government Administration,"「東海大学政治経済学部紀要」28 号, pp. 1-11, 東海大学, 1996.

40　横田　清 (編) Yokota Kiyoshi (ed.),『住民投票 I』 *Referenda I*, 256 pp., 公人社, 1997.

41　村上　弘 Murakami Hiroshi, スイスの住民投票 "Referenda in Switzerland,"「立命館法学」250 号, pp. 313-330, 立命館大学法学会, 1996.

　　Now that referenda have actually been held in Japan—e.g., in Maki, Niigata prefecture (4 Aug. 1996; see III-53), and Okinawa (8 Sept. 1996) —there has been growing interest in the referendum system, and III-40

62

and -41 are the first studies of referenda to have appeared in Japan. A report brought out by the Residents' Participation System Study Group in Tokyo (July 1996) also provides a multifaceted examination of the referendum system.

42　駒井　洋（監）Komai Hiroshi (supvr.), 渡戸一郎（編）Watado Ichirō (ed.),『自治体政策の展開と NGO』*Developments in Local Government Policies and NGOs*, 337 pp., 明石書店, 1996.

43　日詰一幸 Hizume Kazuyuki, 都市行政と市民のボランタリズム "Urban Administration and Citizens' Volunteerism,"「法政研究」1 巻 1 号, pp. 349-377, 静岡大学法経学会, 1996.

III-6. Overseas Research and Case Studies

44　高寄昇三 Takayose Shōzō,『現代イギリスの地方自治』*Local Government in Contemporary Great Britain*, vi＋204 pp., 勁草書房, 1996.

45　横田　清 Yokota Kiyoshi,『アメリカにおける自治・分権・参加の発展』*The Development of Self-Government, Decentralization and Participation in America*, vii＋264 pp., 敬文堂, 1997.

46　木佐茂夫　Kisa Shigeo,『豊かさを生む地方自治』*Local Government Conducive to Prosperity*, x＋187 pp., 日本評論社, 1996.

47　御厨　貴 Mikuriya Takashi,『東京──首都は国家を超えるか』*Tokyo: Can the Capital Transcend State*, 334 pp., 読売新聞社, 1996.

48　五十嵐敬喜・野口和雄・池上修一 Igarashi Takayoshi, Noguchi Kazuo and Ikegami Shūichi,『いきづく町をつくる　美の条例──真鶴町一万人の選択』*Beautification Regulations for Creating a Vibrant Town: The Choice Made by 10,000 People in Manazuru*, 288 pp., 学芸出版社, 1996.

49　横浜市立大学大学院（編）Yokohama City University Graduate School (ed.),『都市経営の科学』*The Science of Urban Management*, 4＋233 pp., 中央経済社, 1997.

50　大震災と地方自治研究会（編）Large Earthquakes and Local Government Study Group (ed.),『大震災と地方自治』*Large Earthquakes and Local Government*, 270 pp., 自治体研究社, 1996.

51　広原盛明（編）Hirohara Moriaki (ed.),『震災・神戸都市計画の検証』*Earthquake: An Examination of Kobe's Urban Planning*, 182 pp., 自治体研究社, 1996.

III-7. Actual Conditions

52　鈴木俊一 Suzuki Shun'ichi,『回想・地方自治五十年』*Recollections of Fifty Years in Local Government*, 320 pp., ぎょうせい, 1997.

53　新潟日報報道部 Niigata Nippō News Department,『原発を拒んだ町』*The Town That Rejected a Nuclear Power Station*, ix＋251 pp., 岩波書

店，1997.

54　中川　徹 Nakagawa Tōru,『行政の不良資産』*The Bad Assets of Public Administration*, 223 pp., 自治体研究社，1996.

55　毎日新聞社会部 Mainichi Shimbun City News Department,『醜い官僚たち』*The Ugly Bureaucrats*, 197 pp., 毎日新聞社，1996.

56　廣中克彦 Hironaka Katsuhiko,『お役人のことがよくわかる 50 ヶ条』*Fifty Rules for Understanding Government Officials*, 257 pp., 講談社，1996.

INTERNATIONAL RELATIONS

Yamakage Susumu
The University of Tokyo

INTRODUCTION

Interest in Japan's stance on international relations has changed considerably during the latter part of the 1990s. Namely, the fiftieth anniversary of the end of World War II passed, and the review period (1996–97) was a time that saw notable destabilization of the international order in the post-Cold War period and vague but increasing anxiety about the approaching fin-de-siecle. Japan, a country that had but a limited number of options at its disposal under the Cold War structure, despite being now in a position to consider various possibilities, has not been able to put forward any clear choices in the face of the intransparency and fluidity of the post-Cold War international environment. In particular, what can be described as vestiges of the Cold War structure, i.e., questions concerning the Taiwan Strait and the Korean Peninsula, cast a large shadow over Japan's security policy. Furthermore, the political crisis that was initiated by the Asian financial crisis in 1997 is not yet over at the time of this writing (spring, 1999). Adequate steps have yet to be taken even against this new crisis.

Research published during the two years 1996–97 appears to reflect the aforementioned international situation in which Japan finds itself. In this survey I will present a general outline of the existing state of research with the focus on books. The survey is divided into four sections: research on prewar diplomacy and the war, postwar Japan-U.S. relations, security (a major part of which overlaps, needless to say, with Japan-U.S. relations), and diplomatic issues in general.

I. PREWAR DIPLOMACY AND THE WAR

In the previous survey (1994–95) I introduced a large number of studies that dealt with the issue of how to interpret prewar Japan's involvement in and invasion of Asia in the light of the fiftieth anniversary of the end of World War II. In this category of research the following noteworthy studies were published during the current review period. Namely, Mitani Hiroshi [I-01] has taken the study of Japanese nationalism one step further by understanding Japan, which began to participate in international society following the opening of the country by the Tokugawa shogunate and the subsequent Meiji Restoration, as a "proto nation-state." Further, Mōri Toshihiko has brought out a general publication [I-02] bringing together the results of his academic work on the Taiwan Expedition of 1874, while Kobayashi Michihiko [I-03] deals with Japan's engagement in Asia (i.e., its "continental policy") from the time of the Sino-Japanese War of 1894-95 to the eve of World War I. Although Hata Ikuhiko's detailed work [I-04] on the Marco Polo Bridge Incident, which sparked the Second Sino-Japanese War, covers the same period as that of his *Nitchū sensō-shi* (A History of the Sino-Japanese War) (1961), it is a major opus that makes maximum use of new materials.

Needless to say, in addition to the war fought on the battlefields of China, Japan also engaged in war against the United States in the Pacific Ocean. A publication edited by Hosoya Chihiro and others [I-05] represents a new genre of research that seeks to link the end of the Pacific War with the construction of the postwar international order in Asia and the Pacific. On the other hand, while focussing on Japanese navy's maneuvers to end the war, Kōketsu Atsushi's work [I-06] reconsiders Japan's postwar conservative ideology, and although concise, raises important issues. Thus, the review period is also noteworthy for the new viewpoints that connect prewar and wartime trends with postwar international

relations and postwar Japanese society. Among ways of interpreting contemporary Japanese society, there is one based on the
concept of "the 1940 regime," and it can be anticipated that in the
field of international relations too research linking the prewar and
postwar eras will increase in the future, as opposed to works that
consider these periods as two separate entities. Iokibe Makoto's
publication [II-01], described below, is an example of this new
approach to research.

As was mentioned in the previous review, recently a large
number of works have been dealing with Japan's southern expansion, and within the period covered by this review the following
publications are worthy of note: a work edited by Kurasawa Aiko
[I-07] that contains contributions from eighteen researchers who
take a multifaceted look at Japan's occupation of different parts of
Southeast Asia; Kurasawa Aiko's compilation [I-08] of interviews with overseas students from Southeast Asia who came to
Japan during the war (i.e., "special foreign students from the
South"); and a work edited by Ikehata Setsuho [I-09] that focusses on the Philippines. Whereas military administration was the
subject of a large number of former studies concerned with Japan's
occupation of Southeast Asia, Hatano Sumio's painstaking work
[I-10] attempts to illuminate, as one aspect of Japanese diplomacy, the meaning of Japan's seemingly contradictory policy of
rule and support for independence in Southeast Asia.

II. POSTWAR JAPAN-U.S. RELATIONS

Japan, following its occupation by the largely American Allied
Forces, regained its sovereignty while maintaining a close relationship with the United States through the postwar period and
proceeded to achieve the status of a major economic power. In this
sense, in Iokibe Makoto's general survey [II-01] of Japanese
politics during the Occupation, Japan's relationship with the
Occupation Army and the United States is an important theme,
and his study represents a significant achievement from the standpoint of research in international relations. While Lee Jong-won
[II-02] analyzes international relations in East Asia during the

early postwar period (i.e., the formation of the Cold War structure), with a focus on the interrelationship between the United States, Japan and Korea.

Japan-U.S. relations involving security will be introduced in the next section, whereas mention will be made of works on Japan-U.S. relations concerning economics and trade in this section. Research on friction between Japan and the United States was prominent during the review period. Nobayashi Takeshi [II-03] deals with the steel industry, an early example of trade friction that has continued to be problem, and he links trends in the U.S. steel industries with Japan-U.S. relations. Journalist Karube Kensuke [II-04] reveals details of how rice, which is considered sacred in Japan yet is a symbol of the trade barrier overseas, was liberalized during the Uruguay Round. Ishiguro Kazunori [II-05] analyzes friction surrounding the Japan-U.S. Air Transport Agreement from the viewpoint of American domination. A publication edited by the American Affairs Division, International Trade Policy Bureau, Ministry of International Trade and Industry (MITI) [II-06] discloses details of how those involved in trade negotiations settled the dispute involving Japan-U.S. automobile friction (mainly focussing on deliberations about automobile parts that took place around 1995). A former senior MITI official, Hatayama Noboru [II-07] recollects his own experience in trade negotiations. Noguchi Hitoshi [II-08] describes financial diplomacy surrounding adjustments to the exchange rate between the yen and the U.S. dollar during the period beginning with the formation of the Plaza Accord (1985) and ending with the Gulf crisis (1990). Taniguchi Masaki [II-09] attempts a theoretical analysis of Japan's trade negotiations with the U.S. based on three case studies.

III. Security

The collapse of the Cold War structure provided an opportunity to gain a new understanding of Japanese security. In concrete terms, this has involved continual requestioning of the basic issue of the meaning of Japan's security with respect to issues such as the reaffirmation of the Japan-U.S. Security Treaty system, bases of

U.S. Forces in Japan, North Korea (i.e., suspicion surrounding its development of nuclear arms and missiles), and participation in United Nations peace-keeping operations. Although works published during the review period did not deal with all of these key questions, significant results were achieved in considering basic issues or in seeking to understand the present situation structurally.

Tanaka Akihiko's general history [III-01] outlines how security has been interpreted in the context of postwar Japanese politics and diplomacy. This is a fundamental text for understanding what kinds of issues have been debated in Japan. The Ministry of Foreign Affairs published a special issue of its public relations magazine *Gaikō Forum* [III-02] in which Japanese security is discussed.

Needless to say, the basis of Japanese security is the Japan-U.S. Security Treaty system. The journal published by the Japan Association of International Relations [III-03] brought out a special issue that focusses on the Japan-U.S. Security Treaty system from an academic viewpoint in an attempt to consider postwar Japanese security. While fundamentally affirming the Japan-U.S. Security Treaty system, Nishihara Masashi and Tsuchiyama Jitsuo [III-04] offer information that is geared toward the general public, yet is objective in its handling of various questions on this topic. In a style that gives the reader a sense of presence, Funabashi Yōichi [III-05] demonstrates how the Japan-U. S. Security Treaty system has become more fluid during the 1990s. Although this is not an academic work, it is required reading for understanding exactly what is occurring in the arena of Japanese-U.S. politics. Because over seventy percent of the land area occupied by U.S. Forces in Japan is located in Okinawa, Okinawa's position in the Japan-U.S. Security Treaty system has always been a major issue, but with the collapse of the Cold War structure it has become the focus of extensive discussion, and Gabe Masaaki presents a systematic study [III-06]; he has also contributed an article to [III-03]. [III-05] is another portrayal of negotiations about U.S. military bases. Furthermore, the volume edited by the Okinawa Times [III-07] offers important information on U.S. military bases and other conflicting issues confronting Okinawa.

IV. JAPANESE DIPLOMACY

In conclusion, I will introduce some works that do not fit into the above three categories. In a commentary on Japanese diplomacy, one of Japan's most distinguished diplomats, Owada Hisashi [IV-01], discusses a wide range of issues in an interview format. Diplomat Ikeda Tadashi [IV-02] considers Japan's involvement in the Cambodian peace process, which was Japan's first postwar instance of full-scale participation in the resolution of an international dispute; it is written from the perspective of someone who was extremely close to the scene of events. The 1997 annual report of the Japanese Political Science Association [IV-03] is a special issue on the theme of Japanese diplomacy in the 1970s.

Other works that deal with issues surrounding recent Japanese diplomacy include Okonogi Masao and Kojima Tomoyuki's analysis [IV-04] of international relations in East Asia, *Kokusai Mondai* (International Affairs) No. 451 [IV-05] that discusses ODA, and *Kokusai Mondai* No. 453 [IV-06] that deals with the problem of global warming. Furthermore, *Kokusai Mondai* Nos. 432 and 444 [IV-07, 08] both review the international situation and Japan during the years 1996 and 1997 respectively. The work edited by Watanabe Akio [IV-09] provides a general survey of the various diplomatic issues that have faced Japan in recent years.

Although the following two studies are not in book form, they are nevertheless important articles indicative of the level and directions of research on Japanese diplomacy: namely, Sakai Tetsuya [IV-10] provides a guide to methods of studying Japanese diplomacy while also developing his ideas on Japanese diplomacy, and Iokibe Makoto [IV-11] reviews research on Japanese diplomacy with a focus on the postwar period. For gaining a bird's-eye view of overall research on Japanese diplomacy, these two studies cannot be overlooked.

BIBLIOGRAPHY

I. Prewar Diplomacy and the War

01 三谷　博 Mitani Hiroshi,『明治維新とナショナリズム——幕末の外交と
政治変動』 *The Meiji Restoration and Nationalism: Diplomacy and
Political Changes in the Bakumatsu Period,* 364 pp., 山川出版社, 1997.

A work that seeks to shed light on the formation of Japan as a nation-
state not in the context of the national integration policies of the Meiji
government, but in the connections between diplomacy and internal
politics during the opening of the coutry in the Bakumatsu period. Making
use of new analytic concepts together with quantitative analysis, this work
contributes to a new understanding of Japan as a nation. It consists of Part
1 "Premises of the Restoration": The formation of the "proto nation-
state," International environment and foreign relations in the first half of
the 19th century; Part 2 "The Decision-Making Process behind the
Opening of the Country": The eve of the opening of the country, Shift
from limited opening to active opening of the country and *daimyos*' views
on foreign relations; Part 3 "Changes in the Political Structure": Plans to
rearm by the Tokugawa shogunate, Attempt to institutionalize "public
discussion" (*kōgi* 公議), and Recruitment of fit persons for higher positions and transformation of the '*ie*' 家; and Part 4 "A Review": The Meiji
Restoration in comparative history. A full bibliography is appended.

02 毛利敏彦 Mōri Toshihiko,『台湾出兵——大日本帝国の開幕劇』 *The
Taiwan Expedition of 1874: The Curtain Raiser of the Empire of Great
Japan* [中公新書], 196 pp., 中央公論社, 1997.

Despite there being an accumulation of works on the Taiwan Expedition of 1874 dating from before the war, according to the author, regard-
less of the numerous detailed works, none of these provides answers to the
basic questions of why Japan dispatched troops and why China took such
a firm line against Japan. The author sees in the Taiwan Expedition of
1874, a confrontation between China seeking to arrest the collapse of the
traditional East Asian order and Japan looking to participate in the
modern international system.

03 小林道彦 Kobayashi Michihiko,『日本の大陸政策 1894-1914』 *Japan's
Continental Policy, 1894-1914,* 318 pp., 南窓社, 1996.

04 秦　郁彦 Hata Ikuhiko,『蘆溝橋事件の研究』 *A Study of the Marco
Polo Bridge Incident,* 419 pp., 東京大学出版会, 1996.

This work examines details of the days before and after this incident
which triggered the outbreak of the Second Sino-Japanese War. Compris-

ing a total of nine chapters, it covers the Japanese invasion of North China, the eve of the Marco Polo Bridge Incident, the actual scene on the night of 7 July, the surrounding locale late that night, the situation at the site from 8-11 July, the process leading up to the dispatch of troops to North China, and Japanese and Chinese perspectives on whether or not to escalate the war. This work, which makes use of new data, could be described as a sequel to the author's earlier publication, 『日中戦争史』 *A History of the Sino-Japanese War* (1961).

05　細谷千博ほか（編）Hosoya Chihiro *et al.* (eds.),『太平洋戦争の終結――アジア・太平洋の戦後形成』 *The End of the Pacific War: The Postwar Formation of Asia and the Pacific*, 439 pp., 柏書房, 1997.

A work bringing together the results of a collaborative study that attempts to grasp in a multifaceted way the significance of the end of the Japan-U.S. War for the international order, as opposed to analyzing the actual process of terminating the war. The complex connections between restoration of the prewar order and entering a new stage in international relations are skillfully revealed. However, it cannot be denied that the treatment of issues surrounding the atomic bombing is somewhat peculiar when the book is considered as a whole. It consists of Part 1 "The International Context of the End of the War": Wartime diplomacy and postwar plans, Japan's peace overtures toward China, The question of Soviet-German peace and Japan, Soviet diplomacy toward Japan and its participation in the Pacific war, American plans for postwar Asia, and The background to and formation of the management structure of the Occupation of Japan; Part 2 "The Atomic Bombing and Its Significance": The origins of atomic bomb diplomacy, The "decision" to drop the bombs, the shock of the atomic bombing and the decision to surrender, and Hiroshima in history; and Part 3 "The Formation of a Regional Order in Postwar Asia": Decolonization and regional order in Southeast Asia, Regional order and the British sphere of influence, Regional order on the Indochina Peninsula, The formation of postwar order in the Philippines, the Korean Peninsula and regional order in postwar East Asia, and The Soviet Union and the formation of the Yalta system. This publication is a compilation of 16 revised papers originally presented at the "International Conference Marking the 50th Anniversary of the End of the Pacific War," sponsored by the International House of Japan.

06　纐纈　厚　Kōketsu Atsushi,『日本海軍の終戦工作――アジア太平洋戦争の再検証』 *The Japanese Navy's Covert Maneuvers to End the War: A Reexamination of the Asia-Pacific War* [中公新書], 208 pp., 中央公

論社, 1996.

A work that attempts to undermine one of Japan's postwar myths, namely, that the army was the villain and the navy was in the right. It attempts to review the role of the navy, starting from the part it played in the decision to wage war through to its maneuvers to end the war, which took into account the establishment of the postwar system. The contents cover the navy's perceptions of the situation, the navy and changes in circumstances in Europe, premises of the outbreak of the Japan-U.S. War, the development of Japan-U.S. negotiations, attempts to overthrow the Tōjō Cabinet, the truth about maneuvers to end the war, and the navy's war responsibility.

07 倉沢愛子 (編) Kurasawa Aiko (ed.), 『東南アジア史のなかの日本占領』 *The Japanese Occupation in the History of Southeast Asia*, 574 pp., 早稲田大学出版部, 1997.

Numerous researchers on Southeast Asian studies participated in this joint work, which attempts to clarify Japan's actions during its occupation of Southeast Asia as a part of the Pacific War and their subsequent influence. This is a highly ambitious work that seeks to grasp what Japan means to Southeast Asia. Part 1 consists of 3 papers on the maintenance and transformation of the ruling structure and leadership; Part 2 comprises 4 papers on how local society coped with mobilization of human and material resources; Part 3 contains 4 papers on culture and society during the Japanese occupation; Part 4 consists of 3 papers on the Japanese occupation in multiethnic societies; and Part 5 is made up of 4 papers on the Japanese occupation in modern history.

08 倉沢愛子 (編) Kurasawa Aiko (ed.), 『南方特別留学生が見た戦時下の日本人』 *Wartime Japanese as Viewed by "Special Foreign Students from the South,"* 270 pp., 草思社, 1997.

This work consists of interviews with nine Indonesians who came to study in Japan under the system of "special foreign students from the South" that emerged as a national state policy to realize the plans for the Greater East Asia Co-Prosperity Sphere.

09 池端雪浦 (編) Ikehata Setsuho (ed.), 『日本占領下のフィリピン』 *The Philippines Under Japanese Occupation*, 387 pp., 岩波書店, 1996.

10 波多野澄雄 Hatano Sumio, 『太平洋戦争とアジア外交』 *The Pacific War and Japanese Diplomacy toward Asia*, 326 pp., 東京大学出版会, 1996.

Although Japan occupied and assumed control of Southeast Asia as part of the Pacific War, at the same time it was compelled to declare approval for the liberation of Asia from colonial rule by Europe and the

United States and for the principle of self-determination. The detailed analysis seen in this work casts light on Japan's plans for postwar order and the concept of a Greater East Asia as part of the pursuit of these plans, and also clarifies the ideals contained in Shigemitsu's diplomacy. The composition of the book is as follows: the outberak of war against Britain, the United States and the Netherlands and plans for ending the war; political maneuvering concerning the advance into "West Asia" (British India); the "founding of Greater East Asia" and the Ministry of Greater East Asia (Daitōashō 大東亜省), the development of the "new policy for China"; the "independence" of Burma and the Philippines; the Treaty of Alliance between Japan and China and the "Greater East Asia Policy Guidelines"; the Greater East Asia Conference and the joint declaration; the ripple effect of the Greater East Asia Declaration; Foreign Affairs Minister Shigemitsu Mamoru 重光葵 and "Greater East Asia Diplomacy"; the Soviet Union and China in wartime diplomacy; and Shigemitsu Mamoru and wartime diplomacy.

II. Postwar Japan-U.S. Relations

01   五百旗頭　真 Iokibe Makoto,『20 世紀の日本 3　占領期――首相たちの新日本』 *Japan in the 20th Century 3: The Occupation Period—The Prime Ministers' New Japan*, 430 pp., 読売新聞社，1997.

As the subtitle "The Prime Ministers' New Japan" indicates, this work describes the process of Japan's demise by surrender through to its rebirth from the perspective of the prime ministers' leadership. As regards international relations, it analyzes relations with the Allied Forces and the period when a diplomatic policy line was being established following the restoration of sovereignty. The following topics are covered: Japan's acceptance of Occupation rule, MacArthur and the Emperor, the realization of "Shidehara Kijūrō's 幣原喜重郎 diplomacy," the 1st Yoshida Cabinet, the coalition administration of the Katayama Tetsu 片山哲 and Ashida Hitoshi 芦田均 Cabinets, and the establishment of conservative politics by Yoshida Shigeru 吉田茂. A detailed chronological table, data, and bibliography are appended.

02   李　鐘元 Lee Jong-won,『東アジア冷戦と韓米日関係』 *The Cold War in East Asia and Korea-U.S.-Japan Relations*, 313 pp., 東京大学出版会, 1996.

Rather than being an analysis of the interrelationship between Korea, the United States and Japan, this work could be more accurately described as an account of Japan's significance to U.S.-Korea relations. In concrete terms, it is an analysis of the role played by Cold War structure and

Japan's presence in the development of U.S.-Korea relations in the 1950s. This book sheds light on the Japan factor in the process of priority shifting to economics from a focus on the military in Asian strategy under the Eisenhower regime.

03 野林　健 Nobayashi Takeshi, 『管理貿易の政治経済学――米国の鉄鋼輸入レジーム: 1959-1995』 *The Political Economics of Government-Managed Trade: America's Steel Import Régime, 1959-1995*, 325 pp., 有斐閣, 1996.

The subtitle "America's Steel Import Régime, 1959-1995" indicates the subject of analysis in concrete terms. Although suggestive of an analysis of American politics, the focal theme of this work is in fact trade friction between Japan and the United States. The eight chapters analyze the issues more or less in chronological order: the American steel industry and competitiveness, the germination of government-managed trade, the structuring of government-managed trade, the steel industry in developed countries and the structural crisis, the failure of the price régime, multi-régimes in the steel industry, the era of global quotas, and seeking a replacement régime. A summary makes up the final chapter. This book is a revised edition of the author's previous publication 『保護貿易の政治力学』 (*The Political Dynamics of Protective Trade*, 勁草書房, 1987).

04 軽部謙介 Karube Kensuke, 『日米コメ交渉――市場開放の真相と再交渉への展望』 *Japan-U.S. Rice Negotiations: The Real Facts Behind Opening of the Market and Prospects for Renegotiations* [中公新書], 234 pp., 中央公論社, 1997.

This work describes through a journalist's eyes how a settlement was reached over the liberalization of rice, one of the most important issues for Japan in the Uruguay Round. Although intense negotiations about the liberalization of agricultural products also took place between the United States and EC, this book focusses on negotiations about rice between Japan and the United States.

05 石黒一憲 Ishiguro Kazunori, 『日米航空摩擦の構造と展望』 *The Structure of Japan-U.S. Air Transport Friction and Future Prospects*, 231 pp., 木鐸社, 1997.

06 通商産業省通商政策局米州課（編）Ministry of International Trade and Industry, International Trade Policy Bureau, American Affairs Division (ed), 『日米自動車交渉の軌跡――新たな日米経済関係構築への取り組み』 *The Course of Japan-U.S. Automobile Negotiations: Engaging in the Building of a New Japan-U.S. Economic Relationship*, 398 pp., 通商産業調査会, 1997.

This work consists of Part 1, focussing on essays and comments (five chapters); Part 2, focussing on data (two chapters); Part 3, entitled "A Different Point of View Leads to Different Facts," which is a comparison of Japanese and U.S. PR materials (three chapters); and Part 4, summarizing subsequent developments. In addition to its value as source material, Part 3 is of particular interest for its viewpoint.

07　畠山　襄 Hatayama Noboru,『通商交渉——国益を巡るドラマ』 *Trade Negotiations: The Drama Surrounding National Interests*, 301 pp., 日本経済新聞社, 1996.

Comprised of the memoirs of an official involved in leading the Japanese delegation in trade negotiations, this work covers the principal economic negotiations that took place from the end of the 1980s through to the first half of the 1990s. Its contents are as follows: Japan-U.S. Structural Impediments Initiative (SII) Talks, Japan-U.S. Comprehensive Economic Talks (the rights and wrongs of establishing numerical targets), Japan-U.S. automobile negotiations, regionalism in Asia and the Pacific (establishment of APEC), Japan-EC agreement on automobiles, and security and trade (the Toshiba incident, etc.).

08　野口　均 Noguchi Hitoshi,『日米通貨交渉2000日——大蔵財務官たちの闘い』 *2000 Days in Japan-U.S. Financial Negotiations: The Struggle of the Ministry of Finance's Finance Secretaries*, 441 pp., 日本経済新聞社, 1995.

A report on Japan-U.S. friction surrounding monetary and financial issues from the latter part of the 1980s through to the early 1990s, including the development of the weak dollar in the period from the Plaza Accord (Sept. 1985) to the Christmas Accord (Dec. 1987), Japan-U.S. Structural Impediments Initiative (SII) Talks, and the provision of funds during the Gulf crisis. Although this work was published during the period covered by the previous survey, it has been included here in consideration of the relevance of its subject matter.

09　谷口将紀 Taniguchi Masaki,『日本の対米貿易交渉』 *Japan's Trade Negotiations with the United States*, 296 pp., 東京大学出版会, 1997.

This work consists of three case studies (the opening-up of procurement of supplies by Nippon Telegraph and Telephone Public Corporation, voluntary restraints on automobile exports, and Japan-U.S. automobile talks) and two data-based analyses. The aim of this work is to develop a theoretical framework for policy decisions and negotiations.

III. Security

01　田中明彦 Tanaka Akihiko,『20世紀の日本2　安全保障——戦後50年の

模索』 *Japan in the 20th Century 2: Security—Fifty Years of Postwar Searching*, 382 pp., 読売新聞社, 1997.

This work discusses the question of how to defend what from what from the perspective of strategy and the Constitution. Its content covers Japan's defeat and Article 9 of the Constitution, the Japan-U.S. Security Treaty, the path to rearmament, convergence with Yoshida's line of thinking, the Self-Defence Forces and basic policies of national defense, revision of the Japan-U. S. Security Treaty, security in the 1960s, basic defense capacity and "fundamental principles of the defence program," post-hegemony security, and post-Cold War security. Detailed bibliography and chronological table appended.

02 『緊急増刊、日本の安全保障』 *Special Issue: Japan's Security* [『外交フォーラム』 1996 年 6 月], 180 pp., 都市出版, 1996.

This issue includes an article by Iokibe Makoto 五百旗頭真 on Japan's views on security from the time of its defeat through to the 1950s and an article by Tanaka Akihiko 田中明彦 dealing with the 1970s.

03 『特集、日米安保体制——持続と変容』 *Special Edition: Japan-U.S. Security System —Continuity and Change* [『国際政治』 115 号], 221 pp., 有斐閣, 1997.

In addition to an introduction, this special issue comprises 10 papers, as follows: "Seeking Mutuality in Revision of the Security Treaty," "Revision of the Security Treaty and Japan's Defense Policies," "The Status of Forces Agreement and Okinawa," "The Korean Peninsula and the Japan-U.S. Security Treaty," "The Vietnam War and the Japan-U.S. Security System," "The Japan-U.S. Security System and Dollar Defense Policies," "U. S. Military Strategy and the Japan-U.S. Security System" "The Japan-U. S. Security System in the Post-Cold War Era," "Towards a Stratified Security Structure in Asia and Pacific," and "The Theory of International Politics in the Japan-U.S. Alliance."

04 西原 正・土山實男 (編) Nishihara Masashi and Tsuchiyama Jitsuo (eds.), 『日米同盟 Q & A 100』 *The Japan-U.S. Alliance: 100 Questions and Answers*, 289 pp., 亜紀書房, 1998.

A book for general readers that seeks to deepen understanding of the Japan-U.S. security system. Written mainly by researchers, it is both neutral and objective in content. It consists of Part 1, a multifaceted analysis of the Japan-U.S. alliance (8 chapters, 68 questions), and Part 2, on the history and future development of the Japan-U.S. alliance (5 chapters, 32 questions). Chronological table and reference data appended. Properly speaking, this work should have been included in the next survey, but it has been specially included here on account of its relevance to the themes at hand.

05　船橋洋一 Funabashi Yōichi,『同盟漂流』 *The Alliance Adrift*, 521 pp., 朝日新聞社, 1997.

This detailed report describes how Japan and the United States have deliberated on post-Cold War security cooperation in the midst of various contradictions faced by the Japan-U.S. security system, such as tensions in the surrounding international situation, including suspicions of nuclear weapon development by North Korea and the Taiwan Strait crisis, as well as the questions of U.S. military bases in Okinawa and the rape of a schoolgirl by American servicemen. The result of the author's meticulous collection of data from both the Japanese and U.S. sides, this is a valuable research source. It is divided into 4 parts and contains 20 chapters.

06　我部政明 Gabe Masaaki,『日米関係の中の沖縄』 *Okinawa in the Context of Japan-U.S. Relations*, 237 pp., 三一書房, 1996.

An analysis of key problems involving Okinawa in the context of relations between the United States and Japan. The issues covered include the trusteeship controversy, currency conversion, U.S. plans for returning Okinawa during the 1950s, the introduction of nuclear weapons, and the system of public elections for the top civilian post, etc. It is divided into 5 parts, dealing with separation of Okinawa from Japan, peace with Japan and Okinawa, U.S. military bases in Okinawa and Japan's security, the inside facts of the return of administrative power to Okinawa, and Okinawa and America fifty years after the war.

07　沖縄タイムス社 (編) The Okinawa Times (ed.),『50年目の激動』 *The Upheavals of the Fiftieth Anniversary*, 366 pp., 沖縄タイムス社, 1996.

IV. Japanese Diplomacy

01　小和田　恆 Owada Hisashi (Interviewer: 山室英夫 Yamamuro Hideo),『外交とは何か』 *The Essence of Diplomacy*, 252 pp., NHK 出版, 1996.

This work is a candid expression of opinion by a diplomat on how high-ranking officials in the Ministry of Foreign Affairs view diplomacy and how they go about furthering Japan's activities in international society. Recently, instances of diplomats relating their own personal experiences and opinions concerning diplomacy have been increasing in *Gaikō Forum*, but this particular work gives insights into the plans diplomats are drawing up for Japanese diplomacy in all its aspects.

02　池田　維 Ikeda Tadashi,『カンボジア和平への道――証言　日本外交試練の5年間』 *The Road to Peace in Cambodia: A Testimony—The Five-Year Ordeal of Japan's Diplomacy*, 358 pp., 都市出版, 1996.

These memoirs of the Japanese Minister to Thailand, who was directly involved in this issue, shed light on how the Japanese government was involved in Cambodian peace process from the end of the 1980s through to the beginning of the 1990s, what Japan's diplomatic goals were, and to what extent they were achieved. This work was originally published in serial form in *Gaikō Forum*. Reference materials and chronological table appended.

03 日本政治学会（編）Japanese Political Science Association (ed.),『特集，危機の日本外交──70 年代』*Special Issue: Japanese Diplomacy in Crisis: The 1970s* ［『日本政治学会年報』1997 年］, 254 pp., 岩波書店, 1997.

A collection of seven papers on Japanese diplomacy during the tumultous 1970s from a perspective that views the 1970s as a time of the "miscarried termination of the Cold War." It deals with Japanese diplomacy and U.S.-China relations in the 1970s, Japan and the reorganization of the dollar system, Southeast Asia and Japanese diplomacy in an era of transition, the normalization of diplomatic relations between Japan and Vietnam and Japan-U.S. relations, the development of defense policies, the context of discussions on collective security, and regionalism and Japanese diplomacy.

04 小此木政夫・小島朋之 Okonogi Masao and Kojima Tomoyuki (eds.),『東アジア　危機の構図』*East Asia: The Structure of the Crisis*, 284 pp., 東洋経済新報社, 1997.

A political perspective on the increasingly unstable situation in post-Cold War East Asia. It consists of Part 1 "The Regional Situation and Strategic Trends," dealing with China, the Korean Peninsula, the United States, Russo-Chinese relations, Russo-Japanese relations, and the balance of power in East Asia, and Part 2 "An Analysis of Factors of Instability," dealing with North Korea, military relations between China and Taiwan, Russian exports of arms, issues surrounding the Senkaku Islands and Takeshima, Hong Kong, and the South China Sea. (Note: This book was published before financial crisis erupted in Thailand in July 1997.)

05 焦点：日本の ODA の再構築 "Focal Point: Rebuilding of Japanese ODA,"「国際問題」451 号, pp. 2-64, 日本国際問題研究所, 1997.

06 焦点：地球温暖化と日本の選択 "Focal Point: Japan's Choices Regarding Global Warming,"「国際問題」453 号, pp. 2-70., 日本国際問題研究所, 1997.

07 焦点：国際情勢と日本・1995 "Focal Point: Japan and the International Situation in 1995,"「国際問題」432 号, pp. 2-65, 日本国際問題研究所, 1996.

08　焦点：国際情勢と日本・1996 "Focal Point: Japan and the International Situation in 1996,"「国際問題」444号, pp. 2-79, 日本国際問題研究所, 1997.

09　渡邉昭夫（編）Watanabe Akio （ed.）,『現代日本の国際政策』 *International Policies in Contemporary Japan*, 250 pp., 有斐閣, 1997.

10　酒井哲哉 Sakai Tetsuya, 日本外交論 "On Japanese Diplomacy,"『国際関係研究入門』, pp. 203-223, 東京大学出版会, 1996.

A study combining an introduction and bibliographical guide for graduate students intending to specialize in Japanese diplomacy. It gives clear expression to the importance of a critical stance in considering what exactly is entailed in discussing Japanese diplomacy. Works cited range from the classical through to the contemporary.

11　五百旗頭　真 Iokibe Makoto, 日本外交研究 "The Study of Japanese Diplomacy,"「国際法外交雑誌」96巻, 4・5合併号, pp. 204-222, 国際法学会, 1997.

This article is a revised version of a paper read at a conference commemorating the centennial of the establishment of the Japanese Association of International Law 国際法学会, and it provides an overall view of postwar research trends.

ECONOMICS

Itō Masanao
The University of Tokyo

INTRODUCTION

In the latter part of the 1990s the Japanese economy's long-term recession has assumed serious proportions. As regards non-banks that had become the focus of problems concerning bad assets, in June 1996 a bill was approved to deal with housing loan companies, i.e., *Jūsen*, and it was agreed to use national coffers to cover 680 billion yen of the 6 trillion 410 billion yen in claims requiring settlement. Further, in October of the same year Prime Minister Hashimoto proposed six major administrative reforms, of which the financial "Big Bang" was promoted as the mainstay.

However, despite these countermeasures the situation showed no improvement, and in April of the following year, 1997, a medium-sized life insurance company, Nissan Mutual Life Insurance Co., Ltd., went bankrupt, and at the same time proposals for restructuring because of poor results were announced by Nippon Credit Bank, Ltd., one of the main long-term credit banks, followed in November by the bankruptcies of the Hokkaidō Takushoku Bank, Ltd., and Yamaichi Securities Co., Ltd., with the financil crisis ultimately extending to the city banks and four major securities companies that had constituted the nucleus of the Japanese financial system. Moreover, these occurrences were no more than a passing point in a post-bubble succession of disclosures involving mismanagement of finances and securities, a colossal amount of bad debts on the part of banks, insurance companies and non-banks, etc., and the failure and suspension of business of secondary regional banks, credit associations, and medium-sized life insurance companies. In the following year (1998), management crises were exposed at Yasuda Trust and Banking Co., Ltd., belonging to an industrial conglomerate (*zaibatsu*), and the Long-Term Credit Bank of Japan, Ltd., in April and June respectively, followed by nationalization of the Nippon Credit Bank and Long-Term Credit Bank of Japan from October onward.

In these circumstances the unemployment rate continued to rise slowly, and a decline in sales and profit margins manifested itself not only in the financial sector but also in the manufacturing sector. For this reason, there was an increase in discussion about the need for policies aimed at changing the system and structure as opposed to existing policies for economic recovery that focussed on public investment, and from overseas there was even a comment to the effect that the Japanese model of economic development was no longer valid (vice-executive director of IMF, 5/12/97).

During this period too adjustments of surplus capital stock were not completed, and there was continued slow growth in plant and equipment investment and long-term sluggishness in consumption, especially personal consumption. The abnormally low official rate was also maintained during this period, and although the yen-dollar exchange rate that had depreciated since the summer of 1995 crossed the 120 yen mark, relief from the slump in the Japanese economy was not apparent despite an increase in exports.

In the following sections we shall go into details of the different areas of research on the Japanese economy conducted in 1996 and 1997; however, pure economic theory, research on the economies and economic history of countries other than Japan and work on statistics and annual reports have been excluded, as has information on basic statistics and statistical yearbooks.

I. Economic History

During the two-year review period there continued to be advances in research summarizing the fifty years since the end of the war. On the other hand, it is also noteworthy that the present review period saw the appearance of a large number of outstanding works on the Meiji era, a subject on which research had been sluggish in recent years.

Firstly, as regards research on the postwar period, Okazaki Tetsuji *et al.* [I-05] and Uchida Kōzō [I-06] summarize the activities of economic organizations, while Hayashi Yūjirō *et al.* [I-07] review economic planning under General Headquarters by way of a round-table talk with persons involved in implementing plans during the occupation. Hara Kaoru [I-20] attempts to reinterpret pricing and currency issues during the postwar reform period. The formation of the postwar corporate system and the postwar agricultural structure are summarized by Hashimoto Jurō [I-21] and Ino Ryūichi [I-24] respectively, while Hyōdō Tsutomu [I-31] and Hazama Hiroshi [I-34] summarize changes in labor consciousness, labor content and labor organizations.

As for research on the Meiji era, Ishii Kanji [I-03] and Takamura Naosuke [I-04] attempt a new interpretation of Japan's industrial revolution in the light of its connection with the war and the formation of social overhead capital, areas that had not been dealt with specifically to date. Suzuki Jun [I-15], Takeuchi Tsuneyoshi [I-16] and Nakamura Takafusa [I-17] summarize the endogenous and unique developement structure of medium and small machine industries, small businesses and traditional industries respectively. Furthermore, Iwasaki Masaya [I-22] and Nishimura Takashi [I-26] seek to reinterpret the characteristics of Japanese agriculture during the Meiji period, while Ichihara Hiroshi [I-33] does likewise on the situation surrounding coal-mining labor. Although it cannot be denied that the proliferation of such research on the Meiji era is partly a reaction to the shift in research on economic history over the last twenty years toward research on the history of modern capitalism, more fundamentally speaking, in contrast to the two conflicting tendencies of ready acceptance or criticism of the "Japanese system," a theory that could be described as a trend in recent years, it can be said that there has been a strengthening in moves toward factual reappraisal of Japanese capitalism based on a return to its origins or moves toward criticism of the very concept of a "Japanese system."

84

As Japan's relationship with the Asian economy becomes closer, reexamination of Japan's historical relationship with the Asian economy continues to progress, and in this direction Kobayashi Hideo *et al.* [I-35] and Namikata Shōichi [I-36] examine the system of Japanese wartime administration, Yasutomi Ayumu [I-37] and Tadai Yoshio [I-38] look at the financial system, Hirai Kōichi [I-39] deals with the fiscal structure, and Nishinarita Yutaka [I-40] reviews the composition of the labor force.

In addition, Nishikawa Shunsaku [I-01] summarizes the history of research on the history of the Japanese economy undertaken from the perspective of historical research on quantitative economics, and Minami Ryōshin [I-02] has produced a detailed monograph on income distribution from the same standpoint.

II. The Japanese Economy

With the prolongation and worsening of the recession, there has been a demand for reexamination of not only finances but also the Japanese economic structure and system themselves. As was pointed out in the introduction, criticism of the "Japanese system" has also begun to emerge overseas, and former admiration has undergone a one-hundred-and-eighty degree turnabout. However, the meaning of what constitutes "the Japanese economic system" which is the subject of criticism here varies according to the writer, and there is not necessarily a consensus of opinion. Although it can by no means be regarded as justifiable, there appears to be an implicit premise that the economic system posited by neoclassical economics is the true form of capitalism and any system deviating from this is distorted.

In any case, there can be no analysis of the present state of the Japanese economy as long as this global standard is ignored, and there has been an increase in the number of studies appearing that either support or criticize this standard. Although there are differences in nuance, Otani Kiyoshi [II-01], Nakatani Iwao [II-03], Iwata Kikuo [II-05], Asako Kazumi *et al.* [II-06], Komiya Ryūtarō *et al.* [II-07], Tanaka Naoki [II-08, 09], Itō Motoshige [II-13], and Noguchi Yukio *et al.* [II-22] generally take the former position, emphasizing the need for a change in the Japanese economic system, while Yamamoto Takanori [II-02], Hirano Yasurō [II-04], Baba Hiroji [II-10], Kitahara Isamu et al. [II-11], Shibagaki Kazuo [II-12], Watanabe Hisashi et al. [II-18], and Yoshida Kazuo [II-19] all criticize the aforementioned neoclassical system reform theory from different perspectives such as Marxian economics in a broad sense, the Regulation school, or complex systems.

This issue is also reflected in discussions on the nature of concrete economic policies and deregulation. Ōyama Kōsuke [II-21] and Hirota Hideki [II-23] undertake historical examinations of Japanese industrial policies, while Noguchi Yukio et al. [II-22] and Masamura Kimihiro [II-24] place macro-policies in context both historically and by historical comparison. Suzuki Mamoru [II-25] and the Society for Environmental Economics and Policy Studies [II-26] take up the connections with social overhead capital and the environment, an issue on which there has been a scarcity of research to date. Research on deregulation also took a step forward, progressing from the examination of the merits and demerits and positioning of deregulation in general to the examination of societal regulations as represented by Uegusa Masu [II-29], covering such areas as guarantees of health and sanitation, guarantees of safety and disaster prevention, and prevention of environmental pollution and preservation of the environment.

As regards the question of a shift in the economic system, this shift has become necessary not only in response to the present economic crisis but also because of developments in informationalization and networking. Itō Makoto et al. [II-15], Takeuchi Kei [II-16], and Masuda Yuji et al. [II-17] all present empirical and multifaceted studies on this subject.

III. PUBLIC FINANCE

Since progress began to be made in reforms of the financial system, including administrative and fiscal reforms, decentralization, and deregulation, advances have been made in concrete research on the direction of and ideas behind fiscal reforms. Ihori Toshihiro [III-05], Hayashi Yoshitsugu [III-07], and Takeuchi Nobuhito *et al.* [III-08], while basing their ideas on the neoclassical framework, present in concrete terms what they believe should be the structure of a financial system in which benefits and burdens coincide, Hoshikawa Jun'ichi [III-01], Yamazaki Satoshi *et al.* [III-02], Andō Minoru [III-04], and Ikegami Jun [III-09], on the other hand, propose fiscal reforms based on a new system for public services while criticizing the direction of the present fiscal reforms as market-oriented from the standpoint of Keynesianism and Marxism.

System reform has also required reconsideration of fiscal investment and loans and the taxation system. From various differing viewpoints, Tomita Toshiki [III-10], Yoshida Kazuo *et al.* [III-11], and Kawakita Hidetaka [III-12] all criticize the reform of fiscal investment and loans that is currently in progress, while Konishi Sachio [III-14], Wada Yatsuka [III-15], and Uchiyama Akira [III-16] point out problems in current tax system reforms with a focus on the corporate tax system.

Since the financial crisis is directly linked to a reappraisal of social security and social welfare, there appeared a large number of empirical studies and policy studies in this area too. Shibuya Hiroshi *et al.*[III-27] presents a factual examination of the differences in welfare policies between Japan and the United States in the areas of pensions, medical care, housing and local communites on the basis of a joint study undertaken from a non-neoclassical perspective by Japanese and American public finance researchers, while Sakawaki Akiyoshi *et al.* [III-22] and Miyata Kazuaki [III-20] offer new interpretations of the overall picture pertaining to social welfare policies and social security policies in contemporary Japan, looking at these areas either generally or historically. Further, Sakamoto Shigeo [III-25] and Yashiro Naohiro [III-26] both draw up concrete plans for a system of livelihood security in an aging society and propose diversification of the means of securing livelihood stability for the elderly.

IV. Money and Banking

The impact of the bursting of the bubble economy on the financial sector extended to the core of the financial system, and during this period advances were made in empirical research on the Japanese financial system together with the appearance of a number of studies of monetary policy. As regards the former, Ueda Kazuo *et al.* [IV-02] present a multifaceted analysis of the actual circumstances surrounding the decreasing international competitiveness of Japanese financial institutions and financial markets from an institutional, factual and theoretical viewpoint. Aoki Masahiko *et al.* [IV-03] undertake a detailed examination of Japan's main bank system from the standpoint of comparative institutional analysis, and Yamada Hiroshi *et al.* [IV-08] examine the Japanese financial crisis of the 1990s from the aspect of bank labor.

As for monetary policy, controversy reignited to such a degree that it could almost be described as a reenactment of the banking school and currency school dispute that occurred duing the early nineteenth century. Although this controversy concerns the casual relationship between money supply and base money, in the final analysis it boils down to whether the demand for money is based on endogenous variables or exogenous variables. This issue has been debated for two hundred years, and while Shimizu Yoshinori [IV-11] criticizes Keynesian monetary policies from the standpoint of the theory of rational expectations, Yoshikawa Hiroshi [IV-12] emphasizes the endogenous nature of the money supply from a Keynesian standpoint. Further, Kuroda Akio [IV-13] reviews the debate between policy makers at the Bank of Japan and academics over high-powered money and the money supply, and he includes a detailed analysis of the monetary policies of the central bank from a standpoint close to that of the Bank of Japan.

Factual research on trends in financial markets and management of financial institutions also made progress. Mabuchi Noritoshi [IV-15] and Aizawa Kōetsu [IV-16] both examine the future outlook of inaugural financial holding companies. Tachibanaki Toshiaki *et al.* [IV-18] examine pricing in the capital market, characteristics of the market, the behavior of investors in the market, and the structure of corporate governance, characterizing these as being market-oriented, while Fukaura Atsuyuki [IV-19] makes a factual examination of the practice of creating liquid claims and its significance in the study of economics. As regards international finance and financial internationalization, reference should be made to VIII-4 (international finance) in the Bibliography.

V. INDUSTRY

Because the deepening recession extended to the manufacturing sector, advances were made in research on the economic conditions of individual industries, and among these studies a large number dealt with small businesses, which have been directly affected by the recession. Kobayashi Yasuo *et al.* [V-23] present a comprehensive summary of past research on small businesses in a survey on the history of research on Japanese small businesses by members of the "118th Committee on Industrial Structure and Small Businesses" affiliated to the Japan Society for the Promotion of Science. Momose Shigeo *et al.* [V-22], Kiyonari Tadao *et al.* [V-03], Horiuchi Toshihiro [V-05], and Kimbara Tatsuo [V-04] all put the standpoint of venture businesses to the fore while examining industrial integration, technological developments and management strategies in Japan; Miyata Yukio [V-07] presents a comparative study on joint research and development in high-tech industries; Watanabe Yukio [V-10] undertakes a detailed and factual analysis of subcontractors in the machine industry centered on Ōta-ku, Tokyo, based on many years of research on actual conditions; and Hwang Wan Shung [V-24] and Shimohirao Isao [V-25] present comparative analyses of locally-based industry (*jibasangyō*) by country and region. Also in the area of industrial policy, small business policies were discussed anew, and Matsui Takayuki [V-06] undertakes a factual investigation of policies on production adjustment and industrial regulation together with the policy-making process, while Kurose Naohiro [V-08] summarizes small business policies in general, including protective policies and competitive policies.

Research on a shift in the system from the viewpoint of network companies and a network economy also progressed, and Ueda Kazuhiro [V-01] sheds light in a multifaceted way on changes that the development of technology has brought to social systems. Fujime Setsuo [V-15] looks at the connection between transportation reforms and changes in the regional system, and Tsuji Masatsugu *et al.* [V-19] describe the present situation and point out problems pertaining to Japan's economic, management, and regional networks.

VI. AGRICULTURE

The reappraisal of Japanese agriculture progressed from partial liberalization of rice and implementation of New Foodstuff Law in November 1995 to the appearance during the review period of a bill for the complete revision of the Basic Agriculture Law. For this reason there were advances in reviews of postwar agriculture and various discussions of its future course, and a large number of studies appeared on agricultural policy too. The Rural Culture Association [VI-01] presents an ongoing study that attempts to provide a comprehensive grasp both of the reappraisal of the international value of Japanese agriculture and rural villages and of the international environment that regulates Japanese agriculture by linking these to global undercurrents in agricultural administration and farm management in different parts of the world. Ono Seishi [VI-02], Uehara Nobuhiro [VI-03], and Kajii Isoshi [VI-06] all examine the history and present conditions of Japanese agriculture from the perspective of agriculture undergoing internationalization. In addition, basing himself on a comprehensive analysis of an agricultural census taken in 1995, Usami Shigeru [VI-05] focusses on trends in the allocation of agricultural resources and large-scale management, changes concerning those who bear the burden of farming and in the number of farming households, the current situation regarding mobilization of farming land, and agriculture in hillside and mountain areas.

In the area of agricultural policy, Kawai Kazushige [VI-10] analyzes the situation as regards the dissolution of policies for self-sustaining food supplies, Ishihara Kenji [VI-11] demonstrates on the basis of changes in the agricultural budget a shift to abandonment of agriculture protection policy, and Takenaka Kunio [VI-12] emphasizes the need for a paradigm shift to a decentralized agricultural policy and system. Further, because agricultural organizations were directly impacted by the financial crisis, research on agricultural cooperative (*nōkyō*) finances and agriculture-related finances also progressed. On the basis of an examination of the links between agricultural cooperatives and housing loan companies, which are the chief institutional suppliers of capital sources, Saeki Naomi [VI-21] and Kondō Yasuo *et al*. [VI-08] discuss the need for system reform of agricultural cooperative-affiliated finances. Nishiyama Hisanori [VI-20] and Fujitani Chikuji [VI-22] raise the question of the need for an overall shift in the activities of coopertives, basing themselves on a comprehensive examination of the operations of agricultural cooperatives such as affiliated financial, credit, and mutual aid schemes.

In the area of agricultural production and distribution of agricultural products, the examination of issues involving the rice market progressed, and the Agricultural Marketing Society of Japan [VI-14, 15] and Koike Tsuneo [VI-16] look at the structure of the production, distribution and consumption of rice and at changes in the pricing system under the New Foodstuff Law. Further, as regards farm management, Tabata Tamotsu *et al*. [IV-25] discuss problems and measures concerning those bearing the burden of farming on the basis of a detailed fact-finding survey of agricultural villages throughout Japan. Meanwhile, Ishihara Toyomi [IV-24] examines changes in farming families, and Hobo Takehiko [IV-26] looks for the future development of agricultural and mountainous villages in endogenous growth on the basis of an analysis of the present situation in depopulated agricultural and mountain villages.

VII. LABOR

The deepening recession has given rise to employment insecurity in Japan, a country that by international standards has been characterized by its low unemployment rate. For this reason, the focus of research and discussion turned from gaining a grasp of the characteristics of Japanese labor-management relations to empirical studies on employment and working conditions.

Yuasa Yoshio [VII-14] and Tokita Yoshihisa *et al.* [VII-18] take a diversified look at the relationship between restructuring and production system reforms and between deregulation and labor problems, while Morita Tōichirō [VII-19] and Miyuki Mitsuyoshi [VII-20] examine the relationship between technological growth and labor and management. Meanwhile, Hayakawa Seiichirō [VII-22] reviews the career paths of government officials, and Furugōri Tomoko [VII-21] considers irregular labor and the labor market. There also appeared a large number of studies on changes in the labor market and labor practices. Iwase Takashi [VII-23] analyzes the characteristics of Japanese employment insecurity and fluctuations in the employment system through comparisons with the United States and Europe, while Yashiro Naohiro [VII-27], Chūma Hiroyuki *et al.* [VII-28], Ono Akira [VII-29], Umino Hiroshi [VII-24], Shimada Haruo *et al.* [VII-26], and Mitani Naoki [VII-25] undertake factual analyses of changes in employment practices and the internal promotion system, mobility in the labor market, and changes in the wage structure. The same topics are dealt with in the context of small businesses by Sakasegawa Kiyoshi [VII-09].

The changes outlined above in the labor market and workplace led to reappraisals of the role of labor unions, corporate welfare and social welfare, thereby requiring a reexamination of views on labor. Tomizawa Kenji *et al.* [VII-30], Inoue Masao [VII-31], Shimoyama Fusao [VII-32], and Kuwabara Yasuo *et al.* [VII-33] each discuss future issues and the outlook of the Japanese labor movement from different viewpoints, while Hayashi Yūjirō *et al.* [VII-36] discuss the connections between nonprofit organizations and labor unions. Meanwhile, Fujita Yoshitaka *et al.* [VII-35] and Takahashi Yūkichi [VII-02] take up the relationship between corporate welfare and social security. Further, Nishimura Hiromichi *et al.* [VII-05], Miura Toyohiko [VII-15], Endō Yukio [VII-16], Washida Seiichi [VII-10], and Sugimura

Yoshimi [VII-11] raise theoretically, historically and factually issues concerning views on labor and work ethics.

In addition, research papers on Japanese labor written in Japanese by Japanese researchers between 1945 and 1995 have been brought together in a comprehensive and most useful eleven-volume series compiled by the Japan Institute of Labor [VII-01].

VIII. THE INTERNATIONAL ECONOMY

The dissolution of the socialist bloc and the collapse of the Cold War system brought about a shift in the world system, and there were advances in research looking at the concrete connections between the world system and the Japanese economy because of a perception that Japanese economic trends are linked to this shift. Kamo Takehiko et al. [VIII-01], Tomita Toshiki [VIII-02], and Ōsumi Sōshirō et al. [VIII-04] all consider Japan's position and role with the shift in the world system as their immediate theme. Iwata Katsuo [VIII-06] and Nakakita Tōru [VIII-07] both examine Japan's participation in global standards and problems surrounding this issue, while Asaba Yoshimasa [VIII-09] takes a historical approach to these same issues.

Research on Japan's relations with Asia has also continued to progress, and Zhuo Muzhi [VIII-12], Aoki Takeshi et al. [VIII-13], Shimada Katsumi et al. [VIII-14], and Tokunaga Shōjirō [VIII-15] discuss how Asia's industrialization, Asian investment and regionalism in Asia have influenced Japan. Further, as regards development aid and government aid, Adachi Yoshihiro [VIII-17], Nishikawa Jun [VIII-18], and Satō Hideo [VIII-19] offer comprehensive studies on the transfer of technology and technological cooperation based on the premise that there is a need for a shift from capital aid to social development aid.

In addition, a large number of studies appeared in the field of international finance as a result of Japan's financial crisis being considered to be linked to international finance. Okuda Hiroshi [VIII-20] and Nakao Shigeo [VIII-22] attempt to elucidate the relationship between the yen, dollar and Deutschemark, while Kamikawa Takao et al. [VIII-24] and Kawai Masahiro [VIII-

26] undertake comprehensive studies of internationalization of the yen in Asia, measures undertaken on the part of Japan for internationalization of the yen, and the position of internationalization of the yen within the global system, with the former approaching these subjects from the perspective of the history of international currency in Asia and the latter from the standpoint of open macroeconomics.

BIBLIOGRAPHY

I. Economic History
I-1. General Works

01 西川俊作・尾高煌之助・斎藤 修 (編) Nishikawa Shunsaku, Odaka Kōnosuke and Saitō Osamu (eds.),『日本経済の 200 年』 *Two Hundred Years of the Japanese Economy*, 508 pp., 日本評論社, 1996.

This publication commemorates the 20th anniversary of the founding of the Quantitative Economic History Study Group (数量経済史研究会). A comprehensive study of the growth of the Japanese economy over the last 200 years, it covers areas ranging from resources, population and price fluctuations to public finance, money and banking, land, agriculture, labor, industry, trade, transportation, capital flow, living standards and economic thought. A survey of research history is also included.

02 南 亮進 Minami Ryōshin,『日本の経済発展と所得分布』 *The Economic Development of Japan and Income Distribution* [一橋大学経済研究叢書 45], 218 pp., 岩波書店, 1996.

This work is a theoretical and empirical elucidation of changes in income distribution brought about by economic development; it is written from the perspective of a critical examination of Simon Kuznets's hypothesis and includes primary sources unearthed by the author.

03 石井寛治 Ishii Kanji,『日本の産業革命——日清・日露戦争から考える』 *Japan's Industrial Revolution: From the Perspective of the Sino-Japanese and Russo-Japanese Wars* [朝日選書 581], 290 pp., 朝日新聞社, 1997.

While attributing problems in previous research on the history of the industrial revolution to a lack of research undertaken from the perspective of world history, this work in concrete terms examines links with East Asia and describes the characteristics of Japan's industrial revolution,

94

focussing on its connections with the Sino-Japanese and Russo-Japanese Wars.

04 高村直助（編）Takamura Naosuke (ed.),『明治の産業発展と社会資本』 *Industrial Development and Social Overhead Capital during the Meiji Era*, 394 pp., ミネルヴァ書房, 1997.

Based on three keywords—the industrial revolution, social overhead capital, and the regional economy—this book examines the relationship between concrete trends in the regional economy and the formation and development of social overhead capital, an area concerning which empirical studies have been sparse to date.

05 岡崎哲二・菅山真次・西沢　保・米倉誠一郎 Okazaki Tetsuji, Sugayama Shinji, Nishizawa Tamotsu and Yonekura Seiichirō,『戦後日本経済と経済同友会』*The Postwar Japanese Economy and the Japan Committee for Economic Development*, 325 pp., 岩波書店, 1996.

This work describes the activities of the Japan Committee for Economic Development, which was established in April 1946 and is one of Japan's four main economic organizations, the others being the Federation of Economic Organizations (Keidanren 経団連), the Japan Federation of Employers' Associations (Nikkeiren 日経連), and the Japan Chamber of Commerce and Industry (日本商工会議所). It is divided into four parts covering the periods of economic recovery, high economic growth, stable growth, and recent years. Postwar Japan's economic devolopment and the evolution of its economic system are analyzed by means of a liberal comparative institutional analysis.

06 内田公三 Uchida Kōzō,『経団連と日本経済の50年——もうひとつの産業政策史』*The Federation of Economic Organizations and 50 Years of the Japanese Economy: An Alternative History of Industrial Policies*, 264 pp., 日本経済新聞社, 1996.

A reappraisal of changes in postwar Japan's industrial policies, which saw a shift from protectionism to promoting competition; it is written from the perspective of the proposals and opinions of the Federation of Economic Organizations.

07 林　雄二郎・宮崎　勇・矢野誠也・田中誠一郎・新藤　稔（編）Hayashi Yūjirō, Miyazaki Isamu, Yano Seiya, Tanaka Seiichirō and Shindō Minoru (eds.),『日本の経済計画——戦後の歴史と問題点』*Japan's Economic Planning: Postwar History and Problems*, 397 pp., 日本経済評論社, 1997.

08 森　武麿・大門正克（編）Mori Takemaro and Ōkado Masakatsu (eds.),『地域における戦時と戦後——庄内地方の農村・都市・社会運動』*The*

Wartime and Postwar Periods in Regional Communities: Farming Villages, Cities and Social Movements in the Shōnai District, 354 pp., 日本経済評論社, 1996.

This work examines changes in local communities by looking at the various social movements that took place in cities and villages of the Shōnai district, Yamagata prefecture, from during the war through to the postwar period.

09 高崎経済大学附属産業研究所（編）Takasaki City University of Economics Research Institute of Regional Economy (ed.),『開発の断面——地域・産業・環境』*A Profile of Development: Local Regions, Industry and the Environment*, 338 pp., 日本経済評論社, 1996.

I-2. Finance

10 原　薫 Hara Kaoru,『戦後インフレーション——昭和 20 年代の日本経済』*Postwar Inflation: Japan's Economy during the Third Decade of the Shōwa Era.* 512 pp., 八朔社, 1997.

A detailed work that examines postwar inflation in 1945-49 empirically and chronologically.

11 日本証券経済研究所（編）Japan Securities Research Institute (ed.),『戦後証券史を語る——続』*On the History of Postwar Securities* (*Cont.*), 268 pp., 日本証券経済研究所, 1996.

12 大蔵省財政史室（編）Ministry of Finance Office of Historical Studies (ed.),『昭和財政史——昭和 27〜48 年度』*A Fiscal History of the Shōwa Era: 1952-73*, 東洋経済新報社.

Vol. 4,『予算 2』*The Budget 2*, 581 pp., 1996.

Vol. 7,『国債』*The Government Bond*, 609 pp., 1997.

I-3. Industry

13 高村直助 Takamura Naosuke,『会社の誕生』*The Birth of the Company*, 236 pp., 吉川弘文館, 1996.

14 渡　哲郎 Watari Tetsurō,『戦前期わが国の電力独占体』*Prewar Japan's Electric Power Monopoly*, 224 pp., 晃洋書房, 1996.

15 鈴木　淳 Suzuki Jun,『明治の機械工業——その生成と展開』*The Machine Industry during the Meiji Era: Its Genesis and Development*, 360 pp., ミネルヴァ書房, 1996.

A thorough and detailed factual study that attempts to elucidate the development process and dynamism of the machine industry during the Meiji era, research on which has up until now been lagging behind.

16 竹内常善・阿部武司・沢井　実（編）Takeuchi Tsuneyoshi, Abe Takeshi and Sawai Minoru (eds.),『近代日本における企業家の諸系譜』*The Genealogies of Entrepreneurs in Modern Japan*, 284 pp., 大阪大学出版

会，1996.

A comprehensive analysis of the historical development and activities of small business managers who played such a decisive role in the industrialization of modern Japan during the Meiji and Shōwa eras.

17　中村隆英（編）Nakamura Takafusa (ed.),『日本の経済発展と在来産業』 *Japan's Economic Development and Traditional Industries*, 263 pp., 山川出版社，1997.

This book attempts to shed light on the development of "traditional industries" in Japan from the start of the Meiji era through to the early Shōwa era from the perspective of their relationship with the lowered capacity of farming villages to absorb the population and the expansion of cities. It presents a nationwide analysis based on business tax data, and also discusses Nishijin 西陣 weaving district, female labor, rural textiles, straw products, commercial and industrial adminitration, and information and communications.

18　神立春樹 Kandachi Haruki,『近代産業地域の形成』 *The Formation of Modern Industrial Regions*, 238 pp., 御茶の水書房，1997.

19　四宮俊之 Shinomiya Toshiyuki,『近代日本製紙業の競争と協調——王子製紙、富士製紙、樺太工業の成長とカルテル活動の変遷』 *Competition and Cooperation in Modern Japan's Paper-Manufacturing Industry: The Growth of Ōji Paper Co., Ltd., Fuji Paper Co., Ltd., and Karafuto Kōgyō Co., Ltd. and Changes in Cartel Activities*, 314 pp., 日本経済評論社，1997.

20　麻島昭一・大塩　武 Asajima Shōichi and Ōshio Takeshi,『昭和電工成立史の研究』 *A Study on the History of the Establishment of Shōwa Denkō K. K.*, 452 pp., 日本経済評論社，1997.

21　橋本寿朗 Hashimoto Jurō,『日本企業システムの戦後史』 *A Postwar History of Japan's Corporate System*, 305 pp., 東京大学出版会，1996.

I-4. Agriculture

22　岩崎正弥 Iwasaki Masaya,『農本思想の社会史——生活と国体の交錯』 *A Social History of Physiocracy in Japan: The Interfusion of Daily Life and National Polity*, 368 pp., 京都大学学術出版会，1997.

23　徳永光俊 Tokunaga Mitsutoshi,『日本農法史研究——畑と田の再結合のために』 *A Study on the History of Japan's Agricultural Methods: For the Reunification of Dry Fields and Rice Paddies*, 334 pp., 農山漁村文化協会，1996.

24　井野隆一 Ino Ryūichi,『戦後日本農業史』 *A History of Agriculture in Postwar Japan*, 472 pp., 新日本出版社，1996.

A general overview of agriculture in postwar Japan from the perspective of Marxism rather than Marxian economics. It looks for the main causes behind the present agricultural crisis both in foodstuff domination by the United States and agribusiness, and in the anomalous development of Japanese capitalism.

25 高橋泰隆 Takahashi Yasutaka,『昭和戦前期の農村と満州移民』 *Farming Villages and Emigrants to Manchuria in the Prewar Shōwa Era*, 283 pp., 吉川弘文館, 1997.

26 西村 卓 Nishimura Takashi,『「老農時代」の技術と思想——近代日本農事改良史研究』 *The Technology and Ideas of the "Period of Rōnō ("Master Farmers")" (18-19c.): A Study on the History of Agricultural Improvements in Modern Japan*, 329 pp., ミネルヴァ書房, 1997.

27 山内豊二 Yamauchi Toyoji,『日本農業論考』 *Studies of Japanese Agriculture*, 289 pp., 御茶の水書房, 1997.

28 玉 真之介 Tama Shinnosuke,『主産地形成と農業団体——戦間期日本農業と系統農会』 *The Formation of Chief Producing Districts and Agricultural Organizations: Agriculture in Interwar Japan and the Agricultural Associations Network*, 287 pp., 農山漁村文化協会, 1996.

An attempt to identify the characteristics of prewar Japan's market structure for agricultural products and market policies by examining how the formation of chief producing districts centered on vegetables and fruit developed in prewar Japanese agriculture through the sales activities of Agricultural Associations Network (Keitō Nōkai).

29 坂根嘉弘 Sakane Yoshihiro,『分割相続と農村社会』 *Divided Succession and Agrarian Society*, 215 pp., 九州大学出版会, 1996.

30 西田美昭 Nishida Yoshiaki,『近代日本農民運動史研究』 *A Study on the History of Peasant Movements in Modern Japan*, 321 pp., 東京大学出版会, 1997.

The theme of this work is the historical character of the tenant farmer disputes and farmers' cooperative movement that developed from the 1920s onward and the peasant movement of the postwar land reform period, which it clarifies from the perspective of their connections with management by farmers. While using Kurihara Hakuju's 栗原百寿 (1910-55) concept of "farmers' small-commodity production" as a guideline, the author also responds to criticism by Nakamura Masanori 中村政則.

I-5. Labor

31 兵藤 釗 Hyōdō Tsutomu,『労働の戦後史』 *A Postwar History of Labor*, (2 vols.), 540 pp., 東京大学出版会, 1997.

Dealing with the period from Japan's defeat in the war through to the bubble economy of the late 1980s, this book describes the history of labor-management relations in a broad sense, that is, labor-management relations from the corporate to the state level. Summarizing the author's many years of research on the history of labor-management relations, it offers a well-balanced account of changes in group labor-management relations and individual labor-management relations.

32　加瀬和俊 Kase Kazutoshi,『集団就職の時代――高度成長のにない手たち』 *The Era of Group Hiring: Those Who Bore the Burden of High Economic Growth*, 223 pp., 青木書店, 1997.

33　市原　博 Ichihara Hiroshi,『炭鉱の労働社会史――日本の伝統的労働・社会秩序と管理』 *A Social History of Labor in Coal Mining: Control and Japan's Traditional Labor and Social Order*, 393 pp., 多賀出版, 1997.

An empirical study based on primary sources from both the management and labor sides, focussing mainly on the period from the Meiji era to the 1930s; it clarifies the formation and establishment process of coal-mining labor management, the independent relationships among miners, characteristics of the miners' society, and the formation of mining labor unions.

34　間　宏 Hazama Hiroshi,『経済大国を作り上げた思想――高度経済成長期の労働エートス』 *The Ideas That Created an Economic Superpower: The Work Ethos of the Period of High Economic Growth*, 239 pp., 文真堂, 1996.

A factual study that focusses on the concepts of "corporate community" and "corporate soldier's (*kigyō senshi* 企業戦士) work ethos" during the period of high economic growth in an attempt to understand the industriousness of Japan's workers.

I-6. International Relations

35　小林英夫・柴田善雅 Kobayashi Hideo and Shibata Yoshimasa,『日本軍政下の香港』 *Hong Kong under Japanese Military Administration*, 311 pp., 社会評論社, 1996.

An empirical study of Hong Kong under direct Japanese military administration, which began in 1941, with reference to the administration system, dispersal of its population, the military administration system, dispersal of its population, the military currency economy, advance of Japanese companies, and food rationing.

36　波形昭一（編）Namikata Shōichi (ed.),『近代アジアの日本人経済団体』 *Japanese Economic Organizations in Modern Asia*, 306 pp., 同文館出版, 1997.

This book takes a comprehensive look at the activities of Japanese economic organizations such as the Chamber of Commerce and Industry in Taiwan, Korea, "Manchuria," and all of Southeast Asia.

37　安富　歩 Yasutomi Ayumu,『「満洲国」の金融』*The Finances of "Manchukuo,"* 295 pp. (text), 149 pp. (charts), 創文社, 1997.

With the overall structure of Manchukuo's financial system as its theme, this work attempts to present a complete picture by focussing on the "money flow" in Manchukuo and by understanding chronologically the structure of capital circulation, including both internal and external finances. In concrete terms, the main method employed in this study involves using the financial data of Manchukuo's principal financial institutions, i.e., balance sheets (B/S) and statements of profit and loss (P/L), as a basis and reconstructing the "money flow" from changes in the balance for separate items in each B/S period; this is then verified by looking at trends in the statements of profit and loss.

38　多田井喜生 Tadai Yoshio,『大陸に渡った円の興亡』*The Rise and Fall of the Yen in China*, vol. I, 337 pp., vol. II, 210 pp., 東洋経済新報社, 1997.

39　平井広一 Hirai Kōichi,『日本植民地財政史研究』*A Study of the Fiscal History of the Japanese Colonies*, 282 pp., ミネルヴァ書房, 1997.

Focussing mainly on the interwar period, this work is an examination and analysis of the fiscal structure in the colonies of Taiwan, Korea, Sakhalin, Kwantung and the South Sea Islands.

40　西成田　豊 Nishinarita Yutaka,『在日朝鮮人の「世界」と「帝国」国家』*The "World" of Korean Residents in Japan and the "Empire" State*, 354 pp., 東京大学出版会, 1997.

This book attempts to present an overall picture of the labor and lives of Korean residents in Japan during the years 1900-1950 from the three perspectives of accumulative theory, social training and government policies.

II. The Japanese Economy
II-1. General Works

01　小谷　清 Otani Kiyoshi,『「反」特殊主義の経済学──日本経済論の通説を断つ』*The Economics of "Anti-"Uniqueness: Eliminating the Popular View of Japanese Economy*, 242 pp., 東洋経済新報社, 1996.

Taking the standpoint of F.A.v. Hayek's liberalism, this book adopts an anti-planning and anti-centralization viewpoint in examining problems confronting the Japanese economy, such as cities, distribution, consolidation of social overhead capital, economic friction, and politics.

02　山本孝則 Yamamoto Takanori,『不良資産大国の崩壊と再生──大地か

らの日本再建プロジェクト』 *The Collapse and Rebirth of a Bad Asset Superpower: A Project for the Reconstruction of Japan from the Land*, 346 pp., 日本経済評論社, 1996.

An analysis of the Heisei recession from the viewpoint of Marxian economics; the author's views are close to those of Miyazaki Yoshikazu 宮崎義一. On the basis of a comparative study of Japan and Germany pertaining to land problems, the author suggests that there is a need for a simultaneous solution to Japan's bad debt crisis and problems relating to the housing and urban environment.

03 中谷　巌 Nakatani Iwao,『日本経済の歴史的転換』 *A Historical Shift in Japan's Economy*, 347 pp., 東洋経済新報社, 1996.

04 平野泰朗 Hirano Yasurō,『日本的制度と経済成長』 *The Japanese System and Economic Growth*, 235 pp., 藤原書店, 1996.

An analysis of the Japanese economy based on *théorie de la régulation*. It takes into consideration the relationship between economic development and institutional forms and also the relationship between the choice of social policies and economic growth.

05 岩田規久男 Iwata Kikuo,『日本型平等社会は滅ぶのか——円・土地・デフレの経済学』 *Is Japanese-Style Egalitarian Society Doomed?: The Economics of the Yen, Land and Deflation*, 273 pp., 東洋経済新報社, 1996.

A critique of recent deregulation theories by an author who has for many years advocated the need for deregulation and marketization from the standpoint of orthodox neoclassical theory. He discusses how deregulation should be promoted while overcoming its negative aspects.

06 浅子和美・福田慎一・吉野直行（編）Asako Kazumi, Fukuda Shin'ichi and Yoshino Naoyuki (eds.),『現代マクロ経済分析——転換期の日本経済』 *A Macroeconomic Analysis of the Present Age: The Japanese Economy at a Turning Point*, 374 pp., 東京大学出版会, 1997.

The proceedings of a conference on "Macroeconomics and the Japanese Economy in the Nineties" hosted by the Tokyo Economics Research Center (東京経済研究センター). This work is divided into 3 parts dealing with fiscal and monetary matters, changes in industrial structure, and a new stage in the Japanese economy, and through the participation of both established and younger scholars in the field of orthodox macroeconomics, the whole spectrum of problems confronting the Japanese economy is exposed.

07 小宮隆太郎・佐瀬正敬・江藤　勝（編）Komiya Ryūtarō, Sase Masataka and Etō Masaru (eds.),『21 世紀に向かう日本経済——人口・国際環境・

産業・技術』 *Japan's Economy Heading toward the 21st Century: Population, the International Environment, Industry, and Technology*, 358 pp., 東洋経済新報社, 1997.

08 田中直毅 Tanaka Naoki, 『新しい産業社会の構造』 *The Structure of a New Industrial Society*, 253 pp., 岩波書店, 1996.

This book looks at Japan's economic society from the perspective of a three-tiered structure: contents, platform, and distribution.

09 田中直毅 Tanaka Naoki, 『ビッグバン後の日本経済』 *Japan's Economy after the Big Bang*, 269 pp., 日本経済新聞社, 1997.

This work argues that, for a shift to a new economic and social system to occur in Japan, remedies must be provided with regard to both problems of market instability and the overcoming of social unrest by making improvisations to microstructure-controlled administration.

10 馬場宏二 Baba Hiroji, 『新資本主義論──視角転換の経済学』 *A New Theory of Capitalism: The Economics of a Change in Perspective*, 346 pp., 名古屋大学出版会, 1997.

11 北原 勇・伊藤 誠・山田鋭夫 Kitahara Isamu, Itō Makoto and Yamada Yoshio, 『現代資本主義をどう視るか』 *How to View Contemporary Capitalism*, 259 pp., 青木書店, 1997.

An analysis of contemporary capitalism by three economists from the three viewpoints of Uno Kōzō's 宇野弘蔵 theory, *théorie de la régulation*, and orthodox Marxian economics. This work records the opinions of and discussions held between the authors on the accumulative system during the period of high economic growth, economic crises since the 1970s, and the direction to be taken in restructuring Japan's present economy.

12 柴垣和夫 Shibagaki Kazuo, 『現代資本主義の論理──過渡期社会の経済学』 *The Logic of Contemporary Capitalism: The Economics of a Transitional Society*, 270 pp., 日本経済評論社, 1997.

An analysis of the Japanese economy from the perspective of Uno's theory. It contains articles on corporate capitalism, social security, international relations, and Japan-U.S. economic friction.

13 伊藤元重 Itō Motoshige, 『市場主義』 *Market-ism*, 214 pp., 講談社, 1996.

Defining the advancing changes in all aspects of the economy and society in terms of "marketization," this study is a general description of the changes this brings to corporate structure, the distribution structure, and business relations.

14 吉田和男 Yoshida Kazuo, 『安全保障の経済分析──経済力と軍事力の国際均衡』 *An Economic Analysis of Security: The International Balance Between Economic Power and Military Power*, 313 pp., 日本経済新

聞社，1996．

Based on the concept of the provision of international public assets and using the methods of economic analysis, this work presents a new theoretical interpretation of security. The author also uses this method to analyze the shift in Japan's security policies.

II-2. Informationalization and Networking

15　伊藤　誠・岡本義行（編）Itō Makoto and Okamoto Yoshiyuki (eds.), 『情報革命と市場経済システム――企業と産業の構造転換』 *The Information Revolution and the Market Economy System: Structural Shifts in Corporations and Industry*, 284 pp., 富士通経営研究所，1996．

16　竹内　啓 Takeuchi Kei,『高度技術社会と人間』*High-Tech Society and People*, 246 pp., 岩波書店，1996．

A comprehensive study by researchers who took part in a five-year study on "Perspectives on High-Tech Society." Philosophical foundations, natural and social conditions for continuous development, the global environment, and political and economic systems are examined. Policy proposals are also made for the Japanese economy in the light of its relationship with shifts in the world system.

17　増田祐司・須藤　修（編）Masuda Yūji and Sudō Osamu (eds.),『ネットワーク世紀の社会経済システム――情報経済と社会進化』 *Socio-Economic Systems in the Network Century: The Information Economy and Social Evolution*, 296 pp., 富士通経営研究所，1996．

A collection of articles based on the results of research projects on "The Informationalization of Industrial Society and the Economic System" and "A Study on Information Networks and the Economy." It consists of three parts: Part 1, dealing with "The Shift in Economic Paradigms"; Part 2, dealing with "The Evolution of Social and Industrial Systems"; and Part 3, dealing with "Changes in the Financial System."

II-3. Economic and Management Systems

18　渡辺　尚・W. クレナー（編）Watanabe Hisashi and Klenner, Wolfgang (eds.),『型の試練――構造変化と日独経済』 *The Trials of an Established System: Structural Change and the Economies of Japan and Germany*, 275 pp., 信山社，1998．

A report on the 11th symposium on Japanese and German economics and social sciences held in Tokyo in 1996. It includes joint research and discussions on economic growth and employment, economic systems, foreign aid, pioneering industries, and small businesses in Japan and Germany.

19　吉田和男 Yoshida Kazuo,『複雑系としての日本型システム――新しい

社会科学のパラダイムを求めて』 *The Japanese-Style System as a Complex System: Seeking a Paradigm for the New Social Sciences*, 254 pp., 読売新聞社, 1997.

20 伊藤秀史 （編） Itō Hideshi (ed.),『日本の企業システム』*Japan's Corporate System*, 386 pp., 東京大学出版会, 1996.

A record of joint research presented at two conferences (the so-called "Zushi Conferences") hosted by the Tokyo Economic Research Center in 1994 and 1995. It provides a multifaceted and comprehensive examination of the relationship between Japanese corporations and their marketplace and non-marketplace environment as well as the internal systems of corporations, etc.

II-4. Economic Policy

21 大山耕輔 Ōyama Kōsuke,『行政指導の政治経済学──産業政策の形成と実施』 *The Political Economy of Administrative Guidance: The Formation and Implementation of Industrial Policies*, 284 pp., 有斐閣, 1996.

22 野口悠紀雄・K. ヤマムラ （編） Noguchi Yukio and Yamamura, Kōzō (eds.),『比較日米マクロ経済政策』 *A Comparison of Japan-U.S. Macroeconomic Policies*, 299 pp., 日本経済新聞社, 1996.

A collection of analytical studies undertaken from the perspective of orthodox neoclassical economics that focuss on problems concerning Japanese and U.S. macroeconomic policies and capital flow between the two countries since the 1980s. Following an introduction on hegemonic nations and the hegemony system, issues such as the taxation system, fiscal policies, monetary policies, capital flow regulations, and asset values, etc., are concretely examined.

23 広田秀樹 Hirota Hideki,『テイクオフの経済政策──産業国家離陸の経済政策～ MITI の戦略産業育成政策』*Economic Policies for Taking Off: Economic Policies for the Take-Off of an Industrial Nation—MITI Policies for Fostering Strategic Industries*, 251 pp., 多賀出版, 1996.

This book examines the Ministry of International Trade and Industry's (MITI) postwar policies for the three industrial areas of steel, automobiles and electronics, and includes an analysis of policy methods and the internal and external conditions of these policies designed to nurture strategic industries.

24 正村公宏 Masamura Kimihiro,『現代の経済政策──混合経済における政府の役割』 *Contemporary Economic Policies: The Government Role in a Mixed Economy*, 258 pp., 東洋経済新報社, 1997.

25 鈴木　守 Suzuki Mamoru,『現代日本の公共政策──環境・社会資本・高齢化』 *Contemporary Japan's Public Policies: The Environment, Social*

Overhead Capital, and the Aging of Society, 201 pp., 慶応義塾大学出版会，1997.

This work looks at the future of public policies from the perspective of neoclassical public economic theory, with the environment, social overhead capital and the aging of society as its three keywords.

26 環境経済・政策学会（編）Society for Environmental Economics and Policy Studies (ed.),『環境経済・政策研究のフロンティア』*The Frontiers of Environmental Economics and Policy Research*, 244 pp., 東洋経済新報社，1996.

II-5. Deregulation

27 中村太和 Nakamura Taiwa,『民営化の政治経済学──日英の理念と現実』*The Political Economy of Privatization: The Ideals and Reality in Japan and Great Britain*, 245 pp., 日本経済評論社，1996.

28 規制と自由化問題研究班（編）Study Group for Problems of Regulations and Liberalization (ed.),『規制緩和の研究』*Studies on Deregulation*［研究叢書 98］，298 pp., 関西大学経済・政治研究所，1996.

29 植草　益（編）Uegusa Masu (ed.),『社会的規制の経済学』*The Economics of Societal Regulations*, 463 pp., NTT 出版，1997.

Whereas societal regulations designed mainly to guarantee health and hygiene, safety, disaster prevention, prevention of environmental pollution, and preservation of the environment have not been systematically researched to date, this book is divided into a theoretical section, dealing with the system of societal regulations and the economic theory of societal regulations, and a section providing concrete details of safety regulations, medical regulations, and environmental regulations.

30 三輪芳朗 Miwa Yoshirō,『規制緩和は悪夢ですか──「規制緩和すればいってもんじゃない」と言いたいあなたに』*Is Deregulation a Bad Dream?: A Reply to the View That "Deregulation Is Not the Answer,"* 299 pp., 東洋経済新報社，1997.

III. Public Finance
III-1. General Works

01 星川順一 Hoshikawa Jun'ichi,『日本経済と財政政策──ケインズ政策のすすめ』*The Japanese Economy and Fiscal Policies: A Recommendation of Keynesian Policies*, 273 pp., 晃洋書房，1996.

This work takes the view that as long as the United States continues with the Keynesian policy of budget deficit and Japan follows neoclassical policies, maintaining fiscal balance, Japan will bear the risk of large fluctuations in the exchange rate and the burden of the U.S. budget deficit. These problems are examined theoretically and empirically with reference to Ricardo's neutrality proposition and Weil's proposition on conditions for the secondary burden bearer (*Journal of Public Economics*, Vol. 38, 1989).

02　山崎　怜・藤岡純一（編）Yamazaki Satoshi and Fujioka Jun'ichi (eds.), 『現代の財政──新自由主義の帰趨』*Contemporary Public Finance: The Direction of Neoliberalism*, 256 pp., 昭和堂, 1996.

03　戸崎　肇 Tozaki Hajime,『財政改革への参加型新システム──活力ある経済社会の構築』*A New Participatory System for Fiscal Reform: The Construction of a Dynamic Economic Society*, 205 pp., 東洋経済新報社, 1996.

　　On the basis of an examination of various policies for overcoming the budget deficit, this work looks empirically at the connection between these policies and problems pertaining to administrative and fiscal reforms, decentralization and deregulation, and then makes proposals for a fiscal system modelled on full participation.

04　安藤　実 Andō Minoru,『日本財政の研究』*A Study of Japan's Public Finance*, 279 pp., 青木書店, 1996.

05　井堀利宏 Ihori Toshihiro,『日本の財政改革』*Japan's Fiscal Reforms*, 220 pp., 筑摩書房, 1997.

　　Relying basically on a neoclassical framework, this work suggests on the basis of a reappraisal of policies for intergenerational, interregional and interpersonal redistribution that the formation of a fiscal system in which benefits and burdens coincide is indispensable.

06　片桐正俊（編）Katagiri Masatoshi (ed.),『財政学──転換期の日本財政』*Public Finance: Japan's Public Finance at a Turning Point*, 484 pp., 東洋経済新報社, 1997.

　　Although this is a textbook on public finance, it deals not only with theory, but also includes a comprehensive and detailed examination of institutions, history and policies, in addition to looking at the whole spectrum of problems confronting contemporary Japan's public finance system.

07　林　宜嗣 Hayashi Yoshitsugu,『財政危機の経済学』*The Economics of the Fiscal Crisis*, 220 pp., 日本評論社, 1997.

　　Written from the standpoint of "small government," this work examines problems being faced by Japan's public finances, focussing on public investment, social security, subsidies, and the taxation system.

08　竹内信仁・白井正敏（編）Takeuchi Nobuhito and Shirai Masatoshi (eds.),『公共経済学研究II』*A Study on Public Economics II*, 248 pp., 中京大学経済学部付属経済研究所, 1997.

09　池上　惇　Ikegami Jun, 『現代経済学と公共政策』 *Contemporary Economics and Public Policies*, 222 pp., 青木書店, 1996.

While reviewing the formation of a network society, the author defines autonomous support networks as public and semi-public assets and proposes state and regional fiscal reforms towards this end.

III-2. The Public Finance System and Public Bonds

10　富田俊基 Tomita Toshiki, 『財投解体論批判』 *A Criticism of the Thesis Advocating the Dissolution of Treasury Loans and Investment*, 220 pp., 東洋経済新報社, 1997.

By reinterpreting treasury loans and investments as a brokering system, this work emphasizes the benefits of treasury loans and investment as a cover for "market failures," and then proceeds to criticize proposals for postal service reforms, reforms for the implementation of a voluntary pension scheme, and also reforms for the issue of debentures of treasury loans and investment institutions as exemplifying the advocacy of the dissolution of treasury loans and investment.

11　吉田和男・小西砂千夫 Yoshida Kazuo and Konishi Sachio, 『転換期の財政投融資——しくみ・機能・改革の方向』 *Treasury Loans and Investment at a Turning Point: Their Mechanism, Functions, and the Direction of Reforms*, 256 pp., 有斐閣, 1996.

12　川北英隆 Kawakita Hidetaka, 『財政投融資ビッグバン——入口・出口の矛盾拡大』 *The Treasury Loans and Investment Big Bang: The Expanding Inconsistencies of Its Conception and Implementation*, 221 pp., 東洋経済新報社, 1997.

13　望月正光 Mochizuki Masamitsu, 『公債と政府部門のストック分析——新 SNA からみた累積公債』 *A Stock Analysis of Public Bonds and the Government Sector: Cumulative Public Bonds as Seen from the New SNA* (*System of National Account of the United Nations*), 324 pp., 白桃書房, 1997.

This work is made up of three parts dealing with a theoretical analysis of public bonds, a stock analysis of public bonds, and a stock analysis by the government sector. The focus is on the analysis of cumulative public bonds in the form of stocks, and it includes long-term estimates of real holding gains and losses on assets and liabilities that result from price increases.

III-3. Tax Reform

14　小西砂千夫 Konishi Sachio, 『日本の税制改革——最適課税論によるアプローチ』 *Japan's Tax Reforms: An Approach Using the Optimum Taxation Theory*, 252 pp., 有斐閣, 1997.

This work puts forward policy proposals based on both the extended application to Japan of the optimum taxation theory that has been developing among Western scholars of public finance since the 1970s and an analysis of related issues confronting the Japanese taxation system.

15　和田八束 Wada Yatsuka, 『税制改革の理論と現実』 *The Theory and Reality of Tax Reform*, 269 pp., 世界書院, 1996.

Based on a chronological study of changes in tax reform from 1945 to the present, this work attempts to place the current taxation system in historical perspective.

16　内山　昭 Uchiyama Akira, 『「会社主義」と税制改革』 *"Company-ism" and Tax Reform*, 259 pp., 大月書店, 1996.

Characterizing the Japanese economy as one based on the concept of "company-ism," this work criticizes the tax reforms that have developed with the introduction of the consumption tax and advocates the need for tax reform focussing on the reform of the corporate taxation system.

III-4. Local Finance

17　日本地方財政学会（編）Japan Association for Local Finances (ed.), 『現代地方財政の構造転換』 *The Structural Shift in Contemporary Local Finance* [日本地方財政学会研究叢書], 293 pp., 勁草書房, 1996.

18　桜井良治 Sakurai Ryōji, 『分権的土地政策と財政』 *Decentralized Land Policies and Public Finance*, 304 pp., ぎょうせい, 1997.

19　池田　清 Ikeda Kiyoshi, 『神戸都市財政の研究──都市間競争と都市経営の財政問題』 *A Study of Kobe Municipal Finances: Intercity Competition and the Public Finance Problems of City Management*, 266 pp., 学文社, 1997.

III-5. Social Security and Social Welfare

20　宮田和明 Miyata Kazuaki, 『現代日本社会福祉政策論』 *Social Welfare Policy in Contemporary Japan*, 244 pp., ミネルヴァ書房, 1996.

While looking back on the development of social welfare in postwar Japan from the two perspectives of social welfare policy and social welfare theory, this work examines current issues in social welfare.

21　田中　明 Tanaka Akira, 『企業福祉論』 *Corporate Welfare*, 196 pp., 北大路書房, 1996.

22　坂脇昭吉・中原弘二（編）Sakawaki Akiyoshi and Nakahara Kōji (eds.), 『現代日本の社会保障』 *Social Security in Contemporary Japan*, 276 pp., ミネルヴァ書房, 1997.

23　堀　勝洋 Hori Katsuhiro, 『年金制度の再構築』 *Reconstructing the Pension Plan*, 237 pp., 東洋経済新報社, 1997.

Considering the present pension plan to be at a critical stage, the author

108

presents an empirical study of concrete issues such as benefit standards, the age when a pension is first granted, pensions for women, cost burdens, etc., and also puts forward policy proposals.

24 石田昌夫 Ishida Masao,『政府と社会保障の経済学』 *The Government and the Economics of Social Security*, 207 pp., 中央経済社, 1997.

25 坂本重雄 Sakamoto Shigeo,『社会保障改革——高齢社会の年金・医療・介護』 *Social Security Reforms: Pensions, Medical Care and Nursing Care in an Aging Society*, 179 pp., 勁草書房, 1997.

26 八代尚宏 (編) Yashiro Naohiro (ed.),『高齢化社会の生活保障システム』 *A Livelihood Security System in an Aging Society*, 216 pp., 東京大学出版会, 1997.

An analysis of the social security system from the standpoint of orthodox economics. The author argues that it is possible to diversify the means of stabilizing the livelihood of the elderly by "marketizing" the livelihood security system through active application of the "insurance principle."

27 渋谷博史・井村進哉・中浜 隆 (編) Shibuya Hiroshi, Imura Shin'ya and Nakahama Takashi (eds.),『日米の福祉国家システム——年金・医療・住宅・地域』 *The Welfare State Systems of Japan and the United States: Pensions, Medical Care, Housing, and Local Communities*, 316 pp., 日本経済評論社, 1997.

A joint study by researchers of public finance in Japan and the United States from a non-neoclassical perspective. It provides an empirical examination of the differences in welfare policies between Japan and the United States pertaining to pensions, medical care, housing and local communities, and it sketches the direction welfare states will take in the future.

IV. Money and Banking

IV-1. General Works

01 鹿野嘉昭 Shikano Yoshiaki,『変貌する日本の金融制度』 *Japan's Financial System in Transformation*, 208 pp., 東洋経済新報社, 1996.

02 植田和男・深尾光洋 (編) Ueda Kazuo and Fukao Mitsuhiro (eds.),『金融空洞化の経済分析』 *An Economic Analysis of Financial Hollowing-Out*, [シリーズ現代経済研究 12], 229 pp., 日本経済新聞社, 1996.

A joint study by economists, legal scholars and administrative personnel from the Bank of Japan and other institutions. It presents a multifaceted analysis of the actual circumstances surrounding the declining international competitiveness of Japan's financial institutions and money markets from an institutional, factual and theoretical perspective.

03 青木昌彦・ヒュー・パトリック (編) Aoki Masahiko and Patric, H. (eds.), 東銀リサーチインターナショナル (訳) Tōgin Research Interna-

tional (tr.),『日本のメインバンク・システム』*Japan's Main Bank System*, 495 pp., 東洋経済新報社, 1996.

04 高山憲之・有田富美子 Takayama Noriyuki and Arita Fumiko,『貯蓄と資産形成——家計資産のマイクロデータ分析』*Savings and Asset Formation: A Micro-Data Analysis of Household Assets*, 238 pp., 岩波書店, 1996.

This work analyzes Japan's household assets using diverse micro-data on matters such as the motivation behind maintaining assets, the relationship between savings and inheritance, the scale of asset inflation, the relationship between asset formation and dual-income families or extended families living together, and the intergenerational transfer of assets through public pensions, etc.

05 石田和彦・白川浩道 Ishida Kazuhiko and Shirakawa Hiromichi,『マネーサプライと経済活動』*The Money Supply and Economic Activity*, 185 pp., 東洋経済新報社, 1996.

An analysis of movements in Japan's money supply by seven staff members of the Bank of Japan's Planning and Research Section, Research and Statistics Department.

06 伊藤史朗（編）Itō Shirō (ed.),『日本経済と金融』*Japan's Economy and Finance*, 242 pp., 晃洋書房, 1997.

07 瀧川好夫 Takikawa Yoshio,『現代金融経済論の基本問題——貨幣・信用の作用と銀行の役割』*Fundamental Problems of Contemporary Financial and Economic Theory: The Functions of Currency and Credit and the Role of Banks*[神戸大学経済学叢書・第4輯], 420 pp., 勁草書房, 1997.

08 山田弘史・野田正穂（編）Yamada Hiroshi and Noda Masaho (eds.),『現代日本の金融——破綻の構造と改革の方向』*Contemporary Japan's Finances: The Structure of Bankruptcy and the Direction of Reforms*, 365 pp., 新日本出版社, 1997.

This work examines Japan's financial crises in the 1990s not from the perspective of bank management, but from that of bank employees. It deals with restructuring, rationalization, wage cuts and deregulation in the banking business, and proposes financial democratization.

09 木下信行・日向野幹也・木寅潤一 Kinoshita Nobuyuki, Higano Mikiya and Kitora Jun'ichi,『電子決済と銀行の進化』*Electronic Settlement of Accounts and the Evolution of Banks*, 267 pp., 日本経済新聞社, 1997.

10 堀内昭義（編）Horiuchi Akiyoshi (ed.),『金融の情報通信革命——21世紀の金融機能はこう変わる』*The Finance Information and Communications Revolution: How Finance Functions Will Change in the 21st*

Century, 271 pp., 東洋経済新報社, 1996.

IV-2. Monetary Policy and Financial Administration

11　清水啓典 Shimizu Yoshinori,『マクロ経済学の進歩と金融政策——合理
的期待の政策的意味』 *Advances in Macroeconomics and Monetary
Policies: The Significance of Rational Expectation for Policy Making*,
362 pp., 有斐閣, 1997.

This work introduces the application of the theory of rational expectations to monetary theory, and on the basis of this theory the author
critically examines Japan's financial system and monetary policies since
the 1980s, developing a critique of Keynesian economics and Keynesian
monetary policies.

12　吉川　洋（編）Yoshikawa Hiroshi (ed.),『金融政策と日本経済』 *Monetary Policy and the Japanese Economy*, 237 pp., 日本経済新聞社, 1996.

Looking at the relationship between the money supply and real economy, this work is critical of the recently influential monetarist viewpoint,
and it emphasizes the endogenous character of the money supply from a
Keynesian perspective. It specifies the endogenous demand function for
money from the 1980s onward and undertakes an empirical examination
of the effectiveness of monetary policies in the real economy.

13　黒田晁生 Kuroda Akio,『金融改革への指針——金融システムと政策決
定』 *A Guide to Monetary Reforms: The Financial System and Policy-
Making*, 204 pp., 東洋経済新報社, 1997.

An examination of the central bank's monetary policies, this work
reviews debate between policy makers at the Bank of Japan and academics
concerning the relationship between high-powered money and the money
supply. It provides a detailed analysis of the period of the bubble economy
and its collapse from the latter half of the 1980s through to the early 1990s
from a perspective close to that of the Bank of Japan.

14　千田純一・岡　正生・藤原英郎 Senda Jun'ichi, Oka Masao and Fujiwara Hideo,『日本の金融システム——新たな課題と求められる姿』
Japan's Financial System: New Issues and Its Desirable Form, 210 pp.,
中央経済社, 1997.

A comprehensive and empirical examination of the present state of
Japan's financial system. In concrete terms, it focusses on the role of
financial institutions, management of financial risk, financial inspections
and supervisory administration, and monetary restrictions.

IV-3. Financial Institutions and Money Markets

15　馬淵紀寿 Mabuchi Noritoshi,『金融持株会社——金融システム再編の主
役』 *Financial Holding Companies: Their Leading Role in the Restruc-*

turing of the Financial System, 262 pp., 東洋経済新報社, 1996.

By way of comparison with the United States, the author surveys the outlook for financial holding companies on which a ban was lifted conditionally with the revision of the Anti-Monopoly Law on 18 June 1997. This work is detailed on Japan's institutional positioning.

16　相沢幸悦 Aizawa Kōetsu,『ユニバーサル・バンクと金融持株会社——日本の金融システムの将来像』 *Universal Banks and Financial Holding Companies: A Future Vision of Japan's Financial System*, 252 pp., 日本評論社, 1997.

17　平石裕一 Hiraishi Yūichi,『市場経済下の協同金融——その理念と展開』 *Cooperative Finance under a Market Economy: Its Ideals and Development*, 248 pp., 地域産業研究所, 1997.

An empirical examination of the credit associations such as credit cooperatives, laborers' credit cooperatives and agricultural cooperative associations.

18　橘木俊詔・筒井義郎（編）Tachibanaki Toshiaki and Tsutsui Yoshirō (eds.),『日本の資本市場』 *Japan's Capital Market* [郵政研究所研究叢書], 376 pp., 日本評論社, 1996.

The subjects of analysis in this work include price formation in the capital market, characteristics of the market, the behavior of investors in the market, and the structure of corporate governance. The author characterizes recent changes in Japan's capital market as marketization.

19　深浦厚之 Fukaura Atsuyuki,『債権流動化の経済学——日本の金融市場活性化のために』 *The Economics of Asset Securitization: For the Vitalization of Japan's Financial Markets*, 200 pp., 日本評論社, 1997.

An empirical study of the economic meaning and actual practice of Japan's securitization of assets undertaken in compliance with the "Law Pertaining to Business Scale Related to Special Assets, etc." enacted in 1993.

IV-4. International Finance and Financial Internationalization
　　　(See "International Economics" under VIII-4.)

V. Industry

V-1. General Works and Industrial Policy

01　植田和弘ほか Ueda Kazuhiro *et al.*,『新しい産業技術と社会システム』 *New Industrial Technology and the Social System*, 240 pp., 日科技連出版, 1996.

02　木下　滋 Kinoshita Shigeru,『産業の構造変化と都市——アメリカと日本』 *Changes in the Industrial Structure and Cities: America and Japan*, 290 pp., 産業統計研究社, 1997.

03 清成忠男・橋本寿朗（編）Kiyonari Tadao and Hashimoto Jurō (eds.),
『日本型産業集積の未来像——「城下町型」から「オープン・コミュニテ
ィ型」へ』 *A Future Picture of Japanese-Style Industrial Integration:
From a "Castle-Town Model" to an "Open Community Model,"* 269 pp.,
日本経済新聞社，1997．

This work gives the results of fact-finding surveys of industrial integration in the case of America's Silicon Valley, the textile and packing
machine industries in North Italy, and Asia, based on which it presents a
comparative study of Japan's industrial integration.

04 金原達夫 Kimbara Tatsuo,『成長企業の技術開発分析——中堅・中小企
業の能力形成』 *An Analysis of Technological Development in Growth
Businesses: The Performance Development of Leading Medium-sized
Firms (Chūken Kigyō) and Small Businesses*, 250 pp., 文真堂，1996．

Having classified technological development in Japan's leading
medium-sized firms and small businesses into three types (subcontracting,
joint development, and independent development), the author examines
the relationship between technological development and management
strategy.

05 堀内俊洋 Horiuchi Toshihiro,『ベンチャー企業経済論——自由化・情報
化時代の戦略と政策』 *The Economic Theory of Venture Businesses:
Strategies and Policies for an Age of Liberalization and Informationalization*, 241 pp., 文真堂，1997．

06 松井隆幸 Matsui Takayuki,『戦後日本産業政策の政策過程』 *The Policy
Process of Postwar Japan's Industrial Policy*, 155 pp., 九州大学出版会，
1997．

Focussing on synthetic fibers and biotechnology, this is an empirical
study of the nature of production adjustment, and industrial adjustment
policy, as well as the policy process.

07 宮田由紀夫 Miyata Yukio,『共同研究開発と産業政策』 *Joint Research
and Development and Industrial Policy*, 234 pp., 勁草書房，1997．

A comparative study on joint research and development in the field of
high-tech industries, focussing on the three areas of Japan, the United
States, and Europe. Whereas works to date have analyzed one or the other
of policies to either foster industry or promote competition, the relationship between both types of policy is emphasized in this book.

08 黒瀬直宏 Kurose Naohiro,『中小企業政策の総括と提言』 *A Summary of
and Proposal for Small Business Policy*, 326 pp., 同友館，1997．

V-2. Manufacturing Industries

09 田中 高 Tanaka Takashi,『日本紡績業の中米進出』 *The Advance of*

Japan's Spinning Industry into Central America, 278 pp., 古今書院, 1997.

10 渡辺幸男 Watanabe Yukio, 『日本機械工業の社会的分業構造』 *The Structure of the Social Division of Labor in Japan's Machine Industry*, 377 pp., 有斐閣, 1997.

   A study on the structure of the social division of labor in Japan's machine industry. The main focus of this detailed and factual analysis is the sub-contracting machine industry in Ōta-ku, Tokyo, but it also combines analyses of other areas such as the Suwa region in Nagano prefecture and the Higashi Ōsaka region, etc. An attempt is also made to grasp the situation of the sub-contracting machine industry in East Asian context.

11 十名直喜 Tona Naoki, 『日本型鉄鋼システム──危機のメカニズムと変革の視座』 *The Japanese-style Steel System: The Mechanism of the Crisis and an Outlook on Reform*, 259 pp., 同文館, 1996.

   A work in which the author attempts to understand the production system of the steel industry as a microcosm of the Japanese-style socio-economic system. Part 1 deals with the production system, Part 2 looks at labor-management relations, and Part 3 consists of an international comparison.

12 関 満博・池谷嘉一 (編) Seki Mitsuhiro and Ikeya Kaichi (eds.), 『中国自動車産業と日本企業』 *China's Automobile Industry and Japanese Businesses*, 307 pp., 新評論, 1997.

13 石田光男ほか Ishida Mitsuo *et al*., 『日本のリーン生産方式──自動車企業の実例』 *Japan's Lean Production Methods: A Case Study of the Automobile Industry*, 376 pp., 中央経済社, 1997.

V-3. Non-Manufacturing Industries

14 角本良平 Kakumoto Ryōhei, 『国鉄改革── JR 10 年目からの検証』 *The Reform of the Japan National Railways: An Examination of JR 10 Years After Privatization*, 297 pp., 交通新聞社, 1996.

15 藤目節夫 Fujime Setsuo, 『交通変革と地域システム』 *Transportation Reforms and the Regional System*, 346 pp., 古今書院, 1997.

   Based on the perspective that transportation reforms instigate changes in local regions and systems, which in turn create new transportation demands, the author attempts to shed light empirically and theoretically on transportation reforms pertaining to Japan's roads, railways, marine and air transport, etc., through a comparison with the United States.

16 吉田 茂 Yoshida Shigeru, 『現代海運業研究』 *A Study on the Contemporary Shipping Industry*, 300 pp., 山縣記念財団, 1997.

17 小出鐸男 Koide Takuo, 『現代出版産業論──競争と協調の構造』 *The*

Contemporary Publishing Industry: The Structure of Competition and Cooperation, 236 pp., 日本エディタースクール出版部, 1997.

18　郵政省郵政研究所（編）Institute for Posts and Telecommunications Policy (ed.),『有料放送事業の今後の展望』*The Future Outlook of Fee-Charging Broadcasting Business*, 209 pp., 日本評論社, 1997.

19　辻　正次・西脇　隆 Tsuji Masatsugu and Nishiwaki Takashi,『ネットワーク未来』*The Future of Networks*, 143 pp., 日本評論社, 1996.

　　Based on a theoretical elucidation of the dynamism of networks as regards their economical efficiency, interlinking, competition, mergers, etc., this work points out existing problems in Japan's economic networks, management networks, and regional networks.

20　高宮城朝則（編）Takamiyagi Tomonori (ed.),『卸売企業の経営と戦略』*The Management and Strategies of Wholesale Business*, 216 pp., 同文館, 1997.

V-4. Small Business, Regional Industry and Locally-Based Industry

21　有田辰男 Arita Tatsuo,『中小企業論――歴史・理論・政策』*On Small Businesses: History, Theory, and Policy*, 231 pp., 新評論, 1997.

22　百瀬恵夫・伊藤正昭（編）Momose Shigeo and Itō Masaaki (eds.),『新中小企業論』*A New Study of Small Businesses*, 306 pp., 白桃書房, 1996.

　　A study on Japan's small businesses with its perspective fully focussed on venture businesses.

23　小林靖雄・滝沢菊太郎（編）Kobayashi Yasuo and Takizawa Kikutarō (eds.),『中小企業とは何か――中小企業研究55年』*What Are Small Businesses?: 55 Years of Research on Small Businesses*, 272 pp., 有斐閣, 1996.

　　A survey on the history of research on Japan's small businesses by members of the "118th Committee on Industrial Structure and Small Businesses" of the Japan Society for the Promotion of Science（日本学術振興会）and a record of members' activities.

24　黄　完晟 Hwang Wan Shung,『日本の地場産業・産地分析』*An Analysis of Japan's Locally-Based Industry and Production Centers*, 211 pp., 税務経理協会, 1997.

　　A comparative analysis of locally-based industry (*jibasangyō*) in Japan, Korea, and Taiwan, with a focus on the wooden furniture industry.

25　下平尾　勲 Shimohirao Isao,『地場産業――地域から見た戦後日本経済分析』*Locally-Based Industry: An Analysis of the Postwar Japanese Economy from a Regional Perspective*, 344 pp., 新評論, 1996.

VI. Agriculture

VI-1. General Works

01 農山漁村文化協会 (編) Rural Culture Association (ed.),『全集 世界の食料 世界の農村』 *A Complete Survey of the World's Food and the World's Villages*, 27 vols., 農山漁村文化協会.

Vol. 10, 今村奈良臣・永田恵十郎 (編) Imamura Naraomi and Nagata Keijūrō (eds.),『水資源の枯渇と配分——開発から管理へ』 *The Depletion and Distribution of Water Resources: From Development to Management*, 271 pp., 1996.

Vol. 12, 三輪昌男 Miwa Masao,『農協改革の新視点——法人でなく機能を』 *A New Viewpoint on the Restructuring of Agricultural Cooperatives: As Seen from the Perspective of Function, Not Corporations*, 237 pp., 1997.

Vol. 17, 今村奈良臣 (編) Imamura Naraomi (ed.),『バイオテクノロジーの農業哲学——地域の個性を活かす』 *The Philosophy of Biotechnology in Agriculture: Making the Most of Regional Characteristics*, 252 pp., 1996.

Vol. 21, 今村奈良臣 (編) Imamura Naraomi (ed.),『WTO 体制下の食料農業戦略——米・欧・豪・中と日本』 *Food and Agricultural Strategy under the WTO: A Comparative Study of the U.S., E.U., Australia, China and Japan*, 307 pp., 1997.

Vol. 22, 吉田 忠 (編) Yoshida Tadashi (ed.),『食生活の表層と底流——東アジアの経験から』 *The Surface and Undercurrents of Dietary Patterns: The East Asian Experience*, 238 pp., 1997.

Vol. 26, 嘉田良平 (編) Kada Ryōhei (ed.),『世界の食品安全基準——脅かす要因と安全確保の道すじ』 *Global Food Safety Standards: Causes for Concern and the Way towards Ensuring Safety*, 244 pp., 1997.

These works are further volumes in a series that sets out to provide a comprehensive grasp of the reappraisal of the international value of Japan's agriculture and rural villages, the international environment that regulates Japanese agriculture, global undercurrents in agricultural administration, and farm management in different parts of the world.

02 小野誠志 (編) Ono Seishi (ed.),『国際化時代における日本農業の展開方向』 *The Direction of the Development of Japan's Agriculture in an Age of Internationalization*, 309 pp., 筑波書房, 1996.

03 上原信博 Uehara Nobuhiro,『現代日本資本主義における農業問題』 *Agricultural Problems in Contemporary Japanese Capitalism*, 280 pp., 御茶の水書房, 1997.

An analysis of agricultural issues from the perspective of Marxian economics. This work focusses on the three periods of land reforms, agricultural administration based on the Basic Agriculture Law (農業基本法), and comprehensive liberalization in response to the WTO system. An analysis limited to cultivated farming revolving around rice is included.

04 梶井 功 (編) Kajii Isoshi (ed.), 『農業問題その外延と内包』 *The Ramifications and Implications of Agricultural Problems*, 294 pp., 農山漁村文化協会, 1997.

This is a collection of articles brought out in commemoration of the 99th birthday of Kondō Yasuo 近藤康男, an authority on Japanese agricultural economics. Although the contributors are all over sixty years of age, some of the studies make reference to recent debate on agricultural economics.

05 宇佐美 繁 (編) Usami Shigeru (ed.), 『日本農業：その構造変動——1995年農業センサス分析』 *Japan's Agriculture—Structural Changes: An Analysis of the 1995 Agricultural Census*, 283 pp., 農林統計協会, 1997.

A summary of the results produced by the "Study Group for the Comprehensive Analysis of the 1995 Agricultural Census" that was established within the Association of Agriculture and Forestry Statistics (農林統計協会) by commission of the Ministry of Agriculture, Forestry and Fisheries. This work focusses on agricultural resources and trends in large-scale management, those who bear the burden of farming and changes in the number of farming households, the current situation regarding mobilization of farming land, and agriculture in hillside and mountain areas.

06 梶井 功 Kajii Isoshi, 『国際化農政期の農業問題』 *Agricultural Issues in an Age of Internationalized Agricultural Policy*, 334 pp., 家の光協会, 1997.

An examination and criticism of government documents concerning the direction of agricultural policy released since 1986. The author makes extensive criticism of agricultural policy that has resulted in the abolishment of the Foodstuff Control Law (食糧管理法) (1995) and revision of the Basic Agriculture Law, and he proposes a system of agriculture that stresses preservation of the environment.

07 熊澤喜久男 Kumazawa Kikuo, 『環境保全型農業の展開に向けて』 *Towards the Development of Agriculture Oriented towards Environmental Preservation*, 315 pp., 農林統計協会, 1996.

An examination of Japan's organic agriculture and environmental preservation-oriented agriculture from an international and domestic perspective. It consists of two parts dealing with basic theory and practice respectively.

08 近藤康男ほか（編）Kondō Yasuo *et al.* (eds.)『日本農業年報』*The Annual Report on Japanese Agriculture*, 農林統計協会.

No. 43, 五味健吉（編）Gomi Kenkichi (ed.),『不良債権問題と農協系統金融』*The Problem of Bad Debt and Agricultural Cooperative-Affiliated Finances*, 253 pp., 1996.

No. 44, 今村奈良臣（編）Imamura Naraomi (ed.),『新農基法への視座』*A View of the New Basic Agriculture Law*, 264 pp., 農林統計協会, 1997.

VI-2. Agricultural Policy

09 黒柳俊雄・出村克彦・広政幸生（編）Kuroyanagi Toshio, Demura Katsuhiko and Hiromasa Yukio (eds.),『農業と農政の経済分析』*An Economic Analysis of Agriculture and Agricultural Policy*, 300 pp., 大明堂, 1996.

10 河相一成（編）Kawai Kazushige (ed.),『解体する食糧自給政策』*The Dissolution of the Policy for Self-Sufficiency in Food*, 330 pp., 日本経済評論社, 1996.

Recognizing the present food crisis, this book examines the characteristics, policy-making process, and institutional framework of food supplies in the case of Japan.

11 石原健二 Ishihara Kenji,『農業予算の変容——転換期農政と政府間財政関係』*Changes in the Agricultural Budget: Agricultural Policy at a Turning Point and Intergovernmental Financial Relations*, 285 pp., 農林統計協会, 1997.

Focussing on an examination of changes in the agricultural budget from 1975 to 1992, this is an empirical elucidation of the shift in the agricultural budget towards price policy and curtailments in subsidized businesses following the Provisional Commission on Administrative Reform and the administrative reforms of the 1980s.

12 竹中久仁雄（編）Takenaka Kunio (ed.),『農政の総括とパラダイム転換——新しい基本法への課題』*A Summary of Agricultural Policy and the Paradigm Shift: Issues Related to the New Basic Agriculture Law*, 373 pp., 筑波書房, 1997.

Emphasizing the need for a shift from the hitherto centralized agricultural policy to a framework based on a decentralized system and policy, the author advocates comprehensive changes in policies for food, agriculture, and farming villages.

13 中川聰七郎 Nakagawa Sōshichirō,『農政改革の課題——農業，農村活性

化への道』 *Current Issues in Agricultural Policy Reform: Towards the Vitalization of Agriculture and Farming Villages*, 292 pp., 農林統計協会, 1997.

VI-3. Agricultural Production and Distribution

14　日本農業市場学会（編）Agricultural Marketing Society of Japan (ed.), 『農産物貿易とアグリビジネス』 *Trade in Agricultural Products and Agribusiness*, 154 pp., 筑波書房, 1996.

This book examines the use of information and distribution problems as experienced by multinationals in Japan and analyzes the distribution of individual products including chicken, fruit juices, fruit, vegetables and milk.

15　日本農業市場学会（編）Agricultural Marketing Society of Japan (ed.), 『激変する食糧法下の米市場』 *The Rice Market Under the Rapidly Changing Foodstuff Law*, 255 pp., 筑波書房, 1997.

This work looks at the rice market, taking the position that the New Foodstuff Law has been ineffective with regard to the supply and demand for rice and price stability.

16　小池恒男 Koike Tsuneo,『激変する米の市場構造と新戦略』 *The Rapidly Changing Structure of the Rice Market and New Strategies*, 239 pp., 家の光協会, 1997.

An examination of how the structure of rice production, distribution and consumption and its pricing will change under the New Foodstuff Law and what kind of policies will become necessary.

17　梅沢昌太郎 Umezawa Shōtarō,『ミクロ農業マーケティング──食生活の多様化と事業戦略』*Microagriculture Marketing: The Diversification of Dietary Habits and Business Strategy*, 282 pp., 白桃書房, 1996.

18　辻井　博 Tsujii Hiroshi,『世界の食糧不安と日本農業』 *Global Food Insecurity and Japan's Agriculture*, 227 pp., 家の光協会, 1997.

19　渡久地朝明 Tokuchi Tomoaki,『戦後期における農業生産構造の計量分析』 *An Econometric Analysis of the Postwar Agricultural Production Structure*, 113 pp., 農林統計協会, 1997.

VI-4. Agricultural Organizations

20　西山久徳 Nishiyama Hisanori,『日本農協の論理と課題と展望』 *The Logic, Issues and Prospects of Japan's Agricultural Cooperatives*, 396 pp., 文化書房博文社, 1996.

21　佐伯尚美 Saeki Naomi,『住専と農協』 *Housing Loan Companies (Jūsen) and Agricultural Cooperatives (Nōkyō)*, 272 pp., 農林統計協会, 1997.

Problems concerning the handling of housing loan companies' losses surfaced in 1995, and various arguments took place for over one year following these revelations. Consisting of two parts, Part 1 of this work examines housing loan companies themselves, including their character, their actual business and how these companies were dealt with, while Part 2 discusses the links between housing loan companies and agricultural cooperatives, which were their chief institutional suppliers of capital. The author advocates the need for institutional reform of agricultural cooperative-affiliated finances.

22   藤谷築次（編）Fujitani Chikuji (ed.),『農協運動の展望方向を問う──21 世紀を見据えて』 *Questioning the Direction of the Development of the Agricultural Cooperative Movement: Looking Hard at the 21st Century*, 268 pp., 家の光協会，1997.

This is a comprehensive examination of the operations of agricultural cooperatives, including affiliated financial, credit, and mutual-aid schemes. Reference is also made to contemporary issues confronting agricultural cooperatives, such as regional development activities and broad-based mergers.

VI-5. Agrarian Society and Farm Management

23   西川　治 Nishikawa Osamu,『農村のヒューマン・エコロジー』 *The Human Ecology of Rural Villages*, 316 pp., 古今書院，1996.

24   石原豊美 Ishihara Toyomi,『農家の家族変動──ライフコースの発想を用いて』 *Changes in Farming Families: Utilizing the Concept of a Life Course*, 208 pp., 日本経済評論社，1996.

25   田畑　保・村松功巳・両角和夫（編）Tabata Tamotsu, Muramatsu Katsumi and Morozumi Kazuo (eds.),『明日の農業をになうのは誰か──日本農業の担い手問題と担い手対策』 *Who Will Bear the Burden of Farming in the Future?: Problems and Countermeasures Concerning Those Who Bear the Burden of Japanese Agriculture*, 377 pp., 日本経済評論社，1996.

Based on a fact-finding survey and analysis of the main agricultural areas of the Hokuriku, Shikoku, Tōhoku, Tokyo metropolitan, Kinki and San'yō regions, this is a comprehensive examination of problems and countermeasures concerning those bearing the burden of Japanese agriculture. Subjects covered include management issues such as combined family management and corporate management; labor issues such as measures concerning persons who have left previous employment to take up farming and young farm workers; land issues such as measures pertaining to the mobilization of farmland; and issues concerning capital.

26   保母武彦 Hobo Takehiko,『内発的発展論と日本の農山村』 *Endogenous Development Theory and Japan's Rural and Mountain Villages*, 271

pp., 岩波書店, 1996.

Based on an analysis of the present situation in depopulated rural and mountain villages, the author identifies the direction of the future development of rural and mountain villages in endogenous development and proposes the necessary policy system to this end. He conducted a questionnaire on cities, towns and villages in hillside and mountain regions throughout Japan and includes an analysis of replies sent in by 997 cities, towns, and villages.

VII. Labor
VII-1. General Works

01　日本労働研究機構（編）Japan Institute of Labor (ed.),『リーディングス日本の労働』*Readings on Japanese Labor*, 11 vols., 日本労働研究機構, 1997-99.

Vol. 2, 渡辺博顕・金子能宏・平田周一（編）Watanabe Hiroaki, Kaneko Norihiro and Hirata Shūichi (eds.),『労働市場の経済分析』*An Economic Analysis of the Labor Maket*, 335 pp., 1997.

Vol. 6, 島田睦男・長縄久生・武田圭太・蟹江教子（編）Shimada Mutsuo, Naganawa Hisao, Takeda Keita, and Kanie Noriko (eds.),『職場と人間』*The Workplace and People*, 338 pp., 1997.

Vol. 9, 伊藤　実・中村良二・佐野　哲・銭　小英（編）Itō Minoru, Nakamura Ryōji, Sano Tetsu and Ch'ien Hsiao-ying (eds.),『労働の国際化』*The Internationalization of Labor*, 307 pp., 1997.

Vol. 10, 佐藤　厚・青木章之介・榧野　潤（編）Satō Atsushi, Aoki Shōnosuke and Kayano Jun (eds.),『中小企業』*Small Businesses*, 386 pp., 1997.

This comprehensive collection of articles divided into eleven areas is taken from works on Japanese labor written in Japanese by Japanese researchers between 1945 and 1995.

02　高橋祐吉ほか（編）Takahashi Yūkichi *et al*. (eds.),『技術選択と社会・企業』*Society, Corporations and Choosing Technology* [「社会政策学会年報」第40集], 310 pp., 御茶の水書房, 1996.

03　高橋祐吉ほか（編）Takahashi Yūkichi *et al*. (eds.),『二一世紀の社会保障』*Social Security in the 21st Century* [「社会政策学会年報」第41集], 300 pp., 御茶の水書房, 1997.

04　『社会政策叢書』編集委員会（編）*Social Policy Library* Editorial Committee (ed.),『弾力化・規制緩和と社会政策』*Flexibility, Deregulation and Social Policy* [社会政策学会研究大会社会政策叢書, 第20集], 299 pp., 啓文社, 1996.

05　西村豁通・竹中恵美子・中西　洋（編）Nishimura Hiromichi, Takenaka

Emiko and Nakanishi Yō (eds.),『個人と共同体の社会科学——近代にお
ける社会と人間』*The Social Science of Individuals and the Community: Society and People in Modern Times*, 429 pp., ミネルヴァ書房, 1996.

This work consists of five parts dealing with civil society and individuals, the family community and women, the corporate community and
labor, the regional community and cooperation, and the state and the
humanity. It is a collection of articles commemorating Professor Nishimura's seventieth birthday, with contributions by a wide range of
researchers with the focus on labor economics.

06 渡辺貞雄（編）Watanabe Sadao (ed.),『21世紀への社会政策』*Social
Policy for the 21st Century*, 256 pp., 法律文化社, 1996.

07 本多淳亮 Honda Junryō,『企業社会と労働者』*Corporate Society and
Workers*, 250 pp., 大阪経済法科大学出版部, 1996.

08 永山武夫先生古稀記念論文集編集委員会（編）Collected Articles Commemorating Professor Nagayama Takeo's 70th Birthday Editorial Committee (ed.),『国際化と労働問題』*Internationalization and Labor Issues*,
256 pp., 前野書店, 1996.

09 逆瀬川 潔 Sakasegawa Kiyoshi,『中小企業と労働問題——労働時間・
最低賃金・退職金』*Small Businesses and Labor Issues: Working Hours,
the Minimum Wage and Retirement Allowance*, 346 pp., 日本労働研究機
構, 1996.

An empirical analysis of the reduction of working hours, restructuring
of the minimum wage system, and the retirement allowance system in
Japan's small businesses.

10 鷲田清一 Washida Seiichi,『だれのための仕事——労働 VS 余暇を超え
て』*Working for Whom?: Transcending the Concept of Work Versus
Leisure*, 181 pp., 岩波書店, 1996.

11 杉村芳美 Sugimura Yoshimi,『「良い仕事」の思想——新しい仕事倫理の
ために』*The Concept of a "Good Job": For the Sake of a New Work
Ethic*, 235 pp., 中央公論社, 1997.

12 中央労働委員会事務局（編）Secretariat of the Central Labor Relations
Commission (ed.),『労働委員会五十年の歩み』*Fifty Years of the Central Labor Relations Commission*, 564 pp., 全国労働委員会連絡協議会,
1996.

A publication commemorating 50 years of the Central Labor Relations
Commission. It consists of four parts comprising a commemorative symposium, essays, general meeting, and ceremony, together with relevant
materials. The symposium is particularly rich in content.

13 労働省労働基準局（編）The Ministry of Labor, Labor Standards Bureau

(ed.),『労働基準行政50年の回顧』 *Fifty Years of Labor Standards Administration in Retrospect*, 431 pp., 日本労務研究会, 1997.

A detailed explanation of changes in the supervisory administration of labor standards and changes in the reduction of working hours, the minimum wage system, safety and hygiene administration, and compensation for workers' accidents as seen from the standpoint of the administration.

VII-2. The Labor Process and Human Resources

14　湯浅良雄 Yuasa Yoshio,『現代の労働過程——リストラクチュアリングと生産システムの改革』 *The Contemporary Labor Process: Restructuring and Reforms in the Production System*, 260 pp., 柏書房, 1997.

15　三浦豊彦 Miura Toyohiko,『労働観のクロニクル——働くことは生活だった』 *Chronicles of an Outlook on Work: Working Was Life*, 202 pp., 労働科学研究所出版部, 1996.

16　遠藤幸男 Endō Yukio,『就業構造の変化と労働者の生活——労働科学の諸問題として』 *Changes in the Employment Structure and Workers' Lifestyles: Its Problems in Labor Science*, 198 pp., 労働科学研究所出版部, 1996.

17　鈴木幸毅・池内守厚（編）Suzuki Kōki and Ikeuchi Moriatsu (eds.),『バーナード理論と労働の人間化』 *Bernard's Theory and the Humanization of Labor* [工業経営研究学会創立10周年記念出版2], 235 pp., 税務経理協会, 1997.

18　戸木田嘉久・三好正巳（編）Tokita Yoshihisa and Miyoshi Masami (eds.),『規制緩和と労働・生活』 *The Effects of Deregulation on Labor and Livelihood*, 245 pp., 法律文化社, 1997.

Consisting of two parts, one dealing with deregulation and labor issues, and the other with deregulation and social security and social welfare, this is a multifaceted examination, incorporating an international perspective, of the problems deregulation policy has brought to labor and livelihood.

19　森田統一郎 Morita Tōichirō,『オートメーションと労働組織』 *Automation and Labor Organizations*, 401 pp., 税務経理協会, 1997.

A mainly theoretical examination of the influence technological growth has had on labor since World War II. The focus is on a critical reappraisal of H. Braverman's and J. R. Bright's theories of unskillfulness and demotion, etc.

20　幸　光善 Miyuki Mitsuyoshi,『現代企業労働の研究——技術発展と労働・管理の視点を中心に』 *A Study on Contemporary Corporate Labor: With a Focus on the Perspectives of Technological Growth and of Labor and Management*, 349 pp., 法律文化社, 1997.

21 古郡鞆子 Furugōri Tomoko,『非正規労働の経済分析』 *An Economic Analysis of Irregular Labor*, 268 pp., 東洋経済新報社, 1997.

22 早川征一郎 Hayakawa Seiichirō,『国家公務員の昇進・キャリア形成』 *The Promotion and Career Formation of Civil Servants*, 386 pp., 日本評論社, 1996.

VII-3. Labor Markets and Employment Practices

23 岩瀬 孝 Iwase Takashi,『大失業回避への戦略』*Strategies for Avoiding Mass Unemployment*, 386 pp., 日本労働研究機構, 1996.

An analysis and examination of the characteristics of Japan's employment insecurity, uncertainty in the employment system, and new employment strategies through a comparison between Japan, the United States and Europe.

24 海野 博 Umino Hiroshi,『賃金の国際比較と労働問題』 *An International Comparison of Wages and Labor Issues*, 236 pp., ミネルヴァ書房, 1997.

Part 1 puts forward new estimates on the basis of a critical appraisal of existing studies on international wage comparisons by Fujimoto Takeshi 藤本武, Itō Yōichi 伊藤陽一, the Ministry of Labor, and Nikkeiren (Japan Federation of Employers' Associations). Part 2 deals with concrete issues in management and labor, covering such areas as the employment and working environment, employment of the elderly, part-timers, and pensions, etc.

25 三谷直紀 Mitani Naoki,『企業内賃金構造と労働市場』 *The Corporate Wage Structure and the Labor Market*, 262 pp., 勁草書房, 1997.

26 島田晴雄・太田 清 (編) Shimada Haruo and Ōta Kiyoshi (eds.),『労働市場改革――管理の時代から選択の時代へ』 *Labor Market Reforms: From an Age of Control to an Age of Choice*, 240 pp., 東洋経済新報社, 1997.

27 八代尚宏 Yashiro Naohiro,『日本的雇用慣行の経済学――労働市場の流動化と日本経済』*Economics of Japanese Employment Practices: Mobility in the Labor Market and the Japanese Economy*, 264 pp., 日本経済新聞社, 1997.

28 中馬宏之・駿河輝和 (編) Chūma Hiroyuki and Suruga Terukazu (eds.),『雇用慣行の変化と女性労働』 *Changes in Employment Practices and Female Labor*, 339 pp., 東京大学出版会, 1997.

29 小野 旭 Ono Akira,『変化する日本的雇用慣行』 *Changing Japanese Employment Practices*, 287 pp., 日本労働研究機構, 1997.

A comparative analysis of employment practices in foreign affiliates and Japanese firms, this work examines internal promotion systems, mobility in the labor market, and the wage structure.

VII-4. Labor-Management Relations and the Labor Movement

30 富沢賢治・中川雄一郎・柳沢敏勝（編）Tomizawa Kenji, Nakagawa Yūichirō and Yanagizawa Toshikatsu (eds.),『労働者協同組合の新地平──社会的経済の現代的再生』 *New Horizons in Workers' Cooperatives: The Contemporary Rejuvenation of a Social Economy*, 325 pp., 日本経済評論社, 1996.

31 井上雅雄 Inoue Masao,『社会変容と労働──「連合」の成立と大衆社会の成熟』 *Social Changes and Labor: The Formation of the "Rengō" (Japanese Trade Union Confederation) and the Maturing of Mass Society*, 416 pp., 木鐸社, 1997.

32 下山房雄 Shimoyama Fusao,『現代世界と労働運動──日本とフランス』 *The Contemporary World and the Labor Movement: Japan and France*, 414 pp., 御茶の水書房, 1997.

33 桑原靖雄・連合総合生活開発研究所（編）Kuwabara Yasuo and Japanese Trade Union Confederation Research Institute for the Advancement of Living Standards (eds.),『労働の未来を創る──グローバル化時代の労働組合の挑戦』 *Building the Future of Labor: The Challenges of Labor Unions in an Age of Globalization*, 323 p., 第一書林, 1997.

A joint study by researchers in the fields of economics, sociology and labor surveys. It makes proposals for changes in the objective situation and policies for subjective movements aiming at a strategy for the realization of an "advanced welfare society," a "decentralized and diversified society," and a "transparent and just society."

VII-4. Social Security and Welfare

34 佐藤　守（編）Satō Mamoru (ed.),『福祉コミュニティの研究』 *A Study on the Welfare Community*, 457 pp., 多賀出版, 1996.

35 藤田至孝・塩野谷祐一（編）Fujita Yoshitaka and Shionoya Yūichi (eds.),『企業内福祉と社会保障』 *Corporate Welfare and Social Security*, 366 pp., 東京大学出版会, 1997.

36 林　雄二郎・連合総合生活開発研究所（編）Hayashi Yūjirō and Japanese Trade Union Confederation Research Institute for the Advancement of Living Standards (eds.)『新しい社会セクターの可能性── NPO と労働組合』 *The Potential of New Sectors in Society: Nonprofit Organizations (NPOs) and Labor Unions*, 206 pp., 第一書林, 1997.

A comprehensive discussion of the involvement of labor unions in the nonprofit sector and the expanding activities of nonprofit organizations.

VIII. International Economy

VIII-1. General Works

01 鴨　武彦・伊藤元重・石黒一憲（編）Kamo Takehiko, Itō Motoshige and Ishiguro Kazunori (eds.),『国際政治経済システム——リーディングス』*The International Political and Economic System: Readings*, 有斐閣.
Vol. 1,『主権国家を超えて』*Beyond the Sovereign Nation*, 375 pp., 1997.
Vol. 3,『相対化する国境』*The Relativization of Borders*, 323 pp., 1997.

02 富田俊基 Tomita Toshiki,『冷戦後の世界経済システム——協調と対立のゲーム理論』*The World Economic System in the Post-Cold War Era: The Game Theory of Cooperation and Confrontation*, 202 pp., 東洋経済新報社, 1996.

Based on both Charles P. Kindleberger's and Robert Gilpin's theory of hegemonic states and the game theory, this work interprets the direction of the structure of the world system in the post-Cold War period as an intermingling of multilateralism and bilateralism.

03 清水嘉治 Shimizu Yoshiharu,『世界経済の統合と再編』*The Integration and Restructuring of the World Economy*, 278 pp., 新評論, 1996.

This work is divided into three parts: Part 1 deals with international issues in environmental economics; Part 2 covers the three regional economic blocs in the world economy; and Part 3 discusses economic friction, currency crises and imbalanced growth. The current state of China's economy is also examined in a supplementary section.

04 大住荘四郎・井内正敏 Ōsumi Sōshirō and Iuchi Masatoshi,『制度・システム変革の国際経済学』*The International Economics of Institutional and System Reforms*, 236 pp., 日本評論社, 1996.

05 渡辺福太郎 Watanabe Fukutarō,『世界経済の流れを知る』*Understanding the Course of the World Economy*, 143 pp., 文真堂, 1996.

06 岩田勝雄（編）Iwata Katsuo (ed.),『21世紀の国際経済——グローバル・リージョナル・ナショナル』*The International Economy in the 21st Century: Global, Regional and National Economies*, 279 pp., 新評論, 1997.

07 中北　徹 Nakakita Tōru,『世界標準の時代——市場制覇の新たな条件』*The Age of Global Standards: New Conditions for Marketplace Domination*, 208 pp., 東洋経済新報社, 1997.

08 降旗節雄（編）Furihata Setsuo (ed.),『世界経済の読み方』*Interpreting the World Economy*, 259 pp., 御茶の水書房, 1997.

09 浅羽良昌（編）Asaba Yoshimasa (ed.),『国際経済史——欧米とアジア』*An International Economic History: The West and Asia*, 270 pp., ミネルヴァ書房, 1996.

The aim of this work is to clarify the driving force and mechanisms behind the economic growth of various countries (Great Britain, Ger-

many, the United States, Japan, Korea, Taiwan and Singapore) by
historical comparison.

VIII-2. Trade and Economic Friction

　10　花崎正晴 Hanazaki Masaharu,『アメリカの貿易赤字日本の貿易黒字——
金融国際化と不均衡調整問題』 *America's Trade Deficit and Japan's
Trade Surplus: Financial Internationalization and the Question of
Imbalance Adjustments*, 220 pp., 東洋経済新報社, 1996.

　11　吉信　粛 Yoshinobu Susumu,『国際分業と外国貿易』 *The International
Division of Labor and Foreign Trade*, 241 pp., 同文館出版, 1997.

　12　周　牧之 Zhuo Muzhi,『メカトロニクス革命と新国際分業——現代世界
経済におけるアジア工業化』 *The "Mechatronics Revolution" and the
New International Division of Labor: Asian Industrialization in the
Contemporary World Economy*, 245 pp., ミネルヴァ書房, 1997.

　　　Based on a fact-finding survey of factories in Japan, China, America and
Southeast Asia, this work demonstrates that the advancing "mechatronics
revolution" is forming new relationships in the international division of
labor in these regions.

　13　青木　健・馬田啓一（編）Aoki Takeshi and Umada Keiichi (eds.),『日
米経済関係——新たな枠組みと日本の選択』 *Japan-U.S. Economic Rela-
tions: A New Framework and Japan's Choices*, 248 pp., 勁草書房, 1996.

　　　An examination of Japan-U.S. economic relations based on the recognition that America's policy of regionalism has shown active growth with
NAFTA as leverage and that in response to this a new regionalism has
come to the fore in Asia, resulting in a new stage in Japan-U.S. relations.

　14　島田克美・藤井光男・小林英夫（編）Shimada Katsumi, Fujii Mitsuo
and Kobayashi Hideo (eds.),『現代アジアの産業発展と国際分業』 *Industrial Growth and the International Division of Labor in Contemporary
Asia*, 276 pp., ミネルヴァ書房, 1997.

　15　徳永正次郎（編）Tokunaga Shōjirō (ed.),『多国籍企業のアジア投資と
円の国際化——日韓企業の海外事業活動と貿易決済の変容に関する実態
調査』 *Asian Investment by Multinational Corporations and the Internationalization of the Yen: A Fact-Finding Survey on Changes in the
Overseas Business Activities of Japanese and Korean Firms and the
Settlement of Trade Accounts*, 171 pp., 税務経理協会, 1996.

VIII-3. Development Assistance and Developing Countries

　16　矢内原　勝（編）Yanaihara Katsu (ed.),『発展途上国問題を考える』
Thinking about Issues Related to Developing Nations, 326 pp., 勁草書房,
1996.

　17　足立芳寛 Adachi Yoshihiro,『開発技術学入門』 *An Introduction to*

Development Technology, 321 pp., オーム社, 1996.

A comprehensive examination of the transfer of technology and technological cooperation in the field of engineering based on the recognition
that, rather than the simple capital assistance which had been the norm to
date, a need has arisen in the sphere of development assistance for the
development of a methodology and technology system that allows growth
limits to be surmounted.

18 西川 潤（編）Nishikawa Jun (ed.),『社会開発──経済成長から人間中
心型発展へ』*Social Development: From Economic Growth to People-
Oriented Development*, 232 pp., 有斐閣, 1997.

The concepts, theories and policies of social development in the field of
international development have come under renewed scrutiny during the
1990s, and this work attempts to clarify these areas through an empirical
examination based on various regions and institutions.

19 佐藤秀雄 Satō Hideo,『ODA の世界──国際社会の中の日本を考える』
*The World of ODA: Looking at Japan as Part of International
Society*, 395 pp., 日本図書刊行会, 1997.

VIII-4. International Finance

20 奥田宏司 Okuda Hiroshi,『ドル体制と国際通貨──ドルの後退とマル
ク、円』*The Dollar System and Internatinal Currency: The Retreat of
the Dollar, and the Yen and Deutschemark*, 270 pp., ミネルヴァ書房,
1996.

This is an attempt to elucidate the relationship between the dollar,
Deutschemark and yen based on a system the author refers to as the
"dollar system," which he defines as the international monetary system
formed by a medium and long-term international credit chain centered on
the dollar, the nonconvertible currency that functions as the international
currency. Japan's overseas investments, the position of the yen in Asia, and
the role of the yen in Japan's overseas transactions are also examined.

21 白石 孝・馬田啓一（編）Shiraishi Takashi and Umada Keiichi (eds.),
『為替レートと日本経済──国際経済学の立場から』*The Exchange
Rate and the Japanese Economy: From the Perspective of International
Economics*, 207 pp., 東洋経済新報社, 1996.

Based on an analysis focussing on external factors such as Japan's trade
and direct investment during the 10 years of yen appreciation following
the Plaza Accord, this work emphasizes the high adaptability of the
Japanese economy to the appreciation of the yen.

22 中尾茂夫 Nakao Shigeo,『円とドルの存亡──国際通貨史からみた日本
の行方』*The Fate of the Yen and Dollar: Japan's Destiny as Seen from*

the History of Internationl Currency, 380 pp., 三田出版会, 1996.

The author understands in historical terms the interdependent relationship between the yen and dollar in the 20th century from the perspective of hegemonic currency and reviews the internationalization of the yen in the Asian economy during the 1990s.

23 行天豊雄 Gyōten Toyoo,『「円」はどこへ行くのか──体験的為替論』 *The Yen: Destination Unknown—A Personal Perspective*, 214 pp., 講談 社, 1996.

A recollection of international monetary negotiations by the writer, who was the Director of the International Finance Bureau of the Ministry of Finance in 1984 and also had experience as the Vice Minister of Finance for International Affairs（財務官）in 1986.

24 上川孝夫・今松英悦 Kamikawa Takao and Imamatsu Eietsu,『円の政治 経済学──アジアと世界システム』 *The Political Economics of the Yen: Asia and the World System*, 326 pp., 同文館, 1997.

This is a comprehensive examination of the internationalization of the yen in Asia, Japan's responses to this internationalization, and the position of the internationalized yen in the global system from the perspective of the history of international currency in Asia.

25 向　寿一 Mukai Juichi,『多国籍企業・銀行論──大競争時代へのサバイ バル戦略』 *Multinational Corporations and Banks: Survival Strategies in an Age of Cutthroat Competition*, 209 pp., 中央経済社, 1997.

An empirical analysis of financing and fund operations by multinational corporations and banks in Japan.

26 河合正弘・QUICK 総合研究所アジア金融研究会（編）Kawai Masahiro and QUICK General Research Institute Asian Finance Study Group (eds.),『アジアの金融・資本市場──自由化と相互依存』 *Asias' Financial and Capital Markets: Liberalization and Mutual Interdependence*, 324 pp., 日本経済新聞社, 1996.

BUSINESS ADMINISTRATION

Takahashi Nobuo
The University of Tokyo

INTRODUCTION

Regarding trends in business administration in the period in question, 1996~1997, due to the slump in the Japanese economy following the bursting of the bubble and the loss of confidence in the Japanese-style system we cannot expect such trends to break away from the gloomy atmosphere which is prevailing over the business world. While the mass media, especially in reports in the economic press, was dominated by a pessimistic view, much praise, by contrast, was continually heaped upon the American-style system, as represented by various new ventures. Thus in the somewhat confused atmosphere generated by the mass media which surrounded the Japanese-style economic system, management studies circles could offer solutions with relatively sober arguments on Japanese-style business administration which comprises the main current of their studies. So this chapter, rather than being classified by narrowly defined academic fields, will attempt to arrange the trends found in management studies circles as a whole, differentiated by topics, in four major currents.

The first current, responding to the demands of society, comprises discussions on Japanese firms. In particular, studies positioning Japanese-style management within the development of internationalization, along with analyses of the organization of Japanese firms and organizational decision-making are worthy of note. A peculiarity of Japanese management studies in the 1990s is the development of original arguments based on primary sources in Japanese firms.

The second current comprises the evolution theory of management systems. In order to explain how the Japanese-style system emerged, they discuss the evolution of management systems. Already from the 1980s, the term "evolution theory" itself was generally favored by many Japanese management studies scholars. In the latter half of the nineties, however, they may be said to have gone beyond simple analogy to establishing evolution theories empowered to explain empirical management phenomena in Japanese firms in theoretical terms.

The third current comprises organizational activation aimed at suggesting prescriptions to remedy unhealthy Japanese firms. After the oil shock of the 1970s onwards, the Japanese economy moved from high growth to low growth to stable growth. Japanese firms might have been calling out for organizational activation to regain in some way or another the dynamic organizational situation that existed in the period of high economic growth. So far, while the suggested remedies have not necessarily brought success, halfway through the nineties, during the prolonged recession in the Japanese economy, organizational activation has again come to be discussed from various angles.

The fourth current comprises corporate governance which has suddenly come to the fore in the mid-nineties. Unexpected movements have increased uneasy feelings among management studies scholars. According to one interpretation, it may be said that after the bubble burst, the think tanks attached to the securities companies which were involved in creating the securities bubble, foisted their responsibility for the bubble on the corporate management disregarding the shareholders. In order to lay the blame elsewhere, they took the opportunity to offer up corporate governance by way of sacrifice. Of course, there were also, however, many overseas studies of corporate governance, and contributions in the fields of business history and accounting are apparent. Whichever one is chosen for study this will undoubtedly be an important theme in the future.

I. JAPANESE FIRMS

Seki Mitsuhiro [I-01] sounded a warning bell on the hollowing-out of the technical basis of machine industries by which the strength of the Japanese economy had come to be sustained. Kiyonari Tadao and Hashimoto Jurō [I-02], taking cognizance of the progressive disintegration of the Japanese industrial agglomeration, carried out factual investigations of the new model of the industrial agglomeration of Silicon Valley in America. They heaped praise on the American system, symbolizing aspirations toward Silicon Valley, representing the other side of the coin of pessimism over the Japanese economy. In particular, mass media reports on the successive births of new ventures in America and the creation there of new industries and employment opportunities carried great influence. Thus for the third venture boom in Japan from the end of 1994 through 1997, the government-driven rapid completion of infrastructure preparation was fundamental to aid in the start up of new ventures [I-03]. Amid the increase in the social demand for studies on such venture industries and venture capital, Hamada Yasuyuki [I-04] and Hata Nobuyuki and Kamijō Masao [I-05] described the history and present state of Japanese venture capital or, the slightly wider subject of venture finance, and made tentative predictions of desirable future manifestations.

In such a mass media-initiated atmosphere, in scholarly circles, dispassionate analyses of Japanese firms were carried out. A representative example is the case study of the internationalization of Matsushita Electric undertaken by Kagono Tadao [I-06]. It is a study which, having confirmed the historical facts concerning the formation in Asia of a large and complex production network of Japanese enterprises and how it came to guide manufacturing industry to success, evaluated it as being at the center of a global axis of coordinates which had expanded the Japanese management style to an international scale. The founder of Matsushita Electric, Matsushita Kōnosuke, at this time became the subject of increased interest from scholars of management studies in Japan and overseas [I-07]. Kasuya Nobuji and the Hōsei University Institute for

Comparative Economic Studies [I-08] also carried out an investigation of the ubiquitous installation of Japanese labor relations and the Japanese system in the diffusion process of East Asian industrialization dynamism.

Indeed, as indicated by Yoshihara Hideki [I-09], every Japanese firm was not necessarily successful at internationalization. As the Japanese economy stagnated, however, while the awareness of Japanese multinationals remained as before without a major change, attempts to place Japanese industry or multinational enterprises relatively theoretically into international relations or the international state system were made not only by scholars of management studies [I-10] but also by political scientists [I-11].

Another distinctive feature of analysis of Japanese firms in the period in question is the trend toward analysis paying attention to organization and decision-making within organizations. Takahashi Nobuo [I-12] advocated the phenomena and actions of Japanese firms, such as the strong growth impetus and lifetime commitment from a theoretical investigation utilizing the model of its actual logical guidance by the "weight of the future," along with over ten years of rich research data. Among discussions on decision-making from a psychological point of view [I-13], which have most recently grabbed attention, Nagase Katsuhiko [I-14] in a dynamic comparative experiment on individual decisions and group decisions, makes it clear that the group decision-making involving many people characteristic of Japanese firms is reactive and unstable.

In the case of strategic decision-making, however, environmental conditions from the outside of the organization are also important [I-15]. Karube Masaru [I-16], with regard to semiconductor processing technology, indicated those differences between Japanese and American enterprise control strategies and resource allocation patterns attributable to differences in economic systems. Furthermore, as regards studies of organization itself, Nakamura Keisuke [I-17] in case studies on large Japanese private enterprise manufacturing businesses, analyzed various types of task organization within the workplace.

II. EVOLUTION THEORY OF MANAGEMENT SYSTEMS

Among studies utilizing the theoretical framework of evolution theory, Fujimoto Takahiro [II-01] analysed Toyota's methods of production, from the viewpoints of evolution in production, product development and sales systems, on the basis of independently gathered data accumulated over a number of years. This research indicated a novel goal insofar as it was a study of "Toyota-ism" (Toyota production system). Hereafter, however, rather than such evolutionary theories akin to biological images, evolutionary theories founded in game theory are likely to represent the mainstream. Evolutionary theories of the game theory type use mathematical models, without reliance on biological images, in an original way to carry out theoretical research into evolution.

Evolutionary theories of the game theory type comprise two currents. One current, of which the work of Aoki Masahiko and Okuno-Fujiwara Masahiro [II-02] is representative, is comparative institutional analysis. It has a profound influence on studies of evolution games in economics. This research has not exerted a direct influence on management studies theory. However, its major concept of "path dependence" has been coming into general use in management studies texts.

The other current consists of those political science theories of the evolution of cooperation known as Axelrod's theory. Regarding these, the work edited by Takahashi Nobuo [II-03] carried out theoretical investigations and indicated that actual management phenomena can be explained by theories of evolution of cooperation. This research, consisting of a collection of articles by young management studies scholars, is the first text to apply Axelrod's theory to management phenomena and suggests the possibility that, hereafter, theories of the evolution of cooperation will become a cornerstone of management theory. Indeed, Shimizu Takashi [II-04] has made a contribution from the theoretical aspect, while subsequently studies of a similar type, such as Arai Kazuhiro's [II-05] discussion of the Japanese firm's lifetime employment system from the standpoint of game theory, principally Axelrod's theory, have been published.

134

III. ORGANIZATIONAL ACTIVATION

"Organizational activation" (*soshiki kasseika*) was not a term borrowed from a foreign language. The term "activation" has been used in Japan since around the mid-1970s principally in the field of organization development as a wide concept covering in an all-embracing way modes of thinking and techniques existing in Japan. Within its wide domain, located close to management strategy theory, Kawai Tadahiko [III-01], on the basis of case studies, argued for spiral management with interactively dual loops of strategy formation process: a top-down type loop and a bottom-up type loop, and analysed activated organizations in which it was realized.

In a Japanese firm, superiors allow their subordinates to side-track problems which are assigned a low priority (*yarisugoshi*). By way of management theory, Takahashi Nobuo [III-02], indicating from rich research data that, thanks to the organizational phenomena in Japanese enterprise of *"yarisugoshi"* and "taking the blame for another person" (*shirinugui*), even with utilizing on-the-job training to the fullest extent, organizational behavior and the system are able to avoid failure, reassessed the existence of organizational activation. Such studies dealing with everyday phenomena in Japanese firms become a rallying call for the restoration of "true Japanese vocabulary" (*Yamato kotoba*) in organizational theory.

As the analytical framework of organizational activation in not specified, various kinds of approaches are possible. Yamashita Hiroshi [III-03] attempted to model organizational activation through the industrial engineering approach, while Tsuchiya Shigehisa [III-04] analysed cases of organizational activation within a framework of organizational learning theory. Sakakibara Kiyonori [III-05] took up organizational activation from the viewpoint of business esthetics. Then again, since originally organizational development techniques take their significance from their grounding in psychology, the approach to organizational activation through organizational psychology must not be ignored. A series of studies centering around Tao Masao [III-06~08] and focusing on company personnel seen from their organizational commitment, the burnout syndrome, and technostress accompanying computerization anticipate developments in theoretical and empirical research in the future.

IV. CORPORATE GOVERNANCE

When in December 1997, the Revised Antimonopoly Law was put in force, the postwar ban prohibiting pure holing companies in Japan was lifted. Shimotani Masahiro [IV-01] touched on discussion up until then surrounding the lifting of the ban on holding companies and the fact of success in avoiding the bad effects of the formation of conglomerates, and regarded it as doubtful whether in fact the lifting of the ban would be effective in economic revitalization. Some Japanese financiers think that holding companies keep a distance from business and the achievement of efficient management. But it is a baseless illusion. Such vague yearnings toward the Anglo-American pattern of financial rivalry (deliberate spending, merger and acquisition) as opposed to the Japanese pattern of industrial rivalry (efficiency of production) [IV-02] are often attached to discussions of corporate governance.

On the historical side, however, Morikawa Hidemasa [IV-03], in indicating the deception of discussions of corporate governance, showed the downfall of what might be expected to be intelligently run commercial capital enterprises. Now in Asia at least, those Japanese manufacturers who continued to adhere to the basic philosophy of solid honesty brought success to their manufacturing [I-06]. Corporate governance as it should be is sure to be no mere passing fad. As indicated by Takamura Naosuke [IV-04], since previously the great merchant families of Japanese modern history practiced separation of ownership and management on a wide scale, it is something which the Japanese built up of their own accord over a long period within Japan [IV-05, 06]. Then again, as indicated by Gotō Masatoshi [IV-07], the obligation in Japan for management to disclose its forecast information is a characteristic institution unique in the world. Even in America proud of leading information publication systems, when in the first half of the 1970s an increase in discussion of systems for forecasts information disclosure occurred, the system of compulsory publication on demand was not established.

Doubtless, along with the existence of the trend which Itō Motoshige [IV-08] calls "market-centrism," company pensions [IV-09], as in America, are bound to increase in importance in Japanese company governance. From the time of the merger and acquisition boom in America beginning in the latter half of the 1960s, however, even within the same company, with company management neither able to appraise concrete suggestions from the operative sections which have been taken over nor able to see performance, communication between the head office manager and the actual site breaks down and ruin becomes a reality. For instance, even if the company makes public exhaustive information, investors and shareholders in the market cannot necessarily do evaluation more precisely than the head office in the same company. Questions of corporate governance are not from start to finish a matter of assertion of the dominance of the shareholder, but in future, they should be considered questions for the whole body of stakeholders in an organizational network far exceeding the boundaries of the firms [IV-10].

V. MISCELLANEOUS

Besides the above, there have been several new developments. Firstly, Nobeoka Kentarō [V-01] has examined multi-project strategy based in the automobile industry. In future, it is possible that in Japan, project management will become a major research topic [V-02]. Besides, with the activities of the volunteers in the Great Hanshin Earthquake of January 1995, the existence of citizen nonprofit organizations (NPOs) has gained great appeal, and research into NPOs, including a trend toward the setting up of study groups, is a sign of their acceptance [V-03~05]. Then, although representing only an initial germination, what Nakamaki Hirochika and Hioki Kōichirō [V-06] call "an anthropology of management" has been attempted up to now here and there in Japanese management studies. Methods of putting together ethnographically aware organizational analyses are awaited as future research developments. Besides, attempts at collating retrospectively major theories [V-07], management scholars [V-08, 09] and sources [V-10] appeared.

BIBLIOGRAPHY

I. Japanese Firms

01 関 満博 Seki Mitsuhiro,『空洞化を超えて——技術と地域の再構築』 *Beyond Deindustrialization: Rebuilding Technology and Regions*, 258 pp., 日本経済新聞社, 1997.

This book points out the demise through "running sores" of the technical basis of machine industries by which the strength of the Japanese economy came to be sustained, and sounds a warning bell over the hollowing-out of technology.

02 清成忠男・橋本寿朗（編）Kiyonari Tadao and Hashimoto Jurō (eds.),『日本型産業集積の未来像』*The Future Appearance of the Japanese-Style Industrial Agglomeration*, 269 pp., 日本経済新聞社, 1997.

Taking cognizance of the progressive disintegration of the Japanese industrial agglomeration, the editors bring together the results of factual investigations of the new model of industry of Silicon Valley in America. Following on from the clarification of the actual state of Silicon Valley and the Asian Connection and a comparison with the northern Italian (Lombardy) industrial region, directions for the rebirth of Japanese industrial agglomeration are explored.

03 松田修一 Matsuda Shūichi,『起業論』*Entrepreneur*, 266 pp., 日本経済新聞社, 1997.

04 浜田康行 Hamada Yasuyuki,『日本のベンチャーキャピタル——未来への戦略投資』*Japanese Venture Capital: Strategic Investment toward the Future*, 318 pp., 日本経済新聞社, 1996.

This book describes the characteristics of Japanese venture capital and the history of Japanese venture finance.

05 秦 信行・上條正夫（編）Hata Nobuyuki and Kamijō Masao (eds.),『ベンチャーファイナンスの多様化』*Diversification of Venture Finance*, 297 pp., 日本経済新聞社, 1996.

After careful consideration of the present state of finance in Japanese small businesses as a whole, this work indicates the history and present condition of Japanese venture capital (VC), then gives a comparison with American VC, the scale of funds, venture capital sources, the business nature of enterprises in which investment is made, stages of growth, and differences and problems in the methods of capital return. Not restricted to VC, on a somewhat wider range of finances, it makes tentative predictions of desirable future developments in Japanese venture finance.

06　加護野忠男 Kagono Tadao,『日本型経営の復権』 *The Resurrection of Japanese-Style Management*, 341 pp., PHP 研究所, 1997.

　　Focusing on a case study of internationalization at Matsushita Electric, this work describes how the Japanese manufacturer, retaining its basic philosophy with the solid honesty of an old-fashioned manufacturer, formed a huge and complex production network in Asia and guided manufacturing industry to success. In contrast, it gives a persuasive description of the historical facts of how astutely clever commercial capitalist firms failed in the bitter rivalries against Japanese firms over the past thirty years and more.

07　松下社会科学振興財団日本的経営研究会（編）The Matsushita Foundation for Management and Social Sciences Japanese Management Study Meeting (ed.),『日本的経営の本流――松下幸之助の発想と戦略』 *Mainstream of Japanese Management: Matsushita Kōnosuke's Ideas and Strategy*, 289 pp., PHP 研究所, 1997.

　　This work attempts to approach the strategy and organization of Matsushita Electric through the ideas and way of thinking of Matsushita Kōnosuke, and to explain the thought and ideas behind Matsushita Electric, as a typical enterprise of Japanese management.

08　法政大学比較経済研究所・粕谷信次（編）Hōsei University Institute for Comparative Economic Studies and Kasuya Nobuji (eds.),『東アジア工業化ダイナミズム――21 世紀への挑戦』 *The Dynamism of East Asian Industrialization: Challenge of the 21st Century*, 330 pp., 法政大学出版局, 1997.

　　Besides looking at the diffusion process of East Asian industrialization dynamism in Thailand, China and India, this work carries out an investigation of the universality of Japanese labor relations and the Japanese system.

09　吉原英樹 Yoshihara Hideki,『未熟な国際経営』 *Immature International Management*, 207 pp., 白桃書房, 1996.

　　In order to examine the present state of international management of Japanese firms, the author carried out a survey of 427 parent companies in Japan and 634 overseas subsidiaries of Japanese enterprises in the U.S.A.,

U.K., Germany, Singapore and Taiwan. The results indicated the following distinctive features: (1) in many cases, the performance of overseas subsidiaries of Japanese enterprises was in general poor or loss-making; (2) especially at the management level, the localization of overseas subsidiaries had not progressed; (3) internationalization (internal internationalization) of Japanese parent companies had not progressed. Thus the designation "immature international management" is used.

10　鈴木典比古 Suzuki Norihiko,『多国籍企業と国際関係の統合理論──グラフによるパラダイム・シフト分析』*The Multinational Business and International Relations: A Graphical Analysis of Paradigm Shift*, 239 pp., 国際書院, 1996.

Combining the three analytical positions of realism, pluralism and globalism, this novel study attempts a theoretical analysis of the activities of multinational enterprises and nation states.

11　恒川惠市 Tsunekawa Keiichi,『企業と国家』*The State and Private Enterprise*, 351 pp., 東京大学出版会, 1996.

This work focuses on State activities which influence private enterprise planning and private enterprise activities which influence State policy, with the power relations between the two. While power relations between the two vary with the timing of industrialization, the nature of society and the State prior to industrialization and the position in the international State system, it suggests that the progress of private enterprise toward a multinational status creates difficulties for the State in the work of economic administration.

12　高橋伸夫 Takahashi Nobuo,『日本企業の意思決定原理』*Principles of Decision-Making in Japanese Firms*, 288 pp., 東京大学出版会, 1997.

The phenomena in Japanese firms of a strong growth impetus and lifetime commitment are seen as apparently irrational from the rational decision-making theories of game theory and decision theory. But, this work perceives them as in fact rational guided by the "weight of the future." Besides a theoretical investigation concluding that a "leaning on the future" paradigm system could survive, it bases its argument on an analysis of more than ten years' rich research data.

13　印南一路 Innami Ichiro,『すぐれた意思決定──判断と選択の心理学』*Excellent Decision-Making: The Psychology of Judgment and Choice*, 325 pp., 中央公論社, 1997.

14　長瀬勝彦 Nagase Katsuhiko, 個人決定と合議決定の乖離に関する動態的分析 "A Dynamic Analysis of Decision-Making by Individuals and Groups,"「組織科学」31 巻 2 号, pp. 60-78, 組織学会, 1997.

Having reviewed sources relevant to group decision-making, the author carried out dynamic comparative experiments on individual and group decisions in a milieu of risk under competitive conditions. As a result, it became clear that when teams consisting of small numbers of people were less influenced by positive and negative feedback, their decision-making was non-reactive and stable.

15 伊藤秀史 (編) Itō Hideshi (ed.),『日本の企業システム』*The Japanese Firm as a System*, 386 pp., 東京大学出版会, 1996.

Scholars, mainly economists, basing their work on the newest standard analytical tools and concepts, analyze the internal organization of Japanese firms and various aspects of the market and non-market environments surrounding firms.

16 軽部　大 Karube Masaru, 日米半導体産業における制度と企業戦略——資源投入の二極分化の可能性について "Institutions and Corporate Strategy in the Japanese and U.S. Semiconductor Industries: Exploring the Possibility of Polarization in Resource Allocation,"「組織科学」31 巻 1 号, pp. 85-98, 組織学会, 1997.

This article indicates the differences between Japanese and American enterprise control strategies and resource allocation patterns with regard to semiconductor processing technology. It advocates that the possibility of externalizing operations through a U.S.-style economic system results in the resource allocation polarizing underdeveloped and developed areas.

17 中村圭介 Nakamura Keisuke,『日本の職場と生産システム』*Japan's Production System and the Organization of Work*, 268 pp., 東京大学出版会, 1996.

Based on the critical investigation of intellectual skill theory and the socio-technical system, this study links Japanese company workplaces and research in the three areas: (1) production management, (2) product development and (3) inter-enterprise relations as regards the division of labor through sub-contracting. Through case studies of large Japanese private enterprise manufacturing businesses, it analyzes all types of task organization within the workplace and reconstructs the Japanese production system as a whole.

II. Evolution Theory of Management Systems

01 藤本隆宏 Fujimoto Takahiro,『生産システムの進化論——トヨタ自動車にみる組織能力と創発プロセス』*The Theory of Evolution of a Production System: Organizational Capability and the Emerging Process in Toyota Motors*, 389 pp., 有斐閣, 1997.

Based on high quality primary source material regarding Toyota

Motors, this work discusses separately the rise and evolution of the emergent formation of production, product development and sales systems and the demonstration of competitiveness on the world market. (1) In regard to new ideas and suggestions, with a vertical internal selection mechanism in which the operation level decides the process with regard to potential customers and "production site first-ism" (*gemba shugi* 現場主義) acts as a mechanism for selection within the organization and (2) with settlement for any concept of a form acceptable in general to top and lower management and the labor unions, a horizontal expansion mechanism through which may be designated a sideways expansion disseminated rapidly to numerous factories is indicated as one key to the dynamic capability of Toyota.

02 青木昌彦・奥野（藤原）正寛（編）Aoki Masahiko and Okuno-Fujiwara Masahiro (eds.),『経済システムの比較制度分析』*Comparative Institutional Analysis: A New Approach to Economic Systems*, 353pp., 東京大学出版会，1996.

In actual economies, there exist, for instance, differing types of enterprises and systems, like Japanese-type enterprises and American-type enterprises. With regard to such phenomena, adopting an evolutionary game approach, in cases where multiple equilibria exist, this work seeks to analyze historical path dependence in terms of evolutionary equilibria with local asymptotic stability. In addition, Japan's main bank system and the relationships between government and industry are also examined.

03 高橋伸夫（編）Takahashi Nobuo (ed.),『未来傾斜原理──協調的な経営行動の進化』*Leaning on Future Principle: Evolution of Cooperative Administrative Behavior*, 250 pp., 白桃書房，1996.

This is a collection of articles which attempts to explain the occurrence of a lukewarm constitution and organizational activation in terms of applying Robert Axelrod's evolution of cooperation theory in the game theory to empirical management phenomena, such as the supplier system in the automobile industry, the research and development alliance in the pharmaceutical industry, and cross-licensing in the semiconductor industry. It is the first text to apply Axelrod's theory to the phenomena of management.

04 清水　剛 Shimizu Takashi, 有限反復囚人のジレンマにおける協調行動の進化 "Evolution of Cooperation in the Finitely Repeated Prisoner's Dilemma,"「行動計量学」24巻1号，pp. 101-111，日本行動計量学会，1997.

Following up Robert Axelrod's computer simulation and making clear the unexpected fact that in the model first used, tit for tat strategy, is not always strong, this work discusses the logic and conditions of the evolution of cooperation.

05 荒井一博 Arai Kazuhiro, 『終身雇用制と日本文化』 *The System of Lifetime Employment and Japanese Cluture*, 191 pp., 中央公論社, 1997.

III. Organizational Activation

01 河合忠彦 Kawai Tadahiko, 『戦略的組織革新』 *Strategic Organizational Innovation*, 277 pp., 有斐閣, 1996.

This work argues for spiral management with interactively used dual loops of the strategy formation process: a top-down type loop and a bottom-up type loop, and analyzes activated organizations in which it has been realized. Beginning with the case of Asahi Beer as an example of the framework employed, it makes a comparative analysis of the cases of the Japanese major electrical appliance manufacturers Sharp, Sony and Matsushita Electric.

02 高橋伸夫 Takahashi Nobuo, 『できる社員は「やり過ごす」』 *Proficient Company Employees "Sidetrack the Problems,"* 200 pp., ネスコ／文藝春秋, 1996.

In Japanese firms, when someone avoid completing his or her assigned tasks long enough, those sometimes become unnecessary. The superiors allow their subordinates to sidetrack the problems assigned a low priority. The author calls this phenomenon *"yarisugoshi"* in Japanese. This book takes its analysis from rich research data on the everyday organizational phenomena such as *"yarisugoshi"* and "taking the blame for another person" (*shirinugui* 尻ぬぐい) in Japanese firms. For example, in Japanese firms, there is a tendency toward tacit agreement that the cost of *"yarisugoshi"* is considered as a training cost or selection cost in the training of future executives or managers. And this is exactly why *"yarisugoshi"* is intended not to be restricted severely in Japanese firms. It is indicated that, thanks to these phenomena, organizational behavior and the system in Japanese firms are able to avoid failure even with utilizing on-the-job training to the fullest extent.

03 山下洋史 Yamashita Hiroshi, 『人的資源管理の理論と実際』 *Theory and Practice of Human Resource Management*, 217 pp., 東京経済情報出版, 1996.

04 土谷茂久 Tsuchiya Shigehisa, 『柔らかい組織の経営──現代社会のあいまいさにどう対応するか』 *Management of Soft Organizations: How Can the Ambiguity of Contemporary Society be Countered ?*, 237 pp., 同文館, 1996.

05   榊原清則 Sakakibara Kiyonori, 『美しい企業　醜い企業』 *Beautiful Enterprise and Ugly Enterprise*, 222 pp., 講談社, 1996.

By means of a comparison between Japanese companies and European companies, this work takes up organizational activation from the viewpoint of companies' esthetics with frequent occurrences of dramatic incidents and emotion-stirring dynamic theatrical-style events.

06   田尾雅夫（編）Tao Masao (ed.), 『「会社人間」の研究——組織コミットメントの理論と実際』 *A Study of "the Company Man": The Theory and Practice of Organizational Commitment*, 334 pp., 京都大学学術出版会, 1997.

A review of literature on the human type called a "company man" and their behavior, and how to discuss organizational commitment. It also examines the small size data using a questionnaire similar to the organizational commitment questionnaire (OCQ).

07   田尾雅夫・久保真人 Tao Masao and Kubo Masato, 『バーンアウトの理論と実際——心理学的アプローチ』 *The Theory and Practice of Burnout: A Psychological Approach*, 184 pp., 誠信書房, 1996.

This work reviews the literature on the symptoms and condition of the burnout syndrome along with the relationship of its causes and effects and its alleviation methods. It also analyzes the data of a questionnaire carried out with approximately one thousand nurses in Kyoto prefecture.

08   田尾雅夫・吉川肇子・高木浩人 Tao Masao, Kikkawa Toshiko, and Takagi Hiroto, 『コンピュータ化の経営管理』 *The Management of Computerization*, 298 pp., 白桃書房, 1996.

A review of studies dealing with organizational changes arising from computerization. It categorizes studies into the domains of bureaucracy, human relations, communication, technostress, and socio-technical systems.

IV. Corporate Governance

01   下谷政弘 Shimotani Masahiro, 『持株会社解禁』 *The Lifting of the Ban on Holding Companies*, 232 pp., 中央公論社, 1996.

This work looks back over past discussion surrounding the lifting of the ban on holding companies, historical developments up until the ban was imposed and the characteristics of postwar Japanese firms' internal organizations and industrial organizations. Japanese large scale companies succeeded in avoiding the bad effects of conglomeration. Therefore it is rather doubtful whether in fact the lifting of the ban will prove effective in economic revitalization.

02   稲上　毅 Inagami Takeshi, 『現代英国経営事情』 *Modern British Manage-*

ment, 299 pp., 日本労働研究機構, 1997.

Taken from the viewpoint of Anglo-American financial rivalry (deliberate spending, merger and acquisition) as opposed to the Japanese viewpoint of industrial rivalry (efficiency of production), this study analyzes modern British management. British-style management is defined as short-run management indifferent to investment in human capital under the strong influence of fickle or unstable shareholding by City-based shareholders. It emphasises the continuity of British-style management through financial control.

03 森川英正 Morikawa Hidemasa,『トップ・マネジメントの経営史』*Business History of Top Management*, 300 pp., 有斐閣, 1996.

In examining how the managerial enterprise emerged from the family company, this work indicates the deception of corporate governance as a source of the downfall of the bubble economy. It raises (1) main bank's pursuit of the profit-first principle having taken advantage of the Plaza Accord in 1985, (2) the big enterprises failed to see through the bubble due to their herd-behavior and (3) the loss of business ethics.

04 高村直助 Takamura Naosuke,『会社の誕生』*The Birth of the Company*, 220 pp., 吉川弘文館, 1996.

This book clarifies the process of formation and diffusion of private corporations in Japan in the latter half of the nineteenth century. The fact of the spread of private corporations in a comparatively short time indicates that, for instance, as the separation of ownership and management was widely practiced by the great merchant families of modern historical times, the prerequisites for the wide acceptance of private corporations had already matured in modern times.

05 宮川隆泰 Miyakawa Takayasu,『岩崎小彌太──三菱を育てた経営理念』*Iwasaki Koyata: The Business Philosophy Fostering Mitsubishi*, 292 pp., 中央公論社, 1996.

This work describes how Iwasaki Koyata, nephew of the Mitsubishi founder Iwasaki Yatarō 岩崎彌太郎, as owner-manager of the Mitsubishi *zaibatsu*, got through the troubled period of the first half of the twentieth century.

06 竹内常善・阿部武司・沢井 実 (編) Takeuchi Tsuneyoshi, Abe Takeshi, and Sawai Minoru (eds.),『近代日本における企業家の諸系譜』*The Genealogies of Entrepreneurs in Modern Japan*, 284 pp., 大阪大学出版会, 1996.

A historical analysis of the development of the Japanese ecomony is carried out through the biographical introduction of several managers of

Japanese small businesses.

07 後藤雅敏 Gotō Masatoshi,『会計と予測情報』*Accounting and Forecast Information*, 205 pp., 中央経済社, 1997.

The obligation in Japan for management to disclose its forecast information is a characteristic institution unique in the world. This work analyses financial news including the short comments, especially the forecasts made by managers, carried in the morning editions of the newspaper *Nihon Keizai Shimbun* 日本経済新聞. Through determination of the extent of influence of these forecasts on stock prices, it makes clear the significance of this system of forecast information disclosure. Regarding this system, even in an America proud of leading information disclosure, when in the first half of the 1970s an increase in the discussion of systems for forecast information disclosure occurred, a system of compulsory publication was not established.

08 伊藤元重 Itō Motoshige,『市場主義』*Market-Centrism*, 214 pp., 講談社, 1996.

09 今福愛志 Imafuku Aishi,『企業年金会計の国際比較』*An International Comparison of Corporate Pension Finance*, 430 pp., 中央経済社, 1996.

This work takes up the problems confronting Japanese company pension finance from an international standpoint. It investigates American, British, Canadian, and German pension finance standards and their practices, as well as international accounting standards, from different viewpoints of accounting theory, accounting systems, and actual facts. Focusing on (1) the interactive processes of pension finance standards and company pension systems and (2) the basic problems of company finance raised by pension finance it explores problematical points in the Japanese system of company pension finance.

10 高橋伸夫 (編) Takahashi Nobuo (ed.),『組織文化の経営学』*Management Theory of Organizational Culture*, 202 pp., 中央経済社, 1997.

According to modern organizational theory, participants of the organization are considered to include not only the workforce, but also stakeholders like employers, customers, and shareholders. Consequently, this work examines the most recent discussions on multinational companies, organizational learning theory, corporate identity, customer satisfaction, and corporate advertizing from the viewpoint of organizational culture which develops along the organizational network beyond the firms' boundary.

11 寺本義也・坂井種次・西村友幸 Teramoto Yoshiya, Sakai Taneji, and Nishimura Tomoyuki,『日本企業のコーポレートガバナンス』*Corporate*

Governance of Japanese Firms, 260 pp., 生産性出版, 1997.

V. Miscellaneous

01 延岡健太郎 Nobeoka Kentarō,『マルチプロジェクト戦略』*Multi-Project Strategy*, 221 pp., 有斐閣, 1996.

Based on automobile production, this book examines multi-project strategies concerned with optimizing the product portfolio of a corporation as a whole, without the loss of appeal of individual products.

02 林 伸二 Hayashi Shinji,『組織が活力を取りもどす──プロジェクトの立案から監査まで』*Recovering the Vitality of an Organization: From Project Preparation to Inspection*, 165 pp., 同友館, 1997.

03 電通総研 (編) Dentsu Institute for Human Studies (ed.),『民間非営利組織 NPO とは何か』*What are Nonprofit Organizations (NPOs)?*, 221 pp., 日本経済新聞社, 1996.

Beginning with a definition of the nonprofit organization, and a comparison between the current Japanese situation and that of the West, this work examines the distinctive features of the organization and the operation of an NPO by contrast with a government agency or private company.

04 三島祥宏 Mishima Yoshihiro,『コミュニティ財団のすべて』*All About Community Foundations*, 236 pp., 清文社, 1996.

This book sets out the history of American community foundations and their current state of activities and operations, such as the tax status, organizational type, capital, donations, and aid functions, followed by the current situation and problems of Japanese community foundations.

05 富沢賢治・川口清史 (編) Tomizawa Kenji and Kawaguchi Kiyofumi (eds.),『非営利・協同セクターの理論と現実──参加型社会システムを求めて』*The Theory and Current State of the Nonprofit and Cooperative Sectors: Toward a Participation Social System*, 440 pp., 日本経済評論社, 1997.

06 中牧弘允・日置弘一郎 (編) Nakamaki Hirochika and Hioki Kōichirō,『経営人類学ことはじめ──会社とサラリーマン』*Toward an Anthropology of Management*, 350 pp., 東方出版, 1997.

Company "ethnographic records" noted by the collaborative research group of the National Museum of Ethnology (国立民族学博物館) generated from the viewpoint of life records made up as synchronic "company records" not as diachronic company histories.

07 経営学史学会 (編) Society for the History of Management Studies (ed.),『アメリカ経営学の潮流』*Trends in American Management Studies* [経営学史学会年報 4], 234 pp., 文真堂, 1997.

08 加藤勝康 Katō Katsuyasu,『バーナードとヘンダーソン──The Func-

tions of the Executive の形成過程』 *Chester I. Barnard and William O. Henderson: The Formation Process of the Functions of the Executive*, 785 pp., 文真堂, 1996.

09 松田裕之 Matsuda Hiroyuki, 『AT&T を創った人びと――企業労務のイノベーション』 *The Founders of AT&T and Innovation in Labor Relations*, 244 pp., 日本経済評論社, 1996.

In a history of AT&T, taking up its subjects Chester I. Barnard, G. Elton Mayo, and Frederick Herzberg, who participated in the domain of personnel and labor relations, this work describes one pattern of the development of labor relations theory with the AT&T as its setting.

10 経営史学会 (編) Business History Society of Japan (ed), 『日本会社史研究総覧――経営史学会創立30周年記念』 *An Overview of Research into Japanese Company Histories: In Commemoration of the Thirtieth Anniversary of the Business History Society of Japan*, 553 pp., 文真堂, 1996.

SOCIOLOGY

Shōji Kōkichi
The University of Tokyo

I. INTRODUCTION

Under the coalition cabinet headed by Hashimoto Ryūtarō, which replaced Murayama Tomiichi's coalition cabinet, the Japanese government in 1996-97 attempted to rebuild Japan's politico-economic system by promoting administrative and financial reforms. But as a result of the rise in the consumption tax in April 1997 and the Asian financial crisis that began in the summer of the same year, the recession was exacerbated, and overall these two years passed in an atmosphere marked by a shift from stagnation to decline. In Okinawa, where the majority of U.S. military bases in Japan are located, there arose an anti-base movement following the rape of a schoolgirl by American servicemen in summer 1995, and in response to this the government succeeded in winning U.S. agreement to return several bases, including Futemma Air Station, but this gave rise to further problems concerning the location and form of substitute bases. In addition, there also emerged problems in the Japan-U.S. security system itself regarding the drawing up of guidelines for the post-Cold War era and the definition of "peripheral circumstances," and these produced fresh points of political contention. At the same time, Yamaichi Securities and many other companies, both large and small, closed down or went bankrupt, there occurred unheard-of incidents of juvenile crime such as the murder and decapitation of an elementary-school pupil by a middle-school student in Kobe, and heated debate about a nursing care insurance system continued as problems affecting the elderly grew more serious. These were all examples of increasing social problems that could be seen to point to a crisis in Japanese society.

Worthy of special mention among the responses of Japanese sociology to this situation was the Japan Sociological Society's annual conference held for the first time in Okinawa in November 1996, with a thematic section devoted to the question of "The Significance of Okinawa for Sociology," which attracted a large audience and saw some keen discussion. Issues raised included how to view Okinawa's twenty-seven years of U.S. military rule after 1945 from the perspective of postcolonialism, whether or not this long period away from Japanese rule had conversely led to the formation of an open viewpoint distinctive of Okinawa, and whether on the other hand it was perhaps the women who had had to bear the brunt of crimes stemming from the U.S. military bases. It should also be noted that the thematic section on the Great Hanshin Earthquake, in its third year since the 1995 annual conference, was brought to a close at the conference held in November 1997 at Chiba University.

The largest publication during the review period was a 27-volume series on contemporary sociology [I-01]. With regard to the history of Japanese sociology, there appeared a catalogue compiled by Kawai Takao [I-02] and a study of Shimmei Masamichi edited by Tanozaki Akio and Yamamoto Shizuo [I-03], while the history of Western sociology was dealt with by Akimoto Ritsuo [I-04]. There was also published a unique intro-duction to sociology compiled by Okumura Takashi with contri-butions by younger researchers [I-05], as well as a textbook on international sociology edited by Kajita Takamichi [I-06]. In the area of classical studies, there appeared a compilation of articles on K. Marx edited by Hosoya Takashi [I-07], two books on M. Weber by Orihara Hiroshi [I-08, 09], and works on American sociology, G. H. Mead and the Chicago school, subsequent devel-opments in Talcott Parsons's functionalism, and so on, by Yazawa Shūjirō [I-10], Kawamura Nozomu [I-11], Hōgetsu Makoto and Nakano Masataka [I-12], Funatsu Mamoru [I-13], Matsumoto Kazuyoshi [I-14], and Suzuki Takeshi [I-15]. In addition, Nasu

Hisashi [I-16] considered movements in the United States with a focus on phenomenological sociology, and Hasegawa Takao [I-17] reexamined the significance of theories of mass society, especially those of Ortega y Gasset. On the theoretical front too there appeared a variety of publications, including works by Sengoku Yoshirō [I-18], who explores new paradigms on the basis of a reexamination of Marxism, Watanabe Masuo [I-19], who aims for a structural grasp of daily life, Kajita Takamichi [I-20], who attempts to extend the horizons of international sociology with a focus on questions of ethnicity, Onda Morio [I-21], who seeks to construct an economic sociology of growth by incorporating the ideas of Karl Polanyi and others, and Tateiwa Shin'ya [I-22], who sets out to fundamentally rethink questions of private ownership from the prespective of control of the body.

II. JAPANESE SOCIETY: STRUCTURE AND CHARACTERISTICS

On the subject of the structure and characteristics of Japanese society, there appeared during the review period several outstanding books that trace Japan's social history from the Meiji era through to the postwar Shōwa era, and there were also published several works that attempt to clarify the problematic nature of Japanese society from the perspective of ethnicity. There also appeared some studies that probe the diversity of Japanese society with reference to historical sociology and life history.

Chief among studies of Japan's social history from the Meiji era through to the postwar Shōwa era were a study of the formulation and historical role of the Imperial Rescript on Education by Soeda Yoshiya [II-01], an account of the formation, development and demise of careerism by Takeuchi Hiroshi [II-02], and a book edited by Suzuki Masahito and Nakamichi Minoru [II-03] which provides a multifaceted analysis of postwar high economic growth and the resulting social changes.

In research on Japanese society from the perspective of ethnicity, Fukuoka Yasunori and Kim Myŏng-su [II-04] shed light on the lives and consciousness of young Korean residents in Japan on the basis of a sampling survey, while Komai Hiroshi and others [II-

05~08] consider in a variety of forms problems and policies relating to foreigners seeking to settle permanently in Japan, and a compilation by Miyajima Takashi and Kajita Takamichi [II-09] deals with issues concerning the citizenship of foreigners. Although somewhat limited in their scope, the books by Yamamoto Takeo [II-10] and Shimpo Mitsuru [II-11] may also be added to these.

In the field of historical sociology and life history, there appeared a volume edited by Tsutsui Kiyotada [II-12] that sheds light on the diversity of Japan's historical sociology on the basis of the classics of sociology, a compilation by the Kyoto Film Festival Executive Committee [II-13] commemorating one hundred years of films in Kyoto that approaches Japanese society from the perspective of period films, and books by Tani Tomio [II-14] and Kobayashi Tazuko [II-15] that consider the significance of life histories as a sociological method, as well as a study by Katagiri Masataka [II-16], who considers the sociology of privacy from his own original perspective. In addition, mention may also be made of books on the social role of education by Tanaka Setsuo [II-17] and by Arimoto Akira and Ehara Takekazu [II-18].

III. POPULATION DYNAMICS AND THE FAMILY

With regard to population dynamics and the family, aging and its influence on the family continued to be the main focus of interest, but at the same time there also appeared some unique studies of the social history of the family, as well as comparative research extending to all of East Asia.

Representative of research on the aging of the population were a report brought out by the Population and Household Study Group [III-01] and a volume edited by Atō Makoto [III-02]. In addition, there also appeared a book by Furuta Takahiko [III-03] and a report by Hiroshima Kiyoshi *et al.* [III-04].

On the subject of the family, the volumes edited by Kumagai Fumie [III-05, 06] deal with the regional characteristics of the family in Japan, while farming families are discussed by Ishihara Toyomi [III-07] and the conditions of the contemporary family in a work edited by Nonoyama Hisaya, Sodei Takako and Shinozaki Masami [III-08]. Muta Kazue [III-09] and Sakamoto Kazue [III-10] both describe the formation of the modern family in Japan and its different aspects from their own unique perspectives. Yamada Masahiro [III-11], Yoshizumi Kyōko [III-12], and Miyamoto Michiko, Iwakami Mami and Yamada Masahiro [III-13], all making use of relevant data, attempt to shed light on changes in marriage, the rise in nonlegal marriages, and parent-child relationships in a society in which greater numbers of people are either not marrying or marrying later in life. In addition, Kasugai Noriko [III-14] discusses relations between mothers and grown-up daughters in the context of the breakup of the family into the separate life courses of its members, while Sechiyama Kaku [III-15] compares the conditions of families in the main countries of East Asia from the perspective of patriarchalism as a feminist concept in an attempt to open up a new field in family and gender studies.

In addition, questions of aging in Japanese society are dealt with in a volume edited by Hamaguchi Haruhiko [III-16] and in a dictionary compiled by Sagaza Haruo *et al.* [III-17]. Hatanaka Munekazu [III-18], on the other hand, considers the type of systems desirable for supporting families with children in a society in which people are having fewer children.

IV. The Community: Rural and Urban

On the subject of rural villages, cities, and local communities formed in between the two or straddling both, there appeared studies that trace the long-term transformation of rural and fishing villages, research attempting to depict the diversity of local communities, and works on the modernization and internationalization of urban society and on palnning geared to the needs of people living in cities.

Starting with rural villages, Kitahara Atsushi [IV-01] reconsiders the significance of Japan's rural communities through a comparison with Thai villages, while Nakano Takashi [IV-02] tries to ascertain the end results of the modernization of Japanese society by delineating the process of four centuries of change in a fishing village in the Hokuriku region. By way of contrast, Hasegawa Akihiko [IV-03] deals in particular with the transformation of rural society in the postwar era, and the book coauthored by Hasegawa, Fujisawa Yawara, Takemoto Tamotsu and Arahi Yutaka [IV-04] and that by Yamamoto Tsutomu [IV-05] discuss the state of underpopulation resulting from rural transformation and related problems.

In research on local society covering both rural and urban areas, Yamamoto Eiji, Takahashi Akiyoshi and Hasumi Otohiko [IV-06] edited a work on towns and villages in Okinawa, an important issue during the review period, and in addition there appeared volumes edited by Seino Masayoshi [IV-07], dealing with a small town in the Tōhoku region, and by Miura Noriko, Suzuki Hiroshi, Kinoshita Kenji and Toyota Kenji [IV-08] on the revitalization of villages and towns throughout Kyushu. Nor should one overlook the study by Kouchi Tōru [IV-09], who essays a typology of local community on the basis of changes in postwar Japan's local community, the book by Iwaki Sadayuki [IV-10] on local society during industrial changes, and the examination of issues in local politics by Kasuga Masashi [IV-11].

As regards cities, there appeared the collected works of Okui Fukutarō [IV-12], a former leading scholar of urban sociology, and a volume edited by Hasumi Otohiko, Nitagai Kamon and Yazawa Sumiko [IV-13], which demonstrates the contributions that the study of the sociology of communities can make to urban sociology. In addition, the volume edited by Satō Kenji [IV-14] considers cities from the perspectives of social history and semantics, while that edited by Yoshihara Naoki [IV-15] addresses the conceptualizing power of urban space, that edited Okuda Michihiro [IV-16] depicts various aspects of cities from the viewpoint of ethnicity, and Hashimoto Kazutaka [IV-17] deals with social planning for the enrichment of the lives of city-dwellers. Mention should also be made of the book compiled by Nakata Minoru [IV-18] on neighborhood associations (*chōnaikai*) and community's self-governing associations (*jichikai*), which underpin the foundations of Japanese cities.

V. INDUSTRY, LABOR, CLASS AND SOCIAL STRATIFICATION

On the subject of industry, labor, class and social stratification, there appeared a new type of research on labor-management relations and organizations, and a study of unions directed by a veteran researcher was also brought to fruition, but generally speaking research in this field was not very productive during the review period.

The only publications on industrial sociology were a volume edited by Inuzuka Susumu [V-01] and a book by Haneda Arata [V-02], apart from which there appeared a volume on business management in an information society edited by Aoyama Hideo and Kojima Shigeru [V-03] and a book on the sociology of organizations by Sawada Zentarō [V-04]. Alone in this field, Ogiso Michio [V-05] could be said to have made a creditable contribution with a study of several Japanese corporations on the basis of his own model of organizations. The study of management conditions in Great Britain by Inagami Takeshi [V-06] is a meticulous work, but it does not deal with management conditions in contemporary Japan.

Yamada Nobuyuki [V-07], on the other hand, takes a broad view of labor-management relations from his own distinctive perspective and attempts to develop a new vision of the sociology of industry and work suited to an age of internationalization. In addition, the social history of white-collar workers by Susato Shigeru [V-08] and the study of Japanese production systems transplanted to the United States by Kumagai Fumie [V-09] should not be overlooked either. About the only notable study on labor was that on union identity and union leaders brought to completion under the direction of Inagami Takeshi [V-10].

As for class and social stratification, nothing of consequence was published, largely because the analysis of the fifth SSM (social stratification and social mobility) survey, conducted in 1995, is still underway. Since the end of the Cold War, studies of class and social stratification with a Marxist orientation have gone completely out of vogue, but some younger researchers taking part in the SSM survey and so on are exploring new possibilities.

156

VI. Mass Communications and Social Consciousness

In the field of mass communications and social consciousness, there appeared a number of works dealing with the changes in information behavior and information life that have accompanied increasing use of multimedia, as well as several noteworthy studies that probe the state of the social consciousness of the Japanese.

On the subject of mass communications and information life, there appeared first of all a work by Hanada Tatsurō [VI-01] that considers questions relating to the public sphere with reference to J. Habermas, as well as a volume edited by Tazaki Tokurō and Funatsu Mamoru [VI-02] that discusses a shift from information society theory to social information theory and a book by Narita Yasuaki [VI-03] on the culture of media space. The volume edited by the University of Tokyo Institute of Socio-Information and Communication Studies [VI-04], on the other hand, examines the information behavior of the Japanese by means of a careful analysis based on a sampling survey, while Mizuno Hirosuke, Nakamura Isao, Korenaga Ron and Kiyohara Keiko [VI-05] and Kojima Kazuto and Hashimoto Yoshiaki [VI-06], using different methods, show how the information life and social life of the Japanese have become more multifaceted and composite with increasing media diversification. In addition, Kobayashi Shūichi [VI-07] inquires into the state of contemporary people, becoming as they are "media people" with the development of different media, while Kawasaki Taisuke and Shibata Tetsuji [VI-08], basing themselves on their experiences as journalists, attempt to expose problems in contemporary Japanese journalism, and both of these books could be said to make original contributions to their respective fields.

As regards social consciousness, firstly the volume edited by Watanuki Jōji and Miyake Ichirō [VI-09] attempts to gain a grasp of changes in the voting behavior of the Japanese on the basis of nationwide panel surveys conducted between 1993 and 1996, and it provides much information that is helpful for understanding the voting behavior and political and social attitudes of the Japanese during this period, which saw the collapse of the 1955 regime. Yoshino Kōsaku [VI-10] has rewritten for Japanese readers his English book mentioned in Volume IX-1 of this series ([II-26]), and it contains sufficient improvements and additions to make it worth rereading as an independent work. Lastly, the book by Mashiko Hidenori [VI-11] deserves to be consulted as a critique of Japanese ideology by an author with his own critical perspective on the Japanese language and Japanese culture.

VII. SOCIAL PROBLEMS AND SOCIAL WELFARE

In the field of social problems and social welfare, not only were a comparatively large number of works published especially on social problems, but there also appeared the results of a new type of research that points to a new direction for the future.

On the subject of social problems, there appeared first of all several works on the Great Hanshin Earthquake, including an examination by Noda Takashi [VII-01] from the basic perspective of the sociology of disasters, a report by Sasaki Masamichi [VII-02] on the actual damage caused by the earthquake, and a volume compiled by Urano Masaki, Ōyane Jun, and Tsuchiya Junji [VII-03]. Next, in the area of environmental sociology there appeared a study by Torigoe Hiroyuki [VII-04] indicative of the level of Japanese environmental sociology, as well as a volume edited by Torigoe [VII-05] on questions pertaining to the environment and life-style, two books by Inoue Takao [VII-06, 07] dealing with the placing of the Shirakami Mountains on the World Heritage List and with the preservation of the environment, and an investigation of the risks surrounding nuclear power generation by Hasegawa Kōichi [VII-08]. As regards questions of discrimination, the most important publication was a series of four books edited by Kurihara Akira [VII-09].

Turning now to crime, the book by Ayukawa Jun [VII-10], although an introductory work, provides an overview of conditions in Japan, while Maniwa Mitsuyuki [VII-11] discusses youth and juvenile crime in postwar Japan in terms of socio-cultural history, and Sakurai Tetsuo [VII-12] touches on the cultural background to juvenile crime in Japan. Also not to be overlooked are the book by Takahara Masaoki [VII-13], who deals with juvenile delinquency from the perspective of social pathology, and the study by Yajima Masami [VII-14], who considers juvenile delinquency in terms of culture. But even more important than these studies are the research by Noguchi Yūji [VII-15], who regards alcoholism as a form of self-addiction and links it to modern ills, the examination of women's dietary disorders in relation to gender issues by Asano Chie [VII-16], and the book by Nakane Mitsutoshi [VII-17], who attempts to present a fresh view of social problems from the vantage point of questions relating to survey techniques and from the perspective of constructivism.

As for social welfare, there appeared a volume compiled by Sodei Takako, Takahashi Hiroshi and Hiraoka Kōichi [VII-18] which brings together the most important articles on social welfare and medical care produced by Japan's postwar sociology, as well as an introduction to welfare in contemporary Japan by Suga Kazuhiko [VII-19]. Welfare for the elderly is dealt with in volumes edited by Nishishita Akitoshi and Asano Hitoshi [VII-20] and Takahashi Yūetsu and Takahagi Tateo [VII-21] and in books by Kaneko Isamu [VII-22] and Ogawa Takeo [VII-23]. In addition, Gotō Sumie [VII-24] discusses the relationship between the contemporary family and welfare, while Hatanaka Munekazu [VII-25] considers questions pertaining to the welfare of families with children as a premise for his study mentioned earlier ([III-18]).

VIII. CULTURAL TRANSFORMATION AND SOCIAL MOVEMENT

On the subject of cultural transformation and social movement, there emerged during the review period several new types of research that could be said to presage the advent of the twenty-first century.

First, with regard to religion, the volume edited by Iida Takeshi, Nakano Takeshi and Yamanaka Hiroshi [VIII-01] discusses the question of nationalism, which has experienced a resurgence since about the same time as the "revival of religion," while Ōsawa

Masachi [VIII-02] inquires into the background to the Aum Shinrikyō incident and probes the darker side of contemporary Japanese society. Also instructive for considering these issues is the book coauthored by Hashizume Daizaburō, Kure Tomofusa, Ōtsuki Takahiro and Mishima Hiroshi [VIII-03]. At the same time, one cannot ignore the fact that questions of the emotions have been attracting the interest of young people in particular, and the book by Okahara Masayuki, Yamada Masahiro, Yasukawa Hajime and Ishikawa Jun [VIII-04] shows that the sociology of emotions has begun to take definite shape in Japan too. Meanwhile, the fact that the books by Takahashi Yoshinori [VIII-05] and Tominaga Shigeki [VIII-06] have been well received by younger people, even though they belong rather to the older type of sociology of literature, probably reflects this change of mood in Japanese society.

Moving on to women and feminism, the volume edited by Ueno Chizuko and Watanuki Reiko [VIII-07] deals with questions of reproductive health in relation to environmental issues, while the study edited by Toshitani Nobuyoshi, Yuzawa Yasuhiko, Sodei Takako and Shinozuka Hideko [VIII-08] addresses the life-style of women who have graduated from women's universities with good academic credentials, and the compilation by Muramatsu Yasuko [VIII-09] discusses ways for women who enter the natural science courses to make the most of their potential. In addition, Amano Masako first deals with "consumers" (*seikatsu-sha*) from the perspective of social history [VIII-10], on the basis of which she then explores ways whereby women can take account of and still transcend feminism and make the most of their historical experiences [VIII-11]. These issues with bearings on social movements have been a long-term focus of Satō Yoshiyuki's research, condensed in a new book [VIII-12] representing a sociology of social movements focussing on consumers' cooperatives, in which women have been the main participants, and this book could be said to exemplify the level reached by research in this field of Japanese sociology. With regard to the sociology of consumer movements, reference can also be made to the study by Ōhashi Matsuyuki [VIII-13].

On the subject of youth, there appeared only a collection of essays by Kurihara Akira [VIII-14], and similarly there appeared little research of note on the sociology of sport apart from a book supervised by Komuku Hiroshi [VIII-15]. However, one cannot overlook the fact that research on sexuality, differing somewhat in its focus from gender studies, is attracting the interest of young people. The book by Akagawa Manabu [VIII-16], dealing with pornography, attempts to open up a new field in social history, while the book edited by Yajima Masami [VIII-17], for the compilation of which many young people were mobilized, brings together the stories of homosexuals, who have until now remained below the surface of Japanese society, and it attempts to alter perceptions of Japanese society by bringing this subculture out into the open. In addition, the study of bathing by Matsudaira Makoto [VIII-18] and the compilation by Kumazawa Makoto, Kiyoshi Mahito and Kimoto Kimiko [VIII-19], seeking to expose one aspect of Japanese society by focussing on the inner world of film buffs, could be described as pioneering works in the field of cultural studies in Japan.

Even more noteworthy is the fact that moves to deal squarely with "metamorphosis," diametrically opposite to "identity," and to construct a sociology of *homo movens*, or man as an inveterate traveller, have been taking definite shape. An example of the former is the volume edited by Miyahara Kōjirō and Ogino Masahiro [VIII-20], which sets out to evaluate metamorphosis, characterized by oblivion, in positive terms, and an example of the latter is the book by Niihara Michinobu [VIII-21], which has the air of a self-portrait of a young sociologist exploring a new society as he makes repeated visits to Sardinia in Italy. Should these new experiments join up with the fruits of researchers who have been searching for links with the third world, as exemplified by the volume compiled by Tsurumi Yoshiyuki and Miyauchi Taisuke [VIII-22], and with works such as that by Tsurumi Kazuko [VIII-23], who has been persistently seeking a form of "endogenous development" uninfluenced by the model of Western modernity, then there is a possibility that there will emerge in Japan too a social movement of young people with new global perspectives.

BIBLIOGRAPHY

I. Introduction

01 井上　俊・上野千鶴子・大澤真幸・見田宗介・吉見俊哉（編）Inoue Shun, Ueno Chizuko, Ōsawa Masachi, Mita Munesuke and Yoshimi Shun'ya (eds.),『岩波講座　現代社会学』*Iwanami Lecture Series: Contemporary Sociology*, 26 vols.+1 sep. vol., 岩波書店, 1995-97.

Vol. 1, 『現代社会の社会学』*The Sociology of Contemporary Society*, 231 pp., 1997.

Vol. 2, 『自我・主体・アイデンティティ』*Self, Subject, and Identity*, 228 pp., 1995.

Vol. 3, 『他者・関係・コミュニケーション』*Others, Relationships, and Communication*, 232 pp., 1995.

Vol. 4, 『身体と間身体の社会学』*The Sociology of Corporality and Intercorporality*, 254 pp., 1996.

Vol. 5, 『知の社会学／言語の社会学』*The Sociology of Knowledge/ The Sociology of Language*, 222 pp., 1996.

Vol. 6, 『時間と空間の社会学』*The Sociology of Time and Space*, 225 pp., 1996.

Vol. 7, 『〈聖なるもの／呪われたもの〉の社会学』*The Sociology of the "Sacred" and the "Cursed,"* 201 pp., 1996.

Vol. 8, 『文学と芸術の社会学』*The Sociology of Literature and Art*, 216 pp., 1996.

Vol. 9, 『ライフコースの社会学』*The Sociology of Life Course*, 221 pp., 1996.

Vol. 10, 『セクシュアリティの社会学』*The Sociology of Sexuality*, 249 pp., 1996.

Vol. 11, 『ジェンダーの社会学』*The Sociology of Gender*, 243 pp., 1995.

Vol. 12, 『こどもと教育の社会学』*The Sociology of Children and Education*, 225 pp., 1996.

Vol. 13, 『成熟と老いの社会学』*The Sociology of Maturity and Old Age*, 214 pp., 1997.

Vol. 14, 『病と医療の社会学』*The Sociology of Illness and Medical Care*, 238 pp., 1996.

Vol. 15, 『差別と共生の社会学』*The Sociology of Discrimination and Symbiosis*, 248 pp., 1996.

Vol. 16, 『権力と支配の社会学』*The Sociology of Power and Control*, 216 pp., 1996.

Vol. 17, 『贈与と市場の社会学』*The Sociology of Gift and the Market*,

194 pp., 1996.

Vol. 18,『都市と都市化の社会学』 *The Sociology of Cities and Urbanization*, 248 pp., 1996.

Vol. 19,『〈家族〉の社会学』 *The Sociology of the "Family,"* 256 pp., 1996.

Vol. 20,『仕事と遊びの社会学』 *The Sociology of Work and Play*, 202 pp., 1995.

Vol. 21,『デザイン・モード・ファッション』 *Design, Modes, and Fashion*, 234 pp., 1996.

Vol. 22,『メディアと情報化の社会学』 *The Sociology of Media and Informationalization*, 256 pp., 1996.

Vol. 23,『日本文化の社会学』 *The Sociology of Japanese Culture*, 233 pp., 1996.

Vol. 24,『民族・国家・エスニシティ』 *Nations, States, and Ethnicity*, 263 pp., 1996.

Vol. 25,『環境と生態系の社会学』 *The Sociology of the Environment and Ecosystem*, 203 pp., 1996.

Vol. 26,『社会構想の社会学』 *The Sociology of the Conceptualization of Society*, 175 pp., 1996.

Sep. Vol.,『現代社会学の理論と方法』 *The Theories and Methods of Contemporary Sociology*, 305 pp., 1997.

02 川合隆男 （編） Kawai Takao (ed.),『近代日本社会学関係雑誌記事目録』 *Catalogue of Journal Articles Related to Modern Japanese Sociology* 19＋444＋296 pp., 龍渓書舎, 1997.

This volume consists of an introductory section (with an introduction, table of contents, explanatory remarks, and specimens of journals included), the catalogue itself, and an author index. It lists the titles and authors of articles, etc., found in more than 30 journals, ranging from the early-Meiji *Meiroku Zasshi*『明六雑誌』(1874-85) to just before the inauguration of *Shakaigaku Hyōron*『社会学評論』(1950), and it is a useful source of information on the activities and achievements of Japanese sociology during this period.

03 田野崎昭夫・山本鎭雄 （編） Tanozaki Akio and Yamamoto Shizuo (eds.),『新明社会学の研究——論考と資料』 *A Study of Shimmei Masamichi's Sociology: Articles and Materials*, v＋473 pp., 時潮社, 1996.

A collection of studies relating to the sociology of Shimmei Masamichi 新明正道, a representative sociologist of Japan who was active from the prewar to postwar period and died in 1984. It provides insights into the significance of Shimmei's sociology and the activities of sociologists who matured under his influence, and it is helpful for understanding the circumstances of Japanese sociology.

04 秋元律郎 Akimoto Ritsuo,『市民社会と社会学思考の系譜』*The Genealogy of Civil Society and Sociological Thinking*, vi＋327＋ix pp., 御茶の水書房, 1997.

An example of how the sociological thought of the West is interpreted from the perspective of Japanese sociology.

05 奥村　隆（編）Okumura Takashi （ed.）,『社会学になにができるか』*What Can Sociology Achieve ?*, xi＋410＋10 pp., 八千代出版, 1997.

06 梶田孝道（編）Kajita Takamichi （ed.）,『国際社会学——国家を超える現象をどうとらえるか』*International Sociology: How to Understand Phenomena That Transcend the State* (2nd ed.), viii＋350 pp., 名古屋大学出版会, 1996.

07 細谷　昂（編）Hosoya Takashi （ed.）,『現代社会学とマルクス』*Contemporary Sociology and Marx*, 495 pp., アカデミア出版会, 1997.

A collection of articles by the leading authority on Marx among Japanese sociologist and by his pupils. It is divided into two parts, the first on Marx and the second on Weber, etc., with each consisting of 8 articles. The overall tone of the volume is set by Hosoya's article "Marx on Future Society," in which he writes: "Influenced by the designation 'Communism', his thesis concerning the social ownership of means of production... has been misunderstood to represent... all of Marx's image of future society,... and Marx's ideas on the flowering of the individual and society have been completely, or almost completely, neglected. This has, I believe, had important consequences in a practical sense too."

08 折原　浩 Orihara Hiroshi,『ヴェーバー「経済と社会」の再構成——「トルソ」の頭』*A Reconstruction of M. Weber's "Economy and Society": The Head of the "Torso,"* vi＋350 pp., 東京大学出版会, 1996.

An attempt to reconstruct M. Weber's *Wirtschaft und Gesellschaft* by the leading authority on Weber in the field of Japanese sociology. "In Japan's academe, which had its beginnings in the acceptance of European scholarship, there is still no end to the local tendency to vie in chasing the latest achievements from Europe and America (including 'positive applications'), but if the steady accumulation of meticulous basic research were to bear fruit so that the classics of the social sciences were promptly reconstructed critically and fundamentally and dispatched back to Europe, then the situation in Japan might perhaps change a little too." (p. 334)

09 折原　浩 Orihara Hiroshi,『ヴェーバーとともに 40 年——社会科学の古

164

典を学ぶ』 *Forty Years in the Company of Weber: Studying the Classics of the Social Sciences*, 208 pp., 弘文堂, 1996.

10 矢澤修次郎 Yazawa Shūjirō, 『アメリカ知識人の思想——ニューヨーク社会学者の群像』 *The Ideas of American Intellectuals: A Tableau of Sociologists in New York*, 325+ix pp., 東京大学出版会, 1996.

11 河村 望 Kawamura Nozomu, 『G. H. ミードと伊波普猷』 *G. H. Mead and Iha Fuyū*, 349 pp., 新樹社, 1996.

This book first examines the philosophy of J. Dewey and Mead, who established American pragmatism, as well as the latter's ideas on communication in particular, and then goes on to consider Yanagita Kunio 柳田國男 and Iha Fuyū, who under the influence of these two Americans set about developing Japanology and the study of Japanese society, and special attention is given to the process whereby Iha founded modern Okinawan studies. It is a painstaking study that will provide many leads for those interested in the significance of Okinawa 沖縄 for Japanese society and also in theories about the Japanese people, Japanese culture and Japanese society.

12 宝月 誠・中野正大 (編) Hōgetsu Makoto and Nakano Masataka (eds.), 『シカゴ社会学の研究——初期モノグラフを読む』 *Studies in the Chicago School of Sociology: Reading the Early Monographs*, xvii+595+xiii pp., 恒星社厚生閣, 1997.

13 船津 衛 (編) Funatsu Mamoru (ed.), 『G. H. ミードの世界』 *The World of G. H. Mead*, 190 pp., 恒星社厚生閣, 1997.

14 松本和良 Matsumoto Kazuyoshi, 『パーソンズの社会学理論』 *Talcott Parsons's Theory of Sociology*, 180+7 pp., 恒星社厚生閣, 1997.

15 鈴木健之 Suzuki Takeshi, 『社会学者のアメリカ——機能主義からネオ機能主義へ』 *The America of Sociologists: From Functionalism to Neo-Functionalism*, v+148+xxviii pp., 恒星社厚生閣, 1997.

16 那須 壽 Nasu Hisashi, 『現象学的社会学への道』 *The Path to Phenomenological Sociology*, 209+xvi+vii pp., 恒星社厚生閣, 1997.

17 長谷川高生 Hasegawa Takao, 『大衆社会のゆくえ——オルテガ政治哲学：現代社会批判の視座』 *The Future of Mass Society: The Political Philosophy of Ortega y Gasset—A Perspective for a Critique of Contemporary Society*, x+278+23 pp., ミネルヴァ書房, 1996.

18 千石好郎 Sengoku Yoshirō, 『社会体制論の模索——パラダイム革新への助走』 *Searching for a Theory of Social Systems: The Run-up to Paradigm Reform*, viii+337 pp., 晃洋書房, 1997.

Consisting of 4 parts divided into 12 chapters, this book discusses the starting point of the Marxist theory of social systems; the development of class theory; state, class, and social systems; and the information revolution and the transformation of social systems. Taking account of the traditions of Marxist social science in postwar Japan, it is a major opus which summarizes the debates about paradigm reform that took place in the area of Neo-Marxism and affiliated fields in the 1970s and 1980s and attempts to apply contemporary Marxism to an understanding of the system underlying contemporary society, marked as it is by advances in the information revolution.

19　渡邊益男 Watanabe Masuo,『生活の構造的把握の理論──新しい生活構造論の構築をめざして』*Theories for a Structural Grasp of Daily Life: Towards the Construction of a New Theory of Life Structure*, x+334 pp., 川島書店, 1996.

20　梶田孝道 Kajita Takamichi,『国際社会学のパースペクティブ──越境する文化・回帰する文化』 *The Perspective of International Sociology: Culture That Crosses Borders and Culture That Comes Back*, 320+iii pp., 東京大学出版会, 1996.

21　恩田守雄 Onda Morio,『発展の経済社会学』*The Economic Sociology of Growth*, 528 pp., 文眞堂, 1997.

22　立岩真也 Tateiwa Shin'ya,『私的所有論』 *On Private Ownership*, xv+445+66 pp., 文眞堂, 1997.

II. Japanese Society: Structure and Characteristics

01　副田義也 Soeda Yoshiya,『教育勅語の社会史──ナショナリズムの創出と挫折』 *The Social History of the Imperial Rescript on Education: The Creation and Breakdown of Nationalism*, x+369 pp., 有信堂, 1997.

A historico-sociological study of the Imperial Rescript on Education (*Kyōiku Chokugo*), which served as the linchpin of ideological control in prewar Japan. It is divided into 6 chapters, dealing with the prehistory of the rescript, textual criticism and characterization of its content, philosophical conflict surrounding the rescript, its functions and effects, supplementary edicts, and its abolition, and Soeda clarifies the formation, expansion and collapse of the prewar Japanese state and society from the perspective of educational control. Based on the perception that "education is politics" and that it was the state bureaucrats of prewar Japan who put this into practice by means of school education, this study also touches on the nature of the Japanese people and Japanese culture, and in this sense it could be said to represent a development of the same author's『日本文化試論』 *A Tentative Theory of Japanese Culture* (see Vol. X-1, [II-07] of this series). Valuable source materials are also cited in the course of the historical accounts and analyses presented by the author, and so it is essential reading for those intending to do research in this field.

02 竹内　洋 Takeuchi Hiroshi,『立身出世主義——近代日本のロマンと欲望』 *Careerism: The Dreams and Desires of Modern Japan,* 332 pp., 日本放送出版協会, 1997.

A social history of modern Japan as seen from the viewpoint of career-ism, divided into 12 chapters. The author describes how "the mechanism of examinees" established in the late Meiji era produced "an educated élite" and, notwithstanding "discord" between this élite and those unable to avail themselves of this apparatus, promoted the modernization of Japan, only to come to an end in "the anomie of an affluent society" that resulted from postwar high economic growth. According to Takeuchi, "type-I examination society," underpinned by a credentialist society and tales of success, still possesses a certain vitality, but "mass examination society (＝type-II examination society)," in which the majority of people become caught up in exams, is "a factory for producing empty subjective entities raised by the system," "resonating" admirably with postmodern thought, which "gives priority to structure rather than subject and to system rather than desires." This too is an indispensable book for con-sidering the present state of Japanese society.

03 鈴木正仁・中道　實（編）Suzuki Masahito and Nakamichi Minoru (eds.),『高度成長の社会学』 *The Sociology of High Economic Growth,* x＋240 pp., 世界思想社, 1997.

The fruit of a joint study by 10 scholars, including the editors, which sets out to reexamine postwar Japan's high economic growth from the perspective of the 1990s. It is divided into three parts, entitled "Building High Economic Growth," "Living through High Economic Growth" and "Looking at High Economic Growth" and consisting of three, five and two articles respectively. Part 1 deals with the history of industrial con-trols, which made high economic growth possible, the development of power resources and the Ministry of Construction's administration of rivers, and the medical industry and the problems of adverse drug reaction; Part 2 discusses questions pertaining to an "affluent" society and the aging of society on the basis of how high economic growth was viewed by economists, homemakers, villagers and youg people; and Part 3 compares Japan's high economic growth with that of China and considers its social and cultural outcomes. There is also a chronological table, and it consti-tutes a handy introduction to the social history of postwar Japan. There is much of interest to researchers of Japanese studies, including Chap. 1 (Aoki Yasuhiro 青木康容), which examines the debate surrounding the

1940 regime and other premises of high economic growth, and Chap. 10 (Suzuki), which discusses the merits and demerits of the changes brought about by high economic growth.

04 福岡安則・金　明秀 Fukuoka Yasunori and Kim Myŏng-su, 『在日韓国人青年の生活と意識』 *The Lives and Consciousness of Young Korean Residents in Japan*, xvi＋226 pp., 東京大学出版会, 1997.

A report on a survey of young Korean residents in Japan conducted in 1993, with 1, 723 samples, of which 800 (46.4%) were returned. The survey covered issues such as social stratification, ethnic education, identity, ethnic associations, attachment to Japan, use of Korean names, desire to become naturalized and retention of Korean nationality, formation of ethnicity, discrimination and ethnicity, and diversity of life-styles, and it provides an outlook for future directions in coexistence. Important facts to come out of this survey are that Japan's labor market is becoming more open to young Koreans; ethnic education is conducted chiefly at home; a sense of ethnic inferiority is often overcome through ethnic education and participation in ethnic associations; there is strong attachment to Japan; 80% use their Japanese names when dealing with Japanese; they are ambivalent about whether to become naturalized or retain their Korean nationality; ethnicity is either transmitted through social relations or acquired through subjective inclination; mediated by a sense of relative deprivation and a sense of ethnic inferiority, experiences of discrimination have an influence on the formation of ethnicity; and life-styles are becoming more and more diversified. As a full-scale survey of an ethnic minority in Japan, this is an extremely useful study.

05 駒井　洋 (編集代表)・石井由香・下平好博・平石正美・若林チヒロ (編) Komai Hiroshi (ed. rep.), Ishii Yuka, Shimodaira Yoshihiro, Hiraishi Masami and Wakabayashi Chihiro (eds.), 『新来・定住外国人がわかる事典』 *A Dictionary for Understanding Newly Arrived and Permanently Settled Foreigners*, 288 pp., 明石書店, 1997.

This book, with contributions by 42 researchers, including the editors, adopts the format of a dictionary to explain improtant matters relating to foreigners who have newly arrived in Japan as well as those who may wish to settle permanently in Japan. It is a useful work for investigating the actual conditions of foreigners in Japan, the legal system as it relates to foreigners, and the responses to foreigners on the part of Japanese society.

06 駒井　洋・渡戸一郎 (編) Komai Hiroshi and Watado Ichirō (eds.), 『自治体の外国人政策──内なる国際化への取り組み』 *Local Government Policies for Foreigners: The Engagement with Internal Internationaliza-*

tion, 466 pp., 明石書店, 1997.

In addition to an introduction and explanatory remarks by the editors, this book describes policies for foreigners in important local governments, with contributions by 15 researchers. The search for systematic policies is exemplified by Kawasaki city, Yokohama city, Kanagawa prefecture, and Tokyo; policies for foreign workers are exemplified by Hamamatsu city, Ōta city, Ōizumi town, and Gumma prefecture; coexistence in inner city areas is exemplified by Shinjuku-ku (Tokyo), Toshima-ku (Tokyo), Osaka city, and Osaka prefecture; and engagement with particular issues is illustrated by the Mogami region (Yamagata prefecture), Kōbe city, Tsukuba city, and Okinawa prefecture.

07 駒井　洋 Komai Hiroshi, 『日本のエスニック社会』 *Ethnic Society in Japan*, 379 pp., 明石書店, 1996.

In this book 11 researchers (exculding the editor) describe the consciousness and behavior of different foreigners living in Japan. It is an example of ethnicity studies in Japan.

08 渡戸一郎 (編) Watado Ichirō (ed.), 『自治体政策の展開と NGO』 *Developments in Local Government Policies and NGOs* [「講座・外国人定住問題」第 4 巻], 337 pp., 明石書店, 1996.

09 宮島　喬・梶田孝道 (編) Miyajima Takashi and Kajita Takamichi (eds.), 『外国人労働者から市民へ――地域社会の視点と課題から』 *From Foreign Workers to Citizens: From the Perspectives and Issues of Local Society*, xiii+237 pp., 有斐閣, 1996.

An examination by 12 researchers (including the editors) of the requisites for foreigners to become citizens of another country. Although overseas examples are also cited, the majority of examples are drawn from Japan. The main topics covered are medical care and social security, housing, family problems, political rights, Japanese-language education and native-language education, gender bias, and the labor market. Also useful are the basic statistics and chronological table.

10 山本剛郎 Yamamoto Takeo, 『都市コミュニティとエスニシティ』 *Urban Communities and Ethnicity*, xiii+355 pp., ミネルヴァ書房, 1997.

11 新保　満 Shimpo Mitsuru, 『石もて追わるるごとく――日系カナダ人社会史』 *Driven Away by Stones: A Social History of Canadians of Japanese Descent* (new ed.), 342 pp., 御茶の水書房, 1996.

12 筒井清忠 (編) Tsutsui Kiyotada (ed.), 『歴史社会学のフロンティア』 *The Frontiers of Historical Sociology*, 262 pp., 人文書院, 1997.

A painstaking work by 29 researchers, including the editor. The second half, which reviews Japanese research undertaken from the perspective of historical sociology in major fields, provides information on the state of research on the family; popular beliefs and new religions; urbanization; rural life and farmers' consciousness; mass culture; media; intellectuals; social stratification; education and selection; Japanese-style human relations, institutions and organizations; social pathology and social problems; and gender.

13 京都映画祭実行委員会（編）・筒井清忠・加藤幹郎（責任編集）Kyoto Film Festival Executive Committee (ed.), Tsutsui Kiyotada and Katō Mikio (gen. eds.),『時代劇映画とはなにか──ニュー・フィルム・スタディーズ』*What Are Period Films ?: New Film Studies*, 269 pp., 人文書院，1997.

14 谷　富夫（編）Tani Tomio (ed.),『ライフ・ヒストリーを学ぶ人のために』*For Those Learning about Life History*, x + 318 pp., 世界思想社，1996.

15 小林多寿子 Kobayashi Tazuko,『物語られる「人生」──自分史を書くということ』*The Narrated "Life": Writing One's Own History*, 241 + 4 pp., 学陽書房，1997.

16 片桐雅隆 Katagiri Masataka,『プライバシーの社会学──相互行為・自己・プライバシー』*The Sociology of Privacy: Interaction, Self, and Privacy*, v + 227 pp., 世界思想社，1996.

This is both a counterpoint to the theory of publicness and a discussion of discommunication, and the author also deals from this perspective with contextualism as a typically Japanese type of relationship.

17 田中節雄 Tanaka Setsuo,『近代公教育──装置と主体』*Modern Public Education: Apparatus and Subjective Agent*, 238 pp., 社会評論社，1996.

18 有本　章・江原武一（編）Arimoto Akira and Ehara Takekazu (eds.),『大学教授職の国際比較』*An International Comparison of the University Professoriate*, 280 pp., 玉川大学出版部，1996.

III. Population Dynamics and the Family

01 人口・世帯研究会（監修）・嵯峨座晴夫 Population and Household Study Group (supvr.) and Sagaza Haruo,『人口高齢化と高齢者──最新国勢調査からみる高齢化社会』*The Aging of the Population and the Elderly: The Aging Society as Seen from the Latest National Census,* vii + 199 pp., 大蔵省印刷局，1997.

As is indicated by its subtitle, this book surveys the present state of the aging of Japanese society and future prospects on the basis of the 1995 census. As regards present conditions, Japan's population on 1 Oct. 1996 was estimated to be 125,860,000, of whom 19,020,000 (15.1%) were 65 years and older. This was the first time that the percentage of the elderly reached 15%, but in international terms this is less than Sweden, Great Britain and other leading European countries. However, it is already higher than the proportion in the United States and is expected to rise rapidly in the future, outstripping the majority of developed nations by 2000 and reaching 27.4% by 2025, far higher than any other nation. On the basis of this premise, this book discusses regional differences in the aging of the population within Japan; the falling birthrate and deathrate, both causes of population aging; household changes resulting from population aging and problems pertaining to households of the elderly; and structural characteristics of the aged population. It also includes many statistics, as well as a bibliography of research on aging, and is an extremely useful study for researchers in this field.

02 阿藤　誠（編）Atō Makoto (ed.),『先進国の人口問題――少子化と家族政策』 *Population Problems in Developed Nations: The Trend towards Fewer Children and Family Policies*, v+277 pp., 東京大学出版会, 1996.

A comparative study of birthrates and family policies in developed nations. Chap. 1 includes an analysis of the reasons for fewer children in Japan and countermeasures as compared with other developed nations.

03 古田隆彦　Furuta Takahiko,『人口波動で未来を読む』 *Reading the Future on tha Basis of Population Waves*, 284 pp., 日本経済新聞社, 1996.

04 廣嶋清志・大江守之・山本千鶴子・鈴木　透・三田房美・小島克久・佐々井　司・坂井博通・大友由紀子　Hiroshima Kiyoshi, Ōe Moriyuki, Yamamoto Chizuko, Suzuki Tōru, Mita Fusami, Kojima Katsuhisa, Sasai Tsukasa, Sakai Hiromichi and Ōtomo Yukiko,『第3回世帯動向調査　1994年人口問題基本調査　現代日本の世帯変動』 *Third Survey of Household Trends, 1994 Basic Survey of Population Problems: Household Changes in Contemporary Japan*, 202 pp., 厚生省人口問題研究所, 1996.

05 熊谷文枝（編）Kumagai Fumie (ed.),『日本の家族と地域性（上）―東日本の家族を中心として』 *Japanese Families and Local Characteristics (1): With a Focus on Families in Eastern Japan*, x+200 pp., ミネルヴァ書房, 1997.

06 熊谷文枝（編）Kumagai Fumie (ed.),『日本の家族と地域性（下）―西日本の家族を中心として』 *Japanese Families and Local Characteristics (2): With a Focus on Families in Western Japan*, x+216 pp., ミネルヴァ書房, 1997.

III-05 and-06 represent the fruits of a joint study by 13 scholars, including the editor, in which they attempt to delineate the local characteristics and diversity of Japanese families. Local differences extracted from household statistics are compounded by cultural factors such as local traditions and customs, thereby resulting in considerable diversity. In addition to the differences between northeastern Japan and southwestern Japan, pointed out already before the war, the transformation of farming in postwar Japan, especially the growth of part-time farming and the expansion of underpopulated areas, the aging of the population, and the transformation of local culture under the influence of these changes have all affected the family, and the contributors consider the current state of Japanese families with reference to numerous statistics and examples. The overall situation is dealt with in the Introduction and Chaps. 1 and 2 of Vol. 1 and the Introduction of Vol. 2, and in addition Vol. 1 deals with rural villages in Hokkaidō, Miyagi prefecture, Yamagata prefecture and Niigata prefecture and with the whole of Ishikawa prefecture, while Vol. 2 covers two cities and outlying islands belonging to metropolitan Tokyo, the whole of Aichi prefecture, underpopulated areas in Shiga prefecture, Shimane prefecture and Kōchi prefecture, the whole of Kagoshima prefecture, and the general characteristics of Okinawan families. Although these two volumes provide information on the general situation regarding Japanese families, in overall content the emphasis is on rural families.

07 石原豊美 Ishihara Toyomi,『農家の家族変動——ライフコースの発想を用いて』 *Family Changes among Farmers: Using the Ideas of Life Course*, 208＋vi pp., 日本経済新聞社, 1996.

08 野々山久也・袖井孝子・篠崎正美（編）Nonoyama Hisaya, Sodei Takako and Shinozaki Masami (eds.),『いま家族に何が起こっているのか——家族社会学のパラダイム転換をめぐって』 *What Is Happening to Families Now ?: On the Paradigm Shift in the Sociology of the Family*, 258＋xvi pp., ミネルヴァ書房, 1996.

09 牟田和恵 Muta Kazue,『戦略としての家族——近代日本の国民国家形成と女性』 *The Family as a Strategy: Women and the Formation of the Nation-State of Modern Japan*, 216 pp., 新曜社, 1996.

10 坂本佳鶴恵 Sakamoto Kazue,『〈家族〉イメージの誕生——日本映画にみる〈ホームドラマ〉の形成』 *The Birth of the Image of the "Family": The Formation of "Home Dramas" as Seen Japanese Films*, vi＋411＋vi pp., 新曜社, 1997.

Approaching the family from the perspective of "images of the family," the author seeks to shed light on both the transformation of the Japanese family and the transformation of Japanese society, and because she makes use of films, this book also represents a history of film culture with a focus on images of the family. It is thus useful for research on the history of modern and contemporary Japan from both these aspects.

11 山田昌弘 Yamada Masahiro,『結婚の社会学——未婚化・晩婚化はつづくのか』 *The Sociology of Marriage: Will the Trend to Remain Unmarried or to Marry Late Continue?*, vii＋180 pp., 丸善ライブラリー, 1996.

Rejecting popular views, the author seeks the reasons for the growing trend in Japanese society to live single or to marry late in "the decrease of opportunities for 'upward marriage by women', with low economic growth as its direct cause," and in "changes in the 'system of love marriage', with the vitalization of contacts between the sexes as its direct cause." According to Yamada, present-day Japan is in a state of transition to the "postmodern couple." This book is helpful for understanding the family and marriage in contemporary Japan.

12 善積京子 Yoshizumi Kyōko,『〈近代家族〉を超える——非法律婚カップルの声』 *Transcending the "Modern Family": The Voices of Non-Legally Married Couples*, 294 pp., 青木書店, 1997.

This book discusses the spread of non-legal marriage in Japan on the basis of survey data, etc., dealing with issues such as motives, the realities of home life, and resultant social changes.

13 宮本みち子・岩上真珠・山田昌弘, Miyamoto Michiko, Iwakami Mami and Yamada Masahiro,『未婚化社会の親子関係——お金と愛情にみる家族のゆくえ』 *Parent-Child Relations in an Unmarried Society: The Future of the Family as Seen in Money and Affection*, xv＋244＋iv pp., 有斐閣, 1997.

Focussing on parent-child relations, the authors examine lifestyles, the future of support and care for aged parents, and the future of young people in contemporary Japanese society, marked as it is by an increasing tendency for people not to marry. A wealth of data is presented in simplified form, thereby facilitating a grasp of the general situation.

14 春日井典子 Kasugai Noriko,『ライフコースと親子関係』 *Life Course and Parent-Child Relations*, iv＋188 pp., 行路社, 1997.

Based on a survey of graduates of a women's university conducted in 1993-94, this book examines relations between mothers and their grown-up daughters from the perspective of life-course theory. Focussing on the intercompensatory nature of parent-child relations, it should provide leads for understanding one aspect of the Japanese family.

15 瀬地山 角 Sechiyama Kaku,『東アジアの家父長制——ジェンダーの比較社会学』 *Patriarchalism in East Asia: A Comparative Sociology of Gender*, x＋348＋xxv pp., 勁草書房, 1996.

16 浜口晴彦（編）Hamaguchi Haruhiko (ed,),『エイジングとは何か――高齢社会の生き方』*What Is Aging?: Living in an Aged Society*, ix＋214 pp., 早稲田大学出版部, 1997.

Although an introductory work, it apprises one to a certain degree of the actualities of the aging of Japanese society and responses to it.

17 嵯峨座晴夫・浜口晴彦ほか（編）Sagaza Haruo, Hamaguchi Haruhiko *et al*, (eds.),『現代エイジング辞典』*A Dictionary of Contemporary Aging*, 584＋xiii pp., 早稲田大学出版部, 1996.

18 畠中宗一 Hatanaka Munekazu,『チャイルドマインディング――もうひとつの子ども家族支援システム』*Child-Minding: Another Support System for Families with Children*, 178 pp., 高文堂出版社, 1997.

The author considers the family from the perspective of childcare and discusses systems for supporting families with children. This book helps one to understand the history and present state of social nursery care centers and support systems for families with children in Japan.

IV. The Community: Rural and Urban

01 北原　淳 Kitahara Atsushi,『共同体の思想――村落開発理論の比較社会学』*The Philosophy of Communities: A Comparative Sociology of Village Development Theory*, vii＋220 pp., 世界思想社, 1996.

02 中野　卓 Nakano Takashi,『鰤網の村の400年――能登灘浦の社会学的研究』*Four Hundred Years in a Village of Yellowtail Net Fishing: A Sociological Study of Nadaura Coast on the Noto Peninsula*, xxvi＋387 pp., 刀水書房, 1996.

The fruit of many years of research on a fishing village in Ishikawa prefecture, this book traces changes in the distinctive organization surrounding yellowtail net fishing (*buri-ami*) and the associated social organization, as well as describing the survival of fishing villages in Japan and their responses to modernization. The long time span, extending from the late 16th century to recent times, has resulted in an outstanding portrayal of early modern and modern Japan as seen from a fishing village in the Hokuriku region. This is a work indicative of the current level of Japanese social history, with its traditions going back to the prewar period.

03 長谷川昭彦 Hasegawa Akihiko,『近代化のなかの村落――農村社会の生活構造と集団組織』*Rural Communities in the Modernization of Japan: Changing Rural Life Structure and Rural Group Organization in Japan*, x＋274 pp., 日本経済評論社, 1997.

One of the few comprehensive studies of Japanese rural society. First summarizing the major changes that have taken place in postwar rural

174

society, the author then describes how a regional society has evolved with changes in the livelihood system and how, on the basis of this, rural collective organizations have been reorganized and what might be described as a regional compound society has been formed.

04 長谷川昭彦・藤沢　和・竹本田持・荒樋　豊 Hasegawa Akihiko, Fujisawa Yawara, Takemoto Tamotsu and Arahi Yutaka,『過疎地域の景観と集団』 *Landscape and Groups in Underpopulated Areas*, 363 pp., 日本経済評論社, 1996.

05 山本　努 Yamamoto Tsutomu,『現代過疎問題の研究』 *A Study of Contemporary Problems in Depopulation*, 270＋vii pp., 恒星社厚生閣, 1996.

06 山本英治・高橋明善・蓮見音彦（編）Yamamoto Eiji, Takahashi Akiyoshi and Hasumi Otohiko (eds.),『沖縄の都市と農村』 *Cities and Villages in Okinawa*, viii＋335 pp., 東京大学出版会, 1995.

A joint study by 7 researchers, including the editors, which represents the results of more than 20 years of research on Okinawa from around the time of its return to Japan in 1972. It describes how the programme to promote development, adopted after its return to Japan, has changed Okinawa with regard to the industrial structure and employment structure, regional problems, town-village relations, the urban formation of Naha, the organization of self-governing associations, "homefolks" associations, depopulation and social and lifestyle changes in northen villages, and the autonomy of villages within U.S. military bases and local culture, and reference is made when necessary to the prewar situation. Changes that accompanied economic growth in postwar Japan, such as the hollowing-out of rural areas and changes in social relations as a result of the concentration of the population in cities, were repeated in Okinawa after its return to Japan, while Okinawa as a whole, with the gravitation of the population to Naha, has been relegated to Japan's "periphery," and these social conditions in Okinawa are critically analyzed in relation to its functions as an enormous military base, which remained even after its return to Japan. This book is essential reading for any inquiry into not only Japan's regional problems but also Japanese society as a whole.

07 清野正義（編）Seino Masayoshi (ed.),『東北の小さな町』 *A Small Town in the Tōhoku Region*, ix＋280 pp., 恒星社厚生閣, 1997.

08 三浦典子・鈴木　広・木下謙治・豊田謙二（編）Miura Noriko, Suzuki Hiroshi, Kinoshita Kenji and Toyota Kenji (eds,),『まちを設計する』 *Designing Towns*, xi＋291 pp., 九州大学出版会, 1997.

A joint study by 13 researchers, including the editors, in which they describe and analyze examples of the town-buildings (*machi-zukuri*) and the revitalization of villages (*mura-okoshi*) in Kyushu. A wide variety of examples are covered, ranging from smaller towns and villages, with examples of coexistence with nature, cultural creativity, vying for visitors, and an emphasis on welfare, to larger towns such as Arita, renowned for its porcelain, and Minamata in the aftermath of the outbreak of Minamata disease, as well as larger cities such as Fukuoka and Kita-Kyūshū.

09　小内　透 Kouchi Tōru,『戦後日本の地域社会変動と地域社会類型——都道府県・市町村を単位とする統計分析を通して』*Change in Local Community and Types of Local Community in Postwar Japan: On the Basis of a Statistical Analysis with Prefectures and Cities, Towns and Villages as Units*, 426＋viii pp., 東信堂, 1996.

10　岩城完之 Iwaki Sadayuki,『産業変動下の地域社会』*Local Community during Industrial Change*, 194 pp., 学文堂, 1996.

11　春日雅司 Kasuga Masashi,『地域社会と地方政治の政治学』*The Political Science of Local Community and Local Politics*, 181＋xi pp., 晃洋書房, 1996.

12　川合隆男・山岸　健・藤田弘夫 (編) Kawai Takao, Yamagishi Ken and Fujita Hiroo (eds.),『奥井復太郎著作集』*Collected Works of Okui Fukutarō*, 大空社, 1996.

Vol. 1,『社会思想論』*Social Thought*, 392 pp.

Vol. 2,『社会政策論』*Social Policy*, 858 pp.

Vol. 3,『都市論 (1) ——都市史・都市社会学』*Urban Studies I: History of Cities and Urban Sociology*, 524 pp.

Vol. 4,『都市論 (2) ——都市社会調査』*Urban Studies II: Urban Social Survey*, 684 pp.

Vol. 5,『都市論 (3) ——現代大都市論』*Urban Studies III: Contemporary Megacities*, 770pp.

Vol. 6,『都市論 (4) ——商店街研究, 国土計画論, 戦時都市論』*Urban Studies IV: Studies on Shopping Streets, National Land Planning, and Wartime Cities*, 970 pp.

Vol. 7,『都市論 (5) ——戦後都市論, 都市と文学』*Urban Studies V: Postwar Cities, City and Literature*, 550pp.

Vol. 8,『国民生活論, 教育論, その他』*Studies on National Life, Education, and Other Essays*, 550 pp.

Sep. Vol., 492 pp.

13　蓮見音彦・似田貝香門・矢沢澄子 (編) Hasumi Otohiko, Nitagai Kamon and Yazawa Sumiko (eds,),『現代都市と地域形成——転換期とその社会形態』*Contemporary Cities and the Formation of Local Communities:*

Societal Modes in Times of Transition, iii＋238 pp., 東京大学出版会, 1997.

A collection of articles by 10 researchers, including the editors. Using the results of community surveys with which many of the contributors have been continuously involved for many years, they discuss new societal modes that are beginning to emerge chiefly in urban areas, dealing with topics such as community groups, families, class and social stratification, residential space, community policies, residents' movements, urban politics, the publicness, community planning, and the social process in cities. This is a study indicative of the level attained by empirical urban and community studies in Japanese sociology.

14 佐藤健二 （編） Satō Kenji (ed.),『都市の解読力』*The Decipherment of Cities* [21 世紀都市社会学第 3 巻], xii＋245 pp., 勁草書房, 1996.

In this book 7 researchers, including the editor, investigate various social phenomena that are unfolding on the stage of urban society. They deal with "tailing" and the understanding of the "individual," urban myths about water and germs, the gay movement and cities, cities and community magazines, cities viewed in terms of sound, town-building and surveys, and social research and cities, and because these all treat of various Japanese cities, this book can also be consulted for research on Japanese cities.

15 吉原直樹 （編） Yoshihara Naoki (ed.),『都市空間の構想力』*The Conceptualizing Power of Urban Space* [21 世紀都市社会学第 5 巻], 280＋xiv pp., 勁草書房, 1996.

16 奥田道大 （編） Okuda Michihiro (ed.),『都市エスニシティの社会学——民族／文化／共生の意味を問う』*The Sociology of Urban Ethnicity: Questioning the Meaning of Ethnos, Culture and Symbiosis*, 4＋297 pp., ミネルヴァ書房, 1997.

A collection of articles by 13 researchers, including the editor, who analyze the different states of ethnicity in various cities. Subjects dealt with include Okinawans in Osaka, Koreans in Yokohama, Chinese in Kobe, foreign residents in Tokyo, and Koreans living in Kita-Kyūshū.

17 橋本和孝 Hashimoto Kazutaka,『ソーシャル・プランニング——市民平活の醸成を求めて』*Social Planning: For the Fostering of Civic Life*, ix＋190 pp., 東信堂, 1996.

18 中田　実ほか （編） Nakata Minoru *et al.* (ed.),『町内会・自治会の新展開』*New Developments in Neighborhood Associations* (*Chōnaikai*) *and Community's Self-Governing Associations* (*Jichikai*), 296 pp., 自治体研究社, 1996.

V. Industry, Labor, Class and Social Stratification

01 犬塚　先（編）Inuzuka Susumu (ed.),『新しい産業社会学——仕事をと おしてみる日本と世界』 *A New Industrial Sociology: Japan and the World Seen through Work*, xxi＋293 pp., 有斐閣, 1996.

Although a textbook, this book provides information on new trends in Japan's industrial sociology, dealing with the demise of seniority-based personnel management, young people's attitudes towards work, gender and labor, questions relating to the mandatory retirement system, the state of labor unions, the formation of new corporations for working people, etc. It should provide leads for further research.

02 羽田　新 Haneda Arata,『産業社会学の諸問題』 *Problems in Industrial Sociology*, 185 pp., 税務経理協会, 1996.

03 青山英男・小島　茂（編）Aoyama Hideo and Kojima Shigeru (eds.),『情報社会と経営』 *Information Society and Business Management,*, viii＋189 pp., 文眞堂, 1997.

04 沢田善太郎 Sawada Zentarō,『組織の社会学——官僚制・アソシエーション・合議制』 *The Sociology of Organizations: The Bureaucracy, Associations, and the Council System*, vi＋264 pp., ミネルヴァ書房, 1997.

05 小木曾道夫 Ogiso Michio,『組織の自己革新——知識集約的部門の現場から』 *The Self-Reform of Organizations: From the Realities of the Knowledge-Intensive Sector*, xiii＋285 pp., 夢窓庵, 1997.

The author first summarizes previous research on organizations, and seeing their essence in the self-organizing model, he devolops a three-dimensional model consisting of formal structure, emergent structure and informal structure and then analyzes the results of his investigations into knowledge-intensive organizations in Japan. He finds that the three structures are independent of each other, that productivity is due more to emergent structures and informal structures than to the environment and formal structures, that Japanese-style management, with the very objectives of organizations now being questioned, is no longer adequate, and that therefore, in order to launch out into a more self-creative type of order-formation, greater recognition should be given to the importance of emergent structures. The author's investigations are focussed on industrial design departments in the manufacturing industry, product development departments, design departments in the apparel industry, and design offices.

06 稲上　毅 Inagami Takeshi,『現代英国経営事情』 *Business Management Conditions in Contemporary Great Britain*, iii＋299 pp., 日本労働研究機

構, 1997.

07 山田信行 Yamada Nobuyuki,『労使関係の歴史社会学——多元的資本主義発展論の試み』 *The Historical Sociology of Labor-Management Relations: An Experiment in Pluralistic Capitalist Growth Theory*, vii+270 pp., ミネルヴァ書房, 1996.

After having redefined labor-management relations in the context of neo-Marxism and world system theory, the author uses this to discuss the pluralistic growth of capitalism, with the United States, Japan and Malaysia as examples. The main points that he makes are that whereas in the United States there has been increasing casualization because of the impasse reached in labor-management relations, resulting in greater dependence on immigrant labor, in Japan casualization has been successfully institutionalized under the flexible organization of labor based on Japanese-style labor-management relations, and in Malaysia the effect of foreign capital has changed from negative to positive and labor-management ralations geared to export-oriented industrialization have evolved. By resituating and reformulating the concepts and theories of labor-management relations within the context of global macroscopic capitalist growth, Yamada attempts to transform them into a theory able to adapt to the major changes taking place in contemporary society, and he points to one direction for the future sociology of industry and labor with a focus on labor-management relations.

08 寿里　茂 Susato Shigeru,『ホワイトカラーの社会史』 *The Social History of White-collar Workers*, iii+259 pp., 日本評論社, 1996.

09 熊谷文枝 Kumagai Fumie,『日本的生産システムイン USA』 *Japanese Production Systems in the U.S.A.*, v+277+vi pp., 日本貿易振興会, 1996.

Based on the experiences of Japanese businesses that have made inroads into the United States, this book is an attempt to examine the cultural friction underlying Japan-U.S. economic friction. On the basis of investigations conducted throughout the United States in 1988-95, the author argues for the establishment of ideals by Japanese corporations, the creation of a hybrid culture, and the setting of objective standards of quality control etc.

10 稲上　毅（編）Inagami Takeshi (ed.),『成熟社会のなかの企業別組合——ユニオン・アイデンティティとユニオン・リーダー』 *Enterprise Unions within a Mature Society: Union Identity and Union Leaders*, vi+348 pp., 日本労働研究機構, 1995.

A joint study by 6 researchers, including the editor, based on the analysis of a questionnaire conducted by post in 1993 on 2,415 unions (with replies from 1,050 unions [43.5%]) in order to gain a grasp of the state of labor unions in contemporary Japan. Major discoveries include the following points: (1) interest in unions is waning, but moves to review the scope of union membership and increase participation in management are continuing; (2) union activities are expanding outwards towards protection of the environment, welfare volunteerism, etc.; (3) symbol reform is conspicuous and the union identity movement is also strong, but this does not mean that traditional roles have been abandoned; (4) there is a strong tendency for union leaders to be elected without any opposing candidates and to make a smooth return to the workplace, but consideration must be given to new methods of leader training; and (5) overall Japanese unions are moving towards seeking a "symbiotic" relationship between labor and management. This is a valuable study among the few works enabling one to gain an understanding of the state of labor unions in contemporary Japan.

VI. Mass Communications and Social Consciousness

01 花田達朗 Hanada Tatsurō, 『公共圏という名の社会空間——公共圏、メディア、市民社会』 *The Social Space Called the Public Sphere: The Public Sphere, Media, and Civil Society*, 337＋xxv pp., 木鐸社, 1996.

A basic inquiry into communication and mass communications based on J. Habermas's theory of *Öffentlichkeit* (publicness), this work demonstrates the theoretical level reached by Japanese sociology in this field. According to the author, the term 'public sphere' must win general acceptance in Japanese society, just as the term 'civil society' has done, and he maintains that there are prospects of this happening.

02 田崎篤郎・船津　衛 (編) Tazaki Tokurō and Funatsu Mamoru (eds.), 『社会情報論の展開』 *Developments in Social Information Theory*, 157 pp., 北樹出版, 1997.

03 成田康昭 Narita Yasuaki, 『メディア空間文化論——いくつもの私との遭遇』 *A Cultural Study of Media Space: Encounters with More Than One "I,"* ix＋252 pp., 有信堂, 1997.

Starting from the current realities of Japanese media space, such as *karaoke*, computer games, pagers, and the Internet, the author discusses the significance of the media and communications, the power of the media to structure reality, and the autonomy of cyberspace and then considers ways of "taming" media space as public sphere. This book is an excellent guide to the realities of contemporary Japanese society, in which media space has been established as a form of culture.

04 東京大学社会情報研究所 (編) University of Tokyo Institute of Socio-In-

formation and Communication Studies (ed.),『日本人の情報行動1995』
The Information Behavior of the Japanese in 1995, x+415 pp., 東京大
学出版会, 1997.

A joint study by 15 researchers headed by Suzuki Hirohisa 鈴木裕久,
based on a survey conducted nationwide in 1995 on a sample of 1,400
people (1,025 returned [73.2%]). Consisting of questions relating to
domicile, basic daily behavior, main information behavior, secondary
information behavior, etc., it provides the following information: as
regards basic daily behavior, on an average the Japanese spend daily
451.8 mins.(31.4%) sleeping, 185.0 mins.(12.8%) dressing, washing, etc.,
102.6 mins.(7.1%) eating and drinking, 78.4 mins.(5.4%) traveling, 303.5
mins.(21.1%) working, 53.2 mins.(3.7%) studying, 69.6 mins.(4.8%)
engaged in hobbies, 160.7 mins.(11.2%) resting, and 35.3 mins.(2.5%)
engaged in other activities; they spend on average 426 mins. daily engaged
in information behavior, which in terms of media patterns consists of mass
media contact (53%), direct information behavior (23%), packaged mass
media contact (14%), personal media utilization (10%), and other types
(1%). An analysis of information behavior according to attributes and
media types is followed by analyses of changes in the information behavior of children and in the use of the media by the Japanese and of the
allocation and typology of time resources relating to information behavior, and the book closes with predictions of future directions. In addition,
the appendixes contain basic data and the original questionnaire, and all
in all this is an indispensable work for the study of the information
behavior of the Japanese.

05 水野博介・中村 功・是永 論・清原慶子 Mizuno Hirosuke, Nakamura
Isao, Korenaga Ron and Kiyohara Keiko,『情報生活とメディア』*Information Life and the Media*, 179 pp., 北樹出版, 1997.

Putting forward the concept of "information life," the authors discuss
changes in information life in postwar Japan, the dissemination of television and its influence on daily life, living conditions and the use of
communications media, networking and changes in information behavior,
and the future of the informationalization of everyday life. It is a useful
work for acquainting oneself with the general state of the information life
of the Japanese.

06 児島和人・橋元良明 (編) Kojima Kazuto and Hashimoto Yoshiaki
(eds.),『変わるメディアと社会生活』*The Changing Media and Social
Life*, xi+256 pp., ミネルヴァ書房, 1996.

A joint study by 17 researchers, including the editors, in which they attempt to gain a multifaceted grasp of the changes in social life accompanying the development and diversification of the media. Although not systematic study, it may be referred to for information on the state of the media in Japanese society.

07 小林修一 Kobayashi Shūichi,『メディア人間のトポロジー』 *The Topology of the Media Person*, 227 pp., 北樹出版, 1997.

08 川崎泰資・柴田鉄治 Kawasaki Taisuke and Shibata Tetsuji,『ジャーナリズムの原点——体験的新聞・放送論』 *The Starting Point of Journalism: An Experiential Study of Newspapers and Broadcasting*, xi+215 pp., 岩波書店, 1996.

A study of problems in Japanese journalism based on the experiences of two newspaper reporters. The main topics include factors that make newspapers lifeless, whether or not television is a form of journalism, whether or not power checks are functioning, and crime coverage and human rights, and it contains on-the-spot information on the current state of journalism in Japan.

09 綿貫譲治・三宅一郎 Watanuki Jōji and Miyake Ichirō,『環境変動と態度変容』 *Changes in the Environment and Changes in Attitude* [「変動する日本人の選挙行動」第2巻], vi+224 pp., 木鐸社, 1997.

An empirical study of the political consciousness of the Japanese, based on analyses of 7 nationwide panel surveys conducted between immediately before the 1993 Lower House elections and immediately after the 1996 Lower House elections. Valid samples numbered 2,682, with the results being compared with data from previous surveys conducted by the authors, and the maintenance and rejection of traditional values according to birth cohort are also analyzed. Other important topics include trust in the system and distrust of politicians, recognition mobilization and the proliferation of policy views, dissatisfaction with and hopes for political reform, the emergence of new political parties and the evaluation of candidates, and changes in the coalition framework and the responses of party supporters, and the authors end by proposing a model for voting participation by the Japanese, according to which there is a high probability that people with considerable political experience, people with a strong sense of duty towards voting, people with a keen interest in the distribution of political power in the Diet, people obtaining concrete benefits through Diet members, and people attached to their local community will vote. It is also pointed out that many Japanese look upon voting as a 'duty' and that Japan's democracy is to a certain extent sustained by this sense of duty. This work is indispensable for the study of the political consciousness and social consciousness of the Japanese.

10 吉野耕作 Yoshino Kōsaku,『文化ナショナリズムの社会学――現代日本のアイデンティティの行方』 *The Sociology of Cultural Nationalism: The Future of the Identity of Contemporary Japan*, vi＋292＋6 pp., 名古屋大学出版会, 1997.

Understanding in terms of cultural nationalism the popular theories about the Japanese (*Nihonjin-ron* 日本人論) that have been in vogue since the late 1960s, the author resituates them on the basis of the results of earlier research on ethnicity and nationalism and analyzes them in particular from the perspective of 'consumption' with reference to the results of a survey conducted in Shizuoka prefecture. In doing so, he criticizes four popular views of *Nihonjin-ron*, which regard it as either a means of deliverance from an identity crisis, an expression of a sense of cultural superiority reflecting economic success and social stability, a form of ruling ideology, or an attachment to identity in terms of Japanese culture. This work represents a new type of research on the social consciousness of the Japanese based on a new theory of nationalism.

11 ましこ・ひでのり Mashiko Hidenori,『イデオロギーとしての「日本」――「国語」「日本史」の知識社会学』 *"Japan" as an Ideology: The Sociology of Knowledge with Regard to the "Japanese Language" and "Japanese History,"* 334 pp., 三元社, 1997.

Taking the view that problems pertaining to Okinawa are Japan's problems and that Japanese history must be reinterpreted from the perspective Ryukyuan and Okinawan history, the author questions the use of the Japanese language and Japanese history as ideological apparatuses. He also takes into account Yoshino Kōsaku's views outlined above ([VI-10]) and is critical of the current situation in which Japanese history has become a "mass consumer item."

VII. Social Problems and Social Welfare

01 野田　隆 Noda Takashi,『災害と社会システム』 *Disasters and Social Systems*, v＋231 pp., 恒星社厚生閣, 1997.

Having first summarized sociological approaches to disasters, the author examines our vulnerability to disasters lurking in everyday society and considers the lessons to be learnt from the Great Hanshin Earthquake. Dividing views on disasters into the theory of the externality of risk, the theory of interaction, and the theory of cultural determination, he adopts the theory of interaction and examines from this perspective emergency social systems and problems relating to disasters and organizations. On the subject of vulnerability to disasters, he carefully points out in particular the pitfalls of disaster-prevention systems and considers the importance and ways of "planning" responses to disasters. With regrd to the Great Hanshin Earthquake, he especially emphasizes the role of the community in coping with unforeseen disasters. This may be regarded as a relatively systematic treatment of the sociology of disasters.

02　佐々木正道 Sasaki Masamichi,『阪神・淡路大震災におけるボランティアの実態調査』 *A Fact-Finding Survey of Volunteers in the Aftermath of the Great Hanshin Earthquake*, 237 pp., 阪神・淡路大震災ボランティア活動調査委員会，1996.

03　浦野正樹・大矢根　淳・土屋淳二（編）Urano Masaki, Ōyane Jun and Tsuchiya Junji (eds.),『阪神・淡路大震災における災害ボランティア活動』 *Disaster-Relief Volunteer Activities after the Great Hanshin Earthquake* [早稲田大学社会科学研究所研究シリーズ 36], 456 pp., 早稲田大学社会科学研究所，1996.

04　鳥越晧之 Torigoe Hiroyuki,『環境社会学の理論と実践』 *The Theory and Practice of Environmental Sociology*, viii＋280 pp., 有斐閣，1997.

　　This book examines the theoretical achievements of Japan's environmental sociology and the results of its practical activities from the vantage point of 'living environmentalism', which seeks to consider environmental issues from the standpoint of people living in the society in question, and the author discusses subjects such as the basic theories of living environmentalism, environmenal rights and ownership, the existence of common rights of possession, the subjective initiative of residents, communities and citizens' participation, the creation of citizens' participation systems by the administration, issues and problems relating to public utilities, movements for creating a living environment in rural areas, pollution resulting from daily life in cities, the living environment and natural environment, and the living environment and historical environment. The chief points made by Torigoe are that Japan's environmental sociology is effective in directly resolving environmental and pollution-related problems; as such it has significance as a critique of the overemphasis of theory and the functionalistic leanings of Japan's sociology; and, unlike natural environmentalism and modern technicism, there is a need to conduct debates on the level of living rather than on the level of existence. This is an excellent work that exemplifies the level reached by Japan's environmental sociology in a manner that is easy to understand.

05　鳥越晧之（編）Torigoe Hiroyuki (ed.),『環境とライフスタイル』 *The Environment and Lifestyles*, 251 pp., 有斐閣，1996.

06　井上孝夫 Inoue Takao,『白神山地と青秋林道──地域開発と環境保全の

社会学』 *The Shirakami Mountains and Seishū (Aomori-Akita) Forest Road: The Sociology of Regional Development and Environmental Protection*, 223＋ix pp., 東信堂, 1996.

07　井上孝夫 Inoue Takao,『白神山地の入山規制を考える』 *Thinking about Restrictions on Entry to the Shirakami Mountains*, 245 pp., 緑風出版, 1997.

Focussing on the Shirakami Mountains, which have been placed on the World Heritage List, this book deals with isses such as what it means in Japanese society to protect the natural environment and the composition of Japanese-style social relations surrounding the management of heritage sites. Together with VII-06, it provides leads for studying issues concerning environmental protection in Japan.

08　長谷川公一 Hasegawa Kōichi,『脱原子力社会の選択——新エネルギー革命の時代』 *Options for Society Breaking Free from Nuclear Energy: An Age of Revolution in New Energy Sources*, iv＋354 pp., 新曜社, 1996.

09　栗原　彬（編）Kurihara Akira (ed.),『講座　差別の社会学』 *Lecture Series: The Sociology of Discrimination*, 弘文堂, 1997.

Vol. 1,『差別の社会理論』 *Social Theories of Discrimination*, 300 pp.

Vol. 2,『日本社会の差別構造』 *The Structure of Discrimination in Japanese Society*, 296 pp.

Vol. 3,『現代世界の差別構造』 *The Structure of Discrimination in the Contemporary World*, 300 pp.

Vol. 4,『共生の方へ』 *Towards Symbiosis*, 300 pp.

This series contains contributions by 72 researchers, including the editor, and Vol. 2 in particular deals with various forms of discrimination in contemporary Japanese society. As well as describing the realities of discrimination against Korean residents in Japan, *buraku* ghettoes, disabled people and their families, victims of pollution-related diseases such as Minamata disease and industrial accidents such as those involving Mitsui Mining, foreigners living in large cities, Okinawa, unmarried people, and sufferers of illnesses, it also discusses issues such as the ethnomethodology of gender-based categories, the dreams and frustrations of the school reform movement, the use of fingerprints in immigration control and discrimination, and the discriminative structure of the care system. It serves as a useful guide for approaching questions of discrimination in Japanese society.

10　鮎川　潤 Ayukawa Jun,『犯罪学入門——殺人・賄賂・非行』 *An Introduction to Criminology: Murder, Bribery, and Delinquency*, 196 pp., 講談社, 1997.

Although an introductory work, this book describes many different aspects of the realities of crime in Japan. Subjects covered include murder, drug-related offences, sexual offences, corporate crime, organizational deviance, criminal organizations, juvenile delinquency, the treatment of offenders and the judicial system, and the victimology and changes in the social environment.

11　間庭充幸 Maniwa Mitsuyuki, 『若者犯罪の社会文化史──犯罪が写し出す時代の病像』 *The Sociocultural History of Youth Crime: The Pathological Image of the Times Reflected in Crime*, xi＋302 pp., 有斐閣, 1997.

Dealing with changes in youth and juvenile crime in postwar Japan, this book describes how the youths who drifted into crime during the postwar liberation came to espouse a strong sense of occlusion as Japanese society became more controlled, turning to "self-destructive crimes" and "game-type crimes," and eventually ended up committing the "game-type crimes of computerniks" based on fabrications such as that of Aum Shinrikyō. It represents a compact social history of crime in postwar Japan.

12　桜井哲夫 Sakurai Tetsuo, 『不良少年』 *Juvenile Delinquents*, 222 pp., 筑摩書房, 1997.

A collection of essays about juvenile delinquency and deviancy in which the author touches on the birth of "juvenile delinquents" in Japan and their postwar history, their treatment in comics, the culture of delinquency, and anti-school culture, and it is helpful for understanding the situation in Japan.

13　高原正興 Takahara Masaoki, 『社会病理学と少年非行』 *Social Pathology and Juvenile Delinquency*, 190 pp., 法政出版, 1996.

14　矢島正見 Yajima Masami, 『少年非行文化論』 *A Cultural Study of Juvenile Delinquency*, 357 pp., 学文社, 1996.

15　野口裕二 Noguchi Yūji, 『アルコホリズムの社会学──アディクションと近代』 *The Sociology of Alcoholism: Addiction and the Modern Age*, viii＋198 pp., 日本評論社, 1996.

According to the author, there are four approaches for dealing with alcoholism—deviancy theory, medical sociology, clinical sociology, and theories of modern society—and he attempts to shed light on various aspects of alcoholism in contemporary Japan from all four approaches. He concludes that, sociologically speaking, alcoholism is an addiction based on co-dependency, and "the fiction of the self," symbolic of the modern age, "now stands buttressed by addiction, playing an outstanding supporting role." This represents a new type of research which, although grounded in social pathology, goes beyond it to develop a critique of modern society.

16　浅野知恵 Asano Chie,『女はなぜやせようとするのか──摂食障害とジェンダー』 *Why Do Women Get a Slim Obsession?: Dietary Disorders and Gender*, 249＋xix pp., 勁草書房, 1996.

17　中根光敏 Nakane Mitsutoshi,『社会学者は 2 度ベルを鳴らす──閉塞する社会空間／熔解する自己』 *Sociologists Ring the Bell Twice: Occlusive Social Space and the Dissolving Self*, 232 pp., 松籟社, 1997.

18　袖井孝子・高橋紘士・平岡公一 (編) Sodei Takako, Takahashi Hiroshi and Hiraoka Kōichi (eds.),『福祉と医療』 *Welfare and Medical Care* [リーディングス日本の社会学 15], vii＋263 pp., 東京大学出版会, 1997.

A collection of articles on welfare and medical care representative of postwar Japanese sociology, divided into three parts dealing with sociological approaches to welfare, various aspects of social welfare, and the sociology of insurance and medical care respectively. The detailed bibliography makes it an indispensable work for research in this field.

19　須賀和彦 Suga Kazuhiko,『現代社会と福祉』 *Contemporary Society and Welfare*, 238 pp., 福村出版, 1997.

20　西下彰俊・浅野 仁 (編) Nishishita Akitoshi and Asano Hitoshi (eds.),『改訂版 老人福祉論』 *On Welfare for the Elderly* (*Rev. Ed.*), 240 pp., 川島書店, 1997.

A textbook by 10 researchers, including the editors, for training social workers and care-workers. It provides an overview of the state of welfare for the elderly in contemporary Japan, dealing with topics such as the aging of Japanese society and the actual state of problems relating to the elderly, the psychology and mental disorders of the elderly, welfare needs, laws pertaining to welfare for the elderly, home-care services, institutional care services, social work, and services for the elderly.

21　高橋勇悦・高萩盾男 (編) Takahashi Yūetsu and Takahagi Tateo (eds.),『高齢化とボランティア社会』 *Aging and a Volunteer Society*, vii＋227 pp., 弘文堂, 1996.

22　金子 勇 Kaneko Isamu,『地域福祉社会学』 *The Sociology of Community Welfare*, 270 pp., ミネルヴァ書房, 1997.

23　小川全夫 Ogawa Takeo,『地域の高齢化と福祉──高齢者のコミュニティ状況』 *The Aging of Local Communities and Welfare: The Community Conditions of the Elderly*, 220 pp., 恒星社厚生閣, 1996.

24　後藤澄江 Gotō Sumie,『現代家族と福祉』 *The Contemporary Family and Welfare*, iv＋180 pp., 有信堂, 1997.

25　畠中宗一 Hatanaka Munekazu,『子ども家族福祉論・序説』 *An Introduc-*

tion to the Study of Welfare for Families with Children, 221 pp., 高文堂出版社, 1996.

VIII. Cultural Transformation and Social Movement

01 飯田剛史・中野　毅・山中　弘（編）Iida Takeshi, Nakano Takeshi and Yamanaka Hiroshi (eds.),『宗教とナショナリズム』*Religion and Nationalism*, vi＋278 pp., 世界思想社, 1997.

A collection of articles by 12 researchers, including the editors, that deal with the links between the revival of religion and the simultaneous resurgence of nationalism. Examples drawn from Japan include the festivals of Korean residents in Japan and their ethnicity, nationalism in modern Japan and the emperor system, anti-secularism and nationalism in contemporary Japan, and cultural nationalism and religious movements.

02 大澤真幸 Ōsawa Masachi,『虚構の時代の果て――オウムと世界最終戦争』*The Outcome of a World of Fictitiousness: Aum Shinrikyō and Armageddon*, 302 pp., 筑摩書房, 1996.

Dealing with the sarin-gas attack on the Tokyo subway system by members of Aum Shinrikyō in March 1995, the author argues that the mutually projected delusions of the members became an aberrant eschatology for an age of fictitiousness, taking the physical form of sarin. According to Ōsawa, in order to prevent the ideal of the end of the world from having destructive results in an age when "transcendence" has been attenuated by the logic of capital in the flow of never-ending time, we must possess a tolerance embracing a "two-tiered relativization" that is able to relativize nihilism too. This book represents a response to a singular incident related to religion in contemporary Japanese society by one of the most acute observers in Japanese sociology.

03 橋爪大三郎・呉　智英・大月隆寛・三島浩司 Hashizume Daizaburō, Kure Tomofusa, Ōtsuki Takahiro and Mishima Hiroshi,『オウムと近代国家』*Aum Shinrikyō and the Modern State*, 311 pp., 南風社, 1996.

04 岡原正幸・山田昌弘・安川　一・石川　准 Okahara Masayuki, Yamada Masahiro, Yasukawa Hajime and Ishikawa Jun,『感情の社会学――エモーション・コンシャスな時代』*The Sociology of Emotions: An Emotion-Conscious Age*, xii＋236 pp., 世界思想社, 1997.

The sociology of emotions has begun to make its presence felt in Japan too, and this book is the best available collection of articles taking into account research developments in the United States. Chap. 6 in particular, by Ishikawa, who links questions of the emotions to questions of intercultural understanding based on cultural relativism, raises hopes for future developments in this field.

05 高橋由典 Takahashi Yoshinori,『感情と行為——社会学的感情論の試み』 *Emotion and Action: A Tentative Sociological Theory of the Emotions*, 262＋viii pp., 新曜社, 1996.

06 富永茂樹 Tominaga Shigeki,『都市の憂鬱——感情の社会学のために』 *The Gloom of Cities: For the Sociology of Emotions*, 302 pp., 新曜社, 1996.

07 上野千鶴子・綿貫礼子（編）Ueno Chizuko and Watanuki Reiko (eds.),『リプロダクティブ・ヘルスと環境——共に生きる世界へ』 *Reproductive Health and the Environment: Towards a Symbiotic World*, 270 pp., 工作舎, 1996.

　　A joint work by 13 researchers, including the editors, who consider worldwide development problems, North-South problems, and ecological problems from the perspective of women's reproductive health and reproductive rights. Among the contributors, Watanuki argues for intergenerational "symbiosis" by viewing women's bodies as "internal nature," while Ueno reviews new developments in feminism relating to reproductive health and rights.

08 利谷信義・湯沢雍彦・袖井孝子・篠塚英子（編）Toshitani Nobuyoshi, Yuzawa Yasuhiko, Sodei Takako and Shinozuka Hideko (eds.),『高学歴時代の女性——女子大学からのメッセージ』 *Women in an Age of High Academic Credentials: A Message from a Women's University*, xiv＋211 pp., 有斐閣, 1996.

　　A joint study by 10 researchers from Ochanomizu University, one of only two national women's universities in Japan. Issues considered include what young women seek from university; Japanese society and female students; changes in domestic science departments; women's studies, gender studies, and university education reform; what companies seek of female students; the hurdles and potential of women researchers; whether women with high academic credentials have shut men out of the labor market; the families and daily life of women with high academic credentials; and how to balance career and home. The appendix contains important related materials arranged in an easy-to-follow manner, and as a whole this book is an excellent introduction to the position and role of women with high academic credentials in contemporary Japan and to their potential for bringing about social change.

09 村松泰子（編）Muramatsu Yasuko (ed.),『女性の理系能力を生かす——専攻分野のジェンダー分析と提言』 *Getting Women to Make Use of Their Abilities in the Natural Sciences: A Gender-Based Analysis of Fields of Specialization and Some Proposals*, 310 pp., 日本評論社, 1996.

10 天野正子 Amano Masako,『生活者とはだれか——自律的市民像の系譜』
*Who Are Consumers (Seikatsusha) ?: The Genealogy of Autonomous
Citizens*, 242 pp., 中央公論社, 1996.

  The author examines the meaning of the word 'consumer' as a key word
of different historical periods by tracing it back to its origins, which she
finds in Miki Kiyoshi's 三木清 theory of a culture of daily living under the
wartime fascist régime. She then traces its postwar developments, critically
examining both economic critiques based on Ōkuma Nobuyuki's 大熊信
行 "consumers' declaration" and Yamazaki Masakazu's 山崎正和 "soft
individualism" and then describing the developments from "theory" to
"movement," exemplified by the experiments of the Peace for Vietnam
Committee (Beheiren ベ平連) and the women's movement centered on the
Seikatsu Club Consumers' Cooperative. Not only is this a social history
of contemporary Japan as seen from the perspectives of consumers and
women, but it is also an outstanding study of gender and social movements in contemporary Japan. It is essential reading for linking feminism
and social movement theory.

11 天野正子 Amano Masako,『フェミニズムのイズムを超えて——女たち
の時代経験』*Transcending the -Ism of Feminism: The Historical Experiences of Women*, 293 pp., 岩波書店, 1997.

12 佐藤慶幸 Satō Yoshiyuki,『女性と協同組合の社会学——生活クラブから
のメッセージ』*The Sociology of Women and Cooperatives: A Message
from the Seikatsu (Livelihood) Club Consumers' Cooperative*, vii+276
pp., 文眞堂, 1996.

  Approaching the issue from the perspective of the rebirth of communities in contemporary industrial society, the author defines the Seikatu
Club Consumers' Cooperative as a "cooperative self-organization of daily
living" and, having first considered the significance of staff work, he then
goes on to discuss women's workers' collectives, consumer cooperatives
and feminism, and the Seikatsu Club Consumers' Cooperative as a form
of social participation for women, as well as touching on environmental
problems and the consumer cooperative movement, staff organization and
the activities of cooperative members as a new social movement, contemporary industrial society and interlocutory communication, and the life-
world and social movements. Satō analyzes in sociological terms the
formation of new human relations in the context of the current questioning of the relationship between the economy, ecology and technology, the
role of women in this, the meaning of utilizing feminism in the consumer
cooperative movement, and the significance of a "representative move-

ment" whereby women use the cooperative movement to advance into politics. He also examines the idea of joint purchasing as a solution to environmental problems insofar that it shows the links between "the kitchen and global environmental problems" and ideas for reforming the organization of cooperatives with reference to the perspective of gender.

13 大橋松行 Ōhashi Matsuyuki,『生活者運動の社会学——市民参加への一里塚』 *The Sociology of the Consumer (Seikatsusha) Movement: A Milestone in Citizens' Participation*, 197 pp., 北樹出版, 1997.

This book deals with subjects such as the movement to stop chemical detergents entering Lake Biwa 琵琶湖, the citizens' movement in the city of Zushi 逗子, and the residents' movement on Miyake Island 三宅島 from the perspectives of the increasing conservatism of young people in an "affluent society," cultural administration, etc.

14 栗原 彬 Kurihara Akira,『〈やさしさ〉の闘い——社会と自己をめぐる思索の旅路で』 *The Struggles of "Gentleness": On a Journey of Musings about Society and Self*, 256 pp., 新曜社, 1996.

15 小椋 博 (監修) Komuku Hiroshi (supvr.),『新・スポーツ文化の創造に向けて』 *Towards the Creation of a New Sports Culture*, 260+45 pp., ベースボールマガジン社, 1996.

16 赤川 学 Akagawa Manabu,『性への自由／性からの自由——ポルノグラフィの歴史社会学』 *Freedom to Sex/Freedom from Sex: The Historical Sociology of Pornography*, 204+13 pp., 青弓社, 1996.

A social history of pornography, with the final two chapters dealing with its history and the current situation in Japan. It is to be hoped that more empirical research on this subject will appear in the future.

17 矢島正見 (編) Yajima Masami (ed.),『男性同性愛者のライフヒストリー』 *The Life Histories of Gays*, viii+491 pp., 学文社, 1997.

One of the few studies of gays in the field of Japanese sociology. It is based on interviews and describes how the interviewees became aware of their homosexuality and how they came to behave as gays. It concludes that in Japan homosexual relations are rooted in consensus, but "this consensus is in fact a typically Japanese vague kind of consensus," and "examining the sexuality of gays has direct bearings on the examination of the future modality of sexuality."

18 松平 誠 Matsudaira Makoto,『入浴の解体新書』 *A New Anatomy of Bathing*, 253 pp., 小学館, 1997.

On the basis of the history and present state of the culture of bathing in Japan, the author develops ideas on comparative culture.

19 熊沢 恂・清 眞人・木本喜美子 Kumazawa Makoto, Kiyoshi Mahito

and Kimoto Kimiko,『映画マニアの社会学——スクリーンにみる人間と社会』 *The Sociology of Film Buffs: People and Society as Seen on the Screen*, 218 pp., 明石書店, 1997.

20 宮原浩二郎・荻野昌弘（編）Miyahara Kōjirō and Ogino Masahiro (eds.),『変身の社会学』 *The Sociology of Metamorphosis*, v+256 pp., 世界思想社, 1997.

This book approaches the human desire for change in contemporary society in terms of the key word 'metamorphosis', arguing that if the power of self-retention can be equated with memory, then the power of metamorphosis is equivalent to oblivion. It represents a new type of sociology that tries to approach society and people from an angle diametrically opposite to that of theories of identity.

21 新原道信 Niihara Michinobu,『ホモ・モーベンス——旅する社会学』 *Homo Movens: The Sociology of Travelling*, 269 pp., 窓社, 1997.

22 鶴見良行・宮内泰介（編）Tsurumi Yoshiyuki and Miyauchi Taisuke (ed.),『ヤシの実のアジア学』 *On Coconuts and Asian Studies*, 349 pp., コモンズ, 1996.

23 鶴見和子 Tsurumi Kazuko,『内発的発展論の展開』 *The Evolution of Endogenous Development Theory*, 318+xiv pp., 筑摩書房, 1996.

GEOGRAPHY

Taniuchi Tōru
The University of Tokyo

I. INTRODUCTION

Geography, broadly speaking, includes the two aspects of physical geography and human geography, but is here limited to human geography.

General trends in research on human geography may be ascertained by referring to the annual reviews mentioned in the Bibliography, I-01~02. Further, in the period covered by this review, along with the publication of an inclusive review and bibliography of literature on economic geography in the first half of the 1990s [I-03] and a special issue of *Geographical Review of Japan* (Series B) in the form of English reviews of research trends in various fields of human geography [I-04], may be added the publication of an inclusive dictionary of human geography [I-05] and of a comprehensive and compact outline of Japanese geography addressed to non-Japanese.

II. POPULATION AND HUMAN ACTIVITIES

Valuable traditional-style contributions to geographical research on Japanese population are studies on internal migration, characteristically macro-studies focusing on metropolises [II-01], along with studies based on intensive fieldwork in specific districts within metropolises [II-02, 03].

Furthermore, studies of policies relating to the aging of resident populations in metropolises [II-04~06] and non-metropolitan cities [II-07, 08], studies of inhabitants' everyday activities viewed by gender [II-09, 10] and of foreign residents [II-11, 12] are increasingly noteworthy as representing important themes in geographical research.

III. CHANGING URBAN SYSTEMS AND URBAN AREAS

Many studies with urban areas as subject have the urban system as their most basic framework. Actual subjects for analysis in urban system studies include many types, but most recently they have been characterised by emphasis upon the location of businesses and offices of public administration [III-01, 02]. In particular, analysis based on economic management function, actually on the location of business offices, may already be said to be established as a most important method of research into urban systems. Furthermore, this method of observation has also become a major technique in studies on metropolitan suburbanization and multinucleation.

IV. CHANGING RURAL AREAS

Most noteworthy with regard to the rich accumulation of studies on depopulated areas, along with progress in research observing central function [IV-01] and public finance [IV-02], is the acquisition of Okahashi Hidenori's research [IV-03], not exclusively restricted to mountain villages as a depopulated area, but argued in terms of structural situation within the nationwide framework. Furthermore, there is a steady advance in research from the viewpoints of communities and organizations [IV-04, 05]. Research into rural areas based on intensive field surveys is important in that it provides an understanding of the Japanese economy based on an understanding of Japanese society. Thus, geography is one field of research able to make a valuable contribution.

V. SPACIAL ORGANIZATION OF ECONOMIC ACTIVITIES

In geographical research related to primary industry, the focus is on research monographs whose premise is an awareness of the question as to how far agricultural regions will survive, given the severe conditions of the international economic environment, such as import liberalization, and interregional agricultural competition within Japan itself [V-01~04]. Furthermore, amid the diminishing tendency to study paddy field cultivation, central to Japanese agriculture, Motoki Yasushi's study of paddy field development [V-05] may be considered an important geographical research contribution on Japanese agricultural policy.

In the case of geographical research on secondary (manufacturing) industry, along with general studies [V-06, 07], in the tradition of past geographical research, there has been a steady accumulation of studies relating to individual categories of industry and individual regions [V-08~14].

In geographical research on tertiary (service) industry, there have appeared studies of transportation [V-15, 16], retailing [V-17, 18], and finance and information [V-19, 20]. Needless to say, such studies are very closely bound up with the research on urban systems and urban areas described in Section III.

VI. HISTORICAL AND CULTURAL STUDIES

By and large, historical studies with regard to geography may be divided into two categories. In the first category are the contributions from geography to historical studies in a wider sense in terms of clarifying geographical conditions in the past [VI-01~04], studies concerning religious beliefs being particularly numerous.

In the second category, comprising studies concerned with the process of modernization in Japan, contributing background to contemporary Japanese society and economy and an insight into problematical issues, may be found empirical research on manufacturing [VI-05, 06], along with urbanization [VI-07] and commodity distribution and transport [VI-08~10]. Furthermore, the findings of research into the historical geography of cities [VI-11] are of value when considering present-day cities.

In association with such historical studies, studies of cultural geography and ecology, such as VI-12~13, are valuable in interpreting the traditional background to Japan's culture and society.

BIBLIOGRAPHY

I. Introduction

01　学会展望（1996 年 1 月～12 月）"A Survey of Geographical Studies in Japan, 1996," 「人文地理」49 巻, pp. 222-275, 人文地理学会, 1997.

02　学会展望（1997 年 1 月～12 月）"A Survey of Geographical Studies in Japan, 1997," 「人文地理」50 巻, pp. 256-308, 人文地理学会, 1998.

03　経済地理学会（編）The Japan Association of Economic Geographers (ed.),『経済地理学の成果と課題　第Ⅴ集』Inventory and Prospects of Economic Geography, Vol. 5, 403 pp., 大明堂, 1997.

04　"Progress in Japanese Human Geography," Geographical Review of Japan, Vol. 69 (Ser. B), Special Issue, 日本地理学会, 1996.

05　山本正三・奥野隆史・石井英也・手塚　章（編）Yamamoto Shōzō, Okuno Takashi, Ishii Hideya and Tezuka Akira (eds.),『人文地理学辞典』Dictionary of Human Geography, 525 pp., 朝倉書店, 1997.

06　矢ケ崎典隆（編）Yagasaki Noritaka (ed.), Japan: Geographical Perspectives on an Island Nation, 184 pp., 帝国書院, 1997.

II. Population and Human Activities

01　磯田則彦 Isoda Norihiko, わが国における 1985～1990 年間の都市間移動パターン "Japanese Interurban Migration Patterns, 1985-1990," 「地理科学」51 巻, pp. 19-33, 地理科学学会, 1996.

02　川口太郎 Kawaguchi Tarō, 郊外世帯の住居移動に関する分析 "Analysis of the Household Relocation Process in a Suburban Setting," 「地理学評論」70 巻 (Ser. A), pp. 108-118, 日本地理学会, 1997.

03　谷　謙二 Tani Kenji, 大都市圏郊外住民の居住経歴に関する分析 "An Analysis of Residential Careers of Metropolitan Suburbanites" 「地理学評論」70 巻 (Ser. A), pp. 263-286, 日本地理学会, 1997.

04　田原裕子・荒井良雄・川口太郎 Tahara Yūko, Arai Yoshio and Kawaguchi Tarō, 大都市圏郊外地域に居住する高齢者の生活空間と定住意思 "Life Space and Residential Preferences of the Elderly in Metropolitan Suburbs 「人文地理」48 巻, pp. 301-316, 人文地理学会, 1996.

05　由井義通 Yui Yoshimichi, 東京都江東区における都営住宅居住者の年齢

別人口構成の変化 "Changing Characteristics of Public Housing Residents in Kōtō-ku, Tokyo," 「季刊地理学」48 巻, pp. 255-275, 東北地理学会, 1996.

06 斎野岳郎 Saino Gakurō, 『大都市の人口高齢化』 *Aging in a Metropolis*, 130 pp., 大明堂. 1997.

07 杉浦真一郎 Sugiura Shin'ichirō, 広島県における高齢者福祉サービスと地域的公正 "Welfare Services for the Elderly and Territorial Justice in Hiroshima Prefecture, Japan," 「地理学評論」70 巻 (Ser. A), pp. 418-432, 日本地理学会, 1997.

08 山下 潤 Yamashita Jun, "Utilization of Elderly Care Facilities by the Non-Institutionalized Elderly in Matsumoto," *Geographical Review of Japan*, Vol. 70 (Ser. B), pp. 1-9, 日本地理学会, 1997.

09 有留順子・小方 登 Aritome Junko and Ogata Noboru, 性差からみた大都市圏における通勤パターン——大阪大都市圏を事例として "Gender Characteristics of Commuting Patterns in the Osaka Metropolitan Area," 「人文地理」49 巻, pp. 47-63, 人文地理学会, 1997.

10 川瀬正樹 Kawase Masaki, 世帯のライフステージから見た千葉県柏市における既婚女性の通勤行動の変化 "Changes in Married Women's Commuting Activity in Terms of Life-Stage in Kashiwa, Chiba Prefecture," 「地理学評論」70 巻 (Ser. A), pp. 699-723, 日本地理学会, 1997.

11 阿部康久 Abe Yasuhisa, 長崎における在日中国人の就業状況の変化と居住地移動 "The Changing Occupations and Residential Mobility of Chinese in Nagasaki," 「人文地理」49 巻, pp. 395-411, 人文地理学会, 1997.

12 清水昌人 Shimizu Masato, 外国人の生活空間行動——東京大都市地域の就学生 "Daily Spatial Activities of Foreign Pre-College Students: A Case Study in the Tokyo Metropolitan Area," 「経済地理学年報」43 巻, pp. 59-71, 経済地理学会, 1997.

III. Changing Urban Systems and Urban Areas

01 森川 洋 Morikawa Hiroshi, わが国主要都市における企業活動と都市システム——1981~91 年の事業所統計の分析から "Firm Activities and Urban Systems in Japanese Main Cities Based on the Analysis of Establishment Census 1981 and 1991," 「地理科学」51 巻, pp. 81-90, 地理科学学会, 1996.

02 坪本裕之 Tsubomoto Hiroyuki, 東京大都市圏におけるオフィス供給と業務地域の成長 "Trend in Office Supply and the Growth of Business Districts in the Tokyo Metropolitan Area," 「人文地理」48 巻, pp. 341-363, 人文地理学会, 1996.

03 石川雄一 Ishikawa Yūichi, 京阪神大都市圏における多核化の動向と郊外

核の特性 "The Trend of Multinucleation and the Characteristics of Suburban Nucleations in the Keihanshin Metropolitan Area," 「地理学評論」69 巻 (Ser. A), pp. 387-414, 日本地理学会, 1996.

IV. Changing Rural Areas

01 作野広和 Sakuno Hirokazu, 過疎的農山村における低次中心地の存立構造 "The Structure of Surviving Lower Order Centers in Depopulated Rural Mountain Regions," 「人文地理」48 巻, pp. 527-549, 人文地理学会, 1996.

02 梶田 真 Kajita Shin, 過疎地域における財政構造の変化と地域変容 "The Local Impact of Changes in the Public Finance System in an Area of Severe Depopulation," 「人文地理」49 巻, pp. 289-302, 人文地理学会, 1997.

03 岡橋秀典 Okahashi Hidenori, 『周辺地域の存立構造——現代山村の形成と展開』 *Transformation of Japan's Peripheral Regions: Development and Peripheralization Process of Mountain Villages*, 401 pp., 大明堂, 1997.

An inclusive study of Japanese mountain villages in terms of their peripheral situation within the reorganization of the nationwide regional structure. This work includes a wealth of case studies from various regions.

04 高橋 誠 Takahashi Makoto, 『近郊農村の地域社会変動』 *Social Changes in Suburban Rural Communities*, 279 pp., 古今書院, 1997.

05 宮澤 仁・菊地俊夫・張 貴民 Miyazawa Hitoshi, Kikuchi Toshio, and Zhang Guimin, 秋田県における農業協同組合合併のプロセスとその地域的性格 "The Process of Amalgamation of Agricultural Cooperatives and Its Regional Characteristics in Akita Prefecture," 「経済地理学年報」43 巻, pp. 165-184, 経済地理学会, 1997.

V. Spatial Organization of Economic Activities

01 川久保篤志 Kawakubo Atsushi, オレンジ果汁輸入自由化による産地の変貌 "Changes in Mandarin Producing Areas with Liberalization of Orange Juice Import," 「人文地理」48 巻, pp. 28-47, 人文地理学会, 1996.

02 荒木一視 Araki Hitoshi, 北海道旭川市における野菜産地の成長——農協の集出荷先対応を中心として "Growth of Vegetable Production in Asahikawa, Hokkaido: Strategies of Shipper's Union," 「人文地理」48 巻, pp. 427-448, 人文地理学会, 1996.

03 張 貴民 Zhang Guimin, 埼玉県岡部町における野菜産地の形成とその持続的基盤 "The Development Mechanism and Its Sustainable Bases in a Vegetable Growing Area in Okabe Town, Saitama Prefecture," 「地理学評論」69 巻 (Ser. A), pp. 223-241, 日本地理学会, 1996.

04   卜部勝彦 Urabe Katsuhiko, 三重県内部川扇状地における植木生産地域
の発展と存立基盤 "The Basis of Development for Nursery Plant Production Areas in the Utsubegawa Fan, Mie Prefecture," 「地理学評論」69 巻
(Ser. A), pp. 327-352, 日本地理学会, 1996.

05   元木　靖 Motoki Yasushi, 『現代日本の水田開発──開発地理学的手法
の展開』 *Paddy Field Development in Modern Japan: A Developmental
Geography Systems Approach*, 275 pp., 古今書院, 1997.

06   竹内淳彦 Takeuchi Atsuhiko, 『工業地域の変動』 *Changing Industrial
Areas in Japan*, 222 pp., 大明堂, 1996.

An analysis of changes to Japanese manufacturing industry since the
latter half of the 1980s, concerning the development of high-tech industries, location changes in the iron and steel industry accompanying
changes in the economic environment, changes in metropolitan industrial
areas, and technopolises.

07   長尾謙吉 Nagao Kenkichi, 製造業における雇用成長の地域差──拡張シ
フトシェア分析を用いて "Regional Employment Changes in Japanese
Manufacturing Industry, 1970-1990: An Extended Shift-Share Analysis,"
「地理学評論」69 巻 (Ser. A), pp. 303-326, 日本地理学会, 1996.

08   北川博史 Kitagawa Hirofumi, わが国主要コンピュータメーカーにおけ
るソフトウェアハウスの展開 "The Development of Large Corporation's
Software Houses," 「人文地理」48 巻, pp. 499-516, 人文地理学会, 1996.

09   水野真彦 Mizuno Masahiko, 機械メーカーと部品サプライヤーの取引関
係とその変化 "Changing Transaction Relationships between Japanese
Manufacturing Firms and Their Parts Suppliers," 「人文地理」49 巻, pp.
525-545, 人文地理学会, 1997.

10   大澤勝文 Ōsawa Katsufumi, 流通構造変化に伴う三条作業工具工業の再
編成 "Reorganization of the Hand-tool Industry in Sanjō City Due to
Changes in Distribution Channels," 「地理学評論」69 巻 (Ser. A), pp.
942-962, 日本地理学会, 1996.

11   水野真彦 Mizuno Masahiko, 自動車産業の事例から見た企業間連関と近
接 "Interfirm Linkages and Proximity: A Case Study of Japanese Automobile Industry," 「地理学評論」70 巻 (Ser. A) pp. 352-369, 日本地理学会,
1997.

12   小田宏信 Oda Hironobu, "The Locational Dynamics of the Japanese
Plastic-Mold Manufacturing Industry during the Microelectronics Innovation," *Geographical Review of Japan*, Vol. 70 (Ser. B), pp. 10-31, 日本
地理学会, 1997.

13   立川和平 Tachikawa Wahei, 福井合繊織物産地の構造変化 "Structural
Change of the Synthetic Textile Industry in Fukui Prefecture," 「経済地理

学年報」43 巻, pp. 18-36, 経済地理学会, 1997.

14 箸本健二 Hashimoto Kenji, 情報ネットワーク化とビール工業における生産・物流体制の変化——キリンビールを事例として "The Influence of Information Network Innovation on the Distribution System of a Japanese Brewery: A Case Study of Kirin Beer,"「経済地理学年報」42 巻, pp.1-19, 経済地理学会, 1996.

15 安積紀雄 Azumi Norio,『営業倉庫の展開と存立基盤——東海・北陸地方を中心として』 The Development of Commercial Warehouses and Locational Bases: Focusing on the Tōkai and Hokuriku Districts, 131 pp., 大明堂, 1996.

16 野尻 亘 Nojiri Wataru, わが国の高速道路における交通流動 "The Traffic Flows on Japanese Express Motorways,"「季刊地理学」48 巻, pp. 115-136, 東北地理学会, 1996.

17 根田克彦 Neda Katsuhiko, "Recent Trends on the Retail Location in the Urban Retailing System: A Case Study of Kushiro, Hokkaido," *Geographical Review of Japan*, Vol. 70 (Ser. B), pp. 41-56, 日本地理学会, 1997.

18 伊藤健司 Itō Kenji, 合理化にともなう事務所機能の空間的再編——大規模小売業者ユニーの事例 "The Spatial Reorganization of Office Functions by Rationalization: A Case Study of 'Uny,' a Large-scale Retailer,"「人文地理」49 巻, pp. 121-141, 人文地理学会, 1997.

19 田中康一 Tanaka Kōichi, 企業の立地と金融の地域構造——雪印の事例より "The Locational Structure of a Corporation and the Regional Structure of Finance: A Case Study of the Snow Brand Milk Products Co.,"「経済地理学年報」42 巻, pp. 20-43, 経済地理学会, 1996.

20 加藤幸治 Katō Kōji, 情報サービスの地域的循環とその東京一極集中——東北地域を事例として "The Regional Circular Flow of Information Services and 'Mono-polarization in Tokyo': A Case Study of the Tōhoku Region,"「地理学評論」69 巻 (Ser. A), pp. 102-125, 日本地理学会, 1996.

VI. Historical and Cultural Studies

01 金子直樹 Kaneko Naoki, 岩木山信仰の空間構造——その信仰圏を中心にして "The Spatial Structure of Mountain Religion: The Case of Mt. Iwaki,"「人文地理」49 巻, pp. 311-330, 人文地理学会, 1997.

02 三木一彦 Miki Kazuhiko, 秩父地域における三峰信仰の展開——木材生産との関連を中心に "Development of the Cult of Mitsumine in the Chichibu Region, Particularly in Relation to Forest Felling,"「地理学評論」69 巻 (Ser. A), pp. 921-941, 日本地理学会, 1996.

03 舩杉力修 Funasugi Rikinobu, 戦国期における伊勢信仰の浸透とその背景——越後国蒲原郡出雲田荘を事例として "Infiltration of Ise Shrine

Worship in the Sengoku Period and Its Background: The Case of Izumoda-no-shō in Kambara District, Echigo Province,"「地理学評論」70 巻 (Ser. A), pp. 491-511, 日本地理学会, 1997.

04 米家泰作 Komeie Taisaku, 前近代日本の山村をめぐる三つの視角とその 再検討 "A Reexamination of Studies of the Mountain Area in Pre-modern Japan, with Special Reference to Cultural, Political, and Economic Viewpoints,"「人文地理」49 巻, pp. 546-566, 人文地理学会, 1997.

05 杉浦芳夫 Sugiura Yoshio, 絹織物工場における電動力織機の普及——福 井市の事例 "Spatial Diffusion of Electric Power Looms in the Fukui Silk Weaving Industry, Modern Japan,"「人文地理」49 巻, pp. 419-441, 人文 地理学会, 1997.

06 青木隆浩 Aoki Takahiro, 近世・近代における埼玉県清酒業の形成過程 "The Formation Process of the *Sake* Brewing Industry in Saitama Prefec- ture during the Early Modern and Modern Ages,"「経済地理学年報」43 巻, pp. 83-99, 経済地理学会, 1997.

07 水内俊雄・綿 久美子 Mizuuchi Toshio and Wata Kumiko, 戦前期開発 の郊外住宅地形成史 "The Study of the Historical Development of Prewar Residential Suburbs,"「地理科学」51 巻, pp. 34-54, 地理科学学会, 1997.

08 葛西大和 Kasai Yamato, 明治・大正期における商品流通の変化 "The Structural Change of Commodity Distribution Patterns in Yamagata Prefecture, 1870-1920,"「歴史地理学」185 号, pp, 1-2, 歴史地理学会, 1997.

09 三木理史 Miki Masafumi, 近代日本の地域交通体系研究——研究方法と 問題点をめぐって "Current Trends and Issues in Studies of Regional Transportation Systems in Modern Japan,"「人文地理」48 巻, pp. 69-88, 人文地理学会, 1996.

10 葛西大和 Kasai Yamato, 近代日本における外国貿易港の配置と貿易額の 地域的構成 "The Location of Ports for International Commerce in Modern Japan and the Regional Structure of Port Trade,"「季刊地理学」 49 巻, pp. 75-93, 東北地理学会, 1997.

11 山田安彦・山崎謹哉（編）Yamada Yasuhiko and Yamazaki Kin'ya (eds.),『歴史のふるい都市群』*Historical Towns in Japan*, 12 Vols., 大明 堂, 1984-1997.
　　Vol. 11,『北九州の都市』*Towns in Northern Kyushu*, 360 pp., 1997.
　　Vol. 12,『南九州の都市』*Towns in Southern Kyushu*, 256 pp., 1997.
　　The latest two volumes in a series published since 1984, which complete the series of twelve. Altogether, the twelve volumes describe the historical geography of 236 Japanese towns.

12 中俣 均 Nakamata Hitoshi, 方言区画論と言語地域区分 "Dialect Divi-

sion Theory (*Hōgen-kukaku-ron*) and the Actual Linguistic Regions,"
「人文地理」49 巻，pp. 20-31，人文地理学会，1997.

13　田和正孝 Tawa Masataka,『漁場利用の生態――文化地理学的考察』*Ecological Study on Fishing Ground Use: An Approach from Cultural Geography*, 402 pp., 九州大学出版会，1997.

CULTURAL ANTHROPOLOGY

Itō Abito
The University of Tokyo

I. GENERAL INTRODUCTION

The area of research to be dealt with here under the title "Cultural Anthropology" covers not only cultural anthropology (or social anthropology) and ethnology in a narrow sense, but also the traditional field of Japanese folklife studies. Interlinked through Japan's historical and social context, these could together be said to have moulded Japanese-style cultural anthropological research, and there would seem to be a need to understand this very nature of cultural anthropology in Japan as one aspect of Japanese society and culture. In addition, the works introduced below include not only books by specialists, but also reports, collections of materials and so on deemed to be useful sources of information for overseas cultural anthropologists.

The supposition that scholarship and research equivalent to what is identified as cultural anthropology in Western society similarly exists in all non-Western societies is fraught with problems. If researchers who have received a specialist education in cultural anthropology within the Western education system, sharing its logical and intellectual systems and having mastered its distinctive methodology, then go on to undertake research on Japan, this undoubtedly represents for Westerners research on Japan grounded in cultural anthropology. But in actual practice all academic disciplines exist within the context of a particular society and culture, and they accordingly undergo distinctive developments. This also applies to cultural anthropology in Japan, and even though it may initially have been introduced from Western society and have continued to be influenced by the West, it has been accepted into Japan's social and cultural context. This means, in other words, that academic disciplines too must be understood as social and cultural processes. In particular, when the Japanese describe and discuss Japan, it is impossible for them to unilaterally apply the overseas paradigms of anthropology in their observations and descriptions. A correct understanding of the nature of cultural anthropology in a broad sense of the term as it exists in Japan would seem to be a prerequisite for anthropological research, both with regard to Japanese society and culture *per se*, and also for utilizing works written by Japanese.

As was pointed out in the previous volume of this series (Vol. XI-1), cultural anthropology in a narrow sense of the term as conceived of by Westerners was introduced to Japan in earnest after World War II under the strong influence of mainly American scholarship, while Japanese folklife studies (*minzokugaku*), on the other hand, has a long history and tradition as an indigenous field of learning, and ethnology, also called *minzokugaku* in Japanese and introduced from the West, has developed against the background of an interest in Asia and internationalization in modern Japan. It was also noted that these three broad academic traditions are each related to different levels of Japanese identity, and together they constitute cultural anthropology in a broad sense as it exists in Japan today.

It is true that today all researchers in Japan with an interest in Japanese culture and society have to some degree been influenced either directly or indirectly by Western anthropology. But this influence varies, and it determines to what degree a piece of research is judged to be anthropological in content. At the same time, even among ordinary Japanese the practice of thinking, talking and writing about their daily lives has constituted an important part of everyday life. For example, already in the eighteenth and nineteenth centuries ethnographic accounts and local gazetteers describing life in different localities were being compiled in large numbers, and even when these were compiled under the direction of the local *han* government, the actual investigations and writing of these works were often entrusted to locals. Many such ethnographic accounts and local gazetteers were also written purely on the initiative of individual intellectuals and other interested persons, who were to be found in every locality, and there were even families in which this interest was handed down from one generation to the next, with journals recording their everyday life being kept over several generations. During the Edo period there was a high rate of literacy even among the commoners when compared with other countries, and even in rural villages there were people with intellectual interests who, on the basis of their own experiences and observations, left records of local life for posterity. In the practical fields of farming, fishing and forestry these have been preserved in the form of voluminous "agricultural writings" (*nōsho*), which are well-known, but it should not be forgotten that in the fields of local history and folklife studies too there were researchers in most localities who were not mere informants and maintained close contacts with specialists. Among those born into wealthy families or experienced farming families, there were some who considered the practice of this popular scholarship to represent a contribution to local society and understood the significance of recording their observations and experiences. They appear to have been aware of the fact that while on the one hand rural life underwent gradual change because of constant exposure to external influences, on the other hand there also existed distinctive local traditions that did not easily change. It could be said that the traditions of people such as these were carried over by local folklife scholars. While engaged in gathering the wealth of unique folk knowledge to be found in each region, they also formed local associations of folklife studies and even published their own journals. Moreover, although they did not possess any theoretical framework based on a logical grasp of their subject matter, as in the case of specialist researchers, they nonetheless had a descriptive framework based on a long-term vision born of the accumulation of practical experience that covered all aspects of local society and culture. Their scholarship may have been lacking in logical systemicity, but it was pluralistic, holistic, experiential and practice-oriented, just like the indigenous knowledge of farmers that is being reevaluated in development paradigms for today's developing societies, and it shows evidence of a stance that would seek to understand society and culture in the context of continual and sustainable change.

These traditions of indigenous learning were to be seen in folklife studies too, as it developed into academic associations with the support of leaders in the main centers during the course of modernization after the Meiji Restoration, and they are also behind the fact that people other than those who have obtained university degrees and become specialist researchers are able to become researchers in local communities. Formerly local writers, supported by the Atic Museum, compiled detailed ethnographies of rural life, exemplified by a record of farming life by a farmer Yoshida Saburō living at the foot of Mt. Kanpū (or Samukaze) on Oga Peninsula, Akita prefecture, and by the records researched and written by school pupils under the guidance of Takeuchi Toshimi, an assistant elementary school teacher, and the compilation of such detailed works by local inhabitants in the 1930s probably has few parallels anywhere else in the world.

Even today it is by no means easy to differentiate clearly between research by specialists and nonspecialists. It is also worth noting that because of the promotion and strong popular awareness of national culture since the Meiji era, the interests of local researchers in specific localities have, through continual comparison with other regions, deepened perceptions of their own regional culture within the nation of Japan as a whole.

In view of the above circumstances, it would be by no means sound to confine this review to research by specialists, and one cannnot neglect books by locals and dilettantes. Even though such books may be overly subjective or lacking in anthropological refinement or systematic discussion, it is the self-perceptions based on the authors' own participation that could be said to be of prime importance. This is all the more so in a society such as that of Japan, which attaches greater importance to pluralistic, inclusive and experiential ideas and feelings than to systematic and logical thought and frameworks. Moreover, introducing these perceptions and descriptions based on the native interests of the Japanese themselves as texts of Japanese culture will probably prove of greater interest to non-Japanese researchers.

During the review period, works dealing with the historical background and problematic nature of cultural anthropology, ethnology and folklife studies in Japan included a study by Mori Masao [I-01], who discusses the relationship between ethnology and Japanese perceptions of Asia since the Meiji era, a report on the wartime Institute of Ethnology (Minzoku Kenkyūjo) by Nakao Katsumi [I-02], and a volume edited by Josef Kreiner [I-03], dealing comprehensively with trends in Japanese ethnology chiefly since the 1980s. In addition, Kuwayama Takami [I-04] raises questions in relation to international anthropology about research on Japan by Japanese in their capacity as local anthropologists, while Aoyagi Machiko [I-05] questions the position of cultural anthropology within the education system in Japan's middle and high schools. As for introductory works on folklife studies published during the same period, there appeared a volume compiled by Fukuda Ajio and Akata Mitsuo [I-06] and an introduction by Sano Kenji *et al*. [I-07]. These apprise one of how researchers in Japan today perceive Japan's social and cultural traditions and how they present these to readers of the younger generation. In addition, the position of folklife studies in Japan's education system is discussed by Tomaru Tokuichi [I-08].

II. REGIONALITY

Under the former *han* system of decentralized rule, Japanese society was marked by major regional differences in language, folk culture and social customs, and during the course of promoting state administration and national integration since the Meiji era these have attracted considerable interest. Not only was this distinctive nature of regional culture recognized from an early stage by folklife scholars as forming part of the identity of local residents, but ethnologists too showed an interest in trying to uncover behind this regionality the process underlying the historical formation of Japan's ethnic culture. This interest in the regionality of Japanese culture formerly evinced by researchers of historical and comparative ethnology is reflected in a volume edited by Josef Kreiner [II-01], which summarizes the points at issue in each field. In addition, the proceedings of a symposium on the cultural traditions of regions to the north of Japan were published [II-02], while Fukuda Ajio [II-03] discusses the social differences between eastern and western Japan.

III. NATURE AND THE ENVIRONMENT

The interests of researchers in Japan may be assumed to strongly reflect reality as perceived by the Japanese, and in particular the high level of interest in uses of the natural environment and in subsistence activities deserves special mention. Rather than the principles of social relationships, the ideals of society, and logical systems, even members of the intellectual élite in Japan have traditionally recognized greater reality in concrete folk knowledge of the natural environment, flora and fauna and in the material culture, folk technology and types of subsistence utilizing this knowledge, and considerable interest has been shown in the modality and durability of lifestyles determined by these factors.

A most comprehensive treatment of the formation of Japanese culture is provided by Sasaki Kōmei [III-01], who focusses on cultural traditions based on subsistence dependent on ecological conditions. Likewise Komuku Jun'ichi [III-02], Sugawara Satoshi [III-03], Yasuda Yoshinori [III-04], Nomoto Kan'ichi and Katsuki Yōichirō [III-05], and Henry Stewart [III-06] all deal with flora and subsistence, while rice-growing culture is discussed by Suwa Haruo and Kawamura Minato [III-07], who include Asia as a whole in their purview, and by Tanaka Kōji [III-08] and Kojima Keizō [III-09]; Kimura Shigemitsu [III-10] and Sakamoto Yasuo [III-11] deal with the culture of dry-field farming. As for fishing, Tanigawa Ken'ichi has compiled collections of materials on river fishing by the Ainu and in the Tōhoku region [III-12] and on whaling and dolphin fishing [III-13].

This interest in the natural environment is not restricted to its role as a mere resource for subsistence activities, and under the impetus of the adverse effects on daily living resulting from the industrialization, development of tourism and residential land formations of recent years there has been renewed interest in the relationship between traditional lifestyles and the environment. Introductions to the environment as a whole from such a perspective are provided by volumes edited by Nomoto Kan'ichi and Fukuda Ajio [III-15] and by Arifuku Kōgaku [III-16], while Deguchi Akiko [III-17] deals with the environment and life along a river valley. In addition Moriyama Hiroshi [III-18], Aoki Kōichirō [IV-34], Komori Haruo [III-19], Inoue Takao [III-20], Shiohama Yasumi [III-21], Miyazaki Takeshi [III-22], and Funai Yukio [III-23] all discuss the revival and growth of local community through the restoration of harmony and symbiosis with the natural environment.

IV. VILLAGES

Formerly villages were the most basic corporate community in Japan's regional society, and for this reason the high degree of autonomy and social integration to be seen in the village have, along with the household (*ie*), attracted the attention of researchers. But in modern times public policies implemented by the administration have come to penetrate villages, while social relationships and spheres of activity have spread beyond village boundaries on account of occupational demands and individual interests, and there is now a tendency for relationships within a village to become conventionalized and be reduced to a mere shell. Furthermore, national consciousness has infiltrated all parts of the country through the development of communications and information media. Today villages and local community tend to be relegated to a peripheral position in the state's political and economic system, but at the same time, as a result of various residents' activities, they are also being rediscovered as a new frame of reference for the identity of local inhabitants, and they are ambivalent in character. Throughout Japan attempts at regional revitalization are now being made by local residents themselves through the revival and invention of local traditions.

Firstly, with regard to rural villages, there appeared a bibliography of postwar research compiled by Ishiyama Hiroshi *et al.* [IV-01], while Hasegawa Akihiko [IV-02] deals with the process of change in rural villages that has accompanied modernization, Iwata Shigenori [IV-03] describes the transformation of young villagers in the process of national integration, Kamimura Masana [IV-04] discusses historical changes in villages, Nakamura Yasuhiko [IV-05] deals with the Matsumoto basin in Nagano prefecture, Takahashi Makoto [IV-06] treats of suburban villages Mori Takemaro and Daimon Masakatsu [IV-07] deal with Yamagata prefecture and Minami Satoshi [IV-08] with the Seto Inland Sea, and the Mainichi Shimbunsha [IV-09] published a report on villages in the Tōhoku region. There also appeared further books by Sakane Yoshihiro [IV-10], Ōta Tadahisa [IV-11], Kimura Motoi and Takashima Rokuo [IV-12], and Harada Shin [IV-13]. Next, fishing villages are dealt with by Nakano Takashi [IV-14], who describes a fishing village on Noto Peninsula, and Kim Byŏng-ch'ŏl [III-14], who reports on a village of boat people in the Seto Inland Sea. In addition, the current state of the depopulation of villages and changes, accompanying the aging of the population are dealt with by Hasegawa Akihiko *et al.* [IV-15] and in a report by the Agricultural Policy Research Committee [IV-16], while Yamaguchi Michiko [IV-17] describes a village submerged under a lake created by a dam, and the journal *Nihon Minzokugaku* (Bulletin of the Folklore Society of Japan) [IV-18] brought out a special issue on the changes that development has brought to local traditions.

At the same time, a distinctive feature of recent years, born of reflections on the present state of villages exposed to these major changes, has been the publication of numerous reports and other books dealing with the revival and revitalization of villages, linked to nostalgia for village life of the past. The theme of the public lectures at the 47th annual conference of the Folklore Society of Japan was "Hometown" [IV-19], while reconstructions of former village life on the basis of interviews are essayed by Ōishi Shinzaburō *et al.* [IV-20], Yano Keiichi [IV-21], Morita Shin'ya [IV-22], and Yasui Manami [IV-23]. Recently there have also been appearing many articles and books providing not just descriptions and analyses of these social changes in villages, but also dealing with village revitalization and redevelopment in which local residents take an active part in revitalizing villages and communities. Such studies include those by Yamamoto Tadamoto [IV-24], Watanabe Nobuo [IV-25], Satō Tōzaburō [IV-26], Soda Osamu et al. [IV-27], Kodama Akito [IV-28], Ono Seishi [IV-29], Usui Susumu [IV-30], Hobo Takehiko [IV-31], Mizuma Yutaka and Ōishi Kaichirō [IV-32], Okahashi Hidenori [IV-33], and Aoki Kōichirō [IV-34], and there also appeared an account of a residents' self-governing association [IV-35].

On the subject of cities, Miyata Noboru [IV-36], availing himself of the results of historical studies, discusses the genesis of towns and cities, while traditional regional cities are dealt with in a book about Takasaki in Gumma prefecture [IV-37], describing its neighborhood associations and festivals, and in a study of Matsushiro in Nagano prefecture [IV-38]. In addition, Nakamura Norikazu [IV-39] discusses the fluidity of society with a focus on urban festivals.

V. RELIGION

In so-called civilized societies interest in religion tends to focus on religions such as Christianity, Buddhism and Islam, which possess scriptures, organizations and institutions. But in the case of Japan, popular beliefs and rites that do not fall under the rubric of such religious organizations and institutions generally occupy an important position. Even in the case of Buddhism, which is considered to have well-developed organizations and institutions, the Buddhist beliefs of the general populace are intricately intertwined with various folk beliefs, making it difficult to gain an overall grasp of Buddhism in Japan. As for Shinto, although the rites presided over by shrine priests display a high degree of modality, the rites performed by village communities and local residents without the participation of priests show many regional differences. Furthermore, any general account of popular beliefs and rites must also take into account calendrical practices and the various practices associated with folk beliefs observed in the home, and it is extremely difficult to describe these in their entirety. Although their organization and institutionalization may be underdeveloped, there is still a high level of interest in these folk beliefs and rites in Japan, and they must in fact be placed at the center of any treatment of religion in Japan.

During the review period publications on religion in general in contemporary Japan included those by Ishii Kenji [V-04], Yamaori Tetsuo [V-02], Tsuda Masao [V-03], Sasaki Kōkan [V-04], Uryū Naka and Shibuya Nobuhiro [V-05], and Akata Mitsuo and Komatsu Kazuhiko [V-06], while Kuno Akira [V-07] describes Japanese views of the otherworld, Takeda Chōshū [V-08] discusses religion in relation to the household, and Serizawa Hiromichi [V-09] deals with religious ethics in connection with modernization and commercial activities.

Shinto, with its basis in indigenous folk beliefs, is dealt with by Wang Chu-hua [V-10], Tani Shōgo [V-11], Yamamura Katsuaki [V-12], Hirano Takakuni [V-13], and Asoya Masahiko [V-14], while Miyata Noboru [V-15] and Den Yoshiyuki [V-16] discuss the distinctive features of Shinto in terms of folk beliefs, Nagasawa Toshiaki [V-17] describes popular beliefs in Edo as an example of the remarkable developments undergone by folk beliefs in cities, and Murayama Shūichi [V-18] deals with the *goryō* belief centered on malevolent spirits. In addition, Hayami Yoshiharu [V-19] considers the beliefs relating to *dōsojin*, a type of deity associated with village boundaries, Mori Takao [V-20] deals with beliefs and rites connected with residential space, and Hirose Kōjirō [V-21] treats of beliefs relating to handicapped people, who represent peripheralized members of society. Spirit possession has long been a subject of considerable interest in folklife studies, and this is discussed by Kawamura Kunimitsu [V-22], while Yamakami Izumo [V-23] traces the history of female shamans.

There appeared a variety of publications on Buddhism too: the Association for Japanese Buddhist Studies [V-24] brought out a volume dealing with various issues in Japanese Buddhism; a volume edited by Takasaki Jikido and Kimura Kiyotaka [V-25] discusses the position of Japanese Buddhism in East Asia; a volume compiled by Itō Yuishin and Fujii Masao [V-26] focusses on the relationship between Buddhism and funeral rites; Minamoto Junko [V-27] and a volume brought out by the International Institute for the Study of Religions [V-28] deal with the position of women in Buddhism; Suzuki Yoshio [V-29] describes the community activities of Buddhism; Takasaki and Kimura [V-30] consider the "new Buddhism" that arose during the Kamakura period; Arimoto Masao [V-31] deals with the social organization of members of the Jōdo Shin sect; Wake Shūjō [V-32] considers the formation and development of the cult centered on Mt. Kōya; and Takada Ryōshin [V-33] traces the history of beliefs associated with the temple Hōryūji.

Mountain asceticism (*shugendō*) is discussed by Miyake Hitoshi [V-34] and Fujita Sadaoki [V-35], and Ushiyama Yoshiyuki [V-36] published a study of Mt. Togakushi. The traditions and influence of Taoism in Japan are dealt with by Kubo Noritada [V-37] and in a volume compiled by Noguchi Tetsurō and Kubo [V-38]. A popular pilgrimage to holly places is discussed by Nakayama Kazuhisa [V-39], and Japanese conceptions of death are dealt with by Tanigawa Ken'ichi [V-40], Yamada Shin'ya [V-41], Wakimoto Tsuneya [V-42], and Asoya Masahiko [V-14].

VI. THE ECONOMY AND BUSINESS MANAGEMENT

Against a background of international interest, economic organizations and the nature of business management in Japan, especially in relation to their sociocultural traditions and economic rationality, remain a fascinating subject of research. An introductory work focussing on Japanese-style management in the workplace and corporations was published by Yoshida Kazuo [VI-01], while Yoshimori Masaru [VI-02] provides comparisons with Europe and America, Takahashi Nobuo [VI-03] considers decision-making, Asanuma Banri [VI-04] draws attention to the custom of long-term trading partnership, Arai Kazuhiro [VI-05] discusses the traditions of Japanese culture to be seen in the system of lifelong employment, and there appeared a volume describing the experiences of Japanese businesses in Asia [VI-06]. In addition, Muroi Wataru [VI-07] takes up hotsprings as an example of business practices in regional localities, Tanaka Mitsuru [VI-08] deals with small businesses in locally-based industry (*jibasangyō*), Seki Mitsuhiro and Hitokoto Noriyuki [VI-09] discuss local entrepreneurs, Morikawa Hidemasa [VI-10] deals with the distinctive features of business management in family businesses as exemplified by the earlier *zaibatsu*, Takeuchi Tsuneyoshi *et al.* [VI-11] probe the characteristics of entrepreneurs during the process of Japan's modernization, Satō Makoto [VI-12] provides an ethnography of the workplace as represented by the company, Nakamura Keisuke [VI-13] points out Japanese characteristics in the production system, and Ichihara Hiroshi [VI-14] deals with Japanese traditional labor practices and business management in coal mining.

VII. THE *IE* AND FAMILY

The *ie* or 'household' is an important organizational unit in the composition of Japanese society, and not only was it important for people's identification, but it was also institutionalized both within traditional community and as a focus of local administration. For this reason the *ie* has attracted considerable interest in cultural anthropology and sociology both with respect to its position in folk culture and as a manifestation of social ideology. At the same time, the concept of 'family' used for analyzing Western society has also been incorporated into research on Japanese society, but when the term 'family' is used in Japan, its usage is not necessarily confined to relationships or to the function of an analytical concept, and it often includes the connotations of the *ie* as organizational entity in folklife. With respect to the *ie*, Ōtō Osamu [VII-01] has published a useful survey of the conditions of peasants in early modern times from the perspective of the history of social institutions, while the character of the *ie* in relation to village communities is discussed in volumes compiled by Iwamoto Yoshiteru and Kunikata Keiji [VII-02] and by Iwamoto and Ōtō [VII-03], and Fujii Masaru [VII-04] considers the *ie* in connection with the group of related households known as *dōzoku* based on kinship (*shinzoku*). There also appeared a work edited by Hasegawa Yoshikazu *et al.* [VII-05] that discusses the *ie* in the context of residential space and against its spiritual background. There were also published many books that consider conditions in Japan from the perspective of the 'family,' including general works by Morioka Kiyomi and Mochizuki Takashi [VII-06] and Amanuma Kaoru [VII-07], a study of the family and domiciles edited by Kishimoto Yukiomi and Suzuki Akira [VII-08], books by Takeyasu Eiko [VII-09] and Sakamoto Kazue [VII-10] on family relationships during the process of modernization, a study focussing on women by Muta Kazue [VII-11], a compilation by Kawai Hayao and Ōba Minako [VII-12] dealing with sex, a book by Ishihara Toyomi [VII-13] describing changes in family composition and relationships in rural villages, and a study by Kameguchi Kenji [VII-14] in which he points out the critical state of family relationships from the vantage point of mental hygiene. On the subject of education in the home and socialization, Fujimoto Kōnosuke *et al.* [VII-15] and Takahashi Satoshi [VII-16] focus on children, and Tanigawa Ken'ichi compiled a volume of ethnographical studies on children in former Japan [VII-17]. In addition, there appeared a volume on child abuse [VII-18], an ethnographical introduction to children and the elderly by Miyata Noboru [VII-19], and works dealing with issues and trends relating to the elderly in the contemporary home by Mitsuoka Kōji [VII-20] and by Uenoya Kayoko and Murakawa Kōichi [VII-21].

VIII. ETHNICITY

In addition to social interest in the indigenous Ainu and in the modern immigrant society of Korean residents in Japan, there has in recent years been widespread interest in issues of human rights, labor, welfare and political participation pertaining chiefly to Asian foreigners, and this has led to a burgeoning of interest in questions of ethnicity in Japan. As a result, there were published many books and reports on this subject during the review period, and this interest will presumably continue to grow against the background of various residents' movements.

Points at issue in ethnicity in Japan and questions of methodology are discussed by Hirota Yasuo [VIII-01], Shiramizu Shigehiko [VIII-02], Okuda Michihiro [VIII-03], Komai Hiroshi [VIII-04], Aoyagi Machiko [VIII-05], and Yoshino Kōsaku [VIII-06], while Harajiri Hideki and Rokutanda Yutaka [VIII-07] and Hamaguchi Yūko [VIII-08] also take into account the historical and international background to these issues.

Among works focussing on Korean residents in Japan, those worthy of special note include an ethnographical introduction to the subject by Harajiri [VIII-09], historical treatments of their migration to Japan by Kim Ch'an-chŏng [VIII-10] and Morita Yoshio [VIII-11], a socioeconomic history by Ha Myŏng-saeng [VIII-12], a volume on the links between Korean residents in Japan and local community [VIII-13], studies of young and third-generation Korean residents by Fukuoka Yasunori and Kim Myŏng-su [VIII-14] and by Yi Ch'ŏng-ya [VIII-15], a report on ancestral ceremonies [VIII-16], and an analysis of expressions of identity by Yi In-ja [VIII-17].

Noteworthy among studies of the Ainu are firstly reconstructions of the historical experiences of the Ainu under the state-sponsored development and settlement policy in Hokkaido and policies for modernization and nationalization as seen from an Ainu perspective by Kayano Shigeru [VIII-18], Miyajima Toshimitsu [VIII-19], and Ogawa Masato [VIII-20], the last of whom focusses on the history of the education system. The present-day conditions of the Ainu as an ethnic minority are described by Nishiura Hiroki [VIII-21] and Nomura Yoshikazu [VIII-22], and there also appeared a survey of the current state of their ethnic culture [VIII-23], while Itō Yasunobu [VIII-24], Kinase Takatsugu [VIII-25], and Kotani Yoshinobu [VIII-26, 27] discuss methods of anthropological research in relation to the current state of the Ainu. Meanwhile, ethnograpohical studies of more classical subject matter are provided by an ecological study of gathering and hunting activities by Endō Kunitoshi [VIII-28], a volume on the Ainu of Sakhalin edited by Haginaka Mie and Udagawa

Hiroshi [VIII-29], and an ethnographical account of the Ainu of Sakhalin and the Kuril Islands compiled by Tanigawa Ken'ichi [VIII-30]. In addition, the Ainu and Okinawans are both discussed in the context of ethnic problems in Japan by Sawada Yōtarō [VIII-31].

In contrast to Ainu studies, there was little research on Okinawa's traditions in relation to ethnicity and national culture during this period, although there did appear a special issue of *Minzokugaku Kenkyū* (The Japanese Journal of Ethnology) providing a methodological examination of the Japanese premises and basic concepts in Okinawan studies, with contributions by Higa Masao [VIII-32], Tsuha Takashi [VIII-33], Takara Kurayoshi [VIII-34], and Ch'oe In-t'aek *et al.* [VIII-35]. At the same time, there has also been strong interest in ethnographical research dealing with Okinawa's cultural traditions, such as religion, music and the performing arts, and in addition to a volume edited by Yamaori Tetsuo [VIII-36], there appeared a study by Ueno Kazuo [VIII-37], an account of the current state of folk beliefs by Tanigawa Ken'ichi [VIII-38], a study of magical practices by Yamazato Jun'ichi [VIII-39], and a comparison with Taoist traditions in China by Kubo Noritada [VIII-40]. As for music and the performing arts, which occupy a special position in Okinawa's cultural traditions and represent a source of Okinawan ethnic identity, Miyagi Shikō [VIII-42] deals with classical music and Sakai Masako [VIII-43] provides an ethnographical study of the songs of Amami.

IX. Migrants, Foreigners, Multiculturalism and Cross-Cultural Education

On the subject of Japanese emigrants in earlier times, Iyotani Toshio and Sugihara Tōru [IX-01] discuss the contemporary social conditions that caused Japanese to emigrate, while a volume compiled by the Emigrants Research Society [IX-02] describes the conditions of emigrants during the war. In addition, Takahashi Yasutaka [IX-03] deals with prewar Japanese immigrants in Manchuria, Okita Kōji [IX-04] and Maeyama Takashi [IX-05,

06] discuss immigrants in Hawaii and Brazil respectively, and Shimpo Mitsuru [IX-07] focusses on immigrant fishermen in Canada. As regards foreign immigrants in Japan, on the other hand, there appeared works dealing with local government policies relating to foreign workers [IX-08], regional industry [IX-09, 10], local community [IX-11], the current state of muliticultural coexistence and future prospects [IX-12], and the political rights of foreigners [IX-13].

In recent years there has been growing interest not only in foreign immigrants in Japan, but also in the types of education experienced by Japanese living overseas. A comparative study of multicultural education conducted by the Research Institute of Comparative Education and Culture at Kyushu University was brought out by Kobayashi Tetsuya and Ebuchi Kazuhiro [IX-14], and an ethnographical study by Ebuchi of the education received by immigrants in other cultures also merits attention [IX-15]. In addition, Kajita Masami [IX-16] deals with American schools as an example of the education received by Japanese children overseas, while Furuoka Toshiyuki [IX-17] discusses the education of returnee children, Takahashi Masao and Sharon S. Vaipae [IX-18] consider the adjustment of foreign pupils to Japan's schools, and Asano Shin'ichirō [IX-19] describes the lives and cultural tranformation of Asian students in Japan.

X. CONCLUDING REMARKS

As we have seen in the above, against the background of various concerns that have surfaced as a result of the social changes faced by Japan in recent years, research directly linked to actual social problems has come to account for the bulk of research published during the review period. The issues taken up include environmental problems and the revival and revitalization of villages and cultural tradition in local community, which is suffering from increasing depopulation and aging of the population, and there also appeared research focussing on the ethnicity and local movements of the indigenous Ainu, on labor, welfare and education as they affect foreign immigrants, on business management, and on the *ie* and family with respect to the welfare of women, children and the elderly in relation to social change. It is clear that during the past few years the study of anthropology and ethnology has, in response to changes in society, been experiencing a major transition, and it is to be expected that in the future interest will focus even more positively on the social problems of contemporary Japan.

BIBLIOGRAPHY

I. General Introduction

01 森　雅雄 Mori Masao, 日本民族学と近代日本の他者認識 "Japanese Ethnology and Perceptions of the Other in Modern Japan," 「民族学研究」62 巻 1 号, pp. 66-85, 日本民族学会, 1997.

02 中生勝美 Nakao Katsumi, 民族研究所の組織と活動──戦時中の日本民族学 "The Organization and Activities of the Institute of Ethnology: Japanese Ethnology during the Second World War," 「民族学研究」62 巻 1 号, pp. 47-65, 日本民族学会, 1997.

As well as describing the establishment and activities of the Institute of Ethnology (Minzoku Kenkyūjo), Nakao points out that the research methods of British social anthropology rather than those of German and Austrian ethnology were adopted, and this facilitated the postwar introduction of American cultural anthropology.

03 ヨーゼフ・クライナー（編）Kreiner, Josef (ed.), 『日本民族学の現在── 1980 年代から 90 年代へ』 *The Current State of Japanese Ethnology: From the 1980s to the 1990s,* 395 pp., 新曜社, 1996.

04 桑山敬己 Kuwayama Takami, 「現地」の人類学者──内外の日本研究を中心に "'Native' Anthropologists: With a Focus on Japanese Studies in Japan and Overseas," 「民族学研究」61 巻 4 号, pp. 517-542, 日本民族学会, 1996.

05 青柳真智子（編）Aoyagi Machiko (ed.), 『中学・高校教育と文化人類学』 *Middle and High School Education and Cultural Anthropology,* 304 pp., 大明堂, 1996.

06 福田アジオ・赤田光男（編）Fukuda Ajio and Akata Mitsuo (ed.), 『社会の民俗』 *The Folkways of Society,* 317 pp., 雄山閣出版, 1997.

07 佐野賢治ほか（編）Sano Kenji *et al.* (eds.), 『現代民俗学入門』 *An Introduction to Contemporary Folklife Studies,* 303 pp., 吉川弘文館,

1996.

An introductory work that also pays attention to new circumstances relating to depopulation and village revitalization, immigrants, the state, education, internationalization, etc.

08 都丸十九一 Tomaru Tokuichi,『民俗学と教育』 *Folklife Studies and Education*, 236 pp., 換乎堂, 1996.

II. Regionality

01 ヨーゼフ・クライナー (編) Kreiner, Josef(ed.),『地域性からみた日本 ──多元的理解のために』 *Japan as Seen from Its Regionality: For a Pluralistic Understanding*, 297 pp., 新曜社, 1996.

This volume contains sections on social organization (Ōbayashi Taryō 大林太良), the present-day economy (Andō Seiichi 安東誠一), family structure (Shimizu Hiroaki 清水浩昭), dialects (Shibuya Katsumi 渋谷勝巳), music (Kojima Tomiko 小島美子), diet (Horii Masaharu 堀井正治), regional cooking (Okumura Takao 奥村彪生), and local organization (Noboru Hideki 昇秀樹).

02 第 10 回「大学と科学」公開シンポ委員会 (編) Committee for the 10th Open Symposium on "The University and Science" (ed.),『北方文化と日本列島』 *Northern Culture and the Japanese Archipelago*, 122 pp., クバプロ, 1996.

03 福田アジオ Fukuda Ajio,『番と衆──日本社会の東と西』 *Kantō's 'Ban' Rotation System for and Kansai's 'Shū' Established System for Presiding over Village Yearly Events: Society in Eastern and Western Japan*, 205 pp., 吉川弘文館, 1997.

III. Nature and the Environment

01 佐々木高明 Sasaki Kōmei,『日本文化の多重構造──アジア的視野から日本文化を再考する』 *The Multilayered Structure of Japanese Culture: Rethinking Japanese Culture from an Asian Perspective*, 334 pp., 小学館, 1997.

The author discusses the formation and multilayered structure of Japan's ethnic culture with reference to ecology, centered on flora, and with a prime focus on the different modes of subsistence and food staples found in laurilignosa culture, rice-growing culture, and the oak-forest culture from the north.

02 小椋純一 Komuku Jun'ichi,『植生からよむ日本人のくらし──明治期を中心に』 *Interpreting the Lifestyle of the Japanese on the Basis of Flora: With a Focus on the Meiji Era*, 246 pp., 雄山閣出版, 1996.

03 菅原 聡 (編) Sugawara Satoshi (ed.),『森林──日本文化としての』 *Forests as Part of Japanese Culture*, 303 pp., 地人書館, 1996.

04 安田喜憲 Yasuda Yoshinori,『森の日本文化——縄文から未来へ』*The Japanese Culture of Forests: From the Jōmon Period to the Future*, 233 pp., 新思索社, 1996.

05 野本寛一・香月洋一郎 (編) Nomoto Kan'ichi and Katsuki Yōichirō (eds.),『生業の民俗』*The Folkways of Subsistence*, 295 pp., 雄山閣出版, 1997.

06 ヘンリ・スチュアート (編) Stewart, Henry (ed.),『採集狩猟民の現在——生業文化の変容と再生』*The Current State of Gatherer-Hunters: The Transformation and Rebirth of Subsistence Culture*, 243 pp., 言叢社, 1996.

07 諏訪春雄・川村 湊 (編) Suwa Haruo and Kawamura Minato (eds.),『アジア稲作文化と日本』*Asia's Rice-Growing Culture and Japan*, 237 pp., 雄山閣出版, 1996.

08 田中耕司 (編) Tanaka Kōji (ed.),『アジアの中の日本稲作文化——需要と成熟』*Japan's Rice-Growing Culture within Asia: Demand and Maturity*, 351 pp., 小学館, 1997.

09 小島慶三・全国小島塾 (編) Kojima Keizō and Nationwide Kojima Private Schools (eds.),『文化としてのたんぼ——日本列島たんぼ賛々』*Paddy Fields as Culture: In Praise of Japan's Paddy Fields*, 230 pp., ダイヤモンド社, 1996.

10 木村茂光 Kimura Shigemitsu,『ハタケと日本人——もう一つの農耕文化』*Dry Fields and the Japanese: Another Kind of Agrarian Culture*, 220 pp., 中央公論社, 1996.

11 坂本寧男 Sakamoto Yasuo,『ムギの民族植物誌——フィールド調査から』*A Botanical Ethnography of Barley: On the Basis of Fieldwork*, 200 pp., 学会出版センター, 1996.

12 谷川健一 (編) Tanigawa Ken'ichi (ed.),『鮭・鱒の民俗』*The Folklore of Salmons and Trouts*, 524 pp., 三一書房, 1996.

13 谷川健一 (編) Tanigawa Ken'ichi (ed.),『鯨・イルカの民俗』*The Folklore of Whales and Dolphins* [日本民俗文化資料集成], 616 pp., 三一書房, 1997.

14 金 柄徹 Kim Byŏng-ch'ol, 船世帯民再考——家船民の陸地との交渉の分析を中心に "Rethinking Sea Nomads: Focussing on an Analysis of the Contacts of *Ebune* Houseboat-Dwellers with Land,"「民族学研究」61 巻 1 号, pp. 28-49, 日本民族学会, 1996.

15 野本寛一・福田アジオ (編) Nomoto Kan'ichi and Fukuda Ajio (eds.),『環境の民俗』*The Folklore of the Environment*, 307 pp., 雄山閣出版, 1997.

16 有福孝岳 (編) Arifuku Kōgaku (ed.),『環境としての自然・社会・文化

――京都大学総合人間学部公開講座』 *Nature, Society and Culture as Environment: Public Lectures of the Faculty of Integrated Human Studies, Kyoto University*, 272 pp., 京都大学学術出版会, 1997.

17　出口晶子 Deguchi Akiko,『川辺の環境民俗学――鮭遡上河川・越後荒川の人と自然』 *An Environmental Folklife Study of Riverbanks: People and Nature along the Arakawa in Echigo, a River Which Salmon Ascend*, 308 pp., 名古屋大学出版会, 1996.

18　守山　弘 Moriyama Hiroshi,『むらの自然をいかす』 *Making the Most of the Natural Environment of Villages*, 128 pp., 岩波書店, 1997.

19　小森治夫 Komori Haruo,『日本型地域開発――水と土地の分化と総合の視点から』 *Japanese-Style Regional Development: From the Perspective of the Differentiation and Amalgamation of Water and Land*, 230 pp., 文理閣, 1997.

20　井上孝夫 Inoue Takao,『白神山地と青秋林道――地域開発と環境保全の社会学』 *The Shirakami Mountains and Seishū (Aomori-Akita) Forest Road: The Sociology of Regional Development and Environmental Protection*, 223 pp., 東信社, 1996.

21　塩浜方美 Shiohama Yasumi,『日本の自然保護思想と産業文化――環境の調和・自然との共生問題』 *Environmental Protection Thought and Industrial Culture in Japan: Questions of Harmony of the Environment and Symbiosis with Nature*, 76 pp., 産業経済研究協会, 1996.

22　宮崎　猛 (編) Miyazaki Takeshi (ed.),『グリーンツーリズムと日本の農村――環境保全による村づくり』 *Green Tourism and Japan's Villages: Development of Villages through Protection of the Environment*, 239 pp., 農村統計協会, 1997.

23　船井幸雄 (編) Funai Yukio (ed.),『「農」の技術革新――「食」を守り、農・山・漁村を蘇らせる』 *Technological Innovation in "Farming": Protecting "Food" and Reviving Farming, Mountain and Fishing Villages*, 173 pp., 東京ビジネス社, 1997.

IV. Villages

01　石山　洋ほか (編) Ishiyama Hiroshi *et al.* (eds.),『農村生活文献目録――戦後日本の農村研究に関する文献目録』 *Bibliography of Rural Life: Bibliography of Research on Rural Villages in Postwar Japan*, 395 pp., 晧星社, 1997.

02　長谷川昭彦 Hasegawa Akihiko,『近代化のなかの村落――農村社会の生活構造と集団組織』 *Rural Communities in the Modernization of Japan: Changing Rural Life Structure and Rural Group Organization in Japan*, 274 pp., 日本経済評論社, 1997.

03　岩田重則 Iwata Shigenori,『ムラの若者, くにの若者――民俗と国民統

合』The Youth of Villages and the Youth of the Nation: Folkways and National Integration, 245 pp., 未来社, 1996.

04 上村正名 Kamimura Masana, 『村落社会の史的研究』A Historical Study of Village Society, 463 pp., 東京堂出版, 1996.

05 中村靖彦 Nakamura Yasuhiko, 『日記が語る日本の農村——松本盆地の畑に八十年』Japanese Villages as Described in Diaries: Eighty Years in the Fields of the Matsumoto Basin, 248 pp., 中央公論社, 1997.

06 高橋　誠 Takahashi Makoto, 『近郊農村の地域社会変動』Social Changes in Suburban Village Communities, 279 pp., 古今書院, 1997.

07 森　武麿・大門正克（編）Mori Takemaro and Daimon Masakatsu (eds.), 『地域における戦時と戦後——庄内地方の農村・都市・社会運動』Wartime and the Postwar Era in Regional Communities: Villages, Cities and Social Movements in the Shōnai District, 354 pp., 日本経済評論社, 1996.

08 南　智 Minami Satoshi, 『瀬戸内農村の変容』The Transformation of Villages around the Seto Inland Sea, 251 pp., 大明堂, 1997.

09 毎日新聞東京本社地方部特報班 Special News Team, Regional News Department, Mainichi Shimbun Tokyo Head Office, 『東北むら半世紀』Tōhoku Villages through Half a Century, 246 pp., 無明舎出版, 1996.

10 坂根嘉弘 Sakane Yoshihiro, 『分割相続と農村社会』Divided Succession and Rural Society, 215 pp., 九州大学出版会, 1996.

11 太田忠久 Ōta Tadahisa, 『米とむら』Rice and Villages, 255 pp., 山陽新聞社, 1996.

12 木村　礎・高島緑雄（編）Kimura Motoi and Takashima Rokuo (eds.), 『村の世界　村の景観』The World of Villages and the Landscape of Villages, 462 pp., 名著出版, 1996.

13 原田　津 Harada Shin, 『むらの原理　都市の原理』The Principles of Villages and the Principles of Cities, 202 pp., 農山漁村文化協会, 1997.

14 中野　卓 Nakano Takashi, 『鰤網の村の400年——能登灘浦の社会学的研究』Four Hundred Years in a Village of Yellowtail Net Fishing (Buriami): A Sociological Study of Nadaura Coast on the Noto Peninsula, 387 pp., 刀水書房, 1996.

15 長谷川昭彦ほか Hasegawa Akihiko et al., 『過疎地域の景観と集団』Landscape and Groups in Depopulated Areas, 363 pp., 日本経済評論社, 1996.

16 農政調査委員会（編）Agricultural Policy Research Committee (ed.), 『人口高齢化と農村集落の構造変化——プロダクティブ・エイジング』The Aging of the Population and Structural Changes in Rural Settlements: Productive Aging, 109 pp., 農政調査委員会, 1997.

17 山口美智子 Yamaguchi Michiko, 『村とダム——水没する秩父の暮らし』

The Village and the Dam: The Lifestyle of Chichibu Submerged under Water, 395 pp., すずさわ書店, 1997.

18 特集 地域開発と民俗変化 "Special Issue: Regional Development and Changes in Folkways," 「日本民俗学」210 号, pp. 1-120, 日本民俗学会, 1997.

Contains the following articles: 小島摩文 Kojima Mabumi, トカラ列島と奄美群島における「地域開発と民俗変化」"'Regional Development and Changes in Folkways' in the Tokara Islands and Amami Islands," pp. 6-15; 永松敦 Nagamatsu Atsushi, 宮崎県椎葉村の民俗変化——外的要因と内的要因について "Changes in Folkways in Shiiba Village, Miyazaki Prefecture: On External Factors and Internal Factors," pp. 15-25; 赤羽正春 Akabane Masaharu, 三面川の河川の変化と民俗 "River Changes and Folkways along the Miomote River," pp. 26-43; 中山正典 Nakayama Masanori, 環境変化に伴う人間とカモシカの関係 "Relations between People and the Serow in the Wake of Environmental Changes," pp. 43-59; 竹内尚武 Takeuchi Naotake, 三谷浜の埋立と三谷祭 "The Reclamation of Miya Beach and the Miya Festival in Aichi Prefecture," pp. 59-70; 喜多村理子 Kitamura Masako, ムラにおける共通の身体感覚の喪失 "The Loss of Shared Physical Feelings in Villages," pp. 71-86; 山田尚彦 Yamada Naohiko, 獅子舞を続けるということ "The Meaning of Continuing the Lion Dance (*Shishimai*)," pp. 86-94; 脇田雅彦 Wakita Masahiko, 美濃・徳山にみる食生活の推移——塚地区を中心に "Changes in Eating Habit to Be Seen in Tokuyama, Mino: With a Focus on the Tsuka Area," pp. 94-108; and 小田嶋政子 Odajima Masako, 生活改善運動と婚姻・葬送儀礼の変化——北海道伊達市の事例から "The Movement for the Improvement of Living Conditions and Changes in Marriage and Funeral Rites: The Example of Date City, Hokkaido," pp. 109-120.

19 特集 故郷を問う "Special Issue: Questions Concerning Hometowns," 「日本民俗学」206 号, pp. 1-55, 日本民俗学会, 1997.

Contains the following articles: 田中宣一 Tanaka Sen'ichi, 故郷および故郷観の変容 "Changes in Hometowns and Views of Hometowns," pp. 2-12; 倉石忠彦 Kuraishi Tadahiko, 都市生活者の故郷観 "City-Dwellers' Views of Their Hometowns," pp. 12-24; 神崎宣武 Kanzaki Noritake, 村おこしの背景 "The Background to Village Revitalization (*Muraokoshi*)," pp. 25-36: and 八木透 Yagi Tōru, 家・女性・墓——女性たちにとっての故郷 "Households, Women, and Graves: Hometowns from the Perspective of Women," pp. 36-55.

20 大石慎三郎・飯田文弥 (監修) Ōishi Shinzaburō and Iida Bun'ya

(supvr.),『ふるさとの人と知恵 山梨』 *The People and Wisdom of Hometowns: Yamanashi* [江戸時代人づくり風土記 19], 348 pp., 農山漁村文化協会, 1997.

21 矢野敬一 Yano Keiichi, 'ふるさとの味' の形成に見る家族の戦後——菖蒲の節句の行事食・笹団子の名産品化を通して "The Postwar Era for Families as Seen in the Formation of 'Hometown Flavours': With Reference to How Rice Dumplings Wrapped in Bamboo Leaves (*Sasa Dango*), Customarily Eaten on Children's Day, Were Transformed into a Specialty Product,"「日本民俗学」209 号, pp. 1-32, 日本民俗学会, 1997.

22 森田真也 Morita Shin'ya, 観光と '伝統文化' の意識化——沖縄県竹富島の事例から "Tourism and Becoming Aware of 'Traditional Culture': The Case of Taketomi Island, Okinawa Prefecture,"「日本民俗学」209 号, pp. 33-65, 日本民俗学会, 1997.

23 安井真奈美 Yasui Manami, 'ふるさと' 研究の分析視角 "The Analytic Angle of 'Hometown' Studies,"「日本民俗学」209 号, pp. 66-88, 日本民俗学会, 1997.

24 山本質素 Yamamoto Tadamoto, 過疎化と村の再生——地域社会の変化と民俗変化 "Depopulation and the Revival of Villages: Changes in Communities and Changes in Folkways,"『現代民俗学入門』 [I-07], pp. 206-215, 1996.

25 渡辺信夫 Watanabe Nobuo,『農とふるさと再生戦略——「共生の時代」を拓く』 *Farming and Strategies for Reviving Hometown Villages: Opening up an "Age of Symbiosis,"* 191 pp., かもがわ出版, 1997.

26 佐藤藤三郎 Satō Tōzaburō,『村に、居る。——新しい文化を創る』 *I'm Staying in the Village: Creating a New Culture*, 204 pp., ダイヤモンド社, 1996.

27 祖田 修・大原興太郎・加古敏之 (編) Soda Osamu, Ōhara Kōtarō and Kako Toshiyuki (eds.),『持続的農村の形成——その理念と可能性』 *The Formation of Enduring Villages: Its Ideals and Possibilities*, 272 pp., 富民協会, 1996.

28 児玉明人 (編) Kodama Akito (ed.),『中山間地域農業・農村の多様性と新展開』 *The Diversity of Agriculture and Villages in Hillside and Mountain Areas and New Developments*, 260 pp., 富民協会, 1997.

29 小野誠志 Ono Seishi,『中山間地域農村の展開——地域産業広域複合経済圏の構築』 *The Development of Villages in Hillside and Mountain Areas: Building a Broad-Based Composite Economic Sphere for Regional Industry*, 230 pp., 筑摩書房, 1997.

30 臼井 晋 (編) Usui Susumu (ed.),『市場再編と農村コミュニティ——地域変革の課題と展望』 *Market Reorganization and Village Communities:*

Issues in Regional Reform and Future Prospects, 127 pp., 高文堂出版社, 1997.

31　保母武彦 Hobo Takehiko,『内発的発展論と日本の農山村』*Endogenous Development Theory and Japan's Rural and Mountain Villages*, 271 pp., 岩波書店, 1996.

32　水間　豊・大石嘉一郎（編）Mizuma Yutaka and Ōishi Kaichirō (eds.), 『文明の選択——農村をどうするのか』*Civilization's Choice: What Is to Be Done about Rural Villages?*, 312 pp., 農林統計協会, 1996.

33　岡橋秀典 Okahashi Hidenori,『周辺地域の存立構造——現代山村の形成と展開』*The Structure Underlying the Existence of Peripheral Regions: The Formation and Development of Contemporary Mountain Villages*, 401 pp., 大明堂, 1997.

34　青木宏一郎 Aoki Kōichirō,『森に蘇る日本文化——過疎化する山村に、高齢者の手を借りて郷土の文化と社会を再構築するための提案書』*Japanese Culture Being Revived in the Forests: A Proposal for Rebuilding Hometown Culture and Society in Depopulated Mountain Villages with the Assistance of the Elderly*, 190 pp., 三一書房, 1996.

35　福谷自治会古里創成誌編集委員会（編）Fukutani Self-Governing Association *Furusato Sōseishi* Editorial Committee (ed.),『古里福谷の創成』*Creating Our Hometown of Fukutani in Kobe*, 447 pp., 福谷自治会, 1997.

36　宮田　登 Miyata Noboru,『歴史と民俗のあいだ——海と都市の視点から』*Links between History and Folkways: From the Perspective of the Sea and Cities*, 202 pp., 吉川弘文館, 1996.

37　高崎市（編）Takasaki Municipal Government (ed.),『旧市域の祭りと町内会——現代の祭りとその背景』*Festivals and Neighborhood Associations (Chōnaikai) in the Old City Precincts: Present-day Festivals and Their Background*, 231 pp., 高崎市, 1996.

38　長野市誌編纂委員会民俗部会（編）Folkways Section, Nagano City Records Compilation Committee (ed.),『城下町松代の民俗』*The Folkways of the Castle Town of Matsushiro*, 166 pp., 長野市, 1996.

39　中村紀和 Nakamura Norikazu, 都市祭礼における流動層——小倉祇園太鼓を事例として "The Fluid Stratum in Urban Festivals: The Case of the Kokura Gion Drummers,"「日本民俗学」205 号, pp. 31-69, 日本民俗学会, 1996.

V. Religion

01　石井研士 Ishii Kenji,『現代日本人の宗教——戦後 50 年の宗教意識と宗教行動』*The Religion of the Contemporary Japanese: Religious Consciousness and Religious Behavior in the 50 Years Since the War*, 238 pp., 新曜社, 1997.

02 山折哲雄 Yamaori Tetsuo, 『近代日本人の宗教意識』 *The Religious Consciousness of the Modern Japanese*, 260 pp., 岩波書店, 1996.

03 津田雅夫 Tsuda Masao, 『文化と宗教——近代日本思想史序論』 *Culture and Religion: An Introduction to the History of Modern Japanese Thought*, 176 pp., 法律文化社, 1997.

04 佐々木宏幹 Sasaki Kōkan, 『神と仏と日本人——宗教人類学の構想』 *Gods, Buddhas, and the Japanese: The Conception of Religious Anthropology*, 272 pp., 吉川弘文館, 1996.

05 瓜生　中・渋谷申博 Uryū Naka and Shibuya Nobuhiro, 『日本宗教のすべて——「混淆し習合する神と仏と人」を探究する』 *All About Japanese Religion: Exploring the Interfusion and Syncretization of Gods, Buddhas and Men*, 303 pp., 日本文芸社, 1996.

06 赤田光男・小松和彦（編）Akata Mitsuo and Komatsu Kazuhiko (eds.), 『神と霊魂の民俗』 *The Folklore of Gods and the Soul*, 267 pp., 雄山閣出版, 1997.

07 久野　昭 Kuno Akira, 『日本人の他界観』 *Japanese Views of the Otherworld*, 181 pp., 吉川弘文館, 1997.

08 竹田聴洲 Takeda Chōshū, 『日本人の「家」と宗教』 *The "Household" and the Religion of the Japanese*, 461 pp., 国書刊行会, 1996.

09 芹沢博通 Serizawa Hiromichi, 『日本の近代化と宗教倫理——近江商人論』 *The Modernization of Japan and Religious Ethics: The Ōmi Merchants*, 342 pp., 多賀出版, 1997.

10 王　守華 Wang Chu-hua, 『日本神道の現代的意義』 *The Contemporary Significance of Japanese Shinto*, 221 pp., 農山漁村文化協会, 1997.

11 谷　省吾 Tani Shōgo, 『神道——その探究への歩み』 *Shinto: The History of Its Exploration*, 407 pp., 国書刊行会, 1997.

12 山村勝明 Yamamura Katsuaki, 『吉田神道の基礎的研究』 *A Basic Study of Yoshida Shinto*, 604 pp., 臨川書店, 1997.

13 平野孝国 Hirano Takakuni, 『神道世界の構造』 *The Structure of the World of Shinto*, 322 pp., ぺりかん社, 1997.

14 阿蘇谷正彦 Asoya Masahiko, 『神道の生死観——神道思想と「死」の問題』 *The Shinto View of Life and Death: Shinto Thought and the Question of "Death,"* 341 pp., ぺりかん社, 1996.

15 宮田　登 Miyata Noboru, 『民俗神道論——民間信仰のダイナミズム』 *Studies in Folk Shinto: The Dynamism of Popular Beliefs*, 289 pp., 春秋社, 1996.

16 田　義幸（編）Den Yoshiyuki (ed.), 『神々の風景と日本人のこころ——自然とは、言葉とは、母子の絆とは』 *The Landscape of the Gods and*

the Mind of the Japanese: Nature, Language, and the Bonds between Mother and Child, 203 pp., PHPエディターズ・グループ, 1996.

17　長沢利明 Nagasawa Toshiaki,『江戸東京の庶民信仰』*Popular Cults in Edo and Tokyo*, 347 pp., 三弥井書店, 1996.

18　村山修一 Murayama Shūichi,『天神御霊信仰』*The Cult of the Tenjin Spirit*, 239 pp., 塙書房, 1996.

19　速水善治 Hayami Yoshiharu,『人形道祖神——境界神の原像』*The Anthropomorphic 'Dōsojin': The Primordial Image of the Gods of Boundaries*, 648 pp., 白水社, 1996.

20　森　隆男 Mori Takao,『住居空間の祭祀と儀礼』*The Ceremonies and Rites of Residential Space*, 385 pp., 岩田書院, 1996.

21　広瀬浩二郎 Hirose Kōjirō,『障害者の宗教民俗学』*Religious Folklife Studies of the Handicapped*, 190 pp., 明石書店, 1997.

22　川村邦光 Kawamura Kunimitsu,『憑依の視座』*The Perspective of Spirit Possession*, 220 pp., 青弓社, 1997.

23　山上伊豆母 Yamakami Izumo,『巫女の歴史——日本宗教の母胎』*The History of Female Shamans: The Matrix of Japanese Religion*, 231 pp., 雄山閣出版, 1996.

24　日本仏教研究会（編）Association for Japanese Buddhist Studies (ed.),『論点・日本仏教』*Points at Issue in Japanese Buddhism* [『日本の仏教』第6巻], 235 pp., 法蔵館, 1996.

25　高崎直道・木村清孝（編）Takasaki Jikido and Kimura Kiyotaka (eds.),『東アジア社会と仏教文化』*East Asian Society and Buddhist Culture*, 314 pp., 春秋社, 1996.

26　伊藤唯真・藤井正雄（編）Itō Yuishin and Fujii Masao (eds.),『葬祭仏教——その歴史と現代的課題』*Funeral Buddhism: Its History and Contemporary Issues*, 405 pp., ノンブル社, 1997.

27　源　淳子 Minamoto Junko,『フェミニズムが問う仏教——教権に収奪された自然と母性』*A Feminist Critique of Buddhism: The Exploitation of Nature and Motherhood by Ecclesiastical Authority*, 201 pp., 三一書房, 1997.

28　国際宗教研究所（編）International Institute for the Study of Religions (ed.),『女性と教団——日本宗教のオモテとウラ』*Women and Religious Organizations: The Public and Private Faces of Japanese Religion*, 187 pp., ハーベスト社, 1996.

29　鈴木良郎 Suzuki Yoshio,『近世仏教と勧化——募縁活動と地域社会の研究』*Early Modern Buddhism and Fund-Raising: A Study of Fund-Raising Activities and Communities*, 356 pp., 岩田書院, 1996.

30　高崎直道・木村清孝（編）Takasaki Jikido and Kimura Kiyotaka (eds.),

『新仏教の興隆』 *The Rise of New Buddhism*, 406 pp., 春秋社, 1997.

31 有元正雄 Arimoto Masao, 『宗教社会史の構想——真宗門徒の信仰と生活』 *A View of the Social History of Religion: The Beliefs and Daily Life of Adherents of the Shin Sect*, 202 pp., 吉川弘文館, 1997.

32 和気秀乗 Wake Shūjō, 『高野山信仰の形成と展開』 *The Formation and Development of the Mt. Kōya Cult*, 335 pp., 法蔵館, 1997.

33 高田良信 (編) Takada Ryōshin (ed.), 『法隆寺の歴史と信仰』 *The History of Hōryūji and Associated Beliefs*, 275 pp., 小学館, 1996.

34 宮家 準 Miyake Hitoshi, 『修験道と日本宗教』 *Shugendō and Japanese Religion*, 224 pp., 春秋社, 1996.

35 藤田定興 Fujita Sadaoki, 『近世修験道の地域的展開』 *The Regional Development of Shugendō in the Early Modern Period*, 481 pp., 岩田書院, 1996.

36 牛山佳幸 Ushiyama Yoshiyuki, 『戸隠信仰の歴史』 *The History of the Togakushi Cult*, 245 pp., 戸隠神社, 1997.

37 窪 徳忠 Kubo Noritada, 『庚申信仰の研究——日中宗教文化交流史』 *A Study of the Kōshin Cult: The History of Religico-Cultural Exchange between Japan and China*, 4 vols. [『窪徳忠著作集』Vols. 1～3, 5], 505 pp. (av.), 第一書房, 1996-98.

38 野口鐵郎・窪 徳忠 (編) Noguchi Tetsurō and Kubo Noritada (eds.), 『中世・近世文化と道教』 *Medieval and Early Modern Culture and Taoism*, 263 pp., 雄山閣出版, 1997.

39 中山和久 Nakayama Kazuhisa, 巡礼と現代——関東三十六不動霊場を中心として "Pilgrimages and the Present Age: With a Focus on the Thirty-Six Pilgrimage Sites Dedicated to Acalanātha in the Kantō Region," 「日本民俗学」211 号, pp., 32-65, 日本民俗学会, 1997.

40 谷川健一 Tanigawa Ken'ichi, 『民俗の思想——常民の世界観と死生観』 *The Thought Behind Folkways: The World View of the General Populace and Their View of Life and Death*, 287 pp., 岩波書店, 1996.

41 山田慎也 Yamada Shin'ya, 死を受容させるもの——輿から祭壇へ "That Which Leads to the Acceptance of Death: From the Portable Shrine to the Altar," 「日本民俗学」207 号, pp. 29-57, 日本民俗学会, 1996.

42 脇本平也 Wakimoto Tsuneya, 『死の比較宗教学』 *A Comparative Religious Study of Death*, 199 pp., 岩波書店, 1997.

VI. The Economy and Business Management

01 吉田和男 Yoshida Kazuo, 『解明日本型経営システム——日本経済を分析する新しい経済学への挑戦』 *Elucidating the Japanese-Style Management System: The Challenge of a New Type of Economics for Analyzing the Japanese Economy*, 254 pp., 東洋経済新報社, 1996.

02 吉森　賢 Yoshimori Masaru,『日本の経営・欧米の経営——比較経営へ
の招待』*Japanese Business Management and Western Business Management: An Invitation to Comparative Business Management*, 254 pp., 放送
大学教育振興会, 1996.

03 高橋伸夫 Takahashi Nobuo,『日本企業の意思決定原理』*The Principles
of Decision-Making in Japanese Corporations*, 288 pp., 東京大学出版会,
1997.

04 浅沼萬里 Asanuma Banri,『日本の企業組織　革新的適応メカニズム——
長期取引関係の構造と機能』*Corporate Organizations in Japan: Their
Innovative Mechanisms of Adaptation—The Structure and Functions
of Long-Term Business Relations*, 379 pp., 東洋経済新報社, 1997.

05 荒井一博 Arai Kazuhiro,『終身雇用制と日本文化——ゲーム論的アプロ
ーチ』*The Lifelong Employment System and Japanese Culture: An
Approach from Game Theory*, 191 pp., 中央公論社, 1997.

06 同志社大学人文科学研究所（編）Dōshisha University Institute for the
Study of Humanities & Social Sciences (ed.),『日本企業とアジア』
Japanese Corporations and Asia, 57 pp., 同志社大学人文科学研究所,
1996.

07 室井　渡 Muroi Wataru,『温泉の開発と経営』*The Development and
Management of Hot Springs*, 366 pp., 地人書館, 1996.

08 田中　充 Tanaka Mitsuru,『日本の経済構造と部落産業——国際化の進
展と中小企業の課題』*Japan's Economic Structure and 'Buraku Industries': Advances in Internationalization and Issues Facing Small Businesses*, 294 pp., 関西大学出版部, 1996.

09 関　満博・一言憲之（編）Seki Mitsuhiro and Hitokoto Noriyuki (eds.),
『地方産業振興と企業家精神』*The Promotion of Regional Industry and
the Entrepreneurial Spirit*, 238 pp., 新評論, 1996.

10 森川英正 Morikawa Hidemasa,『トップ・マネジメントの経営史——経
営者企業と家族企業』*The Business History of Top Management: Entrepreneurial Companies and Family Companies*, 300 pp., 有斐閣, 1996.

11 竹内常善・阿部武司・沢井　実（編）Takeuchi Tsuneyoshi, Abe Takeshi
and Sawai Minoru (eds.),『近代日本における企業家の諸系譜』*The
Genealogies of Entrepreneurs in Modern Japan*, 284 pp., 大阪大学出版
会, 1996.

12 佐藤　信（編）Satō Makoto (ed.),『会社の民俗』*The Folkways of
Companies*, 302 pp., 小学館, 1996.

13 中村圭介 Nakamura Keisuke,『日本の職場と生産システム』*Japan's
Production System and the Organization of Work*, 268 pp., 東京大学出
版会, 1996.

14 市原　博 Ichihara Hiroshi,『炭鉱の労働社会史——日本の伝統的労働、社会秩序と管理』*A Social History of Labor in Coal Mines: Traditional Labor, Social Order and Management in Japan*, 393 pp., 多賀出版, 1997.

VII. The *Ie* and Family

01 大藤　修 Ōtō Osamu,『近世農民と家・村・国家——生活史・社会史の視座から』*Early Modern Peasants and the Household, Village and State: From the Perspectives of Daily-Life History and Social History*, 475 pp., 吉川弘文館, 1996.

02 岩本由輝・国方敬司（編）Iwamoto Yoshiteru and Kunikata Keiji (eds.),『家と共同体——日欧比較の視点から』*Household and Community: From the Perspective of a Comparison between Japan and Europe*, 230 pp., 法政大学出版会, 1997.

03 岩本由輝・大藤　修（編）Iwamoto Yoshiteru and Ōtō Osamu (eds.),『家族と地域社会』*The Family and Community*, 320 pp., 早稲田大学出版部, 1996.

04 藤井　勝 Fujii Masaru,『家と同族の歴史社会学』*The Historical Sociology of the Ie (Household) and Dōzoku (Related Households)*, 358 pp., 刀水書房, 1997.

05 長谷川善計・江守五夫・肥前栄一（編）Hasegawa Yoshikazu, Emori Itsuo and Hizen Eiichi (eds.),『家・屋敷地と霊・呪術』*Households and Residential Properties, Spirits and Magic*, 299 pp., 早稲田大学出版部, 1996.

06 森岡清美・望月　嵩 Morioka Kiyomi and Mochizuki Takashi,『新しい家族社会学』*A New Sociology of the Family*, 196 pp., 培風館, 1997.

07 天沼　香 Amanuma Kaoru,『家族』*The Family*, 323 pp., 東京堂出版, 1997.

08 岸本幸臣・鈴木　晃（編）Kishimoto Yukiomi and Suzuki Akira (eds.),『家族と住居』*The Family and Domiciles*, 265 pp., 東京大学出版会, 1996.

09 竹安栄子 Takeyasu Eiko,『近代化と家族・地域社会』*Modernization in Relation to the Family and Community*, 228 pp., 御茶の水書房, 1997.

10 坂本佳鶴恵 Sakamoto Kazue,『「家族」イメージの誕生——日本映画にみる「ホームドラマ」の形成』*The Birth of the Image of the "Family": The Formation of "Home Dramas" as Seen in Japanese Films*, 411 pp., 新曜社, 1997.

11 牟田和恵 Muta Kazue,『戦略としての家族——近代日本の国民国家形成と女性』*The Family as a Strategy: Women and the Formation of the Nation-State of Modern Japan*, 216 pp., 新曜社, 1996.

12 河合隼雄・大庭みな子（編）Kawai Hayao and Ōba Minako (eds.),『家

族と性』*Families and Sex*, 253 pp., 岩波書店, 1997.

13 石原豊美 Ishihara Toyomi,『農家の家族変動――ライフコースの発想を用いて』*Family Changes among Farmers: Using the Ideas of Life Course*, 208 pp., 日本経済評論社, 1996.

14 亀口憲治 Kameguchi Kenji,『家族の問題――こころの危機と家族のかかわり』*Family Problems: The Psychological Crisis and Its Relation to the Family*, 236 pp., 人文書院, 1997.

15 藤本浩之輔ほか Fujimoto Kōnosuke *et al*.,『子どものコスモロジー――教育人類学と子ども文化』*The Cosmology of Children: Educational Anthropology and Juvenile Culture*, 205 pp., 人文書院, 1996.

16 高橋　敏 Takahashi Satoshi,『家族と子供の江戸時代――躾と消費からみる』*Families and Children during the Edo Period as Seen from Home Discipline and Consumption*, 201 pp., 朝日新聞社, 1997.

17 谷川健一（編）Tanigawa Ken'ichi (ed.),『子供の民俗誌』*The Folkways of Children* [日本民俗資料集成　第 24 巻], 504 pp., 三一書房, 1996.
       Includes accounts of children's games in Ainu villages (Sarashina Genzō 更科源蔵) and children on the island of Amami (Ehara Yoshimori 恵原義盛).

18 日本家族心理学会（編）Japanese Association of Family Psychology (ed.),『児童虐待――家族臨床の現場から』*Child Abuse: From the Actualities of Family Therapy*, 219 pp., 金子書房, 1997.

19 宮田　登 Miyata Noboru,『老人と子供の民俗学』*Folklife Studies of Old People and Children*, 189 pp., 白水社, 1996.

20 光岡浩二 Mitsuoka Kōji,『農村家族の結婚難と高齢者問題』*Difficulties Finding Marriage Partners and Problems Concerning the Elderly in Rural Families*, 275 pp., ミネルヴァ書房, 1996.

21 上野谷加代子・村川浩一（編）Uenoya Kayoko and Murakawa Kōichi (eds.),『高齢者と家族――高齢社会への対応と家族の役割』*The Elderly and Families: Responses to an Aging Society and the Role of the Family*, 271 pp., 中央法規出版, 1996.

VIII. Ethnicity

01 広田康生 Hirota Yasuo,『エスニシティと都市』*Ethnicity and Cities*, 214 pp., 有信堂高文社, 1997.

02 白水繁彦（編）Shiramizu Shigehiko (ed.),『エスニック・メディア――多文化社会日本をめざして』*Ethnic Media: Towards Japan Becoming a Multicultural Society*, 266 pp., 明石書店, 1996.

03 奥田道大（編）Okuda Michihiro (ed.),『都市エスニシティの社会学――民族／文化／共生の意味を問う』*The Sociology of Urban Ethnicity: Questioning the Meaning of Ethnos, Culture and Symbiosis*, 297 pp., ミ

ネルヴァ書房, 1997.

04 駒井　洋（編）Komai Hiroshi (ed.),『日本のエスニック社会』*Ethnic Society in Japan*, 379 pp., 明石書店, 1996.

05 青柳真智子（編・監訳）Aoyagi Machiko (ed. & supv. tr.),『「エスニック」とは何か――エスニシティ基本論文集』*What Is "Ethnic"?: A Collection of Basic Articles on Ethnicity*, 221 pp., 信泉社, 1996.

06 吉野耕作 Yoshino Kōsaku,『文化ナショナリズムの社会学――現代日本のアイデンティティの行方』*The Sociology of Cultural Nationalism: The Future of the Identity of Contemporary Japan*, 292 pp., 名古屋大学出版会, 1997.

07 原尻秀樹・六反田　豊（編）Harajiri Hideki and Rokutanda Yutaka (eds.),『半島と列島のくにぐに――日朝比較交流史入門』*Peninsular and Archipelagic Countries: An Introduction to the Comparative History of Contacts Between Japan and Korea*, 217 pp., 新幹社, 1996.

08 浜口裕子 Hamaguchi Yūko,『日本統治と東アジア社会――植民地期朝鮮と満州の比較研究』*Japanese Rule and East Asian Society: A Comparative Study of Colonial Korea and Manchuria*, 291 pp., 勁草書房, 1996.

09 原尻秀樹（編）Harajiri Hideki (ed.),『日本定住コリアンの日常と生活――文化人類学的アプローチ』*The Everyday Life of Korean Residents in Japan: A Cultural Anthropological Approach*, 213 pp., 明石書店, 1997.

10 金　贊汀 Kim Ch'an-chŏng,『在日こりあん百年史』*The Hundred-Year History of Korean Residents in Japan*, 254 pp., 三五館, 1997.

11 森田芳夫 Morita Yoshio,『数字が語る在日韓国・朝鮮人の歴史』*The History of Korean Residents in Japan as Related by Figures*, 183 pp., 明石書店, 1996.

12 河　明生 Ha Myŏng-saeng,『韓人日本移民社会経済史』*The Economic History of Japan's Korean Immigrant Society*, 215 pp., 明石書店, 1997.

13 会沢　勲（編）Aizawa Isao (ed.),『アジアの交差点――在日外国人と地域社会』*The Crossroads of Asia: Foreign Residents in Japan and Community*, 304 pp., 社会評論社, 1996.

14 福岡安則・金　明秀 Fukuoka Yasunori and Kim Myŏng-su,『在日韓国人青年の生活と意識』*The Lives and Consciousness of Young Korean Residents in Japan*, 226 pp., 東京大学出版会, 1997.

15 李　青若 Yi Ch'ŏng-ya,『在日韓国人三世の胸のうち』*The Sentiments of Third-Generation Korean Residents in Japan*, 221 pp., 草思社, 1997.

16 陳　大哲 Chin Tae-ch'ŏl, 在日韓国・朝鮮人の祖先祭祀における文化変容――理想的祭祀と現実祭祀の事例を通して "Acculturation in the Ancestral Ceremonies of Korean Residents in Japan: With Reference to Ideal Ceremonies and Examples of Actual Ceremonies,"「民族学研究」60

巻 4 号, pp., 342-353, 日本民族学会. 1996.

17 李 仁子 Yi In-ja, 異文化における移住者のアイデンティティ表現の重層性——在日韓国・朝鮮人の墓をめぐって "The Multistratified Nature of Expressions of Identity among Migrants in Foreign Cultures: On the Graves of Korean Residents in Japan,"「民族学研究」61 巻 3 号, pp., 393-422, 日本民族学会, 1996.

18 萱野 茂 Kayano Shigeru,『アイヌ民族から見た近代日本』 *Modern Japan as Seen by the Ainu*, 62 pp., 中央大学人文科学研究所, 1997.

19 宮島利光 Miyajima Toshimitsu,『アイヌ民族と日本の歴史——先住民族の苦難・抵抗・復権』 *The Ainu People and the History of Japan: The Tribulations, Resistance and Rehabilitation of an Indigenous People*, 285 pp., 三一書房, 1996.

20 小川正人 Ogawa Masato,『近代アイヌ教育制度史研究』 *A Study of the History of the Modern Ainu Education System*, 457 pp., 北海道大学図書刊行会, 1997.

21 西浦宏己 Nishiura Hiroki,『アイヌ、いまに生きる』 *The Ainu: Living Now*, 251 pp., 新泉社, 1997.

22 野村義一 Nomura Yoshikazu,『アイヌ民族を生きる』 *Living as Ainu*, 258 pp., 草風館, 1996.

23 札幌学院大学人文学部 (編) Sapporo Gakuin University Faculty of Humanities (ed.),『アイヌ文化の現在』 *The Present State of Ainu Culture*, 335 pp., 札幌学院大学生活共同組合, 1997.

24 伊藤泰信 Itō Yasunobu, アイヌの現在の民族誌に向けて "Towards an Ethnography of the Present State of the Ainu,"「民族学研究」61 巻 2 号, pp. 302-313, 日本民族学会, 1996.

25 木名瀬高嗣 Kinase Takatsugu, 表象と政治性——アイヌをめぐる文化人類学的言説に関する素描 "Representation and Political Nature: A Sketch of Cultural Anthropological Discourse on the Ainu,"「民族学研究」61 巻 1 号, pp. 1-21, 日本民族学会, 1996.

26 小谷凱宣 Kotani Yoshinobu, アイヌ研究の問題点と研究の緊急性 "Points at Issue in Ainu Studies and the Urgency of Research,"「民族学研究」61 巻 2 号, pp. 245-262, 日本民族学会, 1996.

27 小谷凱宣 Kotani Yoshinobu, アイヌ文化 "Ainu Culture,"『日本民族学の現在』 [1-03], pp. 224-237, 1996.

28 遠藤国俊 Endō Kunitoshi,『アイヌと狩猟採集社会——集団の流動性に関する地理学的研究』 *The Ainu and the Society of Hunter-Gatherers: A Geographical Study of Group Fluidity*, 203 pp., 大明堂, 1997.

29 萩中美枝・宇田川 洋 (編) Haginaka Mie and Udagawa Hiroshi (eds.),『北海道東部に残る樺太アイヌ文化』 *The Sakhalin Ainu Culture*

Remaining in Eastern Hokkaido, 137 pp., 常呂町樺太アイヌ文化保存会, 1996.

30 谷川健一 (編) Tanigawa Ken'ichi (ed.), 『北の民俗誌——サハリン・千島の民族』 *Accounts of Northern Folkways: The People of Sakhalin and the Kurils*, 586 pp., 三一書房, 1997.

31 沢田洋太郎 Sawada Yōtarō, 『沖縄とアイヌ——日本の民族問題』 *Okinawa and the Ainu: Japan's Ethnic Problems*, 254 pp., 新泉社, 1996.

32 比嘉政夫 Higa Masao, 琉球列島文化研究の新視角 "A Fresh Perspective on the Study of the Culture of the Ryukyu Islands," 「民族学研究」 61 巻 3 号, pp. 437-448, 日本民族学会, 1996.

33 津波高志 Tsuha Takashi, 対ヤマトの文化人類学 "On the Consciousness of Non-Yamato Identity," 「民族学研究」 61 巻 3 号, pp. 449-462, 日本民族学会, 1996.

34 高良倉吉 Takara Kurayoshi, 琉球史研究からみた沖縄・琉球民俗研究の課題 "Issues in the Study of Okinawan and Ryukyuan Folkways as Seen from the Study of Ryukyuan History," 「民族学研究」 61 巻 3 号, pp. 463-467, 日本民族学会, 1996.

35 崔 仁宅・石川浩之・森 雅文・渋谷 研 Ch'oe In-t'aek, Ishikawa Hiroyuki, Mori Masafumi and Shibuya Ken, 奄美・沖縄はどう語り得るか "How Can Amami and Okinawa Be Described?," 「民族学研究」 61 巻 3 号, pp. 467-481, 日本民族学会, 1996.

36 山折哲雄 (編) Yamaori Tetsuo (ed.), 『日本文化の深層と沖縄』 *The Depths of Japanese Culture and Okinawa* [日文研叢書 12], 151 pp., 国際日本文化研究センター, 1996.

37 上野和男 Ueno Kazuo, 波照間島の祖先祭祀と農耕儀礼——ムシャーマ行事を中心とする盆行事の考察 "Ancestral Ceremonies and Agricultural Rites on Hateruma Island: Observations on the *Bon* Ceremonies Centered on the *Mushāma* Ritual," 「国立歴史民俗博物館研究報告」 第 66 集, pp. 179-200, 国立歴史民俗博物館, 1996.

The author points out that village ceremonies on Hateruma Island, Yaeyama Islands, Okinawa Prefecture, have a dual character, possessing elements of both ancestral ceremonies and agricultural rites.

38 谷川健一 Tanigawa Ken'ichi, 『沖縄——その危機と神々』 *Okinawa: Its Crisis and Deities*, 336 pp., 講談社, 1996.

39 山里純一 Yamazato Jun'ichi, 『沖縄の魔除けとまじない——フーフダ (符礼) の研究』 *Okinawa's Talismans and Spells: A Study of 'Fūfuda'*, 283 pp., 第一書房, 1997.

40 窪 徳忠 Kubo Noritada, 『沖縄の習俗と信仰——中国との比較研究』 *The Customs and Beliefs of Okinawa: A Comparative Study with*

China, 726 pp., 第一書房, 1997.

41　窪　徳忠 Kubo Noritada,『徳之島採集手帖——徳之島民俗の聞き取り資料』 *A Survey Notebook on Tokunoshima in Amami Islands: Oral Materials about the Folkways of Tokunoshima*, 295 pp., 鹿児島短期大学付属南日本文化研究所, 1996.

42　宮城嗣幸 Miyagi Shikō,『琉球古典音楽の源流——屋嘉比、知念、欽定、安室工工四の比較研究』 *The Source of Ryukyuan Classical Music: A Comparative Study of Yakabi, Chinen, Kintei, and Amuro Kūkūshi*, 796 pp., 那覇出版社, 1996.

43　酒井正子 Sakai Masako,『奄美歌掛けのディアローグ——あそび・ウワサ・死』 *Dialogue in the Songs of Amami: Play, Rumours, and Death*, 358 pp., 第一書房, 1996.

IX. Migrants, Foreigners, Multiculturalism and Cross-Cultural Education

01　伊予谷登士翁・杉原　達（編）Iyotani Toshio and Sugihara Tōru (eds.),『日本社会と移民』 *Japanese Society and Emigrants*, 323 pp., 明石書店, 1996.

02　移民研究会（編）Emigrants Research Society (ed.),『戦争と日本人移民』 *War and Japanese Emigrants*, 376 pp., 東洋書林, 1997.
　　This book includes a chronological table relating to the internment of people of Japanese descent in North and South America.

03　高橋泰隆 Takahashi Yasutaka,『昭和戦前期の農村と満州移民』 *Rural Villages and Emigrants to Manchuria during the Prewar Shōwa Era*, 283 pp., 吉川弘文館, 1997.

04　沖田行司 Okita Kōji,『ハワイ日系移民の教育史——日米文化、その出会いと相剋』 *The Educational History of Japanese Immigrants in Hawaii: The Encounter and Confilct between Japanese and American Culture*, 260 pp., ミネルヴァ書房, 1997.

05　前山　隆 Maeyama Takashi,『異邦で「日本」を祀る——ブラジル日系人の宗教とエスニシティ』 *Worshipping "Japan" in a Foreign Country: The Religion and Ethnicity of Japanese Brazilians*, 437 pp., 御茶の水書房, 1997.

06　前山　隆（編）Maeyama Takashi (ed.),『ドナ・マルガリータ・渡辺——移民・老人福祉の五十三年』 *Dona Margarita Watanabe: Fifty-Three Years Spent in Welfare for Immigrants and the Elderly*, 350 pp., 御茶の水書房, 1996.

07　新保　満 Shimpo Mitsuru,『カナダ移民排斥史——日本の漁業移民』 *The History of the Ostracizing of Immigrants in Canada: Japanese Fishing Immigrants*, 241 pp., 未来社, 1996.

08　駒井　洋・渡戸一郎（編）Komai Hiroshi and Watado Ichirō (eds.),『自

治体の外国人政策——内なる国際化への取り組み』 *Local Government Policies for Foreigners: The Engagement with Internal Internationalization*, 466 pp., 明石書店, 1997.

09 吉田良生ほか Yoshida Yoshio *et al.*,『地域産業・社会と外国人労働者』 *Foreign Workers and Regional Industry and Society*, 135 pp., 成文堂, 1997.

10 宮島 喬・梶田孝道（編）Miyajima Takashi and Kajita Takamichi (eds.),『外国人労働者から市民へ——地域社会の視点と課題から』 *From Foreign Workers to Citizens: From the Perspectives and Issues of Local Community*, 237 pp., 有斐閣, 1996.

11 日本労働研究機構（編）Japan Institute of Labor (ed.),『外国人労働者が就業する地域における住民の意識と実態——群馬県大泉町・長野県上田市・宮城県古川市の地域研究』 *The Awareness of Residents in Areas Where Foreign Workers Are Employed and Actual Reality: Area Studies of Ōizumi-machi in Gumma Prefecture, Ueda-shi in Nagano Prefecture, and Furukawa-shi in Miyagi Prefecture*, 242 pp., 日本労働研究機構, 1997.

12 外国人地震情報センター（編）Earthquake Information Centre for Foreigners (ed.),『阪神大震災と外国人——「多文化共生社会」の現状と可能性』 *The Great Hanshin Earthquake and Foreigners: The Current State of a "Society of Multicultural Symbiosis" and Its Possibilities*, 210 pp., 明石書店, 1996.

13 近藤 敦 Kondō Atsushi,『外国人参政権と国籍』 *Political Rights for Foreigners and Nationality*, 194 pp., 明石書店, 1996.

14 小林哲也・江淵一公（編）Kobayashi Tetsuya and Ebuchi Kazuhiro (eds.),『多文化教育の比較研究——教育における文化的同化と多様化』 *A Comparative Study of Multicultural Education: Cultural Assimilation and Diversification in Education*, 362 pp., 九州大学出版会, 1997.

15 江淵一公 Ebuchi Kazuhiro,『異文化間教育学序説——移民・在留民の比較教育民族誌的分析』 *An Anthropological Study of Intercultural Education: A Comparative Ethnographic Analysis of Cross-Cultural Adaptation and Education of Immigrant Ethnic Minorities and Sojourners*, 576 pp., 九州大学出版会, 1997.

16 梶田正巳 Kajita Masami,『異文化に育つ日本の子供——アメリカの学校文化のなかで』 *Japanese Children Growing up in a Foreign Culture: In the School Culture of America*, 222 pp., 中央公論社, 1997.

17 古岡俊之 Furuoka Toshiyuki,『今求められる帰国子女・外国人子女教育』 *The Education for Returnee Children and Foreign Children That Is Now Needed*, 202 pp., 近代文芸社, 1996.

18 高橋正夫・シャロン S. バイパエ Takahashi Masao and Vaipae, Sharon S., 『「ガイジン」生徒がやって来た——「異文化」としての外国人児童・生徒をどう迎えるか』 *"Foreign" Pupils Have Arrived: How Are Foreign Children and Pupils as Embodiments of "Alien Culture" to Be Received?*, 240 pp., 大修館, 1996.

19 浅野慎一郎 Asano Shin'ichirō, 『日本で学ぶアジア系外国人——研修生・留学生・就学生の生活と文化変容』 *Asian Foreigners Studying in Japan: The Life and Acculturation of Trainees, Students and School Pupils*, 482 pp., 大学教育出版, 1997.

EDUCATION

Terasaki Masao
Ōbirin University

I. THE REEXAMINATION OF "EDUCATIONAL RESEARCH" IN POSTWAR JAPAN

"Educational research" or "the study of education" began in Japan under European and American influence immediately after the Meiji Restoration in the Ministry of Education, universities and normal schools. From then until the mid-1940s, although constantly subjected to doubts and criticism about its scientific accuracy, it occupied a corner in Japan's universities and academe, and there also appeared researchers specializing in the study of education.

But it was only after World War II that the study of education acquired a solid footing and began turning out large numbers of specialist researchers, who then began establishing numerous academic societies. The Japan Society for the Study of Education (Nihon Kyōiku Gakkai), founded in 1941 with 188 members, had more than one thousand members by the 1950s, and in the same period there was a mushrooming of academic societies concerned with subjects such as the psychology, sociology and history of education, education for handicapped children, community education, childcare, physical education, and library science. By the mid-1990s some of these had a membership of three thousand or more. Representative of these societies is the Japan Society for the Study of Education, to which the greatest number of researchers in the field of education belong, but recently researchers in areas such as education law, educational administration, comparative education, educational management, school education, university education, and higher education have begun forming satellite societies on its periphery, each of which publishes its own journal and holds its own conferences.

But is it in fact enough for the study of education to adhere only to methods developed in the postwar era? In recent years the need for a paradigm shift has been advocated in Japan not only in the natural sciences but also in the humanities and social sciences. The question of whether this issue should perhaps be considered in the field of education studies began to be raised in a number of societies devoted to the study of education in 1996 and 1997. The works listed in Section I of the Bibliography are representative of this new trend, and their number will no doubt have increased in two years' time when the bibliography for the years 1998–99 is compiled.

II. REASONS BEHIND THIS REEXAMINATION

Needless to say, the direct impetus behind the move in many academic societies concerned with the study of education to begin reexamining research methodology lay, as noted above, in the fact that educational research in postwar Japan had already built up a history of fifty years.

At a commemorative symposium organized by the Society for the Study of Education Law (Kyōikuhō Gakkai), Horio Teruhisa [I-15] and Nagai Ken'ichi [I-14] undertook to reexamine the postwar research paradigm, and their prime interest lay in reconsidering how to comprehend the Fundamental Law of Education (1947), which laid down the basic principles of education in postwar Japan, and the education system that had been created by this law. Horio is critical of the "negation of the modern age" implicit in demands for a paradigm shift, and he argues that a shift in the research paradigm took place already in the years after 1945, when a start was being made to establish postwar Japan's political and education system after the collapse of the Empire of Great Japan as a result of its defeat in the war. According to Horio, what is currently needed is not a paradigm shift but efforts to further develop and add greater depth to postwar research methods. The study of education history was another field in which there has been an active review of research history and reexamination of research methods. At conferences of the Society for the Historical Research of Education (Kyōikushi Gakkai) many researchers in their forties and fifties have been addressing the question of how to evaluate and criticize Marxist methodology, which has exerted enormous influence especially on postwar methods of studying the history of Japanese education, and they have also been considering possible new methods of research. Representative of these are the proposals of Hata Takashi [I-06], a study by Hirota Teruyuki [VII-10], and an article by Satō Manabu [I-10]. Their common concern is to determine the methods by which to study and describe the facts of education history so as to be able to clarify "the true facts of the history of education," and for people such as Hata and Hirota in particular this is a subject that will determine the future of research in the academic societies to which they belong.

However, the shocks that have prompted the reexamination of research methods have not been emanating solely from within academic circles, and further impetus has been provided by the fact that bullying, absenteeism, school phobia and other pathological phenomena have been occurring with increasing frequency in Japan's schools since the mid-1980s. Earlier methods of educational research have been unable to give accurate answers on how to understand these phenomena and resolve the associated problems, and the works listed in Section II of the Bibliography all deal with these issues. The survey conducted by Ishida Yoshikiyo [II-09] in particular apprises us of the measures being taken by municipal boards of education throughout Japan to deal with school absenteeism, while the compilation by Ishikawa Norihiko et al. [II-08] allows us to listen to confessions by young people about their state of mind when they were absenting themselves from school. Watanabe Takashi [II-10], who has for many years been engaged in counselling absentee pupils and has also had contact with their parents, poses the question of whether the act of "attending school" is in fact really necessary, and he provides a radical critique of Japan's system of compulsory education and its school system. These were the main fruits of research in this area in 1996–97, but as a whole it has to be said that this body of research has not yet attained an adequate degree of theoretical refinement and remains at the level of reportages and preliminary studies.

Serious pathological phenomena will no doubt continue to spread in Japan's schools. At the same time, the question of how to discover suitable methods of research will become an increasingly pressing issue for researchers, and the search for such methods will without a doubt continue into the future.

III. RESEARCH ON THE HISTORY OF JAPANESE EDUCATION AND
    UNIVERSITIES

As has been the case for several years now, the history of Japanese education and universities were the fields of research that witnessed the most prolific research activity during the review period. It was pointed out above that the Society for the Historical Research of Education itself published a critical review of postwar research on the history of education, but in addition there also appeared many noteworthy case studies.

Irie Hiroshi [VII-01] describes how commoners in the early modern period transmitted and observed their "household precepts" (*kakun*) and clarifies the relationship between the household and education by means of a careful empirical methodology, and his study is highly original when compared with earlier research on household precepts, which has tended to be confined to the study of the household precepts of warriors, *daimyō* and wealthy merchants in the medieval and early modern periods. In addition, the study by Hirota Teruyuki [VII-10], analyzing the education of officers in the prewar army together with the formation of their distinctive social group, attracted considerable attention. Hirota makes the telling criticism that whereas hitherto research on the history of Japanese education has analyzed in great detail the history of schools and education policy in their capacity as mechanisms for the internalization of the emperor-system ideology, it has failed to consider by what means and to what degree this emperor-system ideology was actually rooted in the minds of the people. By reexamining the paradigm underpinning postwar research into the history of education and gaining an understanding of the social group formed by the "army officer corps," Hirota ultimately succeeds in providing powerful corroboration of the effects of the internalization of the emperor-system ideology.

Many historical studies of education in Japan's colonies have been published during the postwar era, and on the basis of a critique of their methodology Komagome Takeshi [VII-12] also published a study that drew widespread interest. Hirota was born in 1959 and Komagome in 1962. This new generation, born at the start of Japan's high economic growth, is beginning to produce new methods in the area of research on the history of Japanese education.

The reason that research on universities is growing is of course that Japan's universities have been undergoing immense change since 1992. The decline in the number of eighteen-year-olds and the underlying tendency for people to have fewer children have forced all universities to make greater efforts to ensure their own survival. Within universities, the establishment of new faculties and reforms of the curriculum are proceeding on a scale greater than ever before since the inauguration of the new university system after the war.

Amano Ikuo, who has published many studies in the past few years, again made an outstanding contribution to research in this field through the publication of a historical study of the system of higher education [I-03] and a study of the problems facing universities [VIII-02]. Worthy of special note is the fact that the focus of both Amano's research and the study by Tachi Akira [VIII-03] lies in university reform, especially reform of undergraduate education. A collection of articles on university education was also brought out by the Liberal and General Education Society of Japan [VIII-01]. The reform of university education will be accelerated in the future, and at the same time many more studies will no doubt be produced, exerting a certain amount of influence on the current of reform.

IV. EXPECTATIONS FOR THE REFORM OF SCHOOL EDUCATION AND
CLASSROOM RESEARCH

Japanese schools are beset with many problems. But nonetheless
the overwhelming majority of children study at school and spend
much of their daily lives there, and it is there too that they obtain
information on choices affecting their future lives. Even though
schools may give rise to many pathological phenomena, people
cannot just abandon their hopes and expectations for actual
schools in their immediate vicinity. What is called for is real results
of school innovation by teachers, parents and pupils and testimony
thereof.

In 1996-97 we were fortunate in that several such records were
made public. The account of school reforms undertaken at Mitsuke
Elementary School in Niigata prefecture [III-03] and the account
of the recent history of Hokusei Gakuen Yoichi High School in
Hokkaido [III-04] are both valuable records of innovations in
education carried out at these schools. Japan's teachers are kept
extremely busy [IV-03], but nonetheless they are making considerable efforts to revitalize schools and give direction to their pupils'
initiative. The fact that many younger researchers discuss schools
from diverse angles in the comprehensive series on the school *per
se* edited by Horio Teruhisa *et al.* [III-01] is an indication that
this issue of school innovation cannot be ignored in present-day
Japan. From the academic year starting in 2002 it is planned to
fully introduce a five-day week in Japan's schools, and, as is
pointed out by Katō Kōji and others [IV-09], this reform will
have major implications for teachers with regard to curriculum
reforms.

Another problem facing educational circles in Japan is how to
train teachers with a keen enthusiasm for school innovation. The
observation by Imazu Kōjirō [IV-01,02], which take into account
teacher training in the United States, are outstanding in that they
advocate a new combination of teacher training at universities and
in-service training and also examine the new abilities and qualities
required of teachers today. But in reality there has been a drastic
reduction in the number of teachers being appointed to elementary,
junior and senior high schools, partly because of the decline in the

number of children and the financial difficulties of local government, and the Minister of Education has announced that the number of students to be admitted annually to education departments at national universities is to be cut by five thousand from 1997 for three years. Today universities, important places for training teachers, find themselves in most difficult circumstances, and this measure will doubtless become a topic of future debate as a new obstacle to university reform.

Classroom lessons form a major part of the work of teachers, and Akita Kiyomi [IV-08] has conducted a valuable comparative study of how teachers' images of classroom lessons change in accordance with the length of their teaching experience. Young, inexperienced teachers look upon classroom lessons as a flowing stream, and some describe it as a process of providing various forms of knowledge in regular sequence, similar to a dinner in which set dishes are served as successive courses. This resembles the image embraced by university students without any teaching experience. But veteran teachers with long teaching careers conceive of classroom lessons as a never-ending process in which the teacher joins the children in thinking about what they are learning. This study by Akita suggests an important goal, namely, that the reforms involving classroom innovations should not be conducted with the aim of increasing the efficiency of teaching, as is popularly believed, but should be undertaken as a process whereby teachers create a community of learning together with their pupils. Classroom research in greater depth could be described as the area in educational research for which the greatest future expectations are held in Japan.

BIBLIOGRAPHY

I. General Studies

01　堀尾輝久 Horio Teruhisa,『現代社会と教育』 *Contemporary Society and Education*, 248 pp., 岩波書店, 1997.

02　天野郁夫（編）Amano Ikuo (ed.),『教育への問い——現代教育学入門』 *Questions for Education: An Introduction to the Contemporary Study of*

Education, 321 pp., 東京大学出版会, 1996.

03 天野郁夫 Amano Ikuo,『日本の教育システム』*Japan's Education System*, 438 pp., 東京大学出版会, 1996.

04 天野郁夫 Amano Ikuo,『教育と近代化——日本の経験』*Education and Modernization: Japan's Experience*, 430 pp., 東京大学出版会, 1997.

05 今津孝次郎・樋田大二郎（編）Imazu Kōjirō and Hida Daijirō (eds.),『教育言説をどう読むか』*How to Read Educational Discourse*, 264 pp., 新曜社, 1997.

06 羽田貴史 Hata Takashi, 戦後教育と教育学 "Postwar Education and the Study of Education,"「教育学研究」63 巻 3 号, pp. 238-245, 日本教育学会, 1996.

07 国祐道広 Kunisuke Michihiro, 公教育研究の今日的意義と課題 "The Contemporary Significance of and Issues in Research on Public Education,"「日本教育行政学会年報」23 号, pp. 3-15, 日本教育行政学会, 1997.

08 平原春好（編）Hirahara Haruyoshi (ed.),『教育と教育基本法』*Education and the Fundamental Law of Education*, 604 pp., 勁草書房, 1996.

09 教育史学会機関誌編集委員会（編）Editorial Committee for the Organ of the Society for the Historical Research of Education (ed.),『教育史学会 40 周年記念誌』*Commemorative Issue for the 40th Anniversary of the Society for the Historical Research of Education*, 260 pp., 教育史学会, 1997.

This volume was published to commemorate the 40-year history of the Society for the Historical Research of Education, which began with an inaugural meeting at Tokyo Gakugei University in 1956 and its first conference at Waseda University in 1957. It is composed of (1) the proceedings of a 40th-anniversary symposium on "Issues and Methods in the Historical Research of Education" held with relatively younger researchers as panelists (21 Sept. 1996); (2) reviews by 12 contributors on research trends during the past 20 years in the history of Japanese education (ancient and medieval times, early modern period, modern period, and contemporary period), the history of Asian education (China, North and South Korea, and Southeast and South Asia), and the history of Western education (United States, Canada and Central and South America, Great Britain and Scandinavia, France and South Europe, Germany and Central Europe, and Russia and East Europe); and (3) a brief history of the Society, a list of articles carried by its journal, etc., thereby shedding light on the Society's history.

10 佐藤 学 Satō Manabu, 教育史像の脱構築へ——「近代教育」の批判的

検討 "Towards the Deconstruction of the Image of the History of Education: A Critical Examination of 'Modern Education'," 「教育学年報」6
号, pp. 117-141, 世織書房, 1997.

11 斉藤利彦 Saitō Toshihiko, 教育史研究の再構築——「学ぶ者」の視座か
ら "The Reconstruction of the Study of the History of Education: From
the Perspective of the 'Learner'," 「教育学年報」6 号, pp. 143-172, 世織書
房, 1997.

12 羽田貴史 Hata Takashi, 戦後教育史像の再構成 "A Reconstruction of the
Postwar Image of the History of Education," 「教育学年報」6 号, pp. 215
-240, 世織書房, 1997.

13 羽田貴史 Hata Takashi, 教育史研究の課題と方法 "Issues and Methods in
the Study of the History of Education," 『教育史学会 40 周年記念誌』[I-
09], pp. 10-18, 教育史学会, 1997.

14 永井憲一 Nagai Ken'ichi, 戦後 50 年と教育法学の展開 "Fifty Years of
the Postwar Era and Developments in the Study of Education Law," 「日
本教育法学会年報」26 号, pp. 4-26, 有斐閣, 1997.

15 堀尾輝久 Horio Teruhisa, パラダイム転換と教育法学 "The Paradigm
Shift and the Study of Education Law," 「日本教育法学会年報」26 号,
pp. 69-86. 有斐閣, 1997.

16 西田亀久夫 Nishida Kikuo, 『教育政策の課題』 *Issues in Education Policy*, 242 pp., 玉川大学出版部, 1996.

17 佐藤 学 Satō Manabu, 実践的探究としての教育学——技術的合理性に
対する批判の系譜 "The Study of Education as a Practical Quest: The
Genealogy of Criticism of Technical Rationality," 「教育学研究」63 巻 3
号, pp. 278-285, 日本教育学会, 1996.

In this article Satō questions the practical nature and effectiveness of the
study of education and describes the genealogy of research that has
explored the relationship between educational praxis and theory. Theoretical formulations of the practical quest involved in the study of education
have been essayed by William James, John Dewey, J. J. Schwab, and D.
A. Schön. James criticized the then popular theorization of praxis, which
applied the analytical techniques of scientific psychology, and advocated
a science for teachers whereby they form a "three-dimensional view" of
children through trial and error. Dewey focussed on the "intellectual
method," dealing with how children's interests and thinking unfold within
the children themselves, while Schön developed "reflective classes" based
on observation and exploration in the course of children's and teachers'
activities. According to Satō, the significance of this history of theorization lies in the surmounting of the dualism of theory and praxis in the

study of education, and today there is a need to rebuild the study of education on the basis of practical endeavours.

18 民間教育史料研究会・中内敏夫・田嶋　一・橋本紀子（編）Society for the Study of Historical Sources on Popular Education, Nakauchi Toshio, Tajima Hajime and Hashimoto Noriko (eds.),『教育科学の誕生──教育科学研究会史』 *The Birth of Education Science: The History of the Society for the Study of Education Science*, 564 pp., 大月書店, 1997.

The Society for the Study of Education Science was a private organization established by people like Kido Mantarō 城戸幡太郎 and Tomeoka Kiyoo 留岡清男 who were critical of the study of education as a normative science, the prevailing current of education studies in prewar Japan, and took a standpoint rooted in scientism and everyday life. It was founded in 1937 and forced to disband after about four years, but although it was rather short-lived, it is a well-known fact that it exerted considerable influence on education in Japan, especially in the postwar period. However, up until now only fragmentary information about its activities had been available. This book redresses this deficiency, describing in great detail the society's establishment, its development into a movement, the various activities undertaken under its aegis in different parts of Japan, and the activities centered on its headquarters.

19 谷川彰英 Tanigawa Akihide,『柳田国男教育論の発生と継承』 *The Origins and Transmission of Yanagita Kunio's Education Theories*, 384 pp., 三一書房, 1996.

II. Pathology of Education: Bullying and Absenteeism

01 深谷和子 Fukaya Kazuko,『「いじめ」世界の子どもたち──教室の深淵』 *Children in the World of "Bullying": The Abyss of the Classroom*, 219 pp., 金子書房, 1996.

02 新潟日報社（編）Niigata Nippō (ed.),『凍った叫び　準君事件といじめの深層』 *A Frozen Cry: The [Itō] Hisashi [Suicide] Incident and the Depths of Bullying*, 223 pp., 新潟日報事業社, 1996.

03 伊藤茂樹 Itō Shigeki,「心の問題」としてのいじめ問題 "The Problem of Bullying as a 'Problem of the Mind'," 「教育社会学研究」59 集, pp. 21-38, 日本教育社会学会, 1996.

04 坪井節子 Tsuboi Setsuko, いじめ問題と子どもの人権 "The Problem of Bullying and the Rights of Children," 「日本教育法学会年報」26 号, pp. 98-107, 有斐閣, 1997.

05 斎藤次郎 Saitō Jirō,『いじめと中学生』 *Bullying and Middle School Pupils*, 166 pp., 明石書店, 1996.

06 三浦正江・坂野雄二 Miura Masae and Sakano Yūji, 中学生における心

理的ストレスの継時的変化 "Sequential Change in the Psychological Stress of Middle School Pupils," 「教育心理学研究」44 巻 4 号, pp. 368-378, 日本教育心理学会, 1996.

07 武者一弘 Musha Kazuhiro, 「教育委員会の責任」に関する考察——公立中学校における「いじめによる生徒の自殺」事件を事例として "An Inquiry into the 'Responsibility of Boards of Education': With Reference to Incidents of 'Suicide by Pupils on Account of Bullying' in Public Middle Schools," 「日本教育行政学会年報」22 号, pp. 110-122, 日本教育行政学会, 1996.

08 石川憲彦ほか (編) Ishikawa Norihiko *et al.* (eds.), 『若ものたちが語る登校拒否』*Young People Talk about Refusing to Attend School*, 513 pp., 世織書房, 1996.

09 石田美清 Ishida Yoshikiyo, 市教育委員会の不登校対策に関する調査報告 "Report on an Investigation into Measures Being Taken by Municipal Boards of Education against School Absenteeism," 「日本教育行政学会年報」22 号, pp. 221-230, 日本教育行政学会, 1996.

10 渡辺 位 Watanabe Takashi, 『子どもはなぜ学校に行くのか』*Why Do Children Go to School?*, 253 pp., 教育史料出版会, 1996.

III. School Reforms and Children

01 堀尾輝久ほか (編) Horio Teruhisa *et al.* (eds.), 『講座学校』*Lectures on Schools*, Vols. 2-7 (270 pp., 254 pp., 270 pp., 229 pp., 246 pp., 270 pp.), 柏書房, 1996.

02 藤枝静正 Fujieda Shizumasa, 『国立大学附属学校の研究』*A Study of Schools Affiliated to National Universities*, 224 pp., 風間書房, 1996.

03 新潟県見附市立見附小学校 (編) Mitsuke Municipal Mitsuke Elementary School, Niigata Prefecture (ed.), 『輝く学校』*A Radiant School*, 155 pp., 日本教育新聞社出版局, 1996.

04 北星学園余市高等学校 (編) Hokusei Gakuen Yoichi High School (ed.), 『学校の挑戦』*One School's Challenge*, 294 pp., 教育史料出版会, 1997.

An account of the past ten-year history of a small, private Christian school in Hokkaido that has been exploring ways of surviving in the face of a rapid decline in the school roll by actively accepting high school dropouts. Describing how the school recovered from the threat of closure, it deals with the school's response to the need to carry out a radical review of its education policies regarding mufti, etc., as a result of the arrival of students from throughout Japan and the teachers' struggles as they coached students in speech contests, ski camps and volunteer activities and attempted to provide classroom lessons geared to individual differences in ability. The school has also published a record of impressions by former students, parents and teachers entitled 『やりなおさないか君らしさのままで』 *Why Not Make a Fresh Start as You Are?* (1995).

05 堀 真一郎 Hori Shin'ichirō,『自由学校の設計』 *The Design of a Free School*, 254 pp., 黎明書房, 1997.

06 赤塚康雄 (編) Akatsuka Yasuo (ed.),『大阪の学童疎開』 *The Evacuation of School Pupils from Osaka during World War II*, 822 pp., クリエイティブ 21, 1996.

07 日外アソシエーツ (編) Nichigai Associates (ed.),『児童文化人名事典』 *Biographical Dictionary of Juvenile Culture*, 591 pp., 日外アソシエーツ (発売・紀伊国屋書店), 1996.

08 深谷昌志 Fukaya Masashi,『子どもの生活史』 *The History of the Everyday Life of Children,* 295 pp., 黎明書房, 1996.

09 上平泰博・田中治彦・中島 純 Kamihira Yasuhiro, Tanaka Haruhiko and Nakajima Jun,『少年団の歴史』 *The History of the Children's Corps* (*Shōnendan*), 350 pp., 萌文社, 1996.

10 栗原 彬 Kurihara Akira,『やさしさの存在証明』 *Proof of the Existence of Gentleness*, 340 pp., 新曜社, 1996.

11 粒来 香 Tsuburai Kaoru, 高卒無業者層の研究 "A Study of Unemployed High School Graduates,"「教育社会学研究」60 集, pp., 185-208, 日本教育社会学会, 1997.

12 喜多明人ほか (編) Kita Akito *et al.* (eds.),『子どもの参加の権利』 *Children's Right of Participation*, 276 pp., 三省堂, 1996.

13 広井多鶴子 Hiroi Tazuko, 親の懲戒権の歴史——近代日本における懲戒権の「教育化」過程 "The History of Parents' Disciplinary Rights: The Process of the 'Educationalization' of Disciplinary Rights in Modern Japan,"「教育学研究」63 巻 2 号, pp. 119-128, 日本教育学会, 1996.

14 鐘ケ江晴彦 Kanegae Haruhiko,『「同和」教育への社会的視座』 *Social Perspectives on "Integration" (Dōwa) Education*, 293 pp., 明石書店, 1996.

15 東上高志 (編) Tōjō Takashi (ed.),『同和教育の終わり』 *The End of Integration (Dōwa) Education*, 366 pp., 部落問題研究所, 1996.

IV. Teachers, Classroom Research, and the Curriculum

01 今津孝次郎 Imazu Kōjirō,『変動社会の教師教育』 *Teacher Education in a Changing Society*, 338 pp., 名古屋大学出版会, 1996.

02 今津孝次郎 Imazu Kōjirō, 岐路に立つ教師教育——教師教育パラダイムの転換を中心に "Teacher Education at a Crossroads: With a Focus on the Paradigm Shift in Teacher Education,"「教育学研究」63 巻 3 号, pp. 294-302, 日本教育学会, 1996.

In this study Imazu reviews the study of education and its framework with reference to past perceptions of teacher education, perceptions of the growth of teachers, and perceptions of the methods and content of teacher education, and he then considers the paradigm of teacher education. He divides the period under consideration into two periods, the first corresponding to the period of the quantitative expansion of school education up until the first half of the 1970s and the second representing the period of the eruption of school education since the second half of the 1970s. During the first period the term "teacher training" (*kyōshi yōsei* 教師養成) was used, but in the second period "teacher education" (*kyōshi kyōiku* 教師教育) has come into general use. This change is a reflection of improvements in the quality of teachers and the emphasis on in-service training in response to criticism of schools and teachers since the 1970s. The understanding of the growth of teachers has also shifted from an "individual teacher model" to a "school innovation model" based on teachers' activities, and therefore research interests have also shifted to the growth and development of practising teachers. According to Imazu, what is needed in current teacher education is a vertically coordinated grasp of both teacher training and in-service training, along with the study and reform of problems facing teachers in which both teachers and outside researchers participate.

03 大阪教育文化センター教師の多忙化調査研究会（編）Group for the Study of Teachers' Busyness, Osaka Centre for Education and Culture (ed.),『教師の多忙化とバーンアウト──子ども・親との新しい関係づくりをめざして』*The Increasing Busyness and Burnout of Teachers: In Search of a New Relationship with Children and Parents*, 335 pp., 法政出版, 1996.

This volume presents the results of a questionnaire and 20 discussion meetings in which 21 researchers and teachers participated. The questionnaire was conducted on teachers at 232 elementary, middle and high schools in Osaka prefecture, and valid replies were obtained from 2,172 teachers. The actual nature of teachers' busyness is delineated in terms of their relations with pupils and their working environment, and it is indicated by means of a burnout index. Issues addressed include the teachers' sense of busyness, factors behind their busyness, relations with pupils (learning activities, life guidance, coaching of club activities), their working environment (school workplace, views of the teaching profession, gender-based division of labour), the teachers' relationship with culture, etc., and the influence exerted on educational activities by busyness is analyzed in great detail. At the same time it is also shown that there are many teachers who, while struggling with overwork, are managing to cope with it and find joy in their work. The results of the questionnaire are tabulated in an appendix.

04 寺崎昌男・「文検」研究会（編）Terasaki Masao and "Teacher Certification" Study Group (eds.),『「文検」の研究——文部省教員検定試験と戦前教育学』 *A Study of "Teacher Certification": The Ministry of Education Teacher Certification Exams and Prewar Pedagogy*, 443 pp., 学文社, 1997.

The Ministry of Education teacher certification exams referred to in the title (*bunken*: 文部省師範学校中学校高等女学校教員検定試験) are those for secondary school teachers at normal schools, middle schools and girls' high schools that were conducted from 1885 through to 1949, although they were discontinued for a time during World War II. This book focusses on the sections on "education" and "principles of education" in these exams and clarifies how the prewar study of education created a particular paradigm of education studies through its involvement with these exams. The "Research" section of this book provides an institutional survey of the exams, analyzes the exam questions on "education" and "principles of education," discusses the academic interests of the examiners and trends in the questions that they set, examines the magazine for examinees called *Kyōiku shūshin kenkyū* 『教育修身研究』 and their association called "Eifuku Dōgaku no Kai" 永福同学の会, and sheds light on the significance of sitting the exams and the process of self-education as seen in questionnaires and magazine articles. The "Materials" section contains a wealth of source materials, including exam questions, the numbers of successful candidates, examination timetables, reference books for examinees, brief sketches of examiners' careers, bibliography, etc.

05 稲垣忠彦・佐藤 学 Inagaki Tadahiko and Satō Manabu,『授業研究入門』 *An Introduction to Classroom Research*, 250 pp., 岩波書店, 1996.

06 佐藤 学 Satō Manabu,『教育方法学』 *The Study of Educational Methods*, 209 pp., 岩波書店, 1996.

07 中田基昭 Nakada Motoaki,『現象学から授業の世界へ』 *From Phenomenology to the World of Classroom Lessons*, 516 pp., 東京大学出版会, 1997.

08 秋田喜代美 Akita Kiyomi, 教える経験に伴う授業イメージの変容——比喩生成課題による検討 "Changes in the Images of Classroom Lessons Attendant upon Teaching Experience: An Examination Based on Analogy Generation,"『教育心理学研究』44 巻 2 号, pp. 176-186, 日本教育心理学

会，1996.

09　加藤幸次・中沢米子（編）Katō Kōji and Nakazawa Yoneko (eds.),『学校五日制と教育課程の創造』*The Five-Day School Week and the Creation of the Curriculum*, 278 pp., 黎明書房，1996.

10　藤岡信勝 Fujioka Nobukatsu,『近現代史教育の改革』*The Reform of the Teaching of Modern and Contemporary History*, 292 pp., 明治図書出版，1996.

11　藤原　彰・森田俊男（編）Fujiwara Akira and Morita Toshio (eds.),『近現代史の真実は何か』*What Is the Truth about Modern and Contemporary History ?*, 269 pp., 大月書店，1996.

12　坂井俊樹 Sakai Toshiki,『韓国・朝鮮と近現代史教育』*North and South Koreas and the Teaching of Modern and Contemporary History*, 253 pp., 大月書店，1997.

13　佐島群巳ほか（編）Sajima Tomomi *et al.* (eds.),『環境教育指導事典』*Dictionary for Guidance in Environmental Education*, 333 pp., 国土社，1996.

14　高村泰雄・丸山　博 Takamura Yasuo and Maruyama Hiroshi,『環境科学教授法の研究』*A Study of Methods of Teaching Environmental Science*, 674 pp., 北海道大学図書刊行会，1996.

15　中島美惠子 Nakajima Mieko,『地域に学ぶ環境教育』*Environmental Education with a Local Focus*, 176 pp., 教育出版，1996.

16　中野重人ほか（編）Nakano Shigeto *et al.* (eds.),『生活科事典』*Dictionary of Life Environment Studies*, 518 pp., 東京書籍，1996.

17　水越敏行・佐伯　胖（編）Mizukoshi Toshiyuki and Saeki Yutaka (eds.),『変わるメディアと教育のありかた』*The Changing Media and the State of Education*, 289 pp., ミネルヴァ書房，1996.

18　君島和彦 Kimijima Kazuhiko,『教科書の思想』*The Philosophy behind Textbooks*, 328 pp., すずさわ書店，1996.

19　林　竹二・灰谷健次郎 Hayashi Takeji and Haitani Kenjirō,『教えることと学ぶこと』*Teaching and Learning*, 237 pp., 儷書房，1996.

V. Gender and Education, Intercultural Education

01　中西祐子・土屋健志 Nakanishi Yūko and Tsuchiya Takeshi,「ジェンダーと教育」研究の動向と課題——教育社会学・ジェンダー・フェミニズム "Trends and Issues in the Study of 'Gender and Education': The Sociology of Education, Gender, and Feminism,"「教育社会学研究」61集，pp. 77-101, 日本教育社会学会，1997.

02　木村淳子 Kimura Junko, 教室におけるジェンダー形成 "Gender Formation in the Classroom,"「教育社会学研究」61集，pp. 39-54, 日本教育社会学会，1997.

03 氏原陽子 Ujihara Yōko, 中学校における男女平等と性差別の錯綜 "The Convolutedness of the Equality of the Sexes and Sexual Discrimination in Middle Schools,"「教育社会学研究」58 集, pp. 29-46, 日本教育社会学会, 1996.

04 冠野　文 Kanno Fumi, 女性エリート輩出にみる戦後改革のインパクト "The Impact of the Postwar Reforms to Be Seen in the Emergence of a Female Elite,"「教育社会学研究」58 集, pp. 103-122, 日本教育社会学会, 1996.

05 山田純恵 Yamada Sumie, 女子公民科をめぐる公民教育論の展開 "The Development of Theories of Civic Education with Respect to Girls' Civics,"「日本の教育史学」40 集, pp. 206-224, 教育史学会, 1997.

06 多賀　太 Taga Futoshi, 青年期の男性性形成に関する一考察 "A Consideration of Male Sexual Formation in Adolescence,"「教育社会学研究」58 集, pp. 47-64, 日本教育社会学会, 1996.

07 片瀬一男・阿部晃士 Katase Kazuo and Abe Kōji, 沿岸地域における学歴主義と教育達成――「利口・家もたず，達者・家もたす」"Credentialism and Educational Achievement in Coastal Districts: 'Clever without a House, Healthy with a House',"「教育社会学研究」61 集, pp. 163-184, 日本教育社会学会, 1997.

08 江淵一公 Ebuchi Kazuhiro,『異文化間教育学序説』 An Introduction to the Study of Intercultural Education, 576 pp., 九州大学出版会, 1997.

09 佐藤郡衛 Satō Gun'ei,『海外・帰国子女教育の再構築』 The Reconstruction of Education for Overseas and Returnee Students, 300 pp., 玉川大学出版部, 1997.

10 山崎瑞紀・平　直樹・中村俊哉・横山　剛 Yamazaki Mizuki, Taira Naoki, Nakamura Shun'ya and Yokoyama Tsuyoshi, アジア系留学生の対日態度及び対異文化態度形成におけるエスニシティの役割 "The Role of Ethnicity in the Formation of Attitudes towards Japan and Attitudes towards Other Cultures among Asian Students in Japan,"「教育心理学研究」45 巻 2 号, pp. 119-128, 日本教育心理学会, 1997.

11 山口和孝 Yamaguchi Kazutaka, 教育と宗教をめぐる現代史の課題 "Issues in Contemporary History Concerning Education and Religion,"「日本の教育史学」40 集, pp. 345-349, 教育史学会, 1997.

This article presents the gist of proposals made at a symposium of the Society for the Historical Research of Education. Yamaguchi understands issues pertaining to education and religion in the present age in terms of the relationship between religion on the one hand and education and schools on the other, and he first examines the principles of modern public education from a contemporary perspective and then discusses the religious problems being faced by present-day public education. Historically speaking, modern public education has developed in a search to establish the public nature of education (secular schools) by breaking away from religion (ecclesiastical power). As regards religious education, children have been subjected to their parents' religion, and this has generally been recognized as part of parental rights in the education of their children. According to Yamaguchi, the relationship between religion and education in Japan is now facing problems concerning respect for individual values (the right of children to break away from their parents' religion, the introduction of religious customs into school education, etc.), and the neutrality and impartiality of schools.

12　岡本洋之 Okamoto Hiroyuki, 中村正直における「異なるものの共存」の思想 "The Idea of the 'Coexistence of Differences' in the Case of Nakamura Masanao (1832-91)," 「日本の教育史学」40集, pp. 39-56, 教育史学会, 1997.

13　嶺井正也 Minei Masaya, 『障害児と公教育』 Handicapped Children and Public Education, 260 pp., 明石書店, 1997.

VI. Decentralization and Education, Local Regions and Education

01　高木英明 Takagi Hideaki, 地教行法体制40年の軌跡と今日の教育行政 "The Course of 40 Years under the Regional Education Administration Law (地方教育行政法) and Today's Educational Administration," 「日本教育行政学会年報」22号, pp. 3-17, 日本教育行政学会, 1996.

02　若井弥一 Wakai Yaichi, 教育行政の地方分権性 "The Decentralized Characters of Educational Administration," 「日本教育行政学会年報」22号, pp. 31-44, 日本教育行政学会, 1996.

03　上野景三 Ueno Keizō, 地方分権, 自治体再編と社会教育法制 "Decentralization, Reorganization of Local Government, and the Judicial System for Adult Education," 「日本の社会教育」40集, pp. 111-123, 日本社会教育学会, 1996.

04　部落解放研究所 (編) Buraku Liberation Research Institute (ed.), 『地域の教育改革と学力保障』 Regional Education Reforms and Guarantees of School Achievement, 278 pp., 部落解放研究所 (発売：解放出版社), 1996.

05　原　貞次郎・勝野　順 Hara Teijirō and Katsuno Jun, 長野県における高校「多様化」と地域高校の復権 "The Diversification' of High Schools in Nagano Prefecture and the Restoration of the Rights of Local High Schools," 「日本教育法学会年報」26号, pp. 142-150, 有斐閣, 1997.

06　小島喜孝・川原茂雄・千田　忠 Kojima Yoshitaka, Kawahara Shigeo and Chida Tadashi, 北海道における高校教育と地方自治的可能性 "High

School Education and the Possibilities of Local Autonomy in Hokkaido,"「日本教育法学会年報」26 号, pp. 151-160, 有斐閣, 1997.

VII. History of Education

01 入江　宏 Irie Hiroshi,『近世庶民家訓の研究』*A Study of Household Precepts among Commoners in the Early Modern Period*, 436 pp., 多賀出版, 1996.

02 梅渓　昇 Umetani Noboru,『緒方洪庵と適塾』*Ogata Kōan and His Private School Tekijuku*, 160 pp., 大阪大学出版会, 1996.

03 幕末維新学校研究会（編）Group for the Study of Schools in the Bakumatsu and Restoration Period (ed.),『幕末維新期における「学校」の組織化』*The Organization Process of "Schools" in the Bakumatsu and Restoration Period*, 647 pp., 多賀出版, 1996.

04 千葉昌弘 Chiba Masahiro,『近代日本地域民衆教育成立過程の研究』*A Study of the Establishment Process of Local Popular Education in Modern Japan*, 334 pp., 梓出版社, 1996.

05 羽田貴史 Hata Takashi, 明治前期官立学校財政政策の展開 "The Development of Financial Policies for Government Schools in the Early Part of the Meiji Era,"「日本の教育史学」39 集, pp. 27-45, 教育史学会, 1996.

06 新谷恭明 Shintani Yasuaki,『尋常中学校の成立』*The Establishment of Jinjō Chūgakkō (The Predecessor of the Old-System Middle Schools)*, 363 pp., 九州大学出版会, 1997.

07 佐藤秀夫（編）Satō Hideo (ed.),『続・現代史資料（10）: 教育——御真影と教育勅語 3』*Materials on Contemporary History, Contd. (10): Education—Imperial Portraits (Goshin'ei) and the Imperial Rescript on Education 3*, 497 pp., みすず書房, 1996.

08 内田純一 Uchida Jun'ichi, 地方改良運動下の「農村教育」観に関する考察 "A Consideration of Views of 'Rural Education' in the Regional Betterment Movement during the Late Meiji Era,"「日本の教育史学」40 集, pp. 112-129, 教育史学会, 1997.

09 岩田一正 Iwata Kazumasa, 明治後期における少年の書字文化の展開 "The Development of the Written Culture of Boys in the Latter Part of the Meiji Era,"「教育学研究」64 巻 4 号, pp. 417-426, 日本教育学会, 1997.

10 廣田照幸 Hirota Teruyuki,『陸軍将校の教育社会史——立身出世と天皇制』*The Social History of the Education of Army Officers: Career Advancement and the Emperor System*, 491 pp., 世織書房, 1997.

11 沖田行司 Okita Kōji,『ハワイ日系移民の教育史——日米文化, その出会いと相剋』*The Educational History of Japanese Immigrants in Hawaii: The Encounter and Conflict between Japanese and American Culture*, 272 pp., ミネルヴァ書房, 1997.

12 駒込 武 Komagome Takeshi, 『植民地帝国日本の文化統合』 *The Cultural Integration of the Colonial Empire of Japan*, 501 pp., 岩波書店, 1996.

What sort of cultural policies did modern Japan implement in order to rule over other nationalities and give a show of multiethnic integration and, conversely, what sort of mechanisms for excluding other cultures did it create so as to prevent the influx of foreign cultures into Japan and preserve the cultural homogeneity of the Japanese people? Komagome explores these issues through a study of Japan's cultural policies in Taiwan, Korea, Manchuria and occupied parts of North China between 1900 and the 1930s, and he concludes that the structure of these cultural policies should be understood from the three perspectives of "linguistic nationalism and consanguineous nationalism," "homeland-extensionism and colonialism" and "adaptation of native culture and cultural assimilation." It is also shown that education both in the colonies and in Japan played a major role in the implementation of these cultural policies. In postwar Japan many researchers have conducted historical research on the conditions and philosophy of "colonial education," but this is an original study that overturns the paradigm of this earlier research.

13 佐藤由美 Satō Yumi, 韓国の近代教育制度の成立と日本——日本人学務官僚による「普通学校令」の制定をめぐって "Japan and the Establishment of a Modern Education System in Korea: On the Enactment of the 'Elementary School Order' by Japanese Educational Bureaucrats,"「日本の教育史学」39 集, pp. 193-211, 教育史学会, 1996.

14 八本木 浄 Happongi Kiyoshi, 『戦争末期の青年学校』 *Youth Schools towards the End of the War*, 313 pp., 日本図書センター, 1996.

15 近藤健一郎 Kondō Ken'ichirō, 沖縄戦における中等・師範学校生徒の戦場動員 "The Mobilization of Secondary and Normal School Students to the Battlefields in the Struggle for Okinawa,"「日本の教育史学」39 集, pp. 157-174, 教育史学会, 1996.

16 荻原克男 Ogihara Katsuo, 『戦後日本の教育行政構造』 *The Structure of Educational Administration in Postwar Japan*, 327 pp., 勁草書房, 1996.

17 中西祐子・中村高康・大内裕和 Nakanishi Yūko, Nakamura Takayasu and Ōuchi Hirokazu, 戦後日本の高校間格差成立過程と社会階層——1985 年 SSM 調査データの分析を通じて "The Formation of Differences between High Schools in Postwar Japan: On the Basis of an Analysis of Data from the 1985 SSM (Social Stratification and Social Mobility) Survey,"「教育社会学研究」60 集, pp. 61-82, 日本教育社会学会, 1997.

VIII. Universities

01　一般教育学会（編）Liberal and General Education Society of Japan (ed.), 『大学教育研究の課題──改革動向への批判と提言』 *Issues in the Study of University Education: Criticism of Reform Trends and Proposals*, 384 pp., 玉川大学出版部, 1997.

　　A collection of 50 representative articles selected from the *Ippan Kyōiku Gakkaishi* 『一般教育学会誌』, the journal of the Liberal and General Education Society of Japan (renamed in Japanese from Ippan Kyōiku Gakkai to Daigaku Kyōiku Gakkai 大学教育学会 in 1997). The overwhelming majority of its members are university professors who either have taught general education subjects at national, public or private universities or have experience in the administration of general education courses. The articles included in this volume date from 1980 through to January 1995, and they therefore provide an overview of how university staff members have understood the issues facing general education in Japanese universities and the need for research on university education, as well as the proposals for reform that they have put forward, during the 15 years surrounding the change to "general rules" with regard to standards for the chartering of universities in 1991. The articles are divided into 7 sections, including "Issues in the Study of University Education," "Combined Subjects and Seminars," "The System of Self-Assessment for Universities" and "Faculty Development," and the volume closes with a report on plans for curriculum reforms at 57 universities.

02　天野郁夫 Amano Ikuo, 『大学に教育革命を』 *Bringing an Educational Revolution to Universities*, 231 pp., 有信堂高文社, 1997.

03　館　昭 Tachi Akira, 『大学改革　日本とアメリカ』 *University Reform in Japan and the United States*, 214 pp., 玉川大学出版部, 1997.

04　宮坂広作 Miyasaka Kōsaku, 『大学改革と生涯学習』 *University Reform and Lifelong Learning*, 412 pp., 明石書店, 1997.

05　島　一則 Shima Kazunori, 昭和50年代前期高等教育計画以降の地方分散政策とその見直しをめぐって "On Policies for Decentralization Since the Higher Education Plans of the Latter Part of the 1970s and Their Review," 「教育社会学研究」59集, pp. 127-144, 日本教育社会学会, 1996.

06　千葉悦子 Chiba Etsuko, 社会に開かれた大学の可能性──福島大学行政社会学部を事例に "The Possibilities of a University Open to Society: With Reference to the Faculty of Administration and Social Sciences at Fukushima University," 「日本の社会教育」40集, pp. 81-90, 日本社会教育学会, 1996.

07　有馬朗人 Arima Akito, 『大学貧乏物語』 *The Destitution of National*

Universities: From My Experiences as President of the University of Tokyo, 249 pp., 東京大学出版会, 1996.

08 天野郁夫 (編) Amano Ikuo (ed.),『大学を語る——22 人の学長』 *Twenty-Two University Presidents Talk about Their Universities*, 321 pp., 玉川大学出版部, 1997.

09 有本　章・江原武一 (編) Arimoto Akira and Ehara Takekazu (eds.),『大学教授職の国際比較』 *An International Comparison of the University Professoriate*, 280 pp., 玉川大学出版部, 1996.

10 加藤　毅 Katō Takeshi, 大学助手職の研究者養成に関する研究 "A Study of the Training of University Teaching Assistants to Become Researchers,"「教育社会学研究」59 集, pp. 109-126, 日本教育社会学会, 1996.

11 苅谷剛彦 Kariya Takehiko, 大衆化時代の大学進学——〈価値多元化社会〉における選抜と大学教育 "Going to University in an Age of Mass Popularization: Selection and University Education in a 'Society of Pluralized Values',"「教育学研究」64 巻 3 号, pp. 327-336, 日本教育学会, 1997.

12 京都大学高等教育教授システム開発センター (編) Kyoto University Research Center for Higher Education (ed.),『開かれた大学授業をめざして』 *Towards Open University Classes*, 182 pp., 玉川大学出版部, 1997.

13 橋本鉱市 Hashimoto Kōichi, 近代日本における「文学部」の機能と構造——帝国大学文学部を中心として "The Functions and Structure of the 'Faculty of Literature' in Modern Japan: With a Focus on the Faculties of Literature at Imperial Universities,"「教育社会学研究」59 集, pp. 91-108, 日本教育社会学会, 1996.

14 中村勝範 (編) Nakamura Katsunori (ed.),『帝大新人会研究』 *A Study of the Shinjinkai (New Man Society) at Tokyo Imperial University*, 511 pp., 慶應義塾大学法学研究会 (発売・慶應義塾大学出版会), 1997.

15 渡辺かよ子 Watanabe Kayoko,『近現代日本の教養論——一九三〇年代を中心に』 *The Evaluation of the Concept of Cultivation in Modern Japan: The Idea of Cultivation in the 1930s*, 263 pp., 行路社, 1997.

The author has a Ph. D. from the University of Illinois for her above English dissertation, and the present Japanese version, representing a major revision of this earlier study, is a challenging study in the history of intellectual thought in which she reexamines the concept of "cultivation" (*kyōyō* 教養), a popular idea in Japan during the 1930s, and the validity of current evaluations of this concept. She demonstrates that the idea of cultivation during this period was not a continuation of the ideas of cultivation initially formed during the Taishō era, but was the product of criticism of these earlier ideas, and she concludes that the interest in cultivation during this period formed a precondition for the acceptance of general education by Japanese universities from the United States after the war.

16 白井　厚（編）Shirai Atsushi (ed.),『大学とアジア太平洋戦争』*Universities and the Asia-Pacific War*, 452 pp., 日本経済評論社, 1996.

17 前川清治 Maekawa Kiyoharu,『三枝博音と鎌倉アカデミア』*Saigusa Hiroto (1892-1963) and the Kamakura Academia*, 213 pp., 中央公論社, 1996.

18 広沢　栄 Hirosawa Sakae,『わが青春の鎌倉アカデミア』*My Youth and the Kamakura Academia*, 212 pp., 岩波書店, 1996.

19 土持ゲーリー法一 Tsuchimochi Garry Hōichi,『新制大学の誕生──戦後私立大学政策の展開』*The Birth of New-System Universities: The Development of Postwar Policies for Private Universities*, 418 pp., 玉川大学出版部, 1996.

20 加藤博和 Katō Hirokazu,『大学・教養部の解体的終焉』*The Disintegrative End of University Departments of Liberal Arts*, 194 pp., 葦書房, 1997.

21 大塚　豊 Ōtsuka Yutaka,『現代中国高等教育の成立』*The Establishment of Higher Education in Contemporary China*, 444 pp., 玉川大学出版部, 1996.

AUTHOR INDEX

Inoue Masao 91, 124
Inoue Shun 161
Inoue Takao 157, 183, 184, 209, 222
Institute for Posts and Telecommunications Policy 114
Institute of Administrative Management 53
International Institute for the Study of Religions 213, 228
Inuzuka Susumu 155, 177
Iokibe Makoto 67, 70, 74, 77, 80
Ippan Kyōiku Gakkai (see Liberal and General Education Society of Japan)
Irie Hiroshi 242, 256
Iseri Hirofumi 49
Ishida Kazuhiko 109
Ishida Masao 108
Ishida Mitsuo 113
Ishida Mitsuru 24
Ishida Takeshi 16
Ishida Yoshikiyo 241, 248
Ishiguro Kazunori 68, 75, 125
Ishihara Kenji 90, 117
Ishihara Toyomi 90, 119, 152, 171, 215, 232
Ishii Hideya 196
Ishii Kanji 83, 93
Ishii Kenji 212, 226
Ishii Ryōsuke 14
Ishii Yuka 167
Ishikawa Hiroyuki 234
Ishikawa Jun 159, 187
Ishikawa Kenji 29
Ishikawa Masumi 50
Ishikawa Norihiko 241, 249
Ishikawa Yūichi 197
Ishio Yoshito 53
Ishiyama Hiroshi 210, 222
Isoda Norihiko 196
Isomura Tamotsu 18
Isozaki Ikuo 44
Itō Hideshi 103, 140
Itō Kazuyoshi 13
Itō Kenji 200

Itō Kunio 22
Itō Makoto 85, 101, 102
Itō Masaaki 114
Itō Masami 8
Itō Masatsugu 61
Itō Minoru 120
Itō Mitsutoshi 43, 44, 45, 46
Itō Motoshige 84, 101, 125, 136, 145
Itō Shigeki 248
Itō Shigeo 16, 17
Itō Shirō 109
Itō Susumu 18
Itō, Terry 58
Itō Yasunobu 216
Itō Yasushi 20
Itō Yuishin 213, 228, 234
Iuchi Masatoshi 125
Iwabuchi Yoshikatsu 53
Iwade Makoto 27
Iwai Tomoaki 44
Iwai Yoshiko 34
Iwakami Mami 153, 172
Iwaki Sadayuki 154, 175
Iwamoto Misako 48
Iwamoto Yoshiteru 214, 231
Iwasaki Masaya 83, 96
Iwase Takashi 91, 123
Iwata Katsuo 92, 125
Iwata Kazumasa 256
Iwata Kikuo 84, 100
Iwata Shigenori 210, 222
Iyasu Tadashi 47
Iyotani Toshio 236

J

Jain, Purnendra C. 46
Japan Association for Local Finances 107
Japan Association for the Study of Local Government 58
Japan Association of Economic Geographers 196
Japan Association of International Relations 69

274

SUBJECT INDEX